Clark M. Zlotchew, Ph.

# Alpha
# Teach Yourself

# Spanish

Second Edition

ALPHA

A member of Penguin Group (USA) Inc.

in 24

hours

# Alpha Teach Yourself Spanish in 24 Hours, Second Edition

**Copyright © 2004 by Clark M. Zlotchew**

International Standard Book Number: 1-59257-288-x
Library of Congress Catalog Card Number: 2004108631

*Printed in the United States of America*

First printing: 2004

07   06          5   4

**Note:** This publication contains the opinions and ideas of its author. It is intended to provide helpful and informative material on the subject matter covered. It is sold with the understanding that the author and publisher are not engaged in rendering professional services in the book. If the reader requires personal assistance or advice, a competent professional should be consulted.

The author and publisher specifically disclaim any responsibility for any liability, loss or risk, personal or otherwise, which is incurred as a consequence, directly or indirectly, of the use and application of any of the contents of this book.

## Trademarks

All terms mentioned in this book that are known to be or are suspected of being trademarks or service marks have been appropriately capitalized. Alpha Books and Penguin Group (USA) Inc. cannot attest to the accuracy of this information. Use of a term in this book should not be regarded as affecting the validity of any trademark or service mark.

Most Alpha books are available at special quantity discounts for bulk purchases for sales promotions, premiums, fund-raising, or educational use. Special books, or book excerpts, can also be created to fit specific needs.

For details, write: Special Markets, Alpha Books, 375 Hudson Street, New York, NY 10014.

**PUBLISHER**
Marie Butler-Knight

**PRODUCT MANAGER**
Phil Kitchel

**SENIOR MANAGING EDITOR**
Jennifer Chisholm

**ACQUISITIONS EDITOR**
Paul Dinas

**DEVELOPMENT EDITOR**
Michael Koch

**PRODUCTION EDITOR**
Janette Lynn

**COPY EDITOR**
Keith Cline

**COVER DESIGNERS**
Charis Santillie
Douglas Wilkins

**BOOK DESIGNER**
Gary Adair

**INDEXER**
Julie Bess

**LAYOUT/PROOFREADING**
Becky Harmon
John Etchison

*I dedicate this book to my wife Marilyn, to my sister Suzi, and to my students.*

# Overview

# Contents

## Appendixes

# Introduction

This book is for anyone who wants to communicate effectively in Spanish but cannot take classes or live and study for an extended period in a Spanish-speaking country. Now you can teach yourself Spanish easily in the privacy of your own home.

Welcome to *Alpha Teach Yourself Spanish in 24 Hours, Second Edition*. Spanish is the official language of 18 independent nations in North America, South America, Central America, and the Caribbean. It is also an official language of one important country in Western Europe: Spain. In addition, it is the native language of millions of U.S. citizens in the Southwest and in our nation's larger cities. This Spanish-speaking community is now the single largest minority in the country. Spanish has unofficially become the second language in the United States.

## HOW TO USE THIS BOOK

All books in the *Alpha Teach Yourself in 24 Hours* series contain 24 chapters, which are designed to be learned in one hour each. It is not suggested, however, that you lose a night's sleep and actually spend 24 consecutive hours studying this book. Set your own pace.

Depending on the time available to you, you might want to learn the material at the rate of one hour per day. If you have a more leisurely approach, you might want to work on this book at the rate of one hour per week. Learning an additional language in 24 days or even 6 months is, after all, quite an undertaking.

*Alpha Teach Yourself Spanish in 24 Hours, Second Edition*, explains the workings of the language in great detail, step by step, one lesson building on the previous one. The text speaks to you the way a good teacher would, explaining how the language functions, providing clear examples, and gradually providing you with the grammatical structures and the vocabulary necessary for communicating effectively in Spanish. The text anticipates questions and problems you might have and answers those questions.

## How This Book Is Organized

The 24 chapters ("hours") of this book are divided into 5 parts. The first two parts revolve almost exclusively around the structure of the language, whereas the last three, still dealing with structure, lean heavily on the vocabulary for the various activities of daily life.

**Part I, "Nuts and Bolts,"** deals with the most basic aspects of grammatical structure necessary for communication in Spanish.

**Part II, "Being,"** comprises Hours 7 through 9. These three hours deal with the difference in usage between two Spanish verbs that mean *to be*.

**Part III, "Interpersonal Activities,"** is comprised of Hours 10 through 13, and is more activity-centered, with useful vocabularies revolving around specific aspects of daily life that involve interaction with other people, while still introducing grammatical material necessary for effective communication.

**Part IV, "Daily Routine,"** is comprised of Hours 14 through 19, and provides you with ways of talking about activities at home, in the office, and at the mall.

**Part V, "Business, Travel, and Service Industries,"** is comprised of Hours 20 through 24 and deals with vocabulary necessary for making travel and hotel arrangements; medical matters (doctors, dentists, hospitals, sickness); business affairs (including writing business letters); banking and finance (savings, loans, investments, mortgages, and so on); and automotive matters (automobiles and their parts, car rentals, purchasing gasoline and oil, and accident terminology).

Last but not least, this book has a lot of miscellaneous cross-references, tips, shortcuts, and warning sidebar boxes to help you learn. Here's how they stack up:

**JUST A MINUTE**

Just a Minute sidebars offer advice or teach an easier way to do something.

**TIME SAVER**

 Time Saver sidebars give you a faster way to do something.

**PROCEED WITH CAUTION**

 Proceed with Caution boxes are warnings. They warn you about potential problems and help you steer clear of trouble.

**GO TO ▶**

This note gives you a cross-reference to another chapter or section in the book to learn more about a particular topic.

## Tips to Get You Started

Read all the explanations carefully for understanding, study the examples provided, and last but not least, drill yourself on the sample phrases and sentences provided. Do *not* "translate"; that is, do not mentally provide the English translation for the Spanish you are learning. When you understand the principles involved in a particular lesson, say the examples provided *aloud*, over and over, but picturing in your mind's eye exactly what is happening. Picture who is doing what to whom, and feel the "when" (at present, in the past, in the future, and so on).

What do you picture when you say the English pronoun *he?* Don't say you picture nothing. Think about it. Perhaps you picture a masculine figure of some kind standing to the side. Whether you can isolate this image or not when speaking English, conjure one up when speaking Spanish. This is the only way you will internalize the language and make it a part of you. In this way, you will end up speaking Spanish the way you speak English: spontaneously, without taking the time to translate the thoughts into another language. You will also be able to converse more fluently because you won't need to translate your thoughts back and forth between languages.

If, while using this book, you can manage to listen to spoken Spanish (movies, television, radio programs, discs, or tapes), you will greatly enhance your ability to understand spoken Spanish. Naturally, at first you'll understand almost nothing, but after increasing exposure you'll start to recognize a word here, another one there, a phrase here, another phrase there. Soon you'll understand whole spoken sentences, and finally you'll find you understand just about everything. The listening will also help you speak more fluently, through imitation.

The grammar of any language is a closed system; the entire system can be learned. Just about the entire Spanish grammatical system is contained in this book. However, the vocabulary of any language is an open system; you keep adding vocabulary all your life. You do this in English, so you can expect to do the same in Spanish. No one—absolutely no one—ever learns or retains the entire vocabulary of a language, his or her native language included.

Work at a pace that you find comfortable. Practice saying the examples aloud until you are comfortable speaking Spanish. Take some time every day to listen to Spanish radio or watch Spanish television. Remember not to translate, but to force yourself to think in Spanish. Good luck! *¡Buena suerte!*

# About the Author

CLARK M. ZLOTCHEW, PH.D., has been a professor of Spanish language and Hispanic literatures and linguistics at SUNY College at Fredonia since 1975. He received his M.A. in Spanish from Middlebury College in Vermont and his Ph.D. in Romance Languages and Literatures from SUNY Binghamton. He has had a dozen books published, ranging from literary criticism to translations of Spanish and Spanish-American authors to interviews with writers of Argentina and Uruguay. He is also the author, under a pen name, of a military/action novel.

# Acknowledgments

Thanks to Dr. Pedro Talavera-Ibarra, Chair of the Department of Modern Languages and Literatures and to Dr. Khalid J. Siddiqui of the Department of Mathematics of SUNY College at Fredonia for helping me to unravel the mysteries of the computer. Thanks to Dr. Paul Schwartz, Dean of Arts and Sciences, SUNY College at Fredonia; and to Dr. Kenneth Lucey, then Chair of the Departments of Philosophy and of Foreign Languages and Literatures, SUNY College at Fredonia, for expediting the repair of my computer, which crashed in the middle of this book; and to Harry W. (Bill) Thomas for actually repairing it in record time. Thanks to my agent, Tim Hays, for securing the contract for this book, and for convincing me to take on the work. Special thanks go to my wife, Marilyn Kocin Zlotchew, for spending a whole summer running to the college to send my material as e-mail attachments to James Petrozello (whom I also thank for his patience and good humor) and to pick up e-mail messages for me while I was chained to the computer writing this book. Thanks to Marilyn as well for looking into the *WordPerfect Manual* to find the method for alphabetizing lists. Thanks, too, to Lisa Jakubowsky, enthusiastic student of Spanish, who volunteered to help me alphabetize the vocabulary, and put in several hours doing this before Marilyn found out how to do it electronically.

# PART I
# Nuts and Bolts

# HOUR 1

# Pronouncing Spanish

## CHAPTER SUMMARY

**LESSON PLAN:**

In this hour, you'll learn ...

- How to pronounce Spanish letters and words so that native speakers can understand you.
- Vocabulary words that are similar to their English counterparts.

People say that Spanish is a phonetic language. What they mean is that the connection between Spanish spelling and Spanish pronunciation is very direct, unlike English, in which letters often have a number of different sounds associated with them. This direct connection between spelling and pronunciation makes it easy for you to read any new Spanish word correctly, even if you've never heard it spoken.

## PRONOUNCE THE VOWELS

The best way to learn the pronunciation of a foreign language is to listen to native speakers in person, in movies, on television and radio, or on tapes. If you're able to do this, by all means do so. Listen to Spanish radio while you do the dishes, or turn the television to the Spanish channel while you cook dinner; take every opportunity to familiarize yourself with the correct pronunciation of the language. It will help you to pronounce the language like a native and understand people in conversation. If you have no access to the language, this hour's lesson will help you pronounce Spanish in a way that native speakers will understand.

## PRONOUNCE SINGLE VOWELS

The following table lists the correct pronunciation of the five Spanish vowels. Practice saying the individual vowel sounds, as well as the word examples you find in the third column.

**Spanish Vowel Sounds**

| Letter | Sound | Example | Sound of Word |
|--------|-------|---------|---------------|
| a | *ah* | gato | GAH-*toh* |
| e | *eh* | pero | PEH-*roh* |
| i | *ee* | mina | MEE-*nah* |
| o | *oh* | solo | SOH-*loh* |
| u | *oo* | mula | MOO-*lah* |

The *ah* sound of the Spanish *a* falls somewhere between the English *a* in father and hat. The *eh* sound of the Spanish *e* falls somewhere between the *ay* sound of say and the *e* of bed.

The *ee* sound of the Spanish *i* is similar to the *e* sound in cheese. The *oh* sound of the Spanish *o* is similar to the *o* in solo. The *oo* sound of the Spanish *u* corresponds to the sound of the *oo* in moolah.

## PRONOUNCE TWO-VOWEL COMBINATIONS

The vowels *a*, *e*, and *o* are called strong; the vowels *i* and *u* are described as weak. These categories relate to the fact that when two vowels are combined in one word, a combination known as a diphthong, the sound of one vowel dominates the other. For example, combining *a* and *i* (*ai*) in Spanish does not result in the sound *ah-ee* because the two vowel sounds don't receive equal time. Instead, the resulting sound is very similar to the way we pronounce the name of the letter *i* in English or the way we pronounce the letter *i* in the greeting, "Hi!" This chapter uses the combination *ahy* to represent that sound. When the order is reversed, the strong vowel still dominates. The combination *ia* is not pronounced *ee-ah*, with equal time for both vowels. Instead, more time is given to the *a* so that the resulting sound is like the *ya* in yacht. Keep in mind that these diphthongs form part of one syllable, not two. (Two strong vowels belong to separate syllables.) The following table lists the pronunciation of the Spanish diphthongs (weak/strong vowel combinations). The first column has the Spanish diphthong, the second column has the symbol I'm using in this book for its pronunciation, the third column has an English word with the closest sound to the Spanish diphthong, the fourth column has a Spanish word containing that diphthong, and the last column gives the pronunciation, using my symbols, of the Spanish word. Practice saying the following examples aloud.

**Spanish Diphthongs**

| Diphthong | Sound | English Word | Spanish Word | Sound |
| --- | --- | --- | --- | --- |
| ai | *ahy* | high | aire | *AHY-reh* |
| ia | *yah* | yacht | piano | *PYAH-noh* |
| ei | *ehy* | say | seis | *sehys* |
| ie | *yeh* | yes | siete | *SYEH-teh* |
| oi | *ohy* | boy | boina | *BOHY-nah* |
| io | *yoh* | yoke | nación | *na-SYOHN* |
| au | *ow* | cow | causa | *KOW-sah* |
| ua | *wah* | wasp | cuatro | *KWAH-troh* |
| eu | *ehw* | — | neurosis | *nehw-ROH-sees* |
| ue | *weh* | sway | bueno | *BWEH-noh* |
| ui | *wee* | sweet | cuidado | *kwee-DAH-doh* |
| iu | *yoo* | beauty | ciudad | *syoo-DAD* |

**JUST A MINUTE**

When the diphthongs *ai, ei, oi,* or *ui* appear at the end of words, their spelling is changed to *ay, ey, oy,* and *uy.*

Notice the last two entries in the preceding table; the two weak vowels combine to form diphthongs, too. Also notice the entry *eu*; there is no sound quite like this diphthong in English. Try saying *EH-oo* repeatedly; each time say it faster, lessening the space between the stressed *EH* and the unstressed *oo*, until the sound is more like *eh* plus a *w* sound (*ehw*).

## PRONOUNCE THE CONSONANTS

Practice the consonant sounds and the sample words in the following table.

**Spanish Consonant Sounds**

| Letter | English Sound | Example | Sound of Word |
|--------|---------------|---------|---------------|
| b | b | bueno | BWEH-noh |
| c | s (before e and i) | cinta | SEEN-tah |
| c | k (elsewhere) | cama | KAH-mah |
| ch | ch | chico | CHEE-koh |
| d | d | dan | dahn |
| f | f | familia | fah-MEE-lyah |
| g | h (before e and i) | general | heh-neh-RAHL |
| g | g (hard, elsewhere) | gol | gohl |
| h | silent | hombre | OHM-breh |
| j | h | jota | HOH-tah |
| k | k | kilo | KEE-loh |
| l | l | libro | LEE-broh |
| ll | y | lleno | YEH-noh |
| m | m | memoria | meh-MOR-yah |
| n | n | nervio | NEHR-byoh |
| ñ | ny | señor | seh-NYOHR |
| p | p | puro | POO-roh |
| qu | k | química | KEE-mee-ka |
| r | r (tap of tongue) | oro | OH-roh |
| r | rr (trill, word start) | radio | RRAH-dyoh |
| rr | rr (trill) | carro | KAH-rroh |
| s | s | sí | see |
| t | t | toro | TOH-roh |
| v | b | violín | byoh-LEEN |
| w | w | Wáshington | WAH-sheeng-tohn |
| x | gs | exacto | eg-SAK-toh |
| y | y | yogurt | yoh-GUR |
| z | s | zorro | SOH-rroh |

## Learn the Sound for *B* and *V*

The letters *b* and *v* have the same pronunciation; their usage is a spelling matter, not one of pronunciation. If you misspelled *cat* as *kat*, it would still be pronounced in the same way. Both *b* and *v* have two pronunciations, depending on what other sounds adjoin them. In most Spanish dialects, both letters are pronounced in much the same way we pronounce the English *b*, if one of the following conditions applies:

- They appear at the beginning of a phrase. This means they come after silence, even if it's just a slight pause in the sentence—the kind that might be represented in writing by a comma.

- They come after the letter *m* or the letter *n*. If either the *b* or the *v* follows the letter *n*, the combination sounds like *mb* rather than *nv*.

### JUST A MINUTE

Any time *m* or *n* precedes *b* or *v*, the resultant sound is *mb* rather than *nv*. This rule is true even if the *m* or *n* is at the end of a word before a word starting with a *b* or *v*.

See the following table for examples.

### Pronunciation of *B* or *V* After Pause and After *M* or *N*

| Phrase | Pronunciation |
| --- | --- |
| Voy a Colombia. | BOH-ya-koh-LOHM-byah |
| Sí, voy. | SEE (pause) BOHY |
| ¡Vamos! | BAH-mos |
| En Venezuela … | em-beh-neh-SWEH-la … |
| envío | em-BEE-oh |
| en busca | em-BOOS-kah |

However, in all other cases, the sound involved is one we don't have in English. To produce this sound, you put your lips close together, as with the English *b*. To produce the English *b*, you close your lips completely for a moment and then let air escape with an explosion. However, to produce the Spanish *b* or *v*, you need to relax your lips, leaving enough space for air to keep passing through the small opening. Try it. It will buzz a little and sound like something between an English *b* and *v*. Even if you don't make this sound yourself, knowing about the pronunciation of *b* and *v* will help you to understand native Spanish speakers. Otherwise, you might not recognize what is being said.

## LEARN THE SOUND FOR *D*

At the beginning of a phrase (after a pause) or after *n* or *l*, the Spanish *d* sounds like the English *d*. In all other cases, it sounds like the *th* in *the* or *this* (but more relaxed). Sometimes, it's so relaxed in careless speech that it becomes silent, especially if it's the last letter of a word or if it's in the word-ending *ado*. See the following list for examples of how the Spanish *d* is pronounced:

| | |
|---|---|
| interesado | *een-teh-reh-SAH-do* or *een-teh-reh-SAH-o* |
| lado | *LAH-do* or *LAH-o* |
| hablado | *ah-BLAH-do* or *ah-BLAH-o* |
| ganado | *gah-NAH-doh* or *gah-NAH-o* |
| helado | *eh-LAH-do or eh-LAH-o* |

## LEARN THE SOUND FOR *R*

The sound of the single *r* in Spanish is achieved with a single tap of the tip of the tongue against the ridge of gums just behind the upper teeth. This sound, however, is almost identical to the English pronunciation (in the United States, at least) of the letters *t* and *d* when the *t* or *d* is between vowels and comes right after the heavily accented syllable. For example, we Americans don't pronounce the *t* in later the way we pronounce the *t* in tell. (Try to pronounce the *t* of tell in the word *later*, and you'll see it sounds like an upper-class British accent.) And we don't pronounce the *d* in ladder as we do the *d* of done. (Try to pronounce the *d* of done in the word *ladder*, and you'll find it sounds very strange.) In American English, latter and ladder are pronounced in exactly the same way. We just flap the tips of our tongues once to produce the sound in question. This is basically the sound of the single Spanish *r*.

**TIME SAVER**

If you have trouble producing the single Spanish *r* in *verde,* saying "better they" quickly will be more recognizable to a Spanish speaker than pronouncing the word with an English *r* sound.

## LEARN THE SOUND FOR *RR*

The sound of *rr*, referred to in the consonant sounds table as a trill, is a sound we do not have in English, but it's similar to the sound children make when imitating the sound of a motor. It's produced by allowing the tip of the tongue to strike the ridge of gums behind the upper teeth from three to seven times. People often associate this rolling *rrrr* sound with the Spanish language.

### PROCEED WITH CAUTION

The *r* versus *rr* distinction is important in Spanish. *Pero* means *but; perro* means *dog.*

Note that when the single letter *r* is the first letter of a word, it is pronounced exactly the same as the double *rr* within words; it is a trill.

# LEARN SPANISH SPELLING

The Spanish spelling system is very straightforward and simple, especially when compared to the English system. Unlike English, there is not a lot of flexibility between spelling and pronunciation. Still, Spanish spelling does have a few quirks.

### JUST A MINUTE

The Spanish spelling system is so simple that spelling is not a subject taught in the school systems of Spanish-speaking countries.

The letter *q* in Spanish is used only in combination with *u* (*qu*), and only in front of the vowels *e* or *i*. To understand the reason behind this combination, first take a look at the pronunciation of the letter *c* in combination with vowels:

| | |
|---|---|
| casa | *KAH-sah* |
| cosa | *KOH-sah* |
| Cuba | *KOO-bah* |
| centro | *SEHN-troh* |
| cita | *SEE-tah* |

Notice that in order to produce the *k* sound, the letter *c* can be combined with the vowels *a*, *o*, or *u*. However, when *c* is combined with *e* or *i*, the resultant sound is *s*. To achieve the *k* sound with these vowels, you must use *qu*, as in the following words:

| quemar | *keh-MAHR* |
| queso | *KEH-soh* |
| máquina | *MAH-kee-nah* |
| Quito | *KEE-toh* |

Something similar happens with the letter *g*. See the pronunciation of this letter when followed by vowels:

| gala | *GAH-lah* |
| goma | *GOH-mah* |
| seguro | *seh-GOO-roh* |
| general | *heh-neh-RAHL* |
| agitar | *ah-hee-TAHR* |

Notice that with the letter *g* plus a vowel, only three combinations are possible to produce the sound *g*: *ga*, *go*, and *gu*. To achieve the phonetic combinations of *geh* and *gee*, a silent *u* is placed between the *g* and the *e* or *I*, forming the combinations *gue* or *gui*. The following words are examples of these combinations in action:

| Guerra | *GEH-rrah* |
| fatigué | *fah-tee-GEH* |
| guitarra | *gee-TAH-rrah* |
| águila | *AH-gee-lah* |

You now know how to write the sounds *gah*, *goh*, *goo*, *geh*, and *gee*. How do you write the sound *gweh* and *gwee*? In the few cases that these sounds are needed in Spanish, a dieresis (¨) is used over the *u* to convert it from a silent letter into a pronounced one.

| apacigüe | *ah-pah-SEE-gweh* |
| güiro | *GWEE-roh* |

**JUST A MINUTE**

Many native speakers have trouble knowing when to use the silent *h* and distinguishing between *b/v*, *y/ll*, and *s/c/z* in writing.

The letter *w* is used only in words that are not Spanish:

| | |
|---|---|
| Wáshington | *WAH-sheeng-tohn* |
| Wéllington | *WEH-leeng-tohn* |
| Wébber | *WEH-behr* |
| Wajay | *wah-HAHY* (town in Cuba, Indian name) |
| whisky (or whiski) | *WEES-kee* |
| walhalla | *wahl-HAH-lah* (mythological Norse Valhalla) |
| wat | *waht* (watt) |
| windsurf | *ween-SOORF* (windsurfing) |

The letter *k* is used only in words borrowed from other languages. In borrowed words, there is usually an alternate spelling:

| | |
|---|---|
| kilómetro/quilómetro | *kee-LOH-meh-troh* (kilometer) |
| kerosén/querosén | *keh-roh-SEHN* (kerosene) |
| kanguro/canguro | *kahng-GOO-roh* (kangaroo) |
| kaki/caqui | *KAH-kee* (khaki) |
| kiosko/quiosko | *KYOHS-skoh* (kiosk, newspaper stand) |

In the Spanish alphabet, *ch*, *ll*, and *rr* are considered separate letters. Words beginning with these letters have separate entries in the dictionary. For example, if you want to look up the word *chico*, you will not find it between *cetro* and *cianato*; it won't be under the listing for *c*. It will have its own listing as *ch*. Even when *ch* comes in the middle of words, it is considered its own letter. For example, *hechicería* won't come between *hecatombe* and *hectárea* in the dictionary. Instead it comes after the word *hectómetro*, where the words beginning with *hech* start. The same type of situation exists for *ll* and *rr*. This alphabetical order has been officially changed by the Royal Academy of the Spanish Language (*La Real Academia de la Lengua Española*) very recently (1998). However, dictionaries written before 1998 list the definitions according to the old order. Furthermore, other dictionaries may or may not choose to follow the Royal Academy's guidelines. The *ñ* (*EHN-yeh*) is still universally considered a separate letter of the Spanish alphabet. Very few words begin with this letter, but it appears within a great many words (*señor*, *año*, *baño*, and so on).

The *n/ñ* distinction is important. The word *ano* means *anus; año* means *year.*

## LEARN SPANISH ACCENTUATION

Up to this point, you have learned how to pronounce every letter of the Spanish alphabet. Only one matter remains before you can look at any word written in Spanish, even if you've never heard it pronounced, and be able to pronounce it with complete confidence: the Spanish accentuation system. Accentuation might seem like a small matter, but if you've ever heard foreigners attempting to learn English, you know that an error in accentuation can make their utterance unintelligible (they put the acCENT on the wrong syLLABle). There are three basic rules of Spanish accentuation. If you give a few minutes of concentrated attention to them, you'll know them for life.

### LEARN RULE I

If a word ends with a vowel, *s,* or *n,* the oral accentuation is placed on the next-to-last syllable automatically. By saying "automatically," I mean that no accent marks are used; you just know the stress is placed on the next-to-last syllable by the fact that the word ends with a vowel or an *s* or an *n.* See the following examples:

| | |
|---|---|
| chico | *CHEE-koh* (boy) |
| muchacho | *moo-CHAH-choh* (boy) |
| bueno | *BWEH-noh* (good) |
| chocolate | *cho-koh-LAH-teh* (chocolate) |
| habla | *AH-blah* (he/she speaks) |

Each of the preceding five words ends with a vowel, so the stress is automatically placed on the next-to-last syllable. The length of the word has no bearing on accentuation; the rule always applies. Because words ending with *n* or *s* are covered by this rule, the following words are still accented automatically on the next-to-last syllable:

| | |
|---|---|
| chicos | *CHEE-kohs* (boys) |
| muchachos | *moo-CHAH-chohs* (boys) |

| | | |
|---|---|---|
| buenos | *BWEH-nohs* (good) | |
| chocolates | *choh-koh-LAH-tehs* (chocolates) | |
| hablan | *AH-blahn* (they speak) | |

You can almost guess the rest.

**GO TO** ▶
With regard to the word *buenos*, see the lesson on agreement of adjectives with nouns they modify in Hour 2.

## LEARN RULE II

Rule I refers to words that end in a vowel, *n*, or *s*; Rule II refers to the other side of the coin: words that end in consonants other than *n* or *s*. These words are stressed automatically on the very last syllable. See the following examples:

| | |
|---|---|
| usted | *oos-TEHD* (you) |
| pared | *pah-REHD* (wall) |
| papel | *pah-PEHL* (paper) |
| profesor | *proh-feh-SOHR* (professor) |
| hablar | *ah-BLAHR* (to speak) |

As you'll see in Hour 2, nouns that end in a consonant add *es* to the end to pluralize them; this will then shift the preceding words into Rule I, and they'll be accented automatically on the next-to-last syllable. For example, *ustedes* is pronounced *oos-TEH-dehs*. All infinitive verbs end with *r*. For this reason, *hablar,* the infinitive form of the verb, is automatically accented on the last syllable, even though *habla* and *hablan*, which are present tense forms of the verb, are accented on the next-to-last syllable, as shown in the list for Rule I.

**GO TO** ▶
For conjugation of regular verbs in the present tense, see Hour 3.

## LEARN RULE III

Rule III is, strictly speaking, a nonrule. It explains what to do with words that break Rules I and II: Use the written accent mark to indicate where the stress (accentuation) is placed. To keep things clear, I will break this rule down into two parts. The first part deals with words that are not covered by either Rule I or Rule II: words stressed on the third-from-the-last syllable. These words are the least frequent type of word in Spanish:

| | |
|---|---|
| último | *OOL-tee-moh* (last) |
| próximo | *PROHG-see-moh* (next) |
| bálsamo | *BAHL-sah-moh* (balm/balsam) |
| carámbano | *kah-RAHM-bah-noh* (icicle) |
| póstumo | *POHS-too-moh* (posthumous) |

The second part covers words that simply go against Rules I and II:

| | |
|---|---|
| capitán | *kah-pee-TAHN* (captain) |
| salí | *sah-LEE* (I left) |
| López | *LOH-pehs* (López) |
| González | *gohn-SAH-lehs* (González) |
| hablé | *ah-BLEH* (I spoke) |

The word *capitán* would have fallen into Rule I because it ends with an *n*; that rule would have led you to believe it should be stressed on the next-to-last syllable. As you see, it is stressed on the last syllable, not the next-to-last one. Because it breaks the rule, it needs the written accent mark to show you exactly where the stress is. The second and fifth examples, *salí* and *hablé*, would also fall under Rule I because they end with a vowel. You would expect them to be accentuated automatically on the next-to-last syllable, but they aren't. They're stressed on the last syllable and therefore take the written accent mark to show this. López and González end with a consonant (but not *n* or *s*), so they would fall under Rule II, which calls for automatic stress on the last syllable. But they're stressed on the next-to-last syllable, breaking Rule II, and take the written accent to show this.

Earlier in this hour, you learned about the diphthong: a combination of a strong vowel with a weak vowel (or the two weak vowels) to form the center of one single syllable. Diphthongs also affect the rules of accentuation, as the following examples show:

| | |
|---|---|
| piano | *PYAH-noh* (piano) |
| radio | *RRAH-dyoh* (radio) |
| salió | *sah-LYOH* (he/she left) |

The words *piano* and *radio* follow the rules. This might not be obvious if you thought each of the two words contained three syllables. But because the *ia* of *piano* is a diphthong, the word has only two syllables. The next-to-last syllable is *pia*, and that's where the word is stressed, following Rule I. In the word *radio*, the *dio* represents one syllable, not two; the next-to-last syllable, then, is *ra*, and it's the one that's accentuated, following Rule I. The word *salió* is composed of two syllables (*sa-lió*). It would belong to Rule I, but it breaks that rule, because rather than the stress being on the next-to-last syllable (*sa*), it's on the last syllable (*lió*). That's why the written accent mark is necessary.

A diphthong can be broken by an accent mark on the weak vowel (the *i* or the *u*). In that case, the weak vowel becomes strong and is in a syllable separate from that of the other vowel. Two adjacent strong vowels are always in two separate syllables. The following examples show diphthongs being broken with an accent mark:

| | |
|---|---|
| librería | *lee-breh-REE-ah* (bookstore) |
| grúa | *GROO-ah* (crane/hoist) |
| continúo | *kohn-tee-NOO-oh* (I continue) |
| manía | *mah-NEE-ah* (mania) |

**JUST A MINUTE**

Accent marks are also used to differentiate between two words that are spelled and pronounced the same, but have different meanings. For example, *si* means *if,* but *sí* means *yes.*

## LEARN WORDS RELATED TO ENGLISH

A considerable number of Spanish words will be easy for you to learn because they're cognates with English words. That is, they come from the same source (mostly, but not exclusively, Latin), so they're similar in their written appearance. Naturally, their pronunciation is not exactly the same as in English. You'll recognize these words easily, and now that you've learned the pronunciation (including the accentuation) of Spanish, you'll quickly be able to make these words part of your Spanish vocabulary. You'll come across cognates throughout this book (and beyond, if you keep up your study of Spanish).

**PROCEED WITH CAUTION**

You can sometimes be fooled. *La librería* is not the library; it's the bookstore. *Embarazada* is not embarrassed; it's pregnant. *El éxito* is not the exit; it's success. *Ropa* is not rope; it's clothing. *Sopa* is not soap; it's soup.

The following list presents a sampling of cognates. It is an extremely small selection taken from the huge vocabulary in Spanish related to English. You'll be adding to your vocabulary as you proceed. Meanwhile, keep in mind how the Spanish words sound. You now know how to pronounce any Spanish word you see. Practice pronouncing these cognates correctly in Spanish according to what you've learned in this hour of study:

| | |
|---|---|
| *abrupto* (abrupt) | *la condición* (condition) |
| *abandonar* (to abandon) | *condicional* (conditional) |
| *la acción* (action) | *la confesión* (confession) |
| *la actitud* (attitude) | *la confusión* (confusion) |
| *activo* (active) | *elegante* (elegant) |
| *la actividad* (activity) | *el hotel* (hotel) |
| *la conexión* (connection) | *el menú* (menu) |
| *el centro* (center) | *la nación* (nation) |
| *central* (central) | *nacional* (national) |
| *la certificación* (certification) | *el piano* (piano) |
| *la circunstancia* (circumstance) | *el presidente* (president) |
| *la comunicación* (communication) | *la radio* (radio) |
| *la concentración* (concentration) | *el restaurante* (restaurant) |

## THE 30-SECOND RECAP

In this first hour, you have learned to pronounce Spanish so that native speakers will understand you. You are now able to pronounce any word in the Spanish language that you see written, even if you have never heard that word before. Additionally, you've learned some vocabulary that seems a lot like English (cognates) and are aware that there are thousands more cognates in Spanish and English.

## HOUR'S UP!

Review this hour once more and then answer the following questions. To really see how you're doing, don't go back and consult the lessons in this hour while taking the test. (You can find the answers in Appendix A.)

1. True or false: There are more vowel sounds in English than in Spanish.
2. True or false: The pronunciation of a Spanish vowel depends on the word it's in.
3. True or false: In the middle of a word, a single *r* is pronounced the same as a double *r*; it's only a question of spelling.

**QUIZ**

**4.** The word *piano* has ...

    **a.** One syllable.

    **b.** Two syllables.

    **c.** Three syllables.

    **d.** None of the above.

**5.** The letter *t* in *later* is pronounced very much like the Spanish sound represented by the letter ...

    **a.** *t.*

    **b.** *d.*

    **c.** *r.*

    **d.** None of the above.

**6.** The letter *r* in the Spanish word *ropa* is ...

    **a.** Pronounced like an English *r*.

    **b.** Pronounced like an English *t*.

    **c.** Silent.

    **d.** None of the above.

**7.** The letter *r* in the Spanish word *rango* is pronounced ...

    **a.** Like the *rr* in *perro*.

    **b.** Like the *r* in *pero*.

    **c.** Like the *l* in *pelo*.

    **d.** Like the *h* in *héroe*.

**8.** The Spanish word *envió* is pronounced ...

    **a.** *ahn-VEE-oh.*

    **b.** *ehn-vee-OH.*

    **c.** *ehm-BEE-oh.*

    **d.** *ehm-BYO.*

QUIZ

# HOUR 2
# Describing Things

**LESSON PLAN:**

In this hour, you'll learn ...

- How to count from 0 to 20 in Spanish.
- How to distinguish masculine nouns from feminine nouns.
- How to describe nouns by making adjectives and articles agree with them.
- How to change adjectives and articles from singular to plural.

Rather than learning all the numbers in one hour, you will learn to count from 0 to 20 in this hour and will gradually progress into the millions by Hour 8. The following table lists the numerals 0 through 20 with their Spanish names beside them. Look at the numerals one at a time and pronounce the Spanish names aloud, until you can establish a mental identification between each numeral and its Spanish name.

Be sure to pronounce these numbers (and any new vocabulary) according to the rules of pronunciation you studied in Hour 1. If you're not sure you remember those rules, you need to review them now, before you work on these numbers. Reviewing the rules of pronunciation will assure you of correct pronunciation and will avoid reinforcement of the wrong pronunciation. Unlearning ingrained habits is always more difficult than learning correctly from the beginning.

A good way to mentally associate the number with its Spanish name is to hold up a group of objects, such as your fingers, while pronouncing the Spanish words for the numbers. Obviously, fingers only work for counting up to 10. Later, when you learn to count up to 52, you might want to use a deck of playing cards instead of your fingers.

**Spanish Numbers 1 Through 20**

| Number | Word | Number | Word |
|--------|------|--------|------|
| 0 | cero | 11 | once |
| 1 | uno | 12 | doce |
| 2 | dos | 13 | trece |
| 3 | tres | 14 | catorce |
| 4 | cuatro | 15 | quince |
| 5 | cinco | 16 | diez y seis (dieciséis) |
| 6 | seis | 17 | diez y siete (diecisiete) |
| 7 | siete | 18 | diez y ocho (dieciocho) |
| 8 | ocho | 19 | diez y nueve (diecinueve) |
| 9 | nueve | 20 | veinte |
| 10 | diez | | |

## RECOGNIZE GENDER OF NOUNS

A noun is a person, place, or thing; boy, Richard, Chicago, and book are all nouns. Richard and Chicago are called proper nouns because one names a specific person and the other names a specific place. In English, nouns are feminine, masculine, and (the majority) neuter. In Spanish, there are no neuter nouns; all nouns are either masculine or feminine.

With reference to people and to animals, this division is logical: The nouns that stand for people or animals of the male sex are grammatically masculine in gender, and the nouns that stand for people or animals of the female sex are grammatically feminine in gender. However, many nouns in Spanish (or any language) do not refer to people or animals, but to inanimate objects (books, tables, plants, fruits, vegetables, trees, flowers, and so on) and animals that are so insignificant to humans that their sex is unimportant to us. For these nouns, gender has no logic and is purely arbitrary; yet you must learn the gender of all nouns in your vocabulary in order to speak Spanish correctly.

It is extremely important to know whether a noun is masculine or feminine because the article accompanying a noun and the adjectives modifying a noun need to be adjusted depending on the noun's gender. This adjustment is referred to as *agreement*. Luckily, you can recognize the gender of a great many Spanish nouns by their endings.

## RECOGNIZE FEMININE ENDINGS

Several noun endings are typically feminine:

- Nouns that end in -*a* are almost always feminine.
- Nouns that end in -*ión* are always feminine.
- Nouns that end in -*d* are always feminine.
- Nouns that end in -*umbre* are always feminine.
- Nouns that end in -*ez* are always feminine.

**PROCEED WITH CAUTION**

Do not confuse *el papá* (masculine), which means *the father; el Papa* (masculine), which means *the Pope;* and *la papa* (feminine), which means *the potato.*

## RECOGNIZE MASCULINE ENDINGS

With no more than three exceptions, the nouns ending in -*o* are masculine. The three exceptions are the feminine nouns: *la radio* (radio), *la mano* (the hand), and *la modelo*, when this last noun refers to *a female fashion model* (the masculine *el modelo* refers mainly to an inanimate object such as a *ship model* or an *airplane model*).

## RECOGNIZE NOUNS WITH TYPICAL ENDINGS

The following tables provide examples of feminine and masculine nouns that have the endings discussed previously as well as their English translations. Learn these nouns along with their definite articles (*la, el*) by pronouncing them aloud many times while creating a mental image of the thing or concept they represent. Picturing tangible items (a wall, a bull, or a piano) is much easier than creating a mental image of an abstraction (freedom, old age, or virtue). You might want to picture a smiling person breaking his or her chains for the concept attached to *la libertad;* an old man with a cane and long white beard for the concept of *la vejez;* or a child wearing a white robe, a smile, a halo, and angel wings for the concept of *la virtud.*

**Feminine Noun Endings**

| Ending | Sample Noun | English Meaning |
|---|---|---|
| *-a* | la cosa | the thing |
| *-ión* | la nación | the nation |
| *-d* | la ciudad | the city |
| *-d* | la libertad | liberty, freedom |
| *-d* | la virtud | virtue |
| *-d* | la pared | the wall |
| *-umbre* | la certidumbre | (the) certainty |
| *-ez* | la vejez | old age |

**Masculine Noun Endings**

| Ending | Sample Noun | English Meaning |
|---|---|---|
| *-o* | el libro | the book |
| *-o* | el piano | the piano |
| *-o* | el oro | (the) gold |
| *-o* | el toro | the bull |

## RECOGNIZE DECEPTIVE MASCULINE NOUNS

Even though the overwhelming majority of words that end in *-a* are feminine, some masculine nouns end with *-a,* such as *el día* (the day) and *el sofá* (the couch). In addition, a whole group of words that come from Greek and end specifically in either *ma, pa,* or *ta* are masculine. Here are a few members of this class of masculine nouns:

*el programa* (the program)     *el mapa* (the map)

*el planeta* (the planet)     *el tema* (the theme)

## IDENTIFY NOUN GENDER BY MEANING

Some nouns have endings that are neither typically feminine nor typically masculine. Although the endings supply no clue whatsoever, these nouns are recognized as either masculine or feminine nouns by a much more logical method: If the noun refers to a person or animal whose sex is female, then the noun is grammatically feminine. If the noun refers to a person or animal whose sex is male, then the noun is masculine. You must know the meaning of this type of noun in order to determine its grammatical gender. For example, the ending of the noun *hombre* offers no clue as to its gender, but if you know *hombre* means *man*, you know it is a masculine noun. The ending of the noun *mujer* offers no clue as to its gender, but if you know *mujer* means *woman*, you know it is a feminine noun.

**JUST A MINUTE**

A noun ending in *-ista* can be either masculine or feminine. *El pianista* refers to a *male pianist* and is therefore masculine; *la pianista* refers to a *female pianist* and is therefore feminine.

## IDENTIFY NOUN GENDER BY ARTICLE

Many nouns give no clue as to their gender either by their endings or by their meanings. For example, *la luz* (the light) is feminine, and *el lápiz* (the pencil) is masculine, although both nouns end with a *-z* and their meanings refer to nonsexual entities. To remember the gender of such nouns, you must learn them with their definite or indefinite articles. The nouns in the vocabulary lists of this book are shown accompanied by the definite article and the indication (m) for masculine or (f) for feminine. Although the (m) and (f) indications are helpful, it is not practical to rely on them when learning vocabulary, because you're not usually going to think of the word with the designation (m) or (f) after it. These indications are useful for checking on gender when you don't know or have forgotten the gender. On the other hand, the gender of the definite article will be an unmistakable indication of the noun's gender and is a natural word to use in conjunction with the noun, because you'll express it aloud in speech.

**GO TO ▶**
See the "Master the Definite Articles" and "Master the Indefinite Articles" sections in this hour for a discussion of definite and indefinite articles.

# PLURALIZE NOUNS

In English, we usually add *-s* or *-es* to the end of a noun to make it plural (book, books; glass, glasses). English also has a minority of nouns with other plural endings (ox, oxen; alumnus, alumni; cherub, cherubim; phenomenon, phenomena; and so on), as well as some nouns with no plural endings at all (deer; sheep). The Spanish system is clear-cut: If a noun ends with a vowel, add -s to make it plural. If it ends with a consonant, add -es. For example, *chico* becomes *chicos*, but *pared* becomes *paredes*. The following list has more examples:

> *hombre, hombres* (man, men)
> *libro, libros* (book, books)
> *cosa, cosas* (thing, things)
> *mujer, mujeres* (woman, women)
> *ciudad, ciudades* (city, cities)
> *nación, naciones* (nation, nations)

If the singular form of the noun ends with the consonant -*z*, change that *z* to *c* before adding -*es*. The following list has some examples of this rule:

> *actriz, actrices* (actress, actresses)
> *luz, luces* (light, lights)
> *vez, veces* (time, times)
> *lápiz, lápices* (pencil, pencils)

## MASTER THE DEFINITE ARTICLES

Both English and Spanish have definite articles. In English, the one and only form of definite article, the, is used with a noun that is specific and concrete (*The man is waiting for you.*) or unique (*the sun*). In Spanish, the definite articles (*el, la, los,* and *las*) are used just as they are in English, but they are also used with abstractions, generic nouns, and titles.

### MATCH DEFINITE ARTICLES TO NOUNS

Because in Spanish, unlike in English, the definite articles must agree in number (singular/plural) and gender (feminine/masculine) with the nouns they accompany, the definite article has four forms:

- **El.** The masculine singular definite article is *el*. For example, the man is *el hombre*, and the book is *el libro*.
- **Los.** The masculine plural definite article is *los*. The men are *los hombres*, and the books are *los libros*.

- **La.** The feminine singular definite article is *la*. For example, the woman is *la mujer,* and the thing is *la cosa.*
- **Las.** The feminine plural definite article is *las*. The women is *las mujeres,* and the things are *las cosas.*

## USE DEFINITE ARTICLES WITH ABSTRACTIONS

In Spanish, the definite articles (English *the*) are used with concrete or unique nouns and abstract nouns, such as those in the following list:

*la vida* (life)

*el amor* (love)

*la libertad* (freedom, liberty)

*la felicidad* (happiness)

*el honor* (honor)

*el respeto* (respect)

## USE DEFINITE ARTICLES WITH GENERIC NOUNS

In Spanish, definite articles are used when referring to nouns in the generic sense. For example, the noun *los hombres* for men (not referring to any specific men) is expressed in the same way as a reference to specific men. See the following list for more examples:

*el hombre* (man)

*las flores* (flowers)

*los españoles* (Spaniards; the Spanish)

*los libros* (books)

*los amigos* (friends)

*las mujeres* (women)

*el agua* (water)

### PROCEED WITH CAUTION

If a feminine noun begins with *a-* or *ha-* and is stressed on that first syllable, the definite article used is *el,* not *la,* and the indefinite article is *un,* not *una,* but the plural articles are *las* and *unas.* For example, the plural form of *el agua* is *las aguas.*

## Use Definite Articles with Titles

**GO TO** ▶
There are some cases in which English employs the indefinite article, but Spanish dispenses with it. See Hour 7 to learn under what circumstances the indefinite article is not used with the verb *ser*.

Another use of the definite article in Spanish where none is used in English is before a title: Mr. López is *el señor López*; Mrs. Herrera is *la señora Herrera*; Professor Díaz is *el profesor Díaz*; Captain Gallegos is *el capitán Gallegos*; President Carreras is *el presidente Carreras*; and so on. Note that the definite article is used with a title only when talking about the person, never when talking to that person. For example, you could say "*El profesor Díaz es peruano*" ("Professor Díaz is Peruvian"), but you would say "*¿Cómo está usted, profesor Díaz?*" ("How are you, Professor Díaz?")

## Master the Indefinite Articles

Both English and Spanish have indefinite articles. English has three forms of the indefinite article: *a*, *an*, and *some*. These indefinite articles are used with nouns that are nonspecific (a man, an apple, some dresses). The indefinite articles in Spanish are used in much the same circumstances as they are in English, but the Spanish indefinite articles come in four forms to match the number and gender of their corresponding nouns:

- **Un.** The masculine singular indefinite article is based on the number *uno* (one), which is shortened to *un*. Therefore, a man is *un hombre*, and a book is *un libro*.

- **Unos.** The masculine plural indefinite article is *unos*. Some men or a few men are *unos hombres*, and some books or a few books are *unos libros*.

- **Una.** In front of a feminine singular noun, the indefinite article is feminized by changing the *o* of *uno* to an *a*, producing *una*. Therefore, a woman is *una mujer*, and a thing is *una cosa*.

- **Unas.** The feminine plural indefinite article is *unas*, so some women or a few women are *unas mujeres*.

Note that the singular indefinite articles also translate as *one*, so *un hombre* and *una mujer* can also mean *one man* and *one woman*.

## Modify a Noun with a Noun

In both English and Spanish, a noun can be used to describe another noun. When this is done in English, it often gives the impression that one of the nouns is an adjective. For example, consider these noun pairs: chicken salad, cotton dress, and gold ring. While describing salads, dresses, and rings, respectively, the words *chicken, cotton,* and *gold* are nouns rather than adjectives. They refer to the materials or substances the salad, the dress, and the ring are made of. This structure (noun plus noun) exists in Spanish (*hombre lobo* means *werewolf,* for example), but it is much less common than it is in English.

The normal procedure for modifying a noun with another noun in Spanish is to have the main noun placed first, the preposition *de* (of or from) second, and the modifying noun third. See the following list for examples:

*ensalada de pollo* (chicken salad; literally, salad of chicken)

*vestido de algodo[as]n* (cotton dress; literally, dress [made] of cotton)

*anillo de oro* (gold ring; literally, ring [made] of gold)

## MAKE ADJECTIVES AND NOUNS AGREE

Adjectives are words that modify nouns. There are two kinds of adjectives: adjectives of quantity and descriptive adjectives. Adjectives of quantity include numbers and words like *mucho* (a lot), *muchos* (many), *poco* (little in quantity, not size), *pocos* (few), and so on. The following list provides some examples of quantifying adjectives modifying nouns:

*mucho pollo* (a lot of chicken)

*muchos pollos* (many chickens)

*mucha virtud* (a great deal of virtue)

*un libro* (one book, a book)

*unos libros* (some books, a few books)

*una silla* (one chair, a chair)

*unas sillas* (some chairs, a few chairs)

*cinco libros* (five books)

*cinco sillas* (five chairs)

*poco movimiento* (little movement, not much movement)

*pocos pollos* (few chickens, not many chickens)

*poca virtud* (not much virtue)

*pocas virtudes* (few virtues, not many virtues)

In English, adjectives have only one form and do not agree with the nouns they modify. The descriptive adjective good, for example, has that single form. A book is good, a man is good, a woman is good, 100 books are good, 100 men are good, and 100 women are good. In Spanish, however, an adjective—just like the articles covered earlier—must agree in number (singular/plural) and gender (feminine/masculine) with the noun it modifies. You may have noticed how the adjectives in the preceding list changed to match the nouns. The following sections outline some rules to follow when matching adjectives to nouns.

## Change Masculine *o* to Feminine *a*

If, and only if, the masculine form of an adjective ends in *o*, then change the *o* to *a* to make it feminine. In Spanish, a tall man is *un hombre alto*. As you can see, the adjective *alto* (tall) ends with an *o* in the masculine form. If it is to modify a feminine noun, you must change that *o* to an *a*. A tall woman is *una mujer alta*.

## Add *a* to Consonants to Feminize

If, and only if, the masculine form of an adjective ends with a consonant and refers to nationality (or the person's origin in a country, province, region, state, city, town), then you add (not change) the letter *a* to the adjective to make it feminine. For example, the masculine form of the Spanish adjective for Spanish is *español*. This adjective fits the two ifs: It is an adjective of nationality (or origin), and it ends with a consonant. You know, then, that to have it modify a feminine noun, you must add the letter *a*. A Spanish man is *un hombre español*; a Spanish woman is *una mujer española*. The following list has more examples:

*un chico español* (a Spanish boy)

*una chica española* (a Spanish girl)

*el caballo andaluz* (the Andalusian horse)

*una rosa andaluza* (an Andalusian rose)

## ADD *A* TO *-DOR* TO FEMINIZE

If the masculine form of an adjective ends with *-dor*, you change it to the feminine form by adding *a*, as in these examples: *un movimiento libertador* (a liberating movement); *una idea libertadora* (a liberating idea).

## ADD *A* TO *-ON* TO FEMINIZE

If the masculine form of an adjective has the augmentative ending *-ón*, then you add the letter *a* to make it agree with a feminine noun. Thus, *un hombre mandón* (a domineering man) becomes *una mujer mandona* (a domineering woman).

## CHANGE *-OTE* TO *-OTA* TO FEMINIZE

If the masculine form of an adjective has the augmentative ending *-ote*, then in order to have it agree with a feminine noun you change (not add) the final *-e* to a final *-a* (changing *grandote* to *grandota*, for example). (The adjectives *grandote* and *grandota* are forms of the adjective *grande* [big] with the final *e* dropped and the augmentative *-ote* [masculine] or *-ota* [feminine] added to make the adjective sound even bigger.)

**TIME SAVER**

Adjectives that end with *-ón* and with *-ote*, which make both adjectives and nouns sound big, are far less common than other adjectives. You might want to come back to them later.

## DO NOT CHANGE ANYTHING

The previous rules use the word *if* a great deal; they refer to certain specific types of adjectives. If you are not dealing with those specific types of adjectives (a masculine form ending with *-o*, *-or*, *-ón*, *-ote*, or an adjective of nationality that ends with a consonant), then do not change the form of the adjective. Many adjectives, such as *inteligente*, *azul*, and *atroz*, do not need different endings in order to modify masculine and feminine nouns. In other words, these adjectives are both masculine and feminine with no modification.

For example, the intelligent man in Spanish is *el hombre inteligente*; the intelligent woman in Spanish is *la mujer inteligente*. The blue book is *el libro azul*; the blue house is *la casa azul*. An atrocious book is *un libro atroz*; an atrocious idea is *una idea atroz*.

## PLURALIZE ADJECTIVES

Up until now, you've been dealing with masculine and feminine forms of adjectives. Because Spanish adjectives agree not only in gender but in number as well, you will now learn how to pluralize adjectives. Fortunately, the procedure for pluralizing adjectives is exactly the same as for pluralizing nouns. You add an *-s* to adjectives that end in a vowel and add *-es* to adjectives that end in a consonant: *el libro azul* (the blue book) becomes *los libros azules* (the blue books); *la chica inteligente* (the intelligent girl) becomes *las chicas inteligentes* (the intelligent girls).

**PROCEED WITH CAUTION**

Exactly as is the case for nouns, if an adjective ends with the consonant *-z*, change that *-z* to *-c* before adding *-es*. For example, *atroz* becomes *atroces*, *capaz* becomes *capaces*, and *feliz* becomes *felices*.

Study the following table to see how adjectives and articles change (or do not change) in order to agree with the nouns they modify.

**Matching Adjectives to Nouns**

| Masculine Adjective | Article/Noun/Adjective | English |
| --- | --- | --- |
| **Ending in -o** | | |
| bueno | un libro bueno | a good book |
| bueno | una silla buena | a good chair |
| bueno | unos libros buenos | some good books |
| bueno | unas sillas buenas | some good chairs |
| **Nationality Ending with a Consonant** | | |
| francés | el vino francés | the French wine |
| francés | la enciclopedia francesa | the French encyclopedia |
| francés | los vinos franceses | the French wines |
| francés | las enciclopedias francesas | the French encyclopedias |

| Masculine Adjective | Article/Noun/Adjective | English |
| --- | --- | --- |
| **Ending with -dor** | | |
| renovador | un movimiento renovador | a renewing movement |
| renovador | una idea renovadora | a renewing idea |
| renovador | movimientos renovadores | renewing movements |
| renovador | ideas renovadoras | renewing ideas |
| **Ending with -ón** | | |
| mandón | un hombre mandón | a domineering man |
| mandón | una mujer mandona | a domineering woman |
| mandón | hombres mandones | domineering men |
| mandón | mujeres mandonas | domineering women |
| **Ending with -ote** | | |
| grandote | el tejano grandote | the great big Texan |
| grandote | la tejana grandota | the great big Texan woman |
| grandote | los tejanos grandotes | the great big Texans |
| grandote | las tejanas grandotas | the great big Texan women |
| **All Other Endings: No Change for the Feminine** | | |
| azul | el cuaderno azul | the blue notebook |
| azul | la casa azul | the blue house |
| azul | los cuadernos azules | the blue notebooks |
| azul | las casas azules | the blue houses |
| inteligente | un hombre inteligente | an intelligent man |
| inteligente | una mujer inteligente | an intelligent woman |
| inteligente | unos hombres inteligentes | some intelligent men |
| inteligente | unas mujeres inteligentes | some intelligent women |

GO TO ▶
See the "Learn Spanish Accentuation" section of Hour 1 for a discussion of the use of accent marks.

## Know Where to Place Adjectives

As in English, adjectives of quantity (*dos, cinco, mucho[s], poco[s], varios*) normally precede the noun in Spanish, as in *las tres chicas* (the three girls), *diez libros* (10 books), *mucho dinero* (a great deal of money), and *muy pocas cosas* (very few things). You have of course noticed from previous examples that in Spanish, unlike in English, *descriptive* adjectives normally follow the noun in Spanish, as in *una chica bonita, un libro importante, una idea estúpida,* and *la mujer inteligente.*

## Change Placement to Change Meaning

You can change the connotation of the adjective by the way you position it. For example, if an adjective has two possible meanings, one literal and one figurative, placing the adjective after the noun indicates you are speaking literally. In this case, *el hombre pobre* (the poor man) refers to a man who has little or no money. On the other hand, placing the adjective before the noun indicates that you are speaking figuratively. *El pobre hombre* (the poor man) does not refer to his financial state at all. The second example might refer to a millionaire, but one who has just been run over by a truck. In other words, *el pobre hombre* indicates sympathy. The concept of *pobre* when the adjective precedes the noun refers to a general lack of fortune, not specifically to poverty. The following list provides other examples of adjectives used literally and figuratively:

| | |
|---|---|
| *un hombre grande* (literal) | a big man (physical size) |
| *un gran hombre* (figurative) | a great man (moral stature) |
| *un amigo viejo* (literal) | an old friend (an elderly friend) |
| *un viejo amigo* (figurative) | an old friend (a long-time friend) |
| *mujeres puras* (literal) | pure women (virgins) |
| *puras mujeres* (figurative) | exclusively women, nothing but women |
| *un coche nuevo* (literal) | a new car (this year's model) |
| *un nuevo coche* (figurative) | a new car (new to the owner or another, different, car: either a replacement or additional car) |

**JUST A MINUTE**

When *grande* is placed before any singular noun, it is shortened to *gran.*

## UTILIZE ADJECTIVE PLACEMENT FOR EMPHASIS

Even when you are dealing with descriptive adjectives that don't have both literal and figurative meanings, the placement of the adjective before or after the noun affects the connotation. As a general rule, the material at the end of a sentence or phrase or clause in Spanish is emphasized more than the material at the beginning. Even in an utterance of only two words, the second word usually has more emphasis than the first. Therefore, when the descriptive adjective follows the noun, as it normally does, that adjective is being emphasized. You are distinguishing the noun that possesses the quality conveyed by the adjective in contrast to those nouns that do not possess that quality.

For example, if you report that an airplane has crashed in *las montañas altas de Colorado* (the high mountains of Colorado), you are contrasting the mountains of Colorado that are high with the mountains of the same state that are relatively low or not quite as high by emphasizing the adjective *altas* by placing it after the noun. You are saying the plane crashed in the high, rather than lower, mountains of Colorado.

When you put the descriptive adjective before the noun, you are emphasizing the noun more than the adjective; you are making no contrast. When you report that the plane has crashed in *las altas montañas de Colorado*, you are making the comment that all the mountains in Colorado are high.

### PROCEED WITH CAUTION

If you ask a man about the health of his *esposa encantadora* (*charming wife*) rather than the more normal *encantadora esposa* (*charming wife*), you imply he has other wives who are not charming.

No one would say *un español caballo* because the aim of a phrase using the noun *caballo* and the adjective *español* would always be to distinguish horses that are Spanish from all other horses, not to say that it is typical of all horses to be Spanish. Because the word *español*, in addition to being an adjective, is also the noun meaning Spaniard, the juxtaposition of those two words could be taken to refer to something like a Spaniard who, for some reason or other, has the qualities of a horse. It would be totally abnormal. A Spanish horse would be *un caballo español*.

## RECOGNIZE ADJECTIVES WHOSE PLACEMENT IS OF NO CONSEQUENCE

With the very commonly used adjectives *bueno* (good) and *malo* (bad), it makes no difference in denotation or connotation whether they are used before or after the noun. There is only a bit more stress on the adjective when it follows the noun. However, when these two adjectives precede a singular masculine noun, they are shortened to *buen* and *mal*, respectively. In their plural forms, both masculine and feminine, they are not abbreviated.

*un hombre bueno* (a good man)

*un buen hombre* (a good man)

*una mujer buena* (a good woman)

*una buena mujer* (a good woman)

*un hombre malo* (a bad man)

*un mal hombre* (a bad man)

## TURN ADJECTIVES INTO NOUNS

In English, you don't bother using a noun you've modified with an adjective if you and the person you're talking to already know what the noun is. If I asked you "Which car do you prefer: the blue car or the red car?" the question would almost sound childish and certainly repetitive. The more normal question would be "Which car do you prefer: the blue one or the red one?"

**JUST A MINUTE**

Many Spanish adjectives are easily turned into nouns by using a definite article. For example, *el viejo* means *the old man*, *la vieja* means *the old woman*, *el joven* means *the young man*, and *la joven* means *the young woman*.

In Spanish, instead of using the word *one*, you turn adjectives into nouns. For example, the question of which car you prefer would be stated "*¿El azul o el rojo?*" ("The blue or the red?") Remember that if it were a feminine noun referred to, you would be using the feminine form of the adjective and the feminine definite article ("*¿La azul o la roja?*"). Likewise, if the noun were plural, the adjectives and articles would be plural as well. See the following table for examples of the nominalization of adjectives.

**JUST A MINUTE**

Adjectives of nationality can become nouns, as in *un español* (a Spaniard) or *una inglesa* (an English woman). In the masculine form only, adjectives can become the names of languages, as in *el español* (Spanish) or *el inglés* (English).

Sometimes, you would want to use the indefinite article instead of the definite article before the adjective. For example, if someone asked you what color car you preferred, instead of saying "the red one," you would probably say "a red one" because you're not talking about a specific car.

Remember how the number *uno* is shortened to *un* when used as an article in front of a singular masculine noun? This rule does not apply in this instance, because you're only using the adjective as though it were a noun, but it still is an adjective and not a noun. The full number *uno* is used instead. Thus, in order to express the idea of the English *a red one*, you would say *uno rojo* (not *un rojo*). It's as though you were thinking "one that is red," but leaving out the words *that is*.

**Adjectives as Nouns**

| With Noun | English | Without Noun | English |
|---|---|---|---|
| el libro nuevo | the new book | el nuevo | the new one |
| los libros nuevos | the new books | los nuevos | the new ones |
| la silla roja | the red chair | la roja | the red one |
| las sillas rojas | the red chairs | las rojas | the red ones |
| un libro nuevo | a new book | uno nuevo | a new one |
| unos libros nuevos | some new books | unos nuevos | some new ones |
| una silla roja | a red chair | una roja | a red one |
| unas sillas rojas | some red chairs | unas rojas | some red ones |

**PROCEED WITH CAUTION**

Certain adjectives have been used as nouns so often that they may be called nouns, which affects the indefinite article used with them if the adjective/noun in question is masculine and singular. For example, *uno joven* means *a young one* and could refer to a person, a dog, a cat, a horse, or any other animal. But *un joven* normally refers to *a young man*.

# THE 30-SECOND RECAP

After having carefully studied this chapter, you should be able to do the following:

- Count from 0 to 20.
- Distinguish a masculine noun from a feminine noun.
- Pluralize nouns.
- Make articles agree with the noun in gender and number.
- Use nouns to modify other nouns.
- Have adjectives agree with the noun they modify in gender and number.
- Understand different connotations of adjectives depending on their position before or after the noun.
- Use adjectives as though they were nouns.

- Use a modest Spanish vocabulary based on words used as examples in this chapter.

## HOUR'S UP!

Check to see how well you've learned the material covered by this hour of study. Try to choose the correct answer in this multiple-choice quiz without rereading any of the material. (You can find the answers in Appendix A.)

**1.** Fill in the blank: _____ *libros*

    **a.** mucho

    **b.** muchos

    **c.** mucha

    **d.** muchas

**2.** Fill in the blank: _____ *vino*

    **a.** poco

    **b.** poca

    **c.** pocos

    **d.** pocas

**3.** Fill in the blank: *unas sillas* _____

    **a.** buena

    **b.** buenos

    **c.** bueno

    **d.** buenas

**4.** Fill in the blank: *la montaña* _____

    **a.** altas

    **b.** alto

    **c.** altos

    **d.** alta

**5.** Fill in the blank: *una idea* _____

    **a.** atroces

    **b.** atroz

    **c.** atroce

    **d.** atroza

**QUIZ**

# HOUR 3

# Actions in the Present Tense

You have already mastered the Spanish numbers from 0 through 20 and are ready to move forward. The following table lists the numbers 21 through 40 with the Spanish word for the numeral beside them. Look at the numerals one at a time and pronounce the Spanish names for them aloud until you can establish a mental identification between the numeral and its Spanish name. Be sure to pronounce these words and any new vocabulary in this lesson according to the rules of pronunciation you studied in Hour 1.

## HANDLE 21 AND 31 WITH NOUNS

In Hour 2, you learned that the number *uno* changes when it is used in front of a noun either as a number or as the indefinite article. You say *un libro* and *una silla*. This rule is true for every number ending in 1 through 91. See the following examples:

*veintiún libros* (21 books)

*veintiuna sillas* (21 chairs)

*treinta y un hombres* (31 men)

*treinta y una mujeres* (31 women)

## CHAPTER SUMMARY

**LESSON PLAN:**

In this hour, you'll learn ...

- How to count from 21 to 40 in Spanish.
- Subject pronouns in English and their Spanish counterparts.
- Spanish verb usage and the multiple applications of the Spanish present tense.
- How to conjugate regular and stem-changing verbs in the present tense.

**Spanish Numbers 21 Through 40**

| Number | Word | Number | Word |
|---|---|---|---|
| 21 | veinte y uno (veintiuno) | 31 | treinta y uno |
| 22 | veinte y dos (veintidós) | 32 | treinta y dos |
| 23 | veinte y tres (veintitrés) | 33 | treinta y tres |
| 24 | veinte y cuatro (veinticuatro) | 34 | treinta y cuatro |
| 25 | veinte y cinco (veinticinco) | 35 | treinta y cinco |
| 26 | veinte y seis (veintiséis) | 36 | treinta y seis |
| 27 | veinte y siete (veintisiete) | 37 | treinta y siete |
| 28 | veinte y ocho (veintiocho) | 38 | treinta y ocho |
| 29 | veinte y nueve (veintinueve) | 39 | treinta y nueve |
| 30 | treinta | 40 | cuarenta |

**PROCEED WITH CAUTION**

Notice that *veinte* (20) ends with an *-e,* but *treinta* (30) ends with an *-a.* Note, too, that the 20s have an alternate spelling (indicating a slight change in pronunciation), but the 30s do not.

## REVIEW ENGLISH PRONOUNS

Because it might have been quite a while since you formally studied English grammar, you might want to review some of the grammatical terms involved in this lesson. The terms are the same whether applied to English or Spanish. The *subject* of a verb is the person, animal, or thing that performs the action of that verb. For example, in the sentence "John gave Mary the book," John is the subject because he is the one who carried out the action of the verb *to give.*

**GO TO ▶**
For a discussion of the object pronouns see Hours 11, 12, 14, 15, and 17.

A *pronoun* is a word that takes the place of a noun. For example, if we already know we're talking about John, we don't keep repeating his name in a conversation about him. Instead, we substitute the pronoun *he.* We substitute a personal (referring to a person) pronoun for the proper noun *John.* Because the pronoun *he* is used only when John is performing the action of the verb, it is a *subject pronoun.* To be very specific grammatically, he is the third person singular subject pronoun. If something were done to or for John, we would use the object pronoun *him.*

In discussing the identity of people, animals, and things, three categories are helpful: first person, second person, and third person. *First person* is the term used to refer to someone speaking of him- or herself. Think of the colloquial expression "I'm looking out for number one." In English, the first person is expressed with I or we. *Second person* refers to the one to whom you are speaking. In English, the second person is expressed as you. *Third person* refers to the person (or animal or thing) about whom you are speaking. He, she, it, and they are all third person pronouns.

In addition to being in either first, second, or third person, subject pronouns are further classified as being either singular or plural and either feminine or masculine. The following list provides the complete description of all the English subject pronouns.

**English Pronouns**

| Pronoun | Description |
| --- | --- |
| I | first person singular |
| you | second person singular |
| he | third person singular, masculine |
| she | third person singular, feminine |
| we | first person plural |
| you | second person plural |
| they | third person plural, masculine |
| they | third person plural, feminine |

Note that *we* is called the first person plural because it is used to refer to yourself joined by others. Note as well that *you* is both the singular and plural form of second person. Note that although the third person singular is divided into masculine (he) and feminine (she), the third person plural combines masculine and feminine into one pronoun (they).

## LEARN THE SPANISH SUBJECT PRONOUNS

Now that you have reviewed the terminology pertinent to the study of subject pronouns, you are ready to learn the subject pronouns used in Spanish. Study the following table. It shows the Spanish subject pronoun in the first column, the description by person, number, and gender in the second column, and the English equivalent in the third column. Note that among the singular subject pronouns, only the third person distinguishes between masculine and feminine.

**Spanish Subject Pronouns**

| Subject Pronoun | Description | English Equivalent |
| --- | --- | --- |
| yo | first person singular | I |
| tú | second person singular, familiar | you |
| usted | second person singular, formal | you |
| él | third person singular, masculine | he |
| ella | third person singular, feminine | she |
| nosotros | first person plural, masculine | we |
| nosotras | first person plural, feminine | we |
| vosotros | second person plural, familiar, masculine | you |
| vosotras | second person plural, familiar, feminine | you |
| ustedes | second person plural, formal | you |
| ellos | third person plural, masculine | they |
| ellas | third person plural, feminine | they |

## DISTINGUISH FORMAL FROM FAMILIAR

As you can see in the preceding table, Spanish has five second person pronouns: *tú, usted, vosotros, vosotras,* and *ustedes.* These pronouns are all equivalent to the one English second person pronoun: you. One reason that there are so many second person pronouns in Spanish is that Spanish makes a distinction between familiar pronouns, which are used in informal situations or with people you know well, and formal pronouns. English uses the same second person pronoun in all situations.

For example, *tú* is a familiar pronoun because you use it when speaking to a close friend, a relative, a person with whom you feel you have a great deal in common (fellow worker, classmate, and so on), or a child. Children and teenagers invariably use *tú* with each other almost everywhere, even when they don't know each other. In many places, people in their 20s use *tú* this way as well.

**JUST A MINUTE**

You usually use *tú* with people with whom you're on a first-name basis and *usted* with people you call Mr., Mrs., Miss, or Ms., plus the family name.

Like *tú, usted* is singular, but it's formal. You use it when addressing a stranger or someone you don't know very well. You should also use it when addressing an older person or someone else who deserves special respect and in formal situations such as business meetings. Using *usted* places a kind of distance between people, whereas using *tú* shows familiarity.

Keep in mind that these usage guidelines are approximate, because the use of *tú* and *usted* varies greatly from region to region in the vast geographical areas in which Spanish is spoken.

**PROCEED WITH CAUTION**

If you suddenly switch from using *tú* when addressing a friend to *usted,* this sudden formality gives the impression that you are distancing yourself from that friend, perhaps because you are angry.

The subject pronoun *vosotros* and its feminine counterpart, *vosotras,* are the plural forms of *tú.* In other words, they are used when talking to more than one person with whom you are familiar. However, the *vosotros* and *vosotras* pronouns are used in normal everyday conversation in Spain only. Most Latin Americans are aware that this pronoun is used all the time in Spain, because they see motion pictures made in Spain.

The pronoun *ustedes* is the plural form of *usted.* It's the formal third person subject pronoun used for groups of people you address formally. The Spanish-speaking countries of Latin America also use *ustedes* as the plural of *tú.*

## KNOW HOW TO USE *NOSOTROS* AND *NOSOTRAS*

*Nosotros* and *nosotras* are the plural forms of *yo.* You use them when referring to yourself and others with you, like the English *we.* A boy or man never uses *nosotras,* because that form of the second person plural subject pronoun is used only by a woman and only when all the others she is including with her are also female.

A man (or boy) always uses *nosotros,* the masculine form, even when he is the only male in the group. A woman uses *nosotros* if there is even one male in her group. Notice the situations in which the two forms would be used.

### *Nosotros* vs. *Nosotras*

| Situation | Form |
| --- | --- |
| A man speaks; only men are in his group. | Nosotros |
| A man speaks; men and women are in his group. | Nosotros |
| A man speaks; he is the only man in his group. | Nosotros |
| A woman speaks; only women are in her group. | Nosotras |
| A woman speaks; there are men and women in her group. | Nosotros |
| A woman speaks on behalf of a group of 1,000 people that contains just one man. | Nosotros |

---

**JUST A MINUTE**

The same rules of gender for *nosotros* also apply to *vosotros*. The only time you would use the feminine *vosotras* is when you are speaking exclusively to women (whether you are a man or woman). Even if you were conversing with a group of 1,000 women and just one man, that man would make it necessary to use the masculine *vosotros*.

## UNDERSTAND SPANISH VERB USAGE

A verb is a word that expresses action (for example, I think), existence (therefore, I am), or condition (I am tired). It connects the subject of a sentence with the predicate.

The English language has a great many peculiarities, as does any language, but its verb system is comparatively simple. On the other hand, the Spanish verb system is much more complex. Spanish verb endings contain a great deal of information; they tell who, how many, and when. In other words, the endings indicate the grammatical person (first person, second person, or third person), number (singular or plural), and tense (present, past, future, and so on).

**PROCEED WITH CAUTION**

It's essential to master the verb system because the subject pronouns are ordinarily left out in Spanish.

In English, it makes no sense to say "eats a lot," because you would not know who is the one doing the eating. You would need to state the subject, whether with a noun (the boy, Tracey) or a pronoun (he, she). However, in Spanish, it very frequently is not necessary to insert a subject pronoun; the verb ending provides enough information by itself.

When conjugating verbs orally, be careful to follow the rules of accentuation studied in Hour 1 or the meaning could be drastically changed. *Hablo* means *I speak,* but *habló* means *he or she spoke.*

You need to know two terms before we can discuss the use of Spanish verbs: *conjugate* and *infinitive.* When you conjugate a verb, you use the endings that show person, number, and tense. When a verb is not conjugated, it is in the infinitive form and does not indicate who is performing the action of the verb or when the performance occurs. In English, the infinitive always starts with the preposition *to,* as in to be, to go, to speak, and to eat. In Spanish, the infinitive form of the verb always ends in the letter *r,* as in *hablar, comer,* and *vivir.*

Although all Spanish infinitives end with the letter *r,* the vowels preceding the letter *r* are different. Based on these endings, Spanish verbs and their conjugations can be grouped into three categories: *-ar, -er,* and *-ir* verbs. The following sections explain how to conjugate these different categories of verbs.

## Learn the Regular Present Tense *-ar* Conjugation

The first step in conjugating a Spanish verb of the present tense is to remove the infinitive ending *-ar* so that just the stem remains. Thus, the verb *hablar* (to speak) becomes the stem *habl-.* The next step is to attach to the stem the ending that shows the person, number, and tense. The following table shows the endings for the present tense *-ar* verbs next to the subject pronoun that corresponds to the ending.

With reference to verbs, *regular* simply means that you're dealing with a verb that adheres to the rules of conjugation for its group. I'll cover the peculiarities of irregular verbs later on in the book.

### Present Tense for *-ar* Verbs Using *Hablar*

| Subject Pronoun | Verb Stem | Ending | Conjugated Verb |
|---|---|---|---|
| yo | habl- | -o | hablo |
| tú | habl- | -as | hablas |
| él | habl- | -a | habla |
| ella | habl- | -a | habla |

*continues*

**Present Tense for *-ar* Verbs Using *Hablar*   (continued)**

| Subject Pronoun | Verb Stem | Ending | Conjugated Verb |
| --- | --- | --- | --- |
| usted | habl- | -a | habla |
| nosotros/as | habl- | -amos | hablamos |
| vosotros/as | habl- | -áis | habláis |
| ellos | habl- | -an | hablan |
| ellas | habl- | -an | hablan |
| ustedes | habl- | -an | hablan |

**JUST A MINUTE**

The subject of verbs in the third person does not need to be a pronoun. Just as in English, it can be a noun or a proper noun (for example, *el hombre, las sillas, María, Carlos y María*).

Notice that the verb endings for *él, ella*, and *usted* are identical; all three end with *-a*, the vowel found in the infinitive ending right before the final *r*. The verb endings for those three subject pronouns will always be identical. The subject of these verbs doesn't have to be human; it can be a thing, an "it." Notice, too, that the verb endings for the plural forms of those three pronouns (*ellos, ellas*, and *ustedes*) are also identical; they always end in *-an*.

Let's make sure you understand the meaning of the conjugated verb. When reviewing foreign language material, it is not a good idea to translate. However, at this stage, in which you're seeing Spanish verbs conjugated for the first time, make sure you thoroughly understand the meaning. The following table lists the English meaning of the verb *hablar* conjugated in the present tense.

| Verb | Meaning |
| --- | --- |
| (Yo) hablo. | I speak. |
| (Tú) hablas. | You (familiar) speak. |
| (Él) habla. | He speaks. |
| (Ella) habla. | She speaks. |
| (Usted) habla. | You (formal) speak. |
| (Nosotros) hablamos. | We speak. |
| (Vosotros) habláis. | You (familiar, plural) speak. |
| (Ellos) hablan. | They (masculine) speak. |
| (Ellas) hablan. | They (feminine) speak. |
| (Ustedes) hablan. | You (formal, plural) speak. |

## DETERMINE THE SUBJECT BY UNDERSTANDING VERB ENDINGS

The subject pronouns in the preceding list are in parentheses to indicate that Spanish speakers very often do not bother to state them because they are implicit in the ending of the conjugated verb. After all, if you say "*Hablo español*," the verb ending *-o* tells the listener you're expressing the thought that in English would be "I speak Spanish." There is no need to use the subject pronoun *yo* because the verb ending reveals the subject.

If you say "*Hablamos francés*," the Spanish speaker knows, without your saying it, that the subject is *nosotros*. He or she knows you are expressing the thought that in English would be "We speak French." The Spanish speaker would also know that the implied subject of *hablas* is *tú* and that the implied subject of *habláis* is *vosotros* or *vosotras* (if you're speaking only to women).

Depending on the context, the endings *-a* and *-an* are a little more problematic, because *habla* could conceivably mean *he speaks, she speaks,* or *you* (formal, singular *usted*) *speak*. By the same token, *hablan* could signify *they speak* or *you* (plural) *speak*. As you might guess, then, the subject pronouns *él, ella, usted, ellos, ellas,* and *ustedes* are used more than the other subject pronouns, in order to avoid confusion. But they're used much less than subject pronouns in English.

### PROCEED WITH CAUTION

Don't be misled into thinking the masculine pronoun *ellos* necessarily refers only to men; it can refer to men and women as a pair or group the same way that *nosotros* can refer to a mixed group.

Any of those six subject pronouns can be avoided (and usually are) because of other signals. For example, if someone tells you "*Habla mucho*," while pointing his thumb at Juan, you know, without his using the pronoun *él*, that he means that Juan talks a lot. On the other hand, if he utters exactly the same words and points at you, the implied pronoun is *usted*, and he's indicating that you are the one who talks a great deal. If you mention Juan and María, and someone says "*Ah, sí, hablan inglés*," you know, just by the natural flow of the conversation, that the implied subject pronoun of *hablan* is not *ustedes* or *ellas*; it is *ellos*. He's saying that they (Juan and María) speak English.

## USE THE SUBJECT PRONOUN FOR EMPHASIS AND CLARITY

When an *-ar* verb is conjugated to end with *-o, -as, -amos,* or *-áis*, you know the subject is *yo, tú, nosotros/as,* or *vosotros/as*, respectively. Even with the forms of the verb that end with -a and -an, there are ways (pointing, context) to avoid having to use the subject pronoun. However, you might choose to use the subject pronoun for various reasons. One is simply for clarity, to avoid any possibility of confusion, especially on the telephone.

To stress the subject pronoun in Spanish, you can place it after the verb, rather than before it. (The closer a word is to the end of a sentence, the more stress it receives.) The following phrases all mean *I speak Spanish*, but they have different levels of emphasis:

- *Hablo español.* This phrase does not emphasize the subject pronoun, and it is a standard way to state this fact.

- *Yo hablo español.* This standard phrase places a slight emphasis on the subject pronoun.

- *¡Hablo yo español!* This phrase places great emphasis on *yo*. In English, it would be similar to saying, "I'm the one who speaks Spanish!"

- *¡Hablo español yo!* This phrase has the same connotation as the preceding sentence.

**JUST A MINUTE**

In Spanish, sentence structure is more flexible than in English; the subject can be placed almost anywhere, with only a difference in emphasis.

## PRACTICE CONJUGATING *-AR* VERBS

Practice conjugating the following regular *-ar* verbs by the same method explained for *hablar*. Make these verbs part of your Spanish vocabulary as well:

*cantar* (to sing)

*llevar* (to carry, to wear, or to take from one place to another)

*llamar* (to call)

*viajar* (to travel)

*usar* (to use)

Here are some sample sentences:

*Canto bien.* (I sing well.)

*Las chicas cantan bien.* (The girls sing well.)

*Llevamos zapatos.* (We wear shoes.)

*Unos hombres llevan zapatos.* (A few men wear shoes.)

*Viajáis mucho.* (All of you travel a lot.)

*Viajas a Bolivia.* (You travel to Bolivia.)

*Ellos usan el coche.* (They use the car.)

## LEARN THE REGULAR PRESENT TENSE CONJUGATION FOR *-ER* VERBS

As with the *-ar* verbs, the first step in conjugating *-er* verbs is to remove the infinitive ending, which in this case is *-er*. Thus, the verb *comer* (to eat) becomes the verb stem *com-*. The next step is to attach to the stem (in this case *com-*) the ending that shows the person, number, and tense.

### TIME SAVER

The only difference between *-ar* and *-er* verb endings is that the vowel added to the stem of the *-er* verbs is *an e* rather than the *a* of the *-ar* verbs.

Study the following table, which shows the endings for the present tense of the *-er* verbs next to the subject pronoun that corresponds to the ending.

**Present Tense for *-er* Verbs Using *Comer***

| Subject Pronoun | Verb Stem | Ending | Conjugated Verb |
|---|---|---|---|
| yo | com- | -o | como |
| tú | com- | -es | comes |
| él | com- | -e | come |
| ella | com- | -e | come |
| usted | com- | -e | come |
| nosotros/as | com- | -emos | comemos |
| vosotros/as | com- | -éis | coméis |
| ellos | com- | -en | comen |
| ellas | com- | -en | comen |
| ustedes | com- | -en | comen |

Notice the similarities between the *-ar* and the *-er* verbs. In both cases, the *yo* form of the verb ends with the vowel *-o*. The *tú* form of both types of verbs ends with the consonant *s*. The *él, ella,* and *usted* forms all end with a vowel. In both cases, the *nosotros/as* form ends with *-mos*, and the *vosotros/as* form ends with an accented vowel plus *is*. The *ellos, ellas,* and *ustedes* forms of both types of verbs end with the consonant *n*. The only difference is that an *e* rather than an *a* precedes the final consonant.

The following table lists the English meaning of the verb *comer* conjugated in the present tense.

| Verb | Meaning |
|------|---------|
| (Yo) como. | I eat. |
| (Tú) comes. | You (familiar) eat. |
| (Él) come. | He eats. |
| (Ella) come. | She eats. |
| (Usted) come. | You (formal) eat. |
| (Nosotros) comemos. | We eat. |
| (Vosotros) coméis. | You (familiar, plural) eat. |
| (Ellos) comen. | They (masculine) eat. |
| (Ellas) comen. | They (feminine) eat. |
| (Ustedes) comen. | You (formal, plural) eat. |

**JUST A MINUTE**

Notice how the Spanish subject pronouns in the plural provide information about the sex of the subject, which English does not.

Practice conjugating the following regular *-er* verbs using the same method used for *comer*. Make these verbs part of your vocabulary:

*leer* (to read)

*creer* (to believe, think)

Read these sample sentences:

*Lees muchos libros.* (You read a lot of books.)

*Unos amigos leen mucho.* (Some friends read a lot.)

*Leemos unas revistas.* (We read a few magazines.)

*Vosotras leéis periódicos.* (You [women] read newspapers.)

## Learn the Regular *-ir* Conjugation

As with the *-ar* and *-er* verbs, the first step in conjugating *-ir* verbs is to remove the infinitive ending. Thus, the verb *vivir* (to live) becomes the verb stem *viv-*. The next step is to attach to the stem (in this case *viv-*) the ending that shows the person, number, and tense of the verb. Study the following table, which shows the endings for the present tense of the -ir verbs next to the subject pronoun that corresponds to the ending.

**Present Tense of -ir Verbs Using Vivir**

| Subject Pronoun | Verb Stem | Ending | Conjugated Verb |
| --- | --- | --- | --- |
| yo | viv- | -o | vivo |
| tú | viv- | -es | vives |
| él | viv- | -e | vive |
| ella | viv- | -e | vive |
| usted | viv- | -e | vive |
| nosotros/as | viv- | -imos | vivimos |
| vosotros/as | viv- | -ís | vivís |
| ellos | viv- | -en | viven |
| ellas | viv- | -en | viven |
| ustedes | viv- | -en | viven |

In the present tense, the -ir verb endings are very similar to the -er verb endings. In fact, you've probably noticed that, with the exception of the nosotros/as and vosotros/as forms, the endings of the -ir verbs are identical to those of the -er verbs.

**TIME SAVER**

The -ir verbs use imos and ís for the nosotros and vosotros endings, whereas the -er verbs use emos and éis. This is the only difference between these two types of verbs in the present tense.

The following table lists the English meaning of the verb vivir conjugated in the present tense.

| Verb | Meaning |
| --- | --- |
| (Yo) vivo. | I live. |
| (Tú) vives. | You (familiar) live. |
| (Él) vive. | He lives. |
| (Ella) vive. | She lives. |
| (Usted) vive. | You (formal) live. |
| (Nosotros) vivimos. | We live. |
| (Vosotros) vivís. | You (familiar, plural) live. |

*continues*

*continued*

| Verb | Meaning |
| --- | --- |
| (Ellos) viven. | They (masculine) live. |
| (Ellas) viven. | They (feminine) live. |
| (Ustedes) viven. | You (formal, plural) live. |

Practice conjugating the following regular *-ir* verbs using the same method used for *vivir*. Make these verbs part of your vocabulary:

*escribir* (to write)

*describir* (to describe)

*recibir* (to receive)

### JUST A MINUTE

You will remember the meaning of *escribir* if you keep in mind the English cognates: scribe, inscribe, describe, scribble, and scrivener.

Read these sample sentences:

*Escribes muchas cartas.* (You write a lot of letters.)

*Escribimos pocas cartas.* (We write few letters.)

*Recibís muchas cartas.* (All of you receive letters.)

*Recibo veintiuna tarjetas postales por mes.* (I receive 21 postcards a month.)

*Describen la casa.* (They describe the house.)

*María describe el caballo.* (María describes the horse.)

## UNDERSTAND PRESENT TENSE USAGE

The uses of the present tense in Spanish may seem self-evident, and you might assume these uses correspond exactly to the uses of the present tense in English. This, however, is not the case.

In English, we don't use the present tense to speak of what is happening at the present time. If you say, for example, "I watch television," you don't mean you're doing it at that very moment; you mean you do it as a general rule. In English, the term *present tense* is a misnomer; it refers to customary acts, not to acts taking place in the present. When you want to refer to an ongoing act in the present, you use what is termed the present progressive tense; instead of "I watch television," you say "I am watching television."

In Spanish, you use the present tense to indicate a customary, habitual behavior. You also use it to express an action that is going on right now. In addition, you can employ the present tense as an affirmation or confession of an action. For example, the Spanish present tense sentence *Uso el teléfono* has several different meanings in English:

**GO TO** ▶
For details on the present progressive tense, see Hour 9.

- Customary action: I use the telephone.
- Ongoing action: I am using the phone.
- An admission or confession: I do use the phone.

Spanish speakers also use the present tense to speak of a future that is considered by the speaker to be the near future. For example, this sentence uses the adverb *mañana* (tomorrow) with the present tense: *Mañana uso el teléfono*. In English, this phrase means, *Tomorrow I'm using the phone*, or *Tomorrow I'll be using the phone*.

## USE STEM-CHANGING VERBS

Earlier in this hour, you learned how to conjugate regular present tense Spanish verbs. Several types of verbs in Spanish do not follow the regular pattern, but have some sort of irregularity. One type of irregularity is called *stem changing*. The stem of the verb is the syllable right before the infinitive ending.

In some verbs, the *e* in the stem changes to *ie* when conjugated in the present tense. In others, the *e* in the stem changes to *i*. In still others, an *o* in the stem changes to *ue*. There is even one verb in which the *u* of the stem changes to *ue*. Note: These stem changes never take place in the *nosotros* and *vosotros* forms.

### CHANGE THE *E* OF THE STEM

The following table lists typical present tense verbs in all three groups (*-ar*, *-er*, and *-ir*) in which the *e* of the stem changes to *ie* or to *i*. Note that the endings of the verbs are perfectly regular.

**Present Tense Stem-Changing Verbs That Change *e* to *ie* or *i***

| Cerrar (To Close) | Perder (To Lose) | Pedir (To Ask For) |
| --- | --- | --- |
| cierro | pierdo | pido |
| cierras | pierdes | pides |
| cierra | pierde | pide |

*continues*

**Present Tense Stem-Changing Verbs That Change _e_ to _ie_ or _i_ (continued)**

| Cerrar (To Close) | Perder (To Lose) | Pedir (To Ask For) |
|---|---|---|
| cerramos | perdemos | pedimos |
| cerráis | perdéis | pedís |
| cierran | pierden | piden |

**PROCEED WITH CAUTION**

Be careful. Many students confuse _perder_ with _pedir_. The meanings differ, they have different stem changes, and they belong to different groups.

Practice conjugating the following stem-changing verbs in which the _e_ changes to _ie_. Use the preceding table as a guide, and take care to note whether the verb ends with _-ar_, _-er_, or _-ir_. Make these verbs part of your vocabulary:

_querer_ (to want, to love)

_pensar_ (to think)

_comenzar_ (to start)

_empezar_ (to start)

_sentir_ (to feel, to sense)

Read these sample sentences:

_Quiero a María._ (I love María.)

_Queremos viajar._ (We want to travel.)

_Siempre piensas mucho._ (You always think a lot.)

_Empezamos mañana._ (We start tomorrow.)

_Comienzan mañana._ (They start tomorrow.)

_Lo siento mucho._ (I'm very sorry. [Literally, I feel it much.])

_Pierdo muchas cosas._ (I lose a lot of things.)

_Pido muchas cosas._ (I ask for a lot of things.)

_Perdemos el autobús._ (We're missing the bus.)

_Pedimos el coche._ (We're requesting the car.)

**JUST A MINUTE**

_Pedir_ does not mean to ask a question; it means _to ask for_—that is, _to request some-thing._ It also means to order (ask for) something in a restaurant. You don't need an answer; you need someone to do something for you.

## CHANGE *O* IN THE STEM TO *UE*

See the following table for present tense verbs, in all three types in which the *o* of the stem changes to *ue*.

**Present Tense Stem-Changing Verbs That Change *o* to *ue***

| Soñar (To Dream) | Soler (To Be Used To) | Dormir (To Sleep) |
| --- | --- | --- |
| sueño | suelo | duermo |
| sueñas | sueles | duermes |
| sueña | suele | duerme |
| soñamos | solemos | dormimos |
| soñáis | soléis | dormís |
| sueñan | suelen | duermen |

### PROCEED WITH CAUTION

Not all verbs with an *e* or an *o* in the stem change. In the vocabulary lists, the verbs that do have a stem change will show (*ie*), (*i*), or (*ue*) after the entry.

The verb *soler* (*ue*) is conjugated and followed by an infinitive verb to signify that you are accustomed to or in the habit of performing the action of the infinitive verb. For example, *Suelo hablar mucho* means *I usually talk a lot* or *I'm accustomed to talking a lot*.

### JUST A MINUTE

One verb in the Spanish language has a stem change from *u* (not *o*) to *ue*. *Jugar* (to play) is conjugated as follows: *juego, juegas, juega, jugamos, jugáis, juegan*.

## THE 30-SECOND RECAP

In this hour, you've learned to use subject pronouns and to speak in the present tense with regular verbs and stem-changing verbs. You also know the various uses for the present tense and have continued counting through 40.

## QUIZ

## HOUR'S UP!

Try to answer the following questions without looking up the answers in this lesson. (You can find the answers in Appendix A.)

1. Fill in the correct form of the verb *comer: Las chicas* _____ *mucho.*

2. Fill in the correct form of the verb *viajar: Yo* _____ *a España mañana.*

3. Fill in the correct form of the verb *pensar: María* _____ *siempre.*

4. Fill in the correct form of the verb *pensar: Nosotros* _____ *a veces.*

5. Fill in the correct form of the verb *pedir: Tú* _____ *más tiempo.*

6. Fill in the correct form of the verb *perder: Yo* _____ *el tiempo.*

7. Fill in the correct form of the verb *vivir: Vosotros* _____ *en San Francisco.*

8. In Spain, the subject pronoun that means you and that is directed at people who are all female and with whom you are very close friends is …

   a. ustedes.

   b. vosotras.

   c. ellas.

   d. nosotras.

9. If a woman is talking about herself and five others with her (four other women and a boy), the subject pronoun she would use is …

   a. nosotras.

   b. vosotras.

   c. vosotros.

   d. nosotros.

10. The subject pronoun *ustedes* refers to …

    a. A person you are talking about.

    b. More than one person you are talking about.

    c. A person you are talking to.

    d. More than one person you are talking to.

# Hour 4

## Actions in Present and Past Tenses

CHAPTER SUMMARY

**LESSON PLAN:**

In this hour, you'll learn ...

- How to count from 41 through 70 in Spanish.
- How to use verbs that are irregular in the present tense.
- How to talk about the future.
- How to form questions and contractions.

You have already mastered the Spanish numbers from 0 through 40 and are ready to move on. The following table lists numbers 41 through 70 in numerals with their Spanish names beside them. Look at the numerals one at a time and pronounce the Spanish name for each aloud until you can establish a mental identification between the numeral and its Spanish name.

**Spanish Numbers from 41 Through 70**

| Number | Name | Number | Name |
|--------|------|--------|------|
| 41 | cuarenta y uno | 56 | cincuenta y seis |
| 42 | cuarenta y dos | 57 | cincuenta y siete |
| 43 | cuarenta y tres | 58 | cincuenta y ocho |
| 44 | cuarenta y cuatro | 59 | cincuenta y nueve |
| 45 | cuarenta y cinco | 60 | sesenta |
| 46 | cuarenta y seis | 61 | sesenta y uno |
| 47 | cuarenta y siete | 62 | sesenta y dos |
| 48 | cuarenta y ocho | 63 | sesenta y tres |
| 49 | cuarenta y nueve | 64 | sesenta y cuatro |
| 50 | cincuenta | 65 | sesenta y cinco |
| 51 | cincuenta y uno | 66 | sesenta y seis |
| 52 | cincuenta y dos | 67 | sesenta y siete |
| 53 | cincuenta y tres | 68 | sesenta y ocho |
| 54 | cincuenta y cuatro | 69 | sesenta y nueve |
| 55 | cincuenta y cinco | 70 | setenta |

# USE IRREGULAR PRESENT TENSE VERBS

In addition to the regular verbs and the stem-changing verbs of the present tense, which you learned about in Hour 3, you need to learn to use several other kinds of irregular verbs in the present tense.

## LEARN *SER* AND *IR*

The two most irregular verbs of the present tense in Spanish are *ser* (to be) and *ir* (to go). As you can guess from their meanings, these verbs are heavily used; therefore, they are extremely important to master. The following table shows the conjugation of *ser* and *ir*.

**Present Tense of Ser and Ir**

| Subject Pronoun | Ser (To Be) | Ir (To Go) |
| --- | --- | --- |
| yo | soy | voy |
| tú | eres | vas |
| él | es | va |
| ella | es | va |
| usted | es | va |
| nosotros/as | somos | vamos |
| vosotros/as | sois | vais |
| ellos | son | van |
| ellas | son | van |
| ustedes | son | van |

**GO TO** ▶

*Ser* and *ir* belong to a small class of verbs that end in *-oy* instead of *-o* in the first person singular. See the "Learn Irregular First Person *-oy* Verbs" section in this lesson.

Without a doubt, *ser* is the most irregular verb of the present tense in the Spanish language. The various conjugated forms look absolutely nothing like the infinitive form or one another. Furthermore, the third person singular form (*es*) is like no other third person singular verb in the Spanish present tense, because it does not end with a vowel.

To learn the conjugations of *ser*, practice saying the following sentences:

*Soy estudiante.* (I'm a student.)

*Eres estudiante.* (You [familiar] are a student.)

*Usted es estudiante.* (You [formal] are a student.)

*Carmen es bonita.* (Carmen is pretty.)

*Somos artistas.* (We're artists.)

*Sois músicos.* (All of you are musicians.)

*Las chicas son norteamericanas.* (The girls are [North] Americans.)

*Ustedes son puertorriqueños.* (You are Puerto Ricans.)

**PROCEED WITH CAUTION**

Although many Hispanics may call us *americanos,* sometimes they are sensitive when we say it, because they are Americans, too (Latin Americans). For the sake of goodwill, you should use the term *norteamericanos* (North Americans).

Although *ir* is not quite as irregular as *ser*, it is irregular in the sense that, like the forms of *ser*, conjugated forms of *ir* look nothing at all like the infinitive form. The conjugated forms do, however, resemble each other, and their endings, except for the *yo* form, are the regular endings for all present-tense verbs in the sense that they follow the *-s*, vowel, *-mos*, *-is*, and *-n* endings for the subject pronouns *tú, él, ella, usted, nosotros, vosotros, ellos, ellas,* and *ustedes*, respectively. However, the conjugated forms of *ir* are peculiar in that they use the *-ar* verb endings even though the infinitive *ir* has an *-ir* ending.

## USE *IR* AND A DESTINATION

You can use the verb *ir* with the preposition *a* (to) plus the name of a place to speak of going to your destination similarly to the way we express the thought, "He's going to New York." Read the following examples:

*Voy a casa.* (I'm going home.)

*¿Vas a casa, también?* (Are you going home, too?)

*¿Vais a la ciudad?* (Are you [familiar, plural] going to the city?)

*¿Van ustedes a la ciudad?* (Are you [formal, plural] going to the city?)

## EXPRESS THE FUTURE WITH *IR*

The verb *ir* plus *a* (to) plus an infinitive verb is used very commonly and frequently as a substitute for the future tense. In fact, it is probably used more frequently than the future tense itself. It is analogous to the English use of *going to*. For example, *Yo voy a comer* means *I'm going to eat.*

### Learn a Special Use of *Vamos*

The *nosotros* form of the present tense of *ir* has a double use. When the subject pronoun is explicitly stated, *vamos* exclusively means *we go* or *we're going*. However, when the pronoun is not used, *vamos* has two possible uses: (1) to report that we go or are going (*Vamos.*), or (2) as an exhortation (*¡Vamos!*, meaning *Let's go!*). *Vamos* plus infinitive verb means *Let's …* (whatever the infinitive verb means). Practice saying the examples in the following list:

> *¡Vamos a comer!* (Let's eat!)
>
> *¡Vamos a viajar!* (Let's travel!)
>
> *¡Vamos a usar el teléfono!* (Let's use the phone!)
>
> *¡Vamos a escribir unas cartas!* (Let's write some letters!)

Keep in mind that the sentences in the preceding list can also be simple declarative statements in the present tense, using the first person plural as the subject: We're going to eat; we're going to travel; we're going to use the phone. As statements, they would probably not carry the exclamation points, but this is not necessarily the case, because the statements could be expressed emotionally, probably gleefully. (We're going to eat!) It all depends on the context.

### Learn Irregular First Person *-oy* Verbs

Certain verbs are regular in the present tense with every subject pronoun except *yo*. One subgroup of these verbs is the one that ends with *-oy* rather than the usual *-o*, as do *ser and ir*. Practice using the examples of these verbs in the following table.

**Present Tense Verbs Ending in -oy in First Person Singular**

| Subject Pronoun | Dar (To Give) | Estar (To Be) |
|---|---|---|
| yo | doy | estoy |
| tú | das | estás |
| él | da | está |
| ella | da | está |
| usted | da | está |
| nosotros/as | damos | estamos |
| vosotros/as | dais | estáis |
| ellos | dan | están |
| ellas | dan | están |
| ustedes | dan | están |

The verb *estar* does have another peculiarity: Except for the *nosotros* form, it is stressed on the last syllable. As you know from the rules of accentuation presented in Hour 1, the forms *estás*, *está*, and *están* require a written accent mark on the letter *a* to indicate this stress. Practice saying the following sentences:

**GO TO** ▶
*Ser* and *estar* both mean *to be* in English. The differences in use between them are detailed in Hours 7 and 9.

> *Damos mucho.* (We give a lot.)
>
> *Los amigos dan mucho.* (Friends give a lot.)
>
> *Dais mucho.* (You [familiar, plural] are giving a lot.)
>
> *Estamos en la calle.* (We're in the street.)
>
> *Estoy en casa.* (I'm at home.)
>
> *Están en la escuela.* (They're at school.)
>
> *¿Estás en el hospital?* (Are you in the hospital?)

## LEARN IRREGULAR FIRST PERSON *-ZCO* VERBS

A group of verbs that end in *-cer* and *-cir* have an irregular *yo* form of the verb that ends in *-zco*, whereas all the other subject pronouns take a perfectly regular form. The conjugations of two of these verbs are shown in the following table.

**Present Tense Verbs Ending with -zco in the Yo Form**

| Subject Pronoun | Conocer (To Know) | Producir (To Produce) |
| --- | --- | --- |
| yo | conozco | produzco |
| tú | conoces | produces |
| él, ella, usted | conoce | produce |
| nosotros/as | conocemos | producimos |
| vosotros/as | conocéis | producís |
| ellos, ellas, ustedes | conocen | producen |

Practice conjugating the *zco* verbs in the following list:

> *crecer* (to grow, increase)
>
> *obedecer* (to obey)
>
> *ofrecer* (to offer)
>
> *parecer* (to seem, to appear)
>
> *reconocer* (to recognize)
>
> *traducir* (to translate)

Practice saying the following sentences that use -*zco* verbs:

*Como y crezco.* (I eat and grow.)

*Él come y crece.* (He eats and grows.)

*Conocemos a Roberto.* (We know Roberto.)

*Yo no conozco a Roberto.* (I don't know Roberto.)

*Ellas conocen a Miguel.* (They [feminine] know Miguel.)

*En Cuba producen azúcar.* (In Cuba, they produce sugar.)

*Reconozco a María.* (I recognize María.)

## LEARN *SABER* AND *VER*

The following table shows two more commonly used verbs that, in the present tense, are irregular only in the *yo* form.

**TIME SAVER**

You can use the abbreviations *Ud.* and *Uds.* instead of writing the full words *usted* and *ustedes.*

**Present Tense of Saber and Ver**

| Subject Pronoun | Saber (To Know) | Ver (To See) |
| --- | --- | --- |
| yo | sé | veo |
| tú | sabes | ves |
| él, ella, Ud. | sabe | ve |
| nosotros/as | sabemos | vemos |
| vosotros/as | sabéis | veis |
| ellos, ellas, Uds. | saben | ven |

These two -*er* verbs are perfectly regular in every person but the first person singular. The *yo* form of *saber* is extremely irregular. In the case of *ver*, what makes the *yo* form irregular is simply that the letter *e* of the infinitive is retained, instead of being dropped, before adding the final *o*.

## USE *SABER* AND *CONOCER*

The verbs *saber* and *conocer* can both be translated by the English verb *to know*, but they do not mean the same thing. *Saber* has the following meanings:

- To have information about something or someone
- To know a subject thoroughly
- To know how to do something
- To know about something or someone

**JUST A MINUTE**

There is no need to use the equivalent of the English word *how* in speaking of know-ing how to do something in Spanish. Just use the verb *saber* plus the infinitive verb representing what the person knows how to do. For example, *Yo sé cocinar* means *I know how to cook*.

Practice saying aloud the following sentences while feeling their meaning:

*Carlos no sabe mucho.* (Carlos doesn't know much.)

*Yo sé mucho.* (I know a lot.)

*¿Sabes?* (You know? or Do you know?)

*Sé que Chicago está en Illinois.* (I know that Chicago is in Illinois.)

*Ella sabe la lección.* (She knows the lesson thoroughly.)

*¿No sabéis escribir en francés?* (Don't you all know how to write in French? or You don't know how to write in French?)

The verb *conocer* means *to know* in the sense of being acquainted with, being familiar with, or having some passing knowledge of or some acquaintance with. Practice saying aloud the following examples:

*Conozco a Magdalena.* (I am acquainted with Magdalena.)

*Conocen Chicago.* (They are familiar with Chicago.)

*Ella conoce la lección.* (She is familiar with the lesson.)

*Conocemos el caso.* (We know vaguely or basically what the case is about.)

*¿Conocéis al profesor?* (Do you all know the professor?)

*¿Tú conoces Nevada, no?* (You're familiar with Nevada, aren't you?)

**GO TO** ▶
For a review of the stem-changing verbs, see the "Use Stem-Changing Verbs" section in Hour 3.

## Learn to Use *Tener* and *Venir*

The following table shows two commonly used verbs that are irregular for two reasons: The *yo* form of the verb has a *g* inserted in its ending, and the other forms (except, as always, the *nosotros* and *vosotros* forms) have the *ie* stem change.

**Present Tense for *Tener* and *Venir***

| Subject Pronoun | Tener (To Have, Hold) | Venir (To Come) |
|---|---|---|
| yo | tengo | vengo |
| tú | tienes | vienes |
| él, ella, Ud. | tiene | viene |
| nosotros/as | tenemos | venimos |
| vosotros/as | tenéis | venís |
| ellos, ellas, Uds. | tienen | vienen |

Note that these two verbs have exactly the same forms (stems as well as endings), making them rhyme perfectly, except for the endings for *nosotros* and *vosotros*. This difference is due to their belonging to two different verb groups (*-er* and *-ir*).

Practice saying the following sentences:

*Tengo mucho tiempo.* (I have a lot of time.)

*¿Tiene usted un cigarrillo?* (Do you have a cigarette?)

*Tú y yo tenemos una cita.* (You and I have a date.)

*¿Qué tienes?* (What do you have?)

*¿Viene usted muchas veces?* (Do you come here often?)

*Vengo a veces.* (I come here sometimes.)

**JUST A MINUTE**

*¿Qué tienes?* literally means *What do you have?* It is also used to mean *What's the matter with you?* or *What's wrong with you?*

## LEARN THE *-IR* VERBS WITH THE EXTRA *Y*

The following table shows the conjugations of three *-ir* verbs that share (except for the *nosotros* and *vosotros* forms) the irregularity of having a y inserted before the usual endings (among other peculiarities).

## Present-Tense -ir Verbs with Extra y

| Subject Pronoun | Construir (To Construct) | Influir (To Influence) | Oír (To Hear) |
|---|---|---|---|
| yo | construyo | influyo | oigo |
| tú | construyes | influyes | oyes |
| él, ella, Ud. | construye | influye | oye |
| nosotros/as | construimos | influimos | oímos |
| vosotros/as | construís | influís | oís |
| ellos, ellas, Uds. | construyen | influyen | oyen |

You will notice that the verb *oír* does not have a y inserted in its *yo* form. Instead, it has a *g*, just as *tener* and *venir* did. But it does have the y in every other form except, as usual, *nosotros* and *vosotros*.

These verbs conjugate in the same way as *construir* and *influir*:

> *obstruir* (to obstruct)
>
> *concluir* (to conclude, to end)
>
> *destruir* (to destroy)

Practice saying the following sentences aloud:

> *Construimos supermercados*. (We build supermarkets.)
>
> *¿Construyen ustedes supermercados?* (Do you [plural] build supermarkets?)
>
> *Él oye muy bien*. (He hears very well.)
>
> *Perdón, no oigo*. (Sorry, I can't hear. Literally, Pardon, I don't hear.)
>
> *¿No oís?* (Don't you [familiar, plural] hear?)
>
> *Destruyen las casas*. (They're destroying the houses.)
>
> *Destruimos las casas*. (We're destroying the houses.)

**GO TO ▶**
For an explanation of methods of asking questions and a study of interrogative words (*what, who, how,* and so on), see the "Ask Questions" section in this hour.

## LEARN OTHER VERBS WITH AN INTERPOSED G

In addition to the verbs *oír, tener,* and *venir*, other verbs contain an interposed *g* in the ending of the *yo* form. The following table shows three of them.

| Subject Pronoun | Decir (To Say, Tell) | Hacer (To Do, Make) | Poner (To Put) |
|---|---|---|---|
| yo | digo | hago | pongo |
| tú | dices | haces | pones |
| él, ella, Ud. | dice | hace | pone |
| nosotros/as | decimos | hacemos | ponemos |
| vosotros/as | decís | hacéis | ponéis |
| ellos, ellas, Uds. | dicen | hacen | ponen |

Note that although *hacer* and *poner* are regular in every way other than having the interposed *g* in the ending, *decir* is, in addition, one of the stem-changing verbs in which the *e* changes into an *i*.

The following verbs also contain a *g* before the final *o* of the ending for the pronoun *yo*:

- **Caer (to fall).** caigo, caes, cae, caemos, caéis, caen
- **Salir (to leave, go out).** salgo, sales, sale, salimos, salís, salen

Practice saying the following sentences aloud:

*¿Qué dices, amigo?* (What are you saying, my friend?)

*No digo nada, hombre.* (I'm not saying anything, man.)

*Ellos me dicen todo.* (They tell me everything.)

*Yo no hago nada.* (I'm not doing anything.)

*¿Sales pronto?* (Are you leaving soon?)

*Sí, salgo muy pronto.* (Yes, I'm leaving very soon.)

## LEARN THE -GER VERBS

There are some verbs that some texts refer to as *irregular*, but that are perfectly regular in the spoken language. The rules of Spanish orthography make it necessary to substitute one letter for another to preserve the sound. In Hour 1, you learned that the Spanish letter *g* is pronounced like the *g* in the English word *go*, but that in front of the letter *e* or *i*, it is pronounced like the English *h*.

This means that in the verb *coger* (to take, grasp, grab, seize, catch), the *g* has an *h* sound. The regular ending for *yo* with that verb would be an *-o*. And that is exactly what it has. However, if the spelling were *cogo*, the pronunciation would be changed to rhyme with *pogo* instead of *koho*. As a result, the spelling has to be changed to *cojo*, because the *j* in Spanish has the sound of the English *h*, no matter what vowel follows it.

The verb *coger* is a legitimate Spanish word in many countries. However, in some countries (such as Argentina, Uruguay, and Mexico), it is the crude colloquial verb for having sexual relations and is taboo in mixed company and polite society. If you want to avoid using *coger,* use other verbs that refer to taking, grasping, and grabbing, such as *tomar* or *agarrar.*

*Coger*, then, is a regular verb in speech that needs a spelling adjustment in the *yo* form. The other forms are what you would expect: *coges, coge, cogemos, cogéis,* and *cogen*. The same is true for the verb *recoger* (to pick up, gather, collect, recover), which is conjugated as follows: *recojo, recoges, recoge, recogemos, recogéis,* and *recogen*.

Note: The meaning of *recoger* is *to pick up*, not in the literal sense of physically lifting something, but of stopping at someone's house, for instance, and taking that person with you somewhere. (I'll pick you up at 8.) It also means *to recover*, not in the intransitive sense of recuperating from an illness, but in the transitive sense of getting something back that was lost or taken. (They recovered the stolen jewelry from the thieves.)

Practice saying the following sentences aloud:

*Siempre cojo el tren número quince.* (I always take train number 15.)

*El policía coge al criminal.* (The policeman seizes the criminal.)

*Ella coge al animal por la cola.* (She grasps the animal by the tail.)

*Ellos recogen los libros.* (They're gathering up the books.)

*Yo recojo el dinero robado.* (I'm recovering the stolen money.)

## LEARN TO SAY *NO*

To turn a Spanish sentence from affirmative to negative, simply place the word *no* in front of the verb. Practice saying aloud the following affirmative and negative sentences:

*Hablo español.* (I speak Spanish.)

*No hablo español.* (I don't speak Spanish.)

*Llegamos tarde.* (We arrive late.)

*No llegamos tarde.* (We don't arrive late.)

*La chica oye la música.* (The girl hears the music.)

*La chica no oye la música.* (The girl doesn't hear the music.)

The preceding even-numbered statements are negative statements. If you are answering a yes/no question in the negative, the most normal response will contain *no* twice. For example, if the negative statements in the preceding list were not just statements, but answers to questions, those questions and answers would be as follows:

Question: *¿Habla usted español?*
Answer: *No, no hablo español.*

Question: *¿Llegan ustedes tarde?*
Answer: *No, no llegamos tarde.*

Question: *¿Oye la chica la música?*
Answer: *No, la chica no oye la música.*

Say these sentences over and over and picture what is happening, until it feels natural to say them correctly without even looking at them.

If you want to say no to the question and then tell what you do as opposed to what you *don't* do, say *no*, pause, and make a positive statement. This is what you do in English as well. See the following examples:

Question: *¿Habla usted español?* (Do you speak Spanish?)
Answer: *No, hablo inglés.* (No, I speak English.)

Question: *¿Llegan ustedes tarde?* (Do you [plural] arrive late?)
Answer: *No, llegamos temprano.* (No, we arrive early.)

**PROCEED WITH CAUTION**

Be careful. There is a world of difference between *No, hablo francés* and *No hablo francés*. It's the comma in writing and the pause in oral speech that makes this great difference. The first sentence means *No, I speak French.* The second means *I don't speak French.*

## ASK QUESTIONS

You've seen examples of questions being asked in this lesson, but without any explanation of the rules for doing so. In this section, you learn the rules concerning questions.

## ASK FOR A YES OR A NO

In Spanish, the most typical way of asking a yes/no question is to reverse the order of the subject and verb. The statement *You speak German* in Spanish is *Usted habla alemán.* The usual way of asking *Do you speak German?* is *¿Habla usted alemán?*

Reversing the subject and verb is the most common way of asking a yes/no question, but it's not the only way. Remember, Spanish sentence structure is extremely flexible. The subject can go almost anywhere: before the verb, immediately after the verb, or at the end of the sentence. And the subject pronoun can be dispensed with altogether. For example, the English question *Do they listen to a great deal of Spanish music?* could be said in Spanish in any of the following ways:

¿Ellos escuchan mucha música española?

¿Escuchan mucha música española ellos?

¿Escuchan ellos mucha música española?

¿Escuchan mucha música española?

Note: You do *not* separate the noun *música* from its two adjectives (*mucha* and *española*) by inserting the subject. They are a package deal. You probably have noticed that written Spanish questions are preceded by an upside-down question mark (¿) and that exclamations are preceded by an upside-down exclamation mark (¡).

## ASK WHAT, WHO, WHEN, WHERE, AND HOW

The following list contains Spanish interrogatives with their meaning in English.

| Spanish | English |
| --- | --- |
| ¿Qué? | What? |
| ¿Quién? | Who (singular)? |
| ¿Quiénes? | Who (plural)? |
| ¿Cómo? | How? |
| ¿Dónde? | Where? |
| ¿Adónde? | Where to? (a + dónde) |
| ¿Cuál? | Which (singular)? |
| ¿Cuáles? | Which (plural)? |
| ¿Cuándo? | When? |

*continues*

*(continued)*

| Spanish | English |
|---------|---------|
| ¿Cuánto/a? | How much? |
| ¿Cuántos/as? | How many? |
| ¿Por qué? | Why (cause)? |
| ¿Para qué? | What for (goal, purpose)? |

Practice asking the following questions:

*¿Qué quiere usted?* (What do you [formal] want?)

*¿Quién es ella?* (Who is she?)

*¿Quiénes son ellas?* (Who are they [feminine]?)

*¿Cómo estás?* (How are you [familiar]?)

*¿Dónde está Carlos?* (Where is Carlos?)

*¿Adónde va Carlos?* (Where is Carlos going?)

*¿Cuál de los libros quieres?* (Which [one] of the books do you want?)

*¿Cuáles de los libros quieres?* (Which [ones] of the books do you want?)

**JUST A MINUTE**

Use *quién* when you refer to one person or when you expect the answer to deal with one person. Use *quiénes* when you refer to more than one person or expect the answer to deal with more than one person.

## LEARN THE VARIOUS USES OF THE PREPOSITION *A*

You have seen the preposition *a* used in many sentences. It usually is equivalent to the English preposition *to* in referring to a destination. For example, *Va a las montañas* means *She's/he's going to the mountains.* You've also seen that it is used after the verb *ir* and before an infinitive verb as the substitute for the future tense. For example, *Va a comer* means *She's/he's going to eat.* You know it's also used in the *Vamos a …* construction to be the exhortation *Let's ….* However, there is another use for this preposition.

### USE THE PERSONAL *A*

One use for the preposition *a* cannot be translated into English. If the direct object of a verb is a specific human being, then the preposition *a* is placed directly after the verb. Practice saying the following examples:

*Veo a María.* (I see María.)

*Oímos a los chicos.* (We hear the boys.)

*¿Conoces a Carlos?* (Do you know Carlos?)

*María quiere a Miguel.* (María loves Miguel.)

*Queremos describir a Tomás.* (We want to describe Tomás.)

Notice the distinction between humans as objects and things as objects in the use or disuse of the preposition *a:*

*Veo la silla.* (I see the chair.)

*Veo a la chica.* (I see the girl.)

*¿Quieres el libro?* (Do you want the book?)

*¿Quieres a María?* (Do you love María?)

*Ella quiere a su gato.* (She loves her cat.)

*Veo los leones.* (I see the lions.)

Note that the verb *querer* usually means *to want* when the object is not human. In this case, an *a* is not required after the verb. When the object is thought of as human, *querer* means *to love* and requires an *a* to be used after the verb.

**JUST A MINUTE**

When *quién* or *quiénes* is the object of the verb, the preposition *a* is employed in front of it because these interrogatives refer only to human beings. *¿A quién veo?* means *Whom do I see?*

The personal *a* is also used with nonhumans that are humanized in the speaker's mind. Dogs, cats, and other pets are usually humanized by people; you'll hear people use the personal *a* with them. For example, *Oigo al perro.* (I hear the dog.) Wild animals and nonmammals in general are usually not humanized and don't carry a personal *a*. However, it depends on the speaker's attitude. In some cases, people are dehumanized, as in talking of killing the enemy. For example, *El Cid mató muchos moros.* (The Cid slew many Moors.)

In some Spanish-speaking countries (for example, Mexico), people use the *a* when a country, region, city, or town is the object of the verb. For example, *Visito a México.* (I visit Mexico.) In other countries (for example, Spain), the *a* is not used in this way. A Spaniard would say, *Visito Madrid.* (I visit Madrid.)

### LEARN CONTRACTIONS

When the preposition *a* appears before the masculine singular definite article, it is *obligatory* to form the contraction *al*. For example, *Veo al profesor* (I see the professor) would never be *Veo a el profesor*. This contraction does *not* affect the other three definite articles: *los*, *la*, and *las*. See the following examples:

> *Veo al chico.* (I see the boy.)
>
> *Veo a la chica.* (I see the girl.)
>
> *Veo a los chicos.* (I see the boys.)
>
> *Veo a las chicas.* (I see the girls.)

**PROCEED WITH CAUTION**

Do not combine *a* with the subject pronoun *él*. *To him* is *a él*.

When the preposition *de* (of, from) appears before the masculine singular definite article *el* (but not with the subject pronoun *él*), you must form the contraction *del*, as in *el estudio del español* (the study of Spanish). This contraction does not affect the other three definite articles. See the following examples:

> *el problema del pueblo* (the town's problem)
>
> *el problema de la ciudad* (the city's problem)
>
> *el problema de los pueblos* (the towns' problem)
>
> *el problema de las ciudades* (the cities' problem)

**JUST A MINUTE**

*Al* and *del* are the only written contractions in the entire Spanish language.

## THE 30-SECOND RECAP

In this hour of study, you have learned …

- To count from 41 through 70.
- To handle irregular present tense verbs.
- To talk about the future using *ir a* plus an infinitive.
- To use the Spanish equivalent of *Let's* (*vamos a* plus an infinitive).

- To say no.
- To ask questions.
- To use the personal *a*.
- To use the only two written Spanish contractions.

## Hour's Up!

Now that you've studied the material in this hour, see how you do on the following questions without going back to the explanations in this lesson. (You can find the answers in Appendix A.)

1. Choose the correct form of the verb *ser*: *Tú ____ norte-americano*.

    a. sois

    b. estás

    c. es

    d. eres

2. Choose the correct form of the verb *ser*: *Nosotros ____ canadienses*.

    a. sois

    b. somos

    c. estamos

    d. son

3. Choose the correct form of the verb *ir*: *¿Adónde ____ tú?*

    a. vas

    b. ves

    c. eres

    d. ís

4. Choose the correct form of the verb *producir*: *Yo ____ muchas cosas*.

    a. produzco

    b. produce

    c. produco

    d. produzo

5. Choose the correct form of the verb *estar:* Yo _____ *bien.*

   **a.** estó

   **b.** soy

   **c.** estoy

   **d.** doy

6. Choose the correct form of the verb hacer: Vosotros _____ mucho.

   **a.** haces

   **b.** hacen

   **c.** hacéis

   **d.** hacís

7. Choose the correct form of the verb hacer: Yo _____ mucho.

   **a.** hago

   **b.** haco

   **c.** hazo

   **d.** haigo

8. Choose the correct form of the verb decir: Yo _____ "¡Buenos diás!"

   **a.** deco

   **b.** dico

   **c.** diego

   **d.** digo

QUIZ

# HOUR 5

# Past Tenses

## CHAPTER SUMMARY

**LESSON PLAN:**

In this hour, you'll learn ...

- How to count from 71 through 100 in Spanish.
- How to speak of the past with the preterit tense.

You have already mastered the Spanish numbers through 70 and are ready to move forward. The following list contains the numbers 71 through 100 with their Spanish names beside them. Look at the numerals one at a time and pronounce their Spanish names aloud. Notice that I have written out the words only for the numerals in the 70s. For numbers 81 through 89, simply follow the word for 80, *ochenta*, with *y* and the word for the appropriate unit's place. For example, 83 is *ochenta y tres* (where *tres* is in the unit's place).

| Number | Spanish Word |
|--------|--------------|
| 71 | setenta y uno |
| 72 | setenta y dos |
| 73 | setenta y tres |
| 74 | setenta y cuatro |
| 75 | setenta y cinco |
| 76 | setenta y seis |
| 77 | setenta y siete |
| 78 | setenta y ocho |
| 79 | setenta y nueve |
| 80 | ochenta |
| 81 | ochenta y uno, y dos, etc. |
| 90 | noventa |
| 91 | noventa y uno, y dos, y tres, etc. |
| 100 | cien |

It might help you to remember *cien* for the numeral 100 if you relate it to these English words: *century, centennial, cent, percent,* and *centipede.*

## SPEAK ABOUT THE PAST

The preterit tense is used in Spanish to speak of an action or state that was completed in the past. Once again, the form of the verb provides information not only about the basic meaning of the verb, but also about the tense, person, and number involved. In this section, you will practice with the most common type of verbs: regular verbs.

### LEARN ADVERBS USEFUL FOR THE PRETERIT

You will want to use several adverbs and adverbial expressions with verbs in the preterit tense. Learn the examples in the following table.

| Adverb | Meaning |
| --- | --- |
| antes | before, previously |
| ayer | yesterday |
| anteayer | the day before yesterday |
| anoche | last night |
| anteanoche | the night before last |
| hace dos días | two days ago |
| hace cinco días | five days ago |
| la semana pasada | last week |
| el mes pasado | last month |
| el año pasado | last year |

To express *ago,* use *hace* (it makes), the duration of time, *que,* and the preterit form of the verb: *Hace cinco horas que canté.* ("I sang five hours ago.")

### LEARN REGULAR PRETERIT *-AR* VERBS

The following table demonstrates how to conjugate regular *-ar* verbs in the preterit tense using *hablar* (to speak, talk) as an example.

**Preterit Tense for *-ar* Verbs Using *Hablar***

| Subject Pronoun | Verb Stem | Ending | Conjugated Verb |
|---|---|---|---|
| yo | habl- | -é | hablé |
| tú | habl- | -aste | hablaste |
| él | habl- | -ó | habló |
| ella | habl- | -ó | habló |
| usted | habl- | -ó | habló |
| nosotros/as | habl- | -amos | hablamos |
| vosotros/as | habl- | -asteis | hablasteis |
| ellos | habl- | -aron | hablaron |
| ellas | habl- | -aron | hablaron |
| ustedes | habl- | -aron | hablaron |

You might have noticed that the *nosotros* form is exactly the same in the preterit tense as it is in the present tense. This is not a problem. We have verbs in English that are the same in the present and the preterit: I always cut bait; Tomorrow I cut bait; I cut bait two days ago. As in English, context clues, especially adverbs, help you determine whether the verb is in the preterit or present tense. The first two examples in the following list are in the present tense; the last two are in the preterit:

> *Siempre hablamos al capitán.* (We always talk to the captain.)
>
> *Mañana hablamos al capitán.* (Tomorrow we talk to the captain.)
>
> *Ayer hablamos al capitán.* (Yesterday we spoke to the captain.)
>
> *La semana pasada hablamos al capitán.* (Last week we spoke to the captain.)

**JUST A MINUTE**

Even though *usted* and *ustedes* are second person pronouns semantically, grammatically they are third person. A similar situation exists in English: You always say *you are* or *you were; you is* or *you was* is wrong.

Notice that except for an accent mark, the third person singular ending (*ó*) is identical to the *yo* form (*o*) you learned for the present tense. Be very careful in writing and when speaking to include the accent. Because in Spanish the subject pronoun is often left out, the difference between *o* and *ó* can be of paramount importance.

For the preterit tense, you can obtain the *vosotros* ending simply by adding *-is* to the *tú* ending: *hablaste* plus *-is* equals *hablasteis*.

In addition to the identical *nosotros* forms, notice the similarities between the present tense and the preterit tense of *-ar* verbs:

- The verb forms for *yo, él, ella,* and *usted* end with vowels.
- The verb forms for *nosotros* and *nosotras* end with *mos*.
- The verb forms for *vosotros* and *vosotras* end with the letters *is*.
- The verb forms for *ellos, ellas,* and *ustedes* end with the letter *n*.

Note that the preterit is the only tense in the Spanish language in which the *tú* form of the verb does not end with the letter *s*.

Practice conjugating other *-ar* verbs that are regular in the preterit tense while thinking of their meanings. See the following list for some of these verbs:

*tomar* (to take, seize, drink)

*mirar* (to look at, to watch)

*escuchar* (to listen)

Practice saying the following sentences aloud while envisioning what they describe:

*María cantó muy bien.* (María sang very well.)

*Yo llevé a María al cine.* (I took María to the movies.)

*¿Ya tomaste café?* (Did you already have coffee?)

*¿Por qué no llamaste?* (Why didn't you call?)

*Ellas viajaron a la China.* (They traveled to China.)

*Yo miré la mesa.* (I looked at the table.)

*Tú miraste a Carmen.* (You looked at Carmen.)

## Learn Regular Preterit *-er* Verbs

The following table demonstrates how to conjugate regular *-er* verbs in the preterit tense using *comer* (to eat) as an example.

**Preterit Tense for -er Verbs Using *Comer***

| Subject Pronoun | Verb Stem | Ending | Conjugated Verb |
|---|---|---|---|
| yo | com- | -í | comí |
| tú | com- | -iste | comiste |
| él | com- | -ió | comió |
| ella | com- | -ió | comió |
| usted | com- | -ió | comió |
| nosotros/as | com- | -imos | comimos |
| vosotros/as | com- | -isteis | comisteis |
| ellos | com- | -ieron | comieron |
| ellas | com- | -ieron | comieron |
| ustedes | com- | -ieron | comieron |

Basically, the regular -er verb endings in the preterit tense are very similar to those of the -ar verbs; however, there is a shift in the vowel sounds. Whereas the -ar verbs with yo end in accented -é, the -er verbs with yo end in accented -í. Instead of ending with aste, the tú form of the -er verbs ends with -iste. The third person ending changes from accented -ó to accented -ió. The -amos becomes -imos, the -asteis becomes -isteis, and -aron becomes -ieron. Note that unlike the -ar verbs, the nosotros form of the -er verbs is different from its form in the present tense. For example, the present tense of comer is comemos, but the preterit tense is comimos.

Practice conjugating other -er verbs that are regular in the preterit tense while thinking of their meaning:

coger (to take, seize)

escoger (to choose, pick, select)

conocer (to know, be acquainted with, meet)

mover (to move something)

**JUST A MINUTE**

When practicing any Spanish sentences aloud, picture a woman performing the action of the verb when you say *ella*, picture a man when you say *él*, picture women with *ellas*, and picture men with *ellos*.

Practice saying the following sentences aloud while envisioning what they depict:

*Cogí el autobús.* (I caught the bus, or I took the bus.)

*¿Cogieron al criminal?* (Did they catch the criminal?)

*Josefina escogió un libro.* (Josefina selected a book.)

*Escogimos al candidato.* (We chose the candidate.)

*¿Dónde conociste a Juana?* (Where did you first meet Juana?)

*Conocí a Roberto en Chicago.* (I first met Robert in Chicago.)

*¿Conocisteis a María?* (Did you make María's acquaintance?)

**PROCEED WITH CAUTION**

Although *conocer* is usually translated as *to know* or *to be acquainted with*, in the preterit tense it refers to meeting someone for the first time. It does not mean *to meet* in the sense of *to happen upon* or *to have an appointment with*.

## LEARN REGULAR PRETERIT *-IR* VERBS

The following table demonstrates how to conjugate regular *-ir* verbs in the preterit tense using *vivir* (to live) as an example.

**Preterit Tense for *-ir* Verbs Using *Vivir***

| Subject Pronoun | Verb Stem | Ending | Conjugated Verb |
|---|---|---|---|
| yo | viv- | -í | viví |
| tú | viv- | -iste | viviste |
| él | viv- | -ió | vivió |
| ella | viv- | -ió | vivió |
| usted | viv- | -ió | vivió |
| nosotros/as | viv- | -imos | vivimos |
| vosotros/as | viv- | -isteis | vivisteis |
| ellos | viv- | -ieron | vivieron |
| ellas | viv- | -ieron | vivieron |
| ustedes | viv- | -ieron | vivieron |

You can see that the endings of the *-ir* verbs in the preterit tense are identical to those of the *-er* verbs. The *nosotros* ending for *-ir* verbs is exactly the same as the present tense *nosotros* ending. As with the *-ar* verbs, context clues will clarify the tense. See the following examples:

*En 1996, vivimos en Bolivia.* (In 1996, we lived in Bolivia.)

*Ahora vivimos en Kánsas.* (Now we live in Kansas.)

Practice conjugating other *-ir* verbs that are regular in the preterit tense while thinking of their meanings:

*salir* (to leave, go out)

*sufrir* (to suffer)

*escribir* (to write)

*recibir* (to receive)

**PROCEED WITH CAUTION**

Many verbs are irregular in the present tense (for example, *salir* and *coger*), but perfectly regular in the preterit tense.

Practice saying the following sentences aloud while envisioning what they depict:

*Ayer salí temprano.* (Yesterday I left early, or yesterday I went out early.)

*Ellas salieron tarde anteayer.* (They left late the day before yesterday, or they went out late the day before yesterday.)

*Salimos anoche.* (We went out last night, or we left last night.)

*¿Sufrió usted mucho el año pasado?* (Did you suffer much last year?)

*Todos sufrimos mucho.* (We all suffered a great deal.)

# LEARN IRREGULAR PRETERIT VERBS

The Spanish preterit tense contains a great many irregular verbs. In this section, you will be dealing with the most commonly used irregular verbs.

## LEARN THE *U* VERBS

A great many of the irregular preterit verbs are not stressed on the last syllable in the first and third persons. Naturally, then, in writing they do not bear an accent mark on the final vowel. For the sake of memory, you might find it convenient to group some of these unstressed irregular preterit verbs together because they contain the letter *u* in the stem. See the following table for the conjugation of *estar*, *poder*, and *poner*.

**Preterit Tense *u* Verbs**

| Pronoun | Estar (To Be) | Poder (To Be Able) | Poner (To Put) |
|---------|---------------|--------------------|----------------|
| yo | estuve | pude | puse |
| tú | estuviste | pudiste | pusiste |
| él | estuvo | pudo | puso |
| nosotros | estuvimos | pudimos | pusimos |
| vosotros | estuvisteis | pudisteis | pusisteis |
| ellos | estuvieron | pudieron | pusieron |

Although these verbs belong to different groups, their preterit endings are identical (*-e*, *-iste*, *-o*, *-imos*, *-isteis*, and *-ieron*). In addition, they all contain a *u* in the stem.

In the present tense, *poder* (*ue*) is a stem-changing verb from *o* to *ue* (*puedo*, *puedes*, *puede*, *podemos*, *podéis*, *pueden*), whereas *poner* is not. However, as you will remember from Hour 4, *poner* is one of those verbs in the present tense with a *g* inserted before the *yo* ending (*pongo*, *pones*, *pone*, and so on).

**JUST A MINUTE**

Take care not to confuse *poder* (to be able, can) with *poner* (to put, place).

Practice saying the following sentences aloud while picturing the meaning:

*Yo estuve en Venezuela el año pasado.* (I was in Venezuela last year.)

*Nosotros estuvimos en Paraguay la semana pasada.* (We were in Paraguay last week.)

*Pusiste el libro en la basura.* (You put the book in the garbage.)

*No, lo puse en la mesa.* (No, I put it on the table.)

**GO TO ▶**
For a full explanation of the word *lo* (which is in the fourth sentence), see "Use Direct Object Pronouns" in Hour 12.

The following table has the conjugation of three more *u* verbs: *tener*, *andar*, and *saber*.

**More Preterit Tense *u* Verbs**

| Pronoun | Tener (To Have) | Andar (To Walk) | Saber (To Know) |
|---------|-----------------|-----------------|-----------------|
| yo | tuve | anduve | supe |
| tú | tuviste | anduviste | supiste |
| él | tuvo | anduvo | supo |
| nosotros | tuvimos | anduvimos | supimos |
| vosotros | tuvisteis | anduvisteis | supisteis |
| ellos | tuvieron | anduvieron | supieron |

Note that *tener* not only has the same endings as *estar*, but also has a nearly identical stem. Another thing to note is that in the preterit tense, *saber* usually means *found out*. (To express *knew*, see the lesson on the imperfect tense in Hour 6.)

Practice saying the following sentences aloud while picturing the meaning:

*Carmen tuvo una buena oportunidad ayer.* (Carmen had a good opportunity yesterday.)

*¿A quiénes tuvo usted en la oficina anteayer?* (Whom did you have in the office the day before yesterday?)

*Anoche tuve buena suerte.* (Last night I had good luck.)

*¿Tuviste un examen la semana pasada?* (Did you have an exam last week?)

*Sin coche, el hombre anduvo, anduvo, anduvo.* (Without a car, the man walked and walked and walked.)

**PROCEED WITH CAUTION**

Depending on context, *andar* can mean *to ride in* or *on* a conveyance such as a car, bicycle, or horse. It can also refer to the functioning of a machine: *El coche no anda.* (The car isn't working.)

## LEARN THE *-DUCIR* VERBS

Verbs whose infinitive form ends with *-ducir* comprise another group of unstressed irregular verbs in the preterit tense. These verbs' present tense *yo* form ends with *duzco*; their preterit stem contains *duj*. The following table has the conjugations of *conducir*, *traducir*, and *reducir*.

### Preterit Tense of the *-ducir* Verbs

| Pronoun | Conducir (To Drive) | Traducir (To Translate) | Reducir (To Reduce) |
|---------|---------------------|-------------------------|---------------------|
| yo | conduje | traduje | reduje |
| tú | condujiste | tradujiste | redujiste |
| él | condujo | tradujo | redujo |
| nosotros | condujimos | tradujimos | redujimos |
| vosotros | condujisteis | tradujisteis | redujisteis |
| ellos | condujeron | tradujeron | redujeron |

**JUST A MINUTE**

Note that the basic meaning of *conducir* is *to conduct, to lead.* In the context of automobiles, it is also the equivalent of *to drive.* In Spanish, a driver can be *conductor.*

See the following list for examples of some other *-ducir* verbs and practice conjugating in the same way:

*deducir* (to deduce, deduct)

*seducir* (to seduce, captivate, charm)

*producir* (to produce)

Practice saying the following sentences aloud:

*¿Condujo el automóvil Carlos?* (Did Carlos drive the automobile?)

*No, conduje yo.* (No, I drove.)

*Todos los caminos condujeron a Roma.* (All roads led to Rome.)

*¿Tradujiste el mensaje al inglés?* (Did you translate the message into English?)

**PROCEED WITH CAUTION**

There are many words for automobile in Spanish, including *coche* and *automóvil.* A popular word in Mexico and the Caribbean is *carro.* However, in other countries (for example, Argentina and Uruguay), the word is taken to mean an ox cart.

Another verb that contains a *j* before the endings in the preterit tense is *traer* (to bring). Because of this *j*, it too adds *-eron* rather than *-ieron* to the stem. The full conjugation of *traer* in the preterit tense is as follows:

| | | |
|---|---|---|
| traje | trajiste | trajo |
| trajimos | trajisteis | trajeron |

Practice saying the following sentences aloud:

*Carlos no trajo la comida.* (Carlos didn't bring the food.)

*Y yo no traje el video.* (And I didn't bring the video.)

*¿Qué trajeron María y Concha?* (What did María and Concha bring?)

## LEARN PRETERIT *I* VERBS

Another group of unstressed irregular verbs in the preterit tense contain the letter *i* in the preterit stem, even though this *i* is absent in the present tense of the verb. These verbs are very commonly used. See the following table for the conjugation of *hacer*, *dar*, and *querer*. The peculiar thing about the preterit form of *dar* is that its endings would be perfectly regular if it were an *-ir* rather than an *-ar* verb.

**Preterit Tense *i* Verbs**

| Hacer (To Do, Make) | Dar (To Give) | Querer (To Want, Love) | Venir (To Come) |
|---|---|---|---|
| hice | di | quise | vine |
| hiciste | diste | quisiste | viniste |
| hizo | dio | quiso | vino |
| hicimos | dimos | quisimos | vinimos |
| hicisteis | disteis | quisisteis | vinisteis |
| hicieron | dieron | quisieron | vinieron |

**JUST A MINUTE**

The third person singular of *hacer* is written with a *z* instead of a *c* because the spelling *co* represents the sound *ko* in Spanish. See Hour 1 for a full review of the relationship between pronunciation and spelling.

The verb *querer* in the preterit tense most often has meanings more active than merely wanting or not wanting. *Quise ir*, rather than merely expressing a past desire, has the force of *I tried to go*, whereas the negative *No quise ir* has the force of *I refused to go*. (To express *I wanted*, see the lesson on the imperfect tense in Hour 6.)

Practice saying the following sentences aloud:

> *¿Qué hiciste tú anoche?* (What did you do last night?)
>
> *¿Yo? Vine acá.* (Me? I came here.)
>
> *¿Y qué hizo María?* (And what did María do?)
>
> *No supo que dimos una fiesta.* (She didn't find out we threw a party.)

## LEARN STEM-CHANGING PRETERIT VERBS

If a verb had a stem change in the present tense (*o* to *ue*; *u* to *ue*; *e* to *ie*; *e* to *i*) and is an *-ar* or *-er* verb, that verb has no stem change in the preterit tense. But if a verb had a stem change in the present tense and is an *-ir* verb, it does have a stem change in the preterit tense. No matter what the change was in the present, the change in the preterit will be from *o* to *u* or from *e* to *i*. Moreover, the change will take place only with *él, ella, usted, ellos, ellas,* and *ustedes*. The other forms are regular.

For example, *mentir* (to lie, tell untruths) has a stem that changes from *e* to *ie* in the present tense and changes from *e* to *i* in the preterit.

### *Mentir*

| Present | Preterit |
| --- | --- |
| miento | mentí |
| mientes | mentiste |
| miente | mintió |
| mentimos | mentimos |
| mentís | mentisteis |
| mienten | mintieron |

Likewise, *dormir* (to sleep) has a stem that changes from *o* to *ue* in the present tense and changes from *o* to *u* in the preterit.

### Dormir

| Present | Preterit |
|---------|----------|
| duermo | dormí |
| duermes | dormiste |
| duerme | durmió |
| dormimos | dormimos |
| dormís | dormisteis |
| duermen | durmieron |

Here are some other stem-changing preterit verbs:

preferir (to prefer)

repetir (to repeat)

pedir (to request)

morir (to die)

## USE PRETERIT SER AND IR

Two verbs in the preterit tense are extremely irregular in more than one way. In addition to the fact that their preterit forms look and sound nothing like their infinitive forms or their present tense forms, the verbs ser (to be) and ir (to go) are identical to each other in their preterit forms. The following table lists the conjugations of these two verbs. Notice that the vowel i is dominant in the yo, tú, nosotros, and vosotros forms, but the vowel e governs the other forms.

### Preterit Tense of Ser and Ir

| Pronoun | Ser (To Be) | Ir (To Go) |
|---------|-------------|------------|
| yo | fui | fui |
| tú | fuiste | fuiste |
| él, ella, Ud. | fue | fue |
| nosotros/as | fuimos | fuimos |
| vosotros/as | fuisteis | fuisteis |
| ellos, ellas, Uds. | fueron | fueron |

Because the verbs ser and ir in the preterit tense are identical, you might be wondering how to know which verb is being used when someone uses the

**GO TO** ▶

In the third sample sentence, the verb cannot be *ser* for another reason. To indicate physical location, *estar*, rather than *ser*, is used. See the section "Understand Different States of Being" in Hour 7.

preterit tense. This is not a problem; the context clearly indicates which is being used. Study the following sentences for understanding. Then practice saying them aloud:

*Fueron al cine.* (They went to the movies.)

*Lincoln fue un gran hombre.* (Lincoln was a great man.)

*¿Adónde fuiste?* (Where did you go?)

*¿Quiénes fueron?* (Who were they? Who went?)

*Fuimos a la ópera.* (We went to the opera.)

*¿Qué fue?* (What was it?)

The first, third, and fifth of these sample sentences couldn't use a verb meaning *to be* because they all refer to going somewhere. If the preposition *a* follows the verb, the verb must be *ir*. There is no situation in which *ser* would be followed by *a*. The same is true when *¿dónde?* becomes *¿adónde?* with the preposition *a* attached. In the same manner, the second and sixth sample sentences could not be referring to a verb of motion.

Completely out of context, the fourth sample sentence is ambiguous; it could refer to either *going* or *being*. However, that ambiguity is purely theoretical; no one speaks out of context. If you're having a conversation about people who went to a certain place, and someone asks "*¿Quiénes fueron?*" you know it means "Who went?" If you see a group of people leaving the room, and your friend asks you "*¿Quiénes fueron?*" you know he has to mean "Who were they?"

## THE 30-SECOND RECAP

In this hour, you've learned …

- To count from 71 to 100.
- To speak of the past by using the preterit tense with regular and irregular verbs.
- Adverbs and other vocabulary often used with the preterit tense.

## HOUR'S UP!

After thoroughly reviewing the material in this lesson, test yourself on a few representative points to see how you do. (You can find the answers in Appendix A.)

1. Choose the correct preterit form of *llegar: Nosotros _____ ayer.*

    **a.** llegamos

    **b.** llegemos

    **c.** lleguemos

    **d.** llegasteis

2. Choose the correct preterit form of *cantar: ¿Cuándo _____ María?*

    **a.** canto

    **b.** cante

    **c.** canté

    **d.** cantó

3. Choose the correct preterit form of *decir: ¿Qué _____ tú?*

    **a.** dijiste

    **b.** dejiste

    **c.** deciste

    **d.** diciste

4. Choose the correct preterit form of *hacer: Los chicos no _____ nada.*

    **a.** hacieron

    **b.** hecieron

    **c.** hicieron

    **d.** hizeron

5. Choose the most appropriate translation of the following sentence: *No supe nada.*

    **a.** I didn't know anything.

    **b.** I didn't find out anything.

    **c.** I didn't have any supper.

    **d.** I didn't have soup.

**QUIZ**

**6.** Choose the most appropriate translation of the following sentence: *No quisieron ir.*

    **a.** They didn't try to go.

    **b.** They didn't want to go.

    **c.** They refused to go.

    **d.** They couldn't go.

# Hour 6

# Imperfect Past and Future Tenses

**LESSON PLAN:**

In this hour, you'll learn ...

- How to count through 500.
- How to speak about the past by using the imperfect tense.
- How to use some common positive and negative expressions.
- How to use the future tense.

You have already mastered the Spanish numbers through 100 and are ready to move into the hundreds. The following list gives the numbers 100 through 500 in numerals with the Spanish name of the number beside it. Look at the numbers one at a time and pronounce their Spanish names aloud.

You don't need to see each number written out for the hundreds, because you can fill in with numbers you already know. For example, 345 consists of the new (for you) number 300 followed by the number 45, with which you are familiar. For the sake of continuity, as well as to contrast the word for 100 alone and the word for 100 when it precedes a lesser number, we'll start with 100.

Notice in the following table that although 100 is *cien*, it becomes *ciento* when followed by numbers smaller than itself. Starting with 200, the endings become pluralized (end with *-s*), and the *dos*, *tres*, and *cuatro* are joined to the *cientos* segment as one word. For example, *tres* and *cientos* are combined to form *trescientos*.

**JUST A MINUTE**

The number 500 does not follow the pattern of 200, 300, and 400. That is, instead of being *cincocientos* (as you might expect), it's *quinientos*. It might help you remember the Spanish word for 500 if you think about the English words *quincentennial* and *quintuplets.*

**Spanish Numbers 100 Through 500**

| Number | Spanish Word | Number | Spanish Word |
|---|---|---|---|
| 100 | cien | 202 | doscientos dos |
| 101 | ciento uno | 298 | doscientos noventa y ocho |
| 102 | ciento dos | 300 | trescientos |
| 125 | ciento veinticinco | 301 | trescientos uno |
| 176 | ciento setenta y seis | 399 | trescientos noventa y nueve |
| 187 | ciento ochenta y siete | 400 | cuatrocientos |
| 200 | doscientos | 401 | cuatrocientos uno |
| 201 | doscientos uno | 500 | quinientos |

Note also that although the 20s through the 90s use the conjunction *y* (and) before attaching a smaller number (for example, 56 is *cincuenta y seis*), the smaller numbers added to the hundreds dispense with the conjunction: 356 is *trescientos cincuenta y seis*. There is no *y* between *trescientos* and *cincuenta*.

The number *cien* in front of nouns, whether masculine plural or feminine plural, stays *cien*, just as it is when you are merely counting. There is no agreement between it and the noun it modifies. See the following examples:

*cien hombres* (100 men)

*cien mujeres* (100 women)

*cien periódicos* (100 newspapers)

*cien casas* (100 houses)

**JUST A MINUTE**

Whether the English is *one hundred* or *a hundred*, the Spanish will be simply *cien* with no form of *uno* before it.

From 200 on, however, the number does agree in gender with the noun it modifies. See the following list for examples:

*seiscientos coches* (600 cars)

*seiscientas sillas* (600 chairs)

*quinientos muchachos* (500 boys)

*quinientas muchachas* (500 girls)

## SPEAK DIFFERENTLY ABOUT THE PAST

In Hour 5, you learned to speak about actions that were conceptualized as having been completed in the past by using the preterit tense. In this hour, you will learn that the Spanish language has two different tenses that refer to the past: the preterit and the imperfect. These two tenses are not interchangeable; they are used to express different aspects of the past. In addition to learning the correct purpose for each of these tenses in this section, you will learn to form the imperfect tense.

The imperfect tense, unlike the complicated preterit (which you have already mastered), is relatively simple; there are only two kinds of regular endings: one for the *-ar* verbs and a second one for both the *-er* and *-ir* verbs. Furthermore, there are only three irregular verbs in the imperfect tense, and two of the three are not all that irregular.

**GO TO ▶**

The conjugations of the three irregular verbs in the imperfect tense are in the "Learn Irregular Imperfect Verbs" section later in this hour.

### LEARN IMPERFECT TENSE *-AR* VERBS

In the imperfect tense, every *-ar* verb is entirely regular. The following table shows how an *-ar* verb is conjugated in the imperfect tense by using *hablar* (to speak) as an example.

**GO TO ▶**

Notice the accent mark over the middle á in the *nosotros* form. For a review of the rules of accentuation, see Hour 1.

**Imperfect Tense Conjugation of *-ar* Verbs Using *Hablar***

| Subject Pronoun | Verb Stem | Ending | Conjugated Verb |
| --- | --- | --- | --- |
| yo | habl- | *-aba* | hablaba |
| tú | habl- | *-abas* | hablabas |
| él, ella, Ud. | habl- | *-aba* | hablaba |
| nosotros/as | habl- | *-ábamos* | hablábamos |
| vosotros/as | habl- | *-abais* | hablabais |
| ellos/as, Uds. | habl- | *-aban* | hablaban |

The *tú* form once more ends in *s*, as it does in every tense except the preterit tense. Notice that the ending for *él/ella/usted* is the same as that of *yo*. This similarity makes it easier to learn the imperfect tense. As you might guess, it also tends to make the use of subject pronouns somewhat more frequent with the imperfect tense than other tenses for the sake of clarity. To reinforce the *-ar* verb conjugation in the imperfect tense, study the three *-ar* verbs presented in the following table; they conjugate in exactly the same way as *hablar*.

**More *-ar* Verbs in the Imperfect Tense**

| Pronoun | Estar | Llegar | Pasar |
| --- | --- | --- | --- |
| yo | estaba | llegaba | pasaba |
| tú | estabas | llegabas | pasabas |
| él | estaba | llegaba | pasaba |
| nosotros | estábamos | llegábamos | pasábamos |
| vosotros | estabais | llegabais | pasabais |
| ellos | estaban | llegaban | pasaban |

You have already been using the verbs *estar* and *llegar*. The verb *pasar* has various meanings and a great many uses, including the following:

- to pass (move beyond, hand something to someone)
- to happen, occur
- to send, transmit
- to cross, go across

Practice saying the following sentences that use the verb *pasar* in present and preterit tenses:

*Esto pasa los límites.* (This goes beyond the limits.)

*Pasó la sal.* (He passed the salt.)

*¿Qué pasa?* (What's happening? What's going on?)

*No pasó nada.* (Nothing happened.)

*Pasaron el mensaje.* (They sent the message.)

*Pasé el río.* (I crossed the river.)

## CONTRAST IMPERFECT AND PRETERIT USE

Now that you've seen how the *-ar* verbs are conjugated in the imperfect tense, we can use examples of these verbs for illustrative purposes to show you the contrasting uses of the two past tenses: the preterit and the imperfect. Although translation into English has some limited use in explaining this dichotomy, it is far from a reliable tool. This is because when we talk about the past in English, we don't necessarily need to distinguish between the two different aspects of the past; it's always possible to use the English past tense. Yet, in Spanish, a choice must be made between the two aspects; you must use either the preterit tense or the imperfect tense every time you speak about the past.

### JUST A MINUTE

Thinking in the imperfect tense is like walking into the middle of a movie and leaving before it's over. Thinking in the preterit tense is like looking at a photograph.

In English, you can say, "I phoned Roberto yesterday" or "I phoned Roberto every day." These are perfectly good English sentences. Yet, in Spanish, the verb *phoned* would be in a different tense for each of those sentences. The first sentence would employ the preterit tense (*yo llamé*); whereas the second one would use the imperfect tense (*yo llamaba*). To understand this difference, you should try to get inside the Spanish-speaker's head and visualize what concepts and mental images are at work. There are several ways to do this, so we're going to go at it from several angles.

Every action or state has three parts: beginning, middle, and end. To the Spanish-speaker, if you can visualize either the beginning or the end (or both) of an action or state in the past, then you use the preterit tense. For example, *Llamé a Roberto ayer* (I called Roberto yesterday). You can visualize the end of this act (perhaps even the beginning). You imagine the speaker calling and hanging up. It was something that happened at a specific time (*ayer*), and in your mind's eye, you see the act finished.

On the other hand, if you don't visualize either the beginning or the end of an act or state, but just the middle, you use the imperfect tense. For example, *Yo llamaba a Roberto todos los días.* (I called Robert every day.) When you say this or hear someone else say it to you, you don't visualize either starting the call or finishing it. This sentence is a case of repeated, habitual action. And because you never visualize either the beginning or the end of the act when speaking of repeated, habitual action, you use the imperfect tense.

There is a possible clue in translation. In English, we often use the expression *used to* to emphasize the fact that we're talking about a repeated, habitual act; for example, I used to call Roberto every day. But you can't depend on this as a clue, because we don't absolutely need to use this expression; we can simply say "I called Roberto every day," and it's understood to be repetitive and habitual. For that reason, you need to think about whether you're visualizing either the beginning or the end of the action. Notice the impossibility of utilizing the expression *used to* in the following sentences:

I used to call Roberto this morning.

I used to speak to María at nine o'clock last night.

We used to play golf last Tuesday morning.

The preceding three sentences are impossible in English; they don't make sense. This is because they contain the expression that specifies repeated, habitual action (used to) while specifically indicating closure by means of a definite and precise end point (this morning, nine o'clock last night, and last Tuesday morning). In these three sentences, the only tense that it would make sense to use is the English preterit tense: I called …; I spoke …; we played ….

Because we visualize an ending to those actions, the preterit tense would have to be utilized to describe those actions in Spanish. See the following sentences:

*Llamé a Roberto esta mañana.* (I called Roberto this morning.)

*Hablé a María anoche a las nueve.* (I spoke to María at 9 last night.)

*Jugamos al golf el martes pasado por la mañana.* (We played golf last Tuesday morning.)

On the other hand, notice how the following English sentences can be said in two ways without changing the meaning because they refer to repeated, habitual action. You don't visualize a beginning or end to these acts:

I called Roberto every day.

I used to call Roberto every day.

I spoke to María all the time last year.

I used to speak to María all the time last year.

Because the underlying image determines whether you use the preterit tense or the imperfect tense, not the English translation, the first and second sentences in the preceding list would have to use the imperfect tense if they were translated into Spanish. The same is true of the other sentences. The Spanish equivalents follow:

Yo llamaba a Roberto todos los días.

Yo hablaba a María todo el tiempo el año pasado.

**TIME SAVER**

Ask yourself if a specific past tense English sentence can be changed into one that employs *used to* without changing the meaning. If it can, then it refers to repeated, habitual action, and you need the Spanish imperfect tense when expressing that idea in Spanish.

Another specific use of the imperfect tense is to express an ongoing action in the past. A definite clue for this use in English is a sentence that uses the past tense of *to be* plus the present participle (an *-ing* form of the verb). See the following examples:

I was singing.

He was studying while his friend was listening to records.

The use of the English *was* plus a verb ending in *-ing* is a definite clue that you are not visualizing either the beginning or the end of the action, but that you are picturing an ongoing middle of the process. In Spanish, those two sentences would be as follows:

Yo cantaba.

Él estudiaba mientras su amigo escuchaba discos.

Yet another way to approach the matter is to think of reading or telling a story. In that situation, you always set the scene for the upcoming narration with the imperfect tense, but narrate the events in the preterit tense. See the following sentences for typical scene setting:

*Nevaba.* (It was snowing.)

*El viento soplaba.* (The wind was blowing.)

*En la casa, María estudiaba.* (In the house, María was studying.)

Those three sentences in the imperfect tense merely set the scene for the narration of events, which will be in the preterit tense:

*Alguien abrió la puerta.* (Someone opened the door.)

*Sacó una pistola y dijo …* ([He] took out a gun and said …)

---

**TIME SAVER**

Description in the past is in the imperfect tense. *The house was red* doesn't mean the house began to be red or finished being red; it was in the middle of being red. In addition, imperfect tense sets the scene.

You see that the two past tenses can be used in telling the same story. Very often, both tenses can appear within the same sentence. For example, *María estudiaba cuando alguien abrió la puerta.* (María was studying when someone opened the door.) The *estudiaba* is in the imperfect tense because we don't visualize her beginning to study or ending her study; we mentally see her in the middle of the process of studying. Her studying in this case is setting the scene for the impending narration.

The *abrió la puerta* is in the preterit tense because we can mentally see both the beginning and the end of this act, though all we need to visualize is either the beginning or the end in order to use the preterit tense.

The following sentence uses the same verb twice: once in the imperfect tense and again in the preterit tense: *Mamá siempre cantaba cuando cocinaba, pero ayer no cantó.* (Mom always sang when she cooked, but yesterday she did not sing.) The imperfect *cantaba* is used in the first part of the sentence because it refers to her repeated, habitual action. The preterit *cantó* is used in the second part of the sentence because it refers to an act (her not singing) we visualize ending at a specific time (yesterday).

---

**JUST A MINUTE**

The imperfect tense is open-ended; the preterit tense presents the action all wrapped up in a box and tied with a bow.

When you just want to sum up an action or event or condition (mentally see the end of it), you use the preterit tense. When you want that action or event or condition to serve as the backdrop (set the scene) for other events, that act is in the imperfect tense. See the following sentences for examples.

*Estuve en (la) Argentina en mayo.* (I was in Argentina in May.)

*Yo estaba en (la) Argentina en mayo cuando ocurrió el incidente.* (I was in Argentina when the incident occurred.)

*Mientras (yo) estaba en (la) Argentina, yo siempre hablaba españo.* (While I was in Argentina, I always spoke Spanish.)

*Estuvieron en México y aprendieron mucho.* (They were in Mexico and learned a great deal.)

*Mientras estaban en México y aprendían mucho, llegó el terremoto.* (While they were in Mexico and were learning a great deal, the earthquake occurred [literally, arrived].)

The first sentence sums up your stay in Argentina; you see the end of it. The second sentence has your stay in Argentina serve as the background for the incident that occurred. The occurrence of the incident is in the preterit tense because we mentally see the end of it; it is narration.

## LEARN IMPERFECT TENSE *-ER* VERBS

In the imperfect tense, only two *-er* verbs are irregular; all the others follow the rules given in the following table, which uses *comer* (to eat) as an example.

**Imperfect Tense Conjugation of *-er* Verbs Using *Comer***

| Subject Pronoun | Verb Stem | Ending | Conjugated Verb |
| --- | --- | --- | --- |
| yo | com- | -ía | comía |
| tú | com- | -ías | comías |
| él, ella, Ud. | com- | -ía | comía |
| nosotros/as | com- | -íamos | comíamos |
| vosotros/as | com- | -íais | comíais |
| ellos, ellas, Uds. | com- | -ían | comían |

Practice saying the following sentences aloud:

*Comíamos mucho en el pasado.* (We used to eat a lot in the past.)

*Carmen comía mientras Roberto leía.* (Carmen ate while Roberto read.)

*Yo no hacía nada.* (I wasn't doing anything.)

**PROCEED WITH CAUTION**

The English *would* does not signify the conditional tense exclusively. It is also synonymous with *used to* in referring to repeated, habitual action. In the first sentence, I could just as well have used the phrase *We would eat a lot in the past.*

Because the imperfect tense form of every *-er* verb in the Spanish language (except for *ser* and *ver*) is regular, you can practice conjugating any *-er* verb in the imperfect tense, with those two exceptions, by using the endings in the preceding table.

## LEARN IMPERFECT *-IR* VERBS

In the imperfect tense, only one *-ir* verb is irregular; all the others follow the rules given in the following table, which uses *vivir* (to live) as an example.

**Imperfect Tense Conjugation of *-ir* Verbs Using *Vivir***

| Subject Pronoun | Verb Stem | Ending | Conjugated Verb |
| --- | --- | --- | --- |
| yo | viv- | -ía | vivía |
| tú | viv- | -ías | vivías |
| él, ella, Ud. | viv- | -ía | vivía |
| nosotros/as | viv- | -íamos | vivíamos |
| vosotros/as | viv- | -íais | vivíais |
| ellos, ellas, Uds. | viv- | -ían | vivían |

The regular endings for the *-ir* verbs of the imperfect tense are exactly the same as those of the *-er* verbs. Because every *-ir* verb in Spanish (except for the verb *ir*) is regular, you can practice conjugating any *-ir* verb in the imperfect, with that one exception, by using the endings in the preceding table.

Practice saying the following sentences aloud:

*¿Dónde vivían Uds.?* (Where did you used to live?)

*Vivíamos en Chicago.* (We used to live in Chicago.)

*Siempre salían de noche.* (They always used to go out at night.)

*¿Qué decía usted?* (What were you saying?)

## LEARN IRREGULAR IMPERFECT VERBS

In the imperfect tense, only three verbs are irregular: *ver* (to see), *ser* (to be), and *ir* (to go). See the following table for their conjugation.

**Imperfect Tense Conjugation of Irregular Verbs**

| Pronoun | Ver | Ser | Ir |
|---------|---------|--------|---------|
| yo | veía | era | iba |
| tú | veías | eras | ibas |
| él | veía | era | iba |
| nosotros | veíamos | éramos | íbamos |
| vosotros | veíais | erais | ibais |
| ellos | veían | eran | iban |

**TIME SAVER**

It might help to remember that the *tú* form of *ser* in the present tense (*eres*) is very similar to the *tú* form in the imperfect tense (*eras*), with a difference in only one vowel, and that all the forms of the imperfect tense are related to each other.

The verb *ir* in the imperfect tense has elements of the *-ir* conjugation (to which it belongs) as well as elements of the *-ar* conjugation (to which it does not belong). The endings have the *ba* typical of *-ar* verbs in the imperfect (but not *aba*), but the verb forms maintain the vowel sounds of the typical *-ir* verbs: stressed *i* plus *a*.

Practice saying the following sentences aloud:

*Cuando yo era joven, iba a la escuela en autobús.* (When I was young, I used to go to school by bus.)

*Veían la televisión todas las noches.* (They used to watch television every night.)

*Yo veía la televisión mientras mamá cocinaba.* (I was watching television while Mom was cooking, or I used to watch television while Mom cooked.)

*Cuando estábamos en España, íbamos con frecuencia a la corrida de toros.* (When we were in Spain, we'd often go to the bullfight.)

*Mientras ella iba a casa, veía pasar a la gente.* (While she would go home, she'd see people passing by.)

*Íbamos al cine todos los sábados cuando éramos niños.* (We used to go to the movies every Saturday when we were children.)

**JUST A MINUTE**

Even though *ver* means *to see,* and *mirar* means *to watch,* the usual Spanish expression for watching television is *ver la televisión.*

## LEARN NEGATIVE AND POSITIVE EXPRESSIONS

You've already learned to turn a positive statement into a negative one by the simple placement of *no* in front of the verb. To further your proficiency, learn the following list of commonly used positive and negative expressions. Notice that the expressions are presented with their opposites.

**Positive and Negative Expressions**

| Spanish | English | Spanish | English |
|---|---|---|---|
| Sí | Yes | No | No |
| Alguien | Someone, somebody | Nadie | No one, nobody |
| Algo | Something | Nada | Nothing |
| Alguno/a/os/as | Some | Ninguno/a | No, none |
| Todo/a/os/as | All, every | | |
| Siempre | Always | Nunca | Never |
| A veces | At times | Jamás | Never |
| Algunas veces | Sometimes | | |
| De vez en cuando | Occasionally | | |
| De cuando en cuando | Once in a while | | |
| De vez en vez | From time to time | | |
| Todo el tiempo | All the time | | |

**PROCEED WITH CAUTION**

If you go to Mr. López's office to see him, and you're told *"El Señor López no está,"* don't be puzzled. It means, *"Mr. López isn't here."* Because you're looking for him at that place, the *aquí* (here) is understood.

Practice saying aloud the following sentences:

*Tengo algo interesante.* (I have something interesting.)

*No tengo nada.* (I don't have anything.)

*Nada tengo.* (I have nothing.)

*Veo a alguien.* (I see someone.)

*No veo a nadie.* (I don't see anyone.)

*A nadie veo.* (I see no one.)

*Algo está en la mesa.* (Something is on the table.)

If you're thinking in terms of English grammar, then the second and fifth sentences probably seem wrong to you. That's because our English grammar books tell us that two negatives make a positive. To make a negative statement in Spanish, you must have something negative in front of the verb, no matter what comes after the verb. You must use the double negative *No tengo nada,* or simply *Nada tengo.* (The double negative form is more common and less literary.)

In the fourth, fifth, and sixth sentences, the personal *a* is used before *alguien* and before *nadie* because these pronouns (even the negative one) refer to humans and are used as direct objects. Do not confuse these pronouns with *algo* and *nada,* which are used when referring to nonhumans.

## Learn *Alguno* and *Ninguno*

*Alguno* is an adjective. This means it must agree in number and gender, just like any other adjective, with the noun(s) it modifies. Because it is based on the number *uno,* it too is shortened in front of a masculine, singular noun to *algún.* The same is true of its negative opposite, *ninguno,* which becomes *ningún.* Used as a pronoun (the noun being understood, not expressed) or placed after the noun, it retains its full masculine singular form: *ninguno.* See the following examples:

*Algún hombre llamó.* (Some man called.)

*Algunos hombres llamaron.* (Some men called.)

*Alguna mujer llegó.* (Some woman arrived.)

*Algunas mujeres llegaron.* (Some women arrived.)

*No tengo ningún libro.* (I don't have any book.)

*No tengo ninguna casa.* (I don't have any house.)

**PROCEED WITH CAUTION**

*Alguno* is very peculiar. It is used as an emphatic negative when placed after the noun: *No tengo libro alguno.* (I have no book at all.)

## Learn *Todo*

*Todo*, the opposite of *ninguno/a/os/as*, means *all*, *every*, or *the whole*. It also agrees in number and gender with the noun(s) it modifies. See the following list for examples:

*Todos los cubanos hablan español.* (All Cubans speak Spanish.)

*Todas las casas son blancas.* (All the houses are white.)

*Todo el libro es interesante.* (The whole book is interesting.)

*Toda la casa es nueva.* (The whole house is new.)

*Todo estudiante quiere estudiar.* (Every student wants to study.)

*Toda actriz quiere ir.* (Every actress wants to go.)

The idiomatic expression *todo el mundo* (literally, the whole world) is commonly used to mean everyone or everybody. The word *todo* is also used as a noun with the meaning all or everything. With the definite article, it means the whole. The plural noun, *todos*, means everyone or everybody. See the following sample sentences:

*Todo el mundo viene.* (Everyone's coming.)

*Veo a todo el mundo.* (I see everyone.)

*Todo está bien.* (All is well.)

*El todo es mayor que sus partes.* (The whole is greater than its parts.)

*Todos vinieron.* (Everyone came.)

Note the importance of the definite article: There is a great difference between *toda la casa* (the whole house) and *toda casa* (every house).

## Learn *Nunca*

The negative adverb *nunca* is somewhat more common than its synonym, *jamás*; both mean *never* or *ever*. Several positive expressions, which were listed in the preceding table, are its opposite. Practice saying the following sentences aloud:

*Voy al teatro algunas veces.* (Sometimes I go to the theater.)

*De vez en cuando como carne.* (Occasionally I eat meat.)

*María siempre quiere bailar.* (María always wants to dance.)

*Carlos habla todo el tiempo.* (Carlos talks all the time.)

*Nosotros nunca salimos de noche.* (We never go out at night.)

*No salimos nunca de noche.* (We don't ever go out at night.)

*No salimos de noche jamás.* (We don't ever go out at night.)

Note that *nunca* and *jamás* can be used in conjunction for emphasis. In this combination, *nunca* always comes first. For example, *María nunca jamás sale con Julio.* (María never ever goes out with Julio.)

# LEARN THE FUTURE TENSE

The future tense is used in Spanish in much the same way as it is in English: to speak of the future. In this section, you will learn to conjugate both regular and irregular verbs in the future tense.

## CONJUGATE THE REGULAR FUTURE TENSE

The Spanish future tense uses a somewhat different formation procedure from the one employed for the present, preterit, and imperfect tenses. Instead of the infinitive ending being removed before the proper conjugated endings are added, the endings are added directly to the infinitive verb. The following table shows the conjugation of a regular verb in the future tense by using *hablar* as an example.

**Future Tense Formation of Regular Verbs Using *Hablar***

| Subject Pronoun | Infinitive Verb | Ending | Conjugated Verb |
|---|---|---|---|
| yo | hablar | -é | hablaré |
| tú | hablar | -ás | hablarás |
| él, ella, Ud. | hablar | -á | hablará |
| nosotros/as | hablar | -emos | hablaremos |
| vosotros/as | hablar | -éis | hablaréis |
| ellos, ellas, Uds. | hablar | -án | hablarán |

The future tense is much easier to master than any of the other tenses you've already studied because the rules of conjugation are the same for *-ar, -er,* and *-ir* verbs. Use the same endings for all three types of verbs; just affix the endings to the infinitive form of the verb. The following table shows how three regular verbs, one of each type, are conjugated in the future tense.

**Future Tense Conjugations**

| Subject Pronoun | *Trabajar* (To Work) | *Ver* (To See) | *Dormir* (To Sleep) |
|---|---|---|---|
| yo | trabajaré | veré | dormiré |
| tú | trabajarás | verás | dormirás |
| él, ella, Ud. | trabajará | verá | dormirá |
| nosotros/as | trabajaremos | veremos | dormiremos |
| vosotros/as | trabajaréis | veréis | dormiréis |
| ellos, ellas, Uds. | trabajarán | verán | dormirán |

Notice the written accent marks on all forms of the future tense, with the exception of the *nosotros* form. Notice, too, that the future tense verbs are stressed on the last syllable, with the exception of the *nosotros* form, in which the next-to-last syllable is stressed.

Practice saying the following sentences aloud:

*¿Dónde trabajará usted?* (Where will you work?)

*Trabajaré en San Juan.* (I'll work in San Juan.)

*¿Qué veréis en Granada?* (What will you see in Granada?)

*Veremos la Alhambra.* (We'll see the Alhambra.)

*¿Dónde dormirán ellos?* (Where will they sleep?)

*Dormirán en un hotel.* (They'll sleep in a hotel.)

*¿Cuándo hablarás con Marta?* (When will you speak with Marta?)

*Hablaré con ella mañana.* (I'll speak with her tomorrow.)

*Irán a Irán.* (They will go to Iran.)

## LEARN IRREGULAR FUTURE VERBS

There is a group of irregular verbs in the future tense. Some of these verbs drop the vowel of the infinitive ending before adding the endings. Others substitute the letter *d* for the vowel. In addition, there are two verbs that are severely abbreviated before the endings are added.

The following three verbs are examples of the type of irregular verb in which the infinitive vowel drops out in the future tense. Notice: When you drop the *e* of *querer*, the two *r*s come together to form the double *rr*.

**Irregular Verbs in the Future Tense**

| Saber (To Know) | Poder (To Be Able, Can) | Querer (To Want, Love) |
|---|---|---|
| sabré | podré | querré |
| sabrás | podrás | querrás |
| sabrá | podrá | querrá |
| sabremos | podremos | querremos |
| sabréis | podréis | querréis |
| sabrán | podrán | querrán |

**PROCEED WITH CAUTION**

Be careful. The only difference between *we want* and *we shall want* in Spanish is the difference in sound between the single *r* and the double *rr* (*queremos* versus *querremos*).

Practice saying the following sentences aloud:

*Mañana sabremos.* (We'll know tomorrow.)

*No sabrán nada.* (They won't find out anything.)

*¿No podrán ustedes cantar?* (You won't be able to sing?)

*No, no podremos.* (No, we won't be able to.)

*¿Qué querrán hacer?* (What will you want to do?)

*Querremos llegar temprano.* (We'll want to arrive early.)

Another type of irregular verb in the future tense is one in which the last vowel of the infinitive is transformed into the letter *d*. Verbs in this category include *salir* (to leave), *poner* (to put), *tener* (to have), and *venir* (to come), all of which are conjugated in the following table. Also included in the category is *valer* (to protect or to be worth).

**More Irregular Verbs in Future Tense**

| Salir | Poner | Tener | Venir |
|---|---|---|---|
| saldré | pondré | tendré | vendré |
| saldrás | pondrás | tendrás | vendrás |

*continues*

**More Irregular Verbs in Future Tense (continued)**

| Salir | Poner | Tener | Venir |
|---|---|---|---|
| saldrá | pondrá | tendrá | vendrá |
| saldremos | pondremos | tendremos | vendremos |
| saldréis | pondréis | tendréis | vendréis |
| saldrán | pondrán | tendrán | vendrán |

Practice saying the following sentences aloud:

*¿Dónde pondremos las flores?* (Where shall we put the flowers?)

*Pondréis las flores en la mesa.* (You'll put the flowers on the table.)

*¿Quién tendrá la oportunidad?* (Who will have the opportunity?)

*Yo tendré la oportunidad.* (I will have the opportunity.)

*¿Cuándo vendrá mi amigo?* (When will my friend come?)

*Vendrán él y otros mañana.* (He and others will come tomorrow.)

*Todos vendremos.* (We'll all come.)

**JUST A MINUTE**

No *-ar* verbs are irregular in the future tense.

## Use Future *Hacer* and *Decir*

Two verbs in the future tense are extremely irregular: *hacer* (to do, make) and *decir* (to say, tell). Before the future endings are added, these verbs are severely shortened. For *hacer* you add the endings to a base of *har,* and for *decir* you add to a base of *dir.* See the following table for the conjugation of these two verbs.

**Future Tense for *Hacer* and *Decir***

| Subject Pronoun | Hacer | Decir |
|---|---|---|
| yo | haré | diré |
| tú | harás | dirás |
| él, ella, Ud. | hará | dirá |
| nosotros/as | haremos | diremos |
| vosotros/as | haréis | diréis |
| ellos, ellas, Uds. | harán | dirán |

Practice saying the following sentences aloud:

*¿Qué hará el jefe?* (What will the boss do?)

*Y, ¿qué haremos nosotros?* (And what will we do?)

*Ellos no harán nada.* (They won't do anything.)

*¿Qué dirá papá?* (What will Dad say?)

*Él y mamá no dirán nada.* (He and Mom won't say anything.)

*Nosotros diremos la verdad.* (We will tell the truth.)

## TALK OF PROBABILITY AND WONDERING

The future tense is used not only to speak of the future, but also to speak of probabilities in the present and to wonder about things in the present. When wondering is involved, the sentence is phrased as a question in the future tense. See the following sentences for the equivalent of wondering:

*¿Quiénes serán?* (I wonder who they are.)

*¿Quién será?* (I wonder who it is.)

*¿Qué harán?* (I wonder what they're doing.)

Notice the difference between *¿Quiénes son?* (Who are they?) and *¿Quiénes serán?* (I wonder who they are?). When you use the present tense in the question, you are asking a direct question. When you use the future tense in the question, you are being more subtle, almost as if you were talking to yourself. With the present tense, you signal that you expect the person you're questioning to have the answer. When you use a future tense question, you're not making this assumption.

The English translations of the three preceding sentences show one way we handle those thoughts in English. We can also translate them with English questions instead of with statements beginning with *I wonder ....* They might be expressed as *Who can they be? Who can it (he, she) be? What can they be doing?* The idea is still the same. Context is important. For example, the third of the previous sample sentences could certainly be taken literally. If you're speaking about the future, it could mean *What will they do?*

**GO TO ▶**
To see how to express wondering and probability with reference to the past, see the section "Use the Conditional Tense" of Hour 7.

**JUST A MINUTE**

Another way to say *I wonder* in Spanish is *Me pregunto* (I ask myself). This phrase can be followed by any interrogative word, or the Spanish word for if (*si*) followed by a verb in any tense.

### Talk of Probability

You can also use the Spanish future tense for indicating probability. If you're not sure of a fact, but think it probably is true, then instead of the present tense, use the future tense in a declarative sentence. For example, one might answer the preceding questions in the following manner:

> *Serán los padres.* (They're probably the parents.)
>
> *Será el jefe.* (He's probably the boss.)
>
> *Jugarán al béisbol.* (They're probably playing baseball.)
>
> *Estará en casa.* (He's probably at home.)
>
> *No tendrán nada.* (Probably nothing's the matter with them.)

Other English idiomatic ways of phrasing the thoughts expressed in the preceding sentences include these sentences: They must be the parents. He (it) must be the boss. They must be playing baseball. He must be at home. Nothing must be the matter with them.

Notice the difference between *Son los padres* (They are the parents) and *Serán los padres* (They're probably the parents). When you use the present tense in these statements, you're indicating that you're sure about your answer. When you use the future tense, you're suggesting that you're not quite sure, but that you think your answer has a good possibility of being true.

## The 30-Second Recap

In this hour, you've learned how to …

- Count through 500.
- Handle the imperfect tense.
- Know when to use the preterit tense and when to use the imperfect.
- Use common positive and negative expressions.
- Use the future tense.

## Hour's Up!

By completing this hour, you've vastly enriched your communicative skills in Spanish. Review the major points, and then test your ability to use these new skills in Spanish by answering the following questions. Try to do this without looking back at the pages of this hour.

1. The preterit tense is used to …
    **a.** Speak of the past.
    **b.** Visualize the start of an action.
    **c.** Visualize the end of an action.
    **d.** Narrate a series of events.
    **e.** All of the above.

2. The imperfect tense is used to …
    **a.** Speak of the past.
    **b.** Visualize the middle of an action.
    **c.** Describe.
    **d.** Set the stage for narration.
    **e.** All of the above.

3. Choose the most appropriate form of *ir: Ayer yo* _____ *al cine.*
    **a.** iba
    **b.** iré
    **c.** fui
    **d.** voy
    **e.** era

4. Choose the correct Spanish form of *ir: El año pasado tú siempre* _____ *a Florida los veranos* (summers).
    **a.** ibas
    **b.** fuiste
    **c.** irás
    **d.** vas
    **e.** ías

5. Choose the correct Spanish form of *ser: Cuando nosotros* _____ *niños,* ….
    **a.** fuimos
    **b.** somos
    **c.** seremos
    **d.** éramos
    **e.** íbamos

**6.** Choose the correct Spanish translation for ser: El general George Wáshington _____ el primer presidente de los Estados Unidos de América (United States of America).

    **a.** era

    **b.** sió

    **c.** es

    **d.** sera

    **e.** fue

**7.** Choose the correct Spanish translation: I don't ever go.

    **a.** Nunca voy.

    **b.** No voy nunca.

    **c.** No voy jamás yo.

    **d.** All of the above.

**8.** Choose the correct Spanish translation: I see nothing.

    **a.** Vedo nada.

    **b.** Veo yo nada.

    **c.** No veo algo

    **d.** Nado veo.

**9.** Provide the opposite expression: nunca.

    **a.** siempre

    **b.** a veces

    **c.** de vez en cuando

    **d.** all of the above

**10.** Provide the opposite expression: No tengo libro alguno.

    **a.** No tengo libro ninguno.

    **b.** Tengo algunos libros.

    **c.** Ningún libro tengo.

    **d.** No tengo ningunos libros yo.

QUIZ

# Part II
## Being

# HOUR 7

# Ser/Estar, Conditional Tense, Adverbs

## CHAPTER SUMMARY

**LESSON PLAN:**

In this hour, you'll learn …

- How to count through 1,000.
- How to form adverbs.
- How to use the conditional tense.
- How to differentiate between *ser* and *estar*.

The numbers from 500 to 999 function similarly to the numbers from 200 to 500, which you've already mastered. There are some small peculiarities in the actual words that represent these numbers. See the following table for representative numbers:

| | |
|---|---|
| 500 quinientos | 706 setecientos seis |
| 501 quinientos uno | 800 ochocientos |
| 502 quinientos dos | 807 ochocientos siete |
| 600 seiscientos | 808 ochocientos ocho |
| 603 seiscientos tres | 900 novecientos |
| 604 siescientos cuatro | 901 novecientos uno |
| 700 setecientos | 909 novecientos nueve |
| 705 setecientos cinco | 1,000 mil |

Note that, like *quinientos*, some of these numbers are a bit different from what you might have anticipated. Based on *siete*, you have **setecientos**. Based on *nueve*, you have **nove**cientos.

As with numbers from 200 through 500, which you have already learned, all the numbers from 500 through 999 agree, in number and in gender, with the nouns they modify. However, the number 1,000 does not: It is simply *mil*, no form of *uno* is used in front of it. See the following examples:

*quinientos libros* (500 books)

*quinientas revistas* (500 magazines)

*setecientos hombres* (700 men)

*setecientas personas* (700 persons)

*novecientos edificios* (900 buildings)

*novecientas casas* (900 houses)

*mil caballos* (1,000 horses)

*mil mujeres* (1,000 women)

*mil gatos* (1,000 cats)

*mil mesas* (1,000 tables)

## USE THE CONDITIONAL TENSE

The conditional tense in Spanish serves the same function as the English tense of the same name. It is used to refer to actions, events, or states which have not taken place and might never take place because they are dependent on certain *conditions*. It's called the conditional tense precisely because it refers to actions whose reality is conditional. In English, the conditional tense uses the auxiliary verb *would* to convey the idea of conditionality: *I would go to the store*.

The following sentences illustrate the conditional state associated with this tense. You can readily comprehend that this tense is employed to speak about *iffy* situations.

I would go *if* they were to invite me.

He'd (he would) be a good worker *if* he weren't a drinker.

We'd go to the beach *if* we knew how to swim.

Who would do such a thing (*if* given the opportunity)?

## UNDERSTAND "PAST FUTURE" IN ENGLISH

A second use of the conditional tense, in both English and Spanish, is to serve as the future of the past, or the past future. Although "past future" sounds contradictory, we commonly use the conditional tense in English to discuss the future of the past. See the following English sentences for examples:

He says he will go.

He said he would go.

I think I'll have lunch later.

I thought I'd have lunch later.

They promise they will.

They promised they would.

The first verb in the first, third, and fifth sentences is in the present tense, and is followed by a verb in the future tense. The future tense is used in these sentences to project what will happen some time after the verb in the present tense. When we shift the sentences from the present to the past, we must use the conditional tense for the second verb. Because the first verb is in the past tense, the verbs that had been in the future tense in the other sentences are shifted to the conditional tense. The conditional tense is used in these sentences to project what would happen some time after the verb in the past tense; that is what we mean by the past future.

**JUST A MINUTE**

The conditional tense in the preceding sentences relates to the past tense the way the future tense relates to the present tense.

## CONJUGATE THE REGULAR CONDITIONAL TENSE

The conditional tense conjugates similarly to the future tense. As with the future tense, instead of removing the infinitive, the endings are added directly to the infinitive verb. See the following table for the conjugation of a regular verb in the conditional tense.

**TIME SAVER**

The conditional endings are not new to you. They are the same as those for the *-er* and *-ir* verbs of the imperfect tense. The difference is that whereas these endings were added to the stem of the verb (of only two conjugations) for the imperfect, they are added to the infinitive for all three conjugations of the conditional.

**Conditional Tense Formation: Regular Verbs**

| Subject Pronoun | Infinitive Verb | Ending | Conjugated Verb |
|---|---|---|---|
| **Singular** | | | |
| yo | hablar | -ía | hablaría |
| tú | hablar | -ías | hablarías |
| él, ella, Ud. | hablar | -ía | hablaría |

*continues*

**Conditional Tense Formation: Regular Verbs**

| Subject Pronoun | Infinitive Verb | Ending | Conjugated Verb |
| --- | --- | --- | --- |
| **Plural** | | | |
| Nosotros/as | hablar | -íamos | hablaríamos |
| vosotros/as | hablar | -íais | hablaríais |
| ellos, ellas, Uds. | hablar | -ían | hablarían |

You will find the conditional tense even easier to master than the future tense. Not only are the rules of conjugation the same for *-ar*, *-er*, and *-ir* verbs, but the yo ending is the same as that of él, ella, and Ud. See the following table, in which three regular verbs, one from each of the three conjugations, are conjugated in the conditional tense.

**Conditional Tense: *Trabajar, Ver, and Dormir***

| Subject Pronoun | Trabajar (To Work) | Ver (To See) | Dormir (To Sleep) |
| --- | --- | --- | --- |
| yo | trabajaría | vería | dormiría |
| tú | trabajarías | verías | dormirías |
| él, ella, Ud. | trabajaría | vería | dormiría |
| nosotros/as | trabajaríamos | veríamos | dormiríamos |
| vosotros/as | trabajaríais | veríais | dormiríais |
| ellos, ellas, Uds. | trabajarían | verían | dormirían |

**JUST A MINUTE**

Most conditional sentences imply a clause beginning with *if*. In other words, if certain conditions were present, then the implied act could take place.

Practice saying the following sentences aloud:

*¿Dónde trabajaría Ud.?* (Where would you work?)

*Trabajaría en San Juan.* (I'd work in San Juan.)

*¿Qué veríais en Granada?* (What would you see in Granada?)

*Veríamos la Alhambra.* (We would see the Alhambra.)

*¿Dónde dormirían ellos?* (Where would they sleep?)

## LEARN IRREGULAR CONDITIONAL VERBS

There is a group of irregular verbs in the conditional tense; these are the very same verbs that were irregular in the future tense. Just as in the future tense, some of these verbs (the same ones as in the future tense) drop the vowel of the infinitive ending before adding the endings. Others substitute the letter *d* for the vowel. In addition, two verbs are severely abbreviated before the endings are added. None of the irregular conditional verbs are *-ar* verbs.

*Saber* is a typical verb in the conditional tense in which the infinitive vowel drops out. See the following list for its conjugation:

1. **Infinitive.** *Saber* (to know)
2. **Drop vowel.** *Sabr-*
3. **Add endings.** *Sabría, sabrías, sabría, sabríamos, sabríais, sabrían*

Other irregular conditional tense verbs that drop the vowel of the infinitive before adding endings include *poder* (to be able, can) whose stem is *podr-* and *querer* (to want, love) whose stem is *querr-*.

The conditional tense of *querer* is most often used in place of the blunt present tense (I want to eat) to soften the means of expression. *Querer* in the conditional tense is a more subtle, polite form of speaking. The phrase *Querría comer*, instead of meaning *I would want to eat*, can be thought of as the more subtle, *I'd like to eat.*

### PROCEED WITH CAUTION

The only difference between the imperfect and the conditional of *querer* is the difference in sound between the single *r* and the double *rr*. Note the difference between the following two sentences: *Yo quería a Juana.* (I loved Juana.) *Yo querría a Juana.* (I would love Juana.)

Practice saying the following sentences aloud:

*Yo no querría hablar con él.* (I wouldn't want [wouldn't like] to talk with him.)

*No sabrían nada si ...* (They wouldn't know [find out] anything if ...)

*¿No podrían Uds. cantar?* (Wouldn't you be able to sing?)

*No, no podríamos.* (No, we wouldn't [be able].)

*Salir* is the type of irregular conditional verb in which the vowel of the infinitive is transformed into the letter *d:*

1. **Infinitive.** *Salir* (to leave, go out)
2. **Vowel changes to d.** *Saldr-*
3. **Add endings.** *Saldría, saldrías, saldría, saldríamos, saldríais, saldrían*

Other irregular conditional tense verbs that transform the vowel of the infinitive into the letter *d* include *poner, tener, venir,* and *valer.* See the following table for the conjugation of the first three of these verbs.

**Conditional Tense: *Poner, Tener,* and *Venir***

| Subject Pronoun | Poner | Tener | Venir |
| --- | --- | --- | --- |
| yo | pondría | tendría | vendría |
| tú | pondrías | tendrías | vendrías |
| él, ella, Ud. | pondría | tendría | vendría |
| nosotros/as | pondríamos | tendríamos | vendríamos |
| vosotros/as | pondríais | tendríais | vendríais |
| ellos, ellas, Uds. | pondrían | tendrían | vendrían |

Practice saying the following sentences aloud:

*¿Dónde pondríamos las flores?* (Where would we put the flowers?)

*Pondríais las flores en la mesa.* (You'd put the flowers on the table.)

*¿Quién tendría la oportunidad?* (Who would have the opportunity?)

*Yo tendría la oportunidad.* (I would have the opportunity.)

**PROCEED WITH CAUTION**

Be careful. It's easy to confuse the conditional tense of *poner* and *poder* (*pondría* versus *podría*). The letter *n* makes the difference.

*Hacer* (to do, make) and *decir* (to say, tell) are extremely irregular in the conditional tense. Before adding the conditional endings, these verbs are severely shortened. For *hacer* add the endings to the stem *har-,* and for *decir* add the endings to the stem *dir-.* See the following table for the conjugation of these two verbs.

**Conditional Tense: *Hacer* and *Decir***

| Subject Pronoun | Hacer (To Do, Make) | Decir (To Say, Tell) |
|---|---|---|
| yo | haría | diría |
| tú | harías | dirías |
| él, ella, Ud. | haría | diría |
| nosotros/as | haríamos | diríamos |
| vosotros/as | haríais | diríais |
| ellos, ellas, Uds. | harían | dirían |

Practice saying the following sentences aloud:

*¿Qué harías tú?* (What would you do?)

*¿Y, qué haríamos nosotros?* (And what would we do?)

*Ellos no harían nada.* (They wouldn't do anything.)

*¿Qué diría papá?* (What would Dad say?)

## TALK OF PROBABILITY AND WONDERING

The conditional tense has still other uses. Just as you've used the future tense to speak of probabilities in the present, and to wonder about things in the present, you can use the conditional tense to speak of probabilities in the past, and to wonder about things in the past.

When wondering is involved, the conditional tense is presented in question form. See the following sentences for the equivalent of wondering:

*¿Quiénes serían?* (I wonder who they were.)

*¿Quién sería?* (I wonder who it was.)

*¿Qué harían?* (I wonder what they were doing.)

**GO TO** ▶
For a review of the future tense, see Hour 6.

Notice the difference between *¿Quiénes fueron?* (Who were they?) and *¿Quiénes serían?* (I wonder who they were.) When you use the preterit tense (or the imperfect) in the question, you are asking a direct question. When you use the conditional tense in the question, you are being more subtle, almost as if you were talking to yourself. With the past tenses, you signal that you expect the person you're questioning to have the answer. When you use the conditional tense question, you're not making this assumption.

The English translations of the five preceding sentences show one way we handle those thoughts in English. We can also translate them with English questions employing the auxiliary verb *could*. In this case, they might be expressed as follows: *Who could they have been? Who could it (he, she) have been? What could they have been doing? Where could Carlos have been? What could have been the matter with them?*

Context is important. For example, the third of the previous sample sentences could certainly be taken literally; it could mean *What would they do?*

## USE THE CONDITIONAL FOR PROBABILITY

You can also use the Spanish conditional tense for indicating probability in the past. If you're not sure of a fact, but think it is probably true, then instead of the preterit or imperfect tense, use the conditional tense in a declarative sentence. For example, one might answer the preceding questions in the following manner:

> *Serían los padres.* (They were probably the parents.)
>
> *Sería el jefe.* (It [he] was probably the boss.)
>
> *Jugarían al béisbol.* (They were probably playing baseball.)
>
> *Estaría en casa.* (He was probably at home.)
>
> *No tendrían nada.* (Probably nothing was the matter with them.)

Another English idiomatic way of phrasing the thoughts expressed in these sentences is this: *They must have been the parents. He (it) must have been the boss. They must have been playing baseball. He must have been home. There must have been nothing the matter with them.*

### JUST A MINUTE

Note the difference between the following two sentences: *Fueron los padres.* (They were the parents.) *Serían los padres.* (They were probably the parents.) The first sentence shows you're absolutely certain, the second does not.

## UNDERSTAND DIFFERENT STATES OF BEING

Two verbs in Spanish are equivalent to the single English verb *to be*. These Spanish verbs—*ser* and *estar*—are *not* equivalent, and are used in very different ways. You have already seen these verbs used in previous chapters, but without much explanation. You will begin to understand these differences and to

use these verbs correctly in this hour, and you will continue learning to
employ them in Hours 8 and 9.

## USE *SER* FOR EXISTENCE

*Ser* refers to existence. *I think, therefore I am* in Spanish is *Yo pienso, por eso
yo soy.* In this usage, *ser* is synonymous with *existir* (to exist).

## USE *SER* FOR IDENTITY

*Ser* is used for identity. It is used to connect the subject of a verb with a noun
or pronoun. *Estar* never does this. Remember this uncomplicated rule, and
you won't have to ponder other factors when you want to connect the subject to a noun or pronoun. You could state this rule in another way: *Ser* tells
(or asks) *who* or *what.*

Say the following sentences aloud:

*¡Somos idiotas!* (We are idiots!)

*¿Quién es usted?* (Who are you?)

*Soy el capitán.* (I'm the captain.)

*¿Y tú, chico, quién eres (tú)?* (And you, boy, who are you?)

*Soy el hijo del capitán.* (I'm the captain's son.)

*¡Es ella!* (It is she! [It's her!])

*Soy yo.* (It is I. [It's me.])

---

**TIME SAVER**

Think of *ser* as a mathematical equals sign between the subject of the verb and a
noun or pronoun (*Carlos es un hombre: Carlos = un hombre*).

Notice that the indefinite article is omitted before the noun when *ser* is used
with a noun of (1) nationality; (2) religion; (3) political affiliation; or (4)
profession or trade, unless that noun is further modified: *Pedro es republicano*
(Pedro is a Republican), but *Pedro es un republicano verdadero* (Pedro is a true
Republican). *María es estudiante* (María is a student), but *María es una estudiante que trabaja mucho* (María is a student who works hard).

## USE *SER* WITH *DE*

The verb *ser* is used in conjunction with the preposition *de* (of, from) to indicate three things: ownership, composition (that something is made of), and origin (where someone or something is originally from). (See later in this hour for an explanation of *estar* and physical location.)

Practice speaking the following questions and answers using *ser* and *de* (noticing which interrogative word is employed for each of the three uses):

> *¿De quién es el libro?* (Whose book is it?)
>
> *El libro es de José.* (The book is José's.)
>
> *¿De qué es (el libro)?* (What is it [the book] made of?)
>
> *(El libro) Es de papel.* ([The book] is [made of] paper.)
>
> *¿De dónde es?* (Where's it from?)
>
> *Es de Madrid.* (It's from Madrid.)

Notice that Spanish does not use an apostrophe, and that *José's* translates literally as *of José*. Notice, too, that the literal translations of the Spanish questions begin with *of whom*, *of what*, and *from where*.

## USE *SER* FOR ACTIVITY LOCATION

The verb *ser* is not used to speak of mere physical location; that's the function of *estar*. However, it is used to refer to the location of an event, a happening, or a situation in which people are interacting or doing things. If *ser* is used to tell or ask where something is, that something is always thought of as activity, not mere physical location. Sometimes there is a clear separation of these two functions, a difference in denotation. At other times, the lines are not as well drawn; it's just a matter of connotation or emphasis. Look at the following examples:

> *¿Dónde es la fiesta?* (Where's the party?)
>
> *La fiesta es en mi casa.* (The party's at my house.)
>
> *¿Dónde será la graduación?* (Where will the graduation be?)
>
> *Va a ser allí.* (It's going to be [held] there.)

In talking about a location, if the verb *to be* refers to an activity *taking place, going on,* or *being held,* use *ser.* If the verb does not refer to a location where an activity takes place, use *estar.*

These sentences are pretty clear cut; they all refer to some kind of activity, interaction, or event. Therefore, you would use the verb *ser.*

## USE *ESTAR* FOR PHYSICAL LOCATION

One of the many uses of the verb *estar* is to ask or tell about the physical location of someone or something. Practice saying the following sentences:

*¿Dónde estás, Eduardo?* (Where are you, Eduardo?)

*Estoy aquí.* (I'm here.)

*¿Dónde estuvo María el mes pasado?* (Where was María last month?)

*Estuvo en París.* (She was in Paris.)

*¿Dónde están los libros?* (Where are the books?)

*Están en el escritorio.* (They're on the desk.)

*Estábamos en Bogotá cuando ocurrió.* (We were in Bogotá when it happened.)

Because there are so many different ways to refer to physical location, it is easy to confuse *ser* and *estar.* As you can see, these sentences refer to physical location and therefore employ *estar.* Study the following sentences until it's clear to you why each one employs *ser* or *estar.* Then practice saying the following sentences until they sound natural to you:

*¿De dónde es Ud.?* (Where are you from? [origin])

*Soy de Honduras.* (I'm from Honduras. [origin])

*¿Dónde está Ud. ahora?* (Where are you now? [physical location])

*Estoy en Nevada.* (I'm in Nevada. [physical location])

*¿De dónde son ellos?* (Where are they from? [origin])

*Son de los Estados Unidos.* (They're from the United States. [origin])

*¿Y, dónde están hoy?* (And where are they today? [physical location])

You can never use *ser* to talk about a person's whereabouts, because a person (or animal, or physical object) cannot be an event, interaction, or activity.

## USE SPANISH ADVERBS

GO TO ▶
For a review of the grammatical term *verb*, see Hour 3. For a review of the grammatical term *noun*, see Hour 2.

An adverb is a word that can perform three functions:

- Modify a verb
- Modify an adjective
- Modify another adverb

Adverbs usually refer to manner, quality, time, place, or degree.

Before moving on to the formation of adverbs in Spanish, take a look at the following English examples of adverbial use. In the following two sentences, the adverbs modify *verbs*. In the first sentence, the adverb *well* modifies the verb *writes*; it tells us *how* Joan writes. In the second sentence, the adverb *atrociously* modifies the verb *speaks*; it tells us *how* Brian speaks.

Joan writes *well*.

Brian speaks *atrociously*.

In the following two sentences, the adverbs modify *adjectives*. In the first sentence, the adverb *very* modifies the adjective *pretty*; it explains to what extent Kate is pretty. In the second sentence, the adverb *incredibly* modifies the adjective *wealthy*; it explains to what extent Mr. Jones is wealthy.

Kate is *very* pretty.

Mr. Jones is *incredibly* wealthy.

In the following two sentences, there are two adverbs; in each sentence, one adverb modifies a verb, and this adverb, in turn, is itself modified by another adverb. In the first sentence, the adverb *well* modifies the verb *writes*, while the adverb *very* modifies the adverb *well*. *Very* informs us to what degree Joan writes well.

Joan writes *very well*.

Brian speaks quite *atrociously*.

In the previous sentence, the adverb *atrociously* modifies the verb *speaks*, while the adverb *quite* modifies the adverb *atrociously*. *Quite* informs us to what degree Brian speaks atrociously.

The most common way to form adverbs in English is to start with an adjective and then add the ending *-ly*. For example:

atrocious (adj.); atrocious*ly* (adv.)

intelligent (adj.); intelligent*ly* (adv.)

sweet (adj.); sweet*ly* (adv.)

quick (adj.); quick*ly* (adv.)

slow (adj.); slow*ly* (adv.)

bad (adj.); bad*ly* (adv.)

---

**TIME SAVER**

In Spanish and English, adverbs answer questions such as *how? when? where? how much? how often?* and *to what extent?*

There are some irregular adverbs in English; some do not even have an adjective parallel. See the following examples:

good (adj.); well (adv.)

fast (adj.); fast (adv.)

_____; soon (adv.)

_____; often (adv.)

_____; seldom (adv.)

_____; very (adv.)

*Well* refers to manner and quality; *fast* refers to manner; *soon* refers to time; *often* and *seldom* refer to time; and *very* refers to degree.

## LEARN TO FORM ADVERBS IN SPANISH

Now that we've reviewed these general concepts about the formation of adverbs in English, as well as the concepts expressed by adverbs in both Spanish and English, you are ready to learn how to form adverbs in Spanish. The regular manner of forming adverbs in Spanish has three steps:

1. Start with the adjective.
2. Use the *feminine* form of the adjective.
3. Add the ending *-mente* to the adjective.

The following table illustrates the transformation of adjectives to adverbs.

### Adjectives to Adverbs

| Masculine Adjective | Feminine Adjective | + -mente | Adverb |
|---------------------|--------------------|----------|--------------|
| rápido | rápida | + -mente | rápidamente |
| lento | lenta | + -mente | lentamente |

*continues*

**Adjectives to Adverbs   (continued)**

| Masculine Adjective | Feminine Adjective | + -mente | Adverb |
|---|---|---|---|
| obvio | obvia | + -mente | obviamente |
| atroz | atroz | + -mente | atrozmente |
| alegre | alegre | + -mente | alegremente |
| sutil | sutil | + -mente | sutilmente |

Practice saying the following sentences:

*El tren anda rápidamente.* (The train moves fast [rapidly].)

*Pancho lee lentamente.* (Pancho reads slowly.)

*Obviamente, Ud. no conoce al presidente.* (Obviously, you don't know the president.)

*Brian habla atrozmente.* (Brian speaks atrociously.)

*Cantaron alegremente.* (They sang merrily.)

*Hiciste todo muy sutilmente.* (You did everything very subtly.)

**GO TO ▶**
For a review of adjective/noun agreement, and the masculine and feminine forms of adjectives, see Hour 2.

Remember that *atroz*, *alegre*, and *sutil* are adjectives that are both masculine and feminine; therefore, they need no adjustment to become feminine. Because they are already feminine, you just add the *-mente* ending to them.

In Spanish, just as in English, there are irregular adverbs. See some of them in the following list:

| Spanish | English |
|---|---|
| bien (from adj. bueno/a) | well |
| mal (from adj. malo/a) | badly, poorly |
| pronto | soon |
| despacio | slowly |

In both Spanish and English, we can use an adverbial phrase instead of an adverb. This is more common in Spanish. The phrase is usually (but not exclusively) introduced by the preposition *con* (with). See the following examples:

*El tren anda con rapidez.* (The train moves with rapidity.)

*Pancho lee con lentitud.* (Pancho reads with slowness.)

*Cantaron con alegría.* (They sang with joy.)

*Hiciste todo con mucha sutileza.* (You did everything with much subtlety.)

*Carlos venía a menudo.* (Carlos used to come often.)

---

**JUST A MINUTE**

*A menudo* is an idiom signifying *often,* and cannot be translated literally.

Of course, you would never say some of the preceding English sentences, which are literal translations of the Spanish, and are used here only to demonstrate how the Spanish sentences work. The first and fourth of the previous sample sentences seem stilted; and the second sample sentence doesn't even sound English. Instead, you would say, "The train moves rapidly (fast)," "Pancho reads slowly," and probably, "You did everything very subtly." The third and fifth sentences, of course, are regular English sentences. However, all five sentences are very common and completely normal in Spanish.

## THE 30-SECOND RECAP

In this hour, you have learned to count through 1,000, to use the conditional tense, to use *ser* and *estar,* and to form adverbs and adverbial phrases.

## HOUR'S UP!

Now test yourself by answering the following questions. Try to do this without looking up the answers in the pages of this hour's lesson. It would be a good idea, however, to go back and review the material before taking the test.

1. The conditional tense is used to speak of …

    **a.** The future.

    **b.** The present.

    **c.** The past future.

    **d.** None of the above.

2. The conditional tense is used to speak of …

    **a.** Conditional realities.

    **b.** Past probabilities.

    **c.** Iffy situations

    **d.** All of the above.

QUIZ

**3.** Choose the correct form of the verb in parentheses in the conditional tense: (*comer*) *Ellos*.

    **a.** comerán

    **b.** comerían

    **c.** comrían

    **d.** comdrían

**4.** Choose the correct form of the verb in parentheses in the conditional tense: (*salir*) *Yo*.

    **a.** saldría

    **b.** saliría

    **c.** salría

    **d.** salrán

**5.** Choose the correct form of the verb in parentheses in the conditional tense: (*hacer*) *Tú* _____ *mucho*.

    **a.** harías

    **b.** hacerías

    **c.** hazrías

    **d.** hicerías

**6.** Choose the correct form of the verb in parentheses in the conditional tense: (decir) María _____ la verdad.

    **a.** dizría

    **b.** deciría

    **c.** diría

    **d.** daría

**7.** Choose the correct form of either ser or estar: Muchos amigos _____ en Colombia.

    **a.** están

    **b.** son

    **c.** sois

    **d.** estáis

**8.** Choose the correct form of either ser or estar: Tú ____ el capitán.

    **a.** estuviste

    **b.** estuvisteis

    **c.** fuiste

    **d.** fuisteis

# HOUR 8

## *Ser* vs. *Estar* with Adjectives

## CHAPTER SUMMARY

**LESSON PLAN:**

In this hour, you'll learn ...

- How to count from 1,001 to 1,000,000.
- How to discuss the weather and temperatures.
- How to use the verb *ser* for telling time.
- How to use the verb *ser* with adjectives to speak of characteristics.
- How to use the verb *estar* with adjectives to speak of conditions.

Study representative numbers from 1,001 through one million:

| | |
|---|---|
| 1.001 mil y uno | 15.505 quince mil quinientos cinco |
| 1.095 mil noventa y cinco | 60.000 sesenta mil |
| 1.110 mil ciento diez | 88.000 ochenta y ocho mil |
| 2.503 dos mil quinientos tres | 99.000 noventa y nueve mil |
| 3.601 tres mil seiscientos uno | 100.000 cien mil |
| 5.999 cinco mil novecientos noventa y nueve | 800.000 ochocientos mil |
| 10.080 diez mil ochenta | 999.000 novecientos noventa y nueve mil |
| 1.000.000 un millón | |

Notice the following:

- The period (not the comma) is used to indicate *thousand*.
- *Mil* is never pluralized.
- After *mil*, you add numbers you already know.
- Unlike *mil*, 1.000.000 starts with *un*.

JUST A MINUTE

In Spanish, the year is always spoken as *mil* .... For example, 1492 is pronounced *mil cuatrocientos noventa y dos*; 1999 is *mil novecientos noventa y nueve*; 2005 is *dos mil cinco*.

Study the following list:

Las Mil y Una Noches (*The Thousand and One Nights*)

*mil y un libros* (1,001 books)

*mil veintiún libros* (1,021 books)

*mil veintiuna mesas* (1,021 tables)

*mil seiscientos pianos* (1,600 pianos)

*mil seiscientas montañas* (1,600 mountains)

*mil trescientos cinco anillos* (1,305 rings)

*mil trescientas cinco casas* (1,305 houses)

*mil quinientos un caballos* (1,501 horses)

*mil quinientas una ciudades* (1,501 cities)

After having studied the preceding list, you will have noticed several things: Even in numbers dealing with 1,000 plus, *uno* is still shortened to *un* before masculine nouns, and feminized to *una* before feminine nouns, but *not* pluralized. The hundreds, which show plural by ending in *-s*, still reflect whether the noun being modified is masculine or feminine, ending with *-os* for the masculine and *-as* for the feminine.

Now that you understand the manner in which these numbers work, go back and practice pronouncing them in Spanish while mentally associating what you're saying with the numerical figures they represent.

PROCEED WITH CAUTION

Numbers are the last elements of a foreign language that students internalize; most people who have acquired fluency in a new language, and even think in it, typically switch to their native language to do arithmetic. So take the time to internalize the numbers.

## TELL TIME WITH *SER*

*Ser* is the verb used to refer to time. In English, we have several ways of speaking of clock time by saying, for example, "It's five o'clock," and if it's not five o'clock on the dot, things like, "It's five after five," or "It's five past five," or "It's five-oh-five," or even "It's five five." We might even take the trouble to say, "It is five minutes after five o'clock." In Spanish there is more than one way, too.

The term for one o'clock is somewhat different from that of all the other hours. Because one o'clock deals with *one* hour, it is singular. The English statement, It's one o'clock, becomes in Spanish *Es la una*. The verb *ser* is conjugated in the third person singular to agree with the unexpressed subject equivalent to the English *it*. So *Es* is here understood to mean *It is* ....

Notice that the feminine form of number one is used: *una*. This is because it is understood that it stands for *una hora* (one hour). But the word *hora* is never used in giving the time. It is, however, employed in asking the time. Notice that not only is the verb *ser* in the *singular* third person, but the feminine definite article is also singular.

To ask what time it is, you would say, "*¿Qué hora es?*" Literally, this means *What hour is (it)?*

**JUST A MINUTE**

In Spanish, the neuter subject pronoun (*it* in English) is understood rather than expressed.

After the one o'clock hour, both the verb *ser* and the feminine definite article are in the *plural*, because you are referring to more than one hour. For the same reason, the verb is plural. For example, *It's two o'clock* in Spanish is *Son las dos*. You are using *son* instead of *es*, and *las* instead of *la*. For example:

*Es la una*. (It's one o'clock.)

*Son las seis*. (It's six o'clock.)

*Era la una*. (It was one o'clock.)

*Eran las seis*. (It was six o'clock.)

*Será la una*. (It will be one o'clock. [It's probably one o'clock.])

*Serían las dos*. (It would be two o'clock. [It was probably two o'clock.])

To express the number of minutes it is after the hour in question, you simply add the conjunction *y* and then the number that stands for the number of minutes it is after the hour. For example, to express *It's five after nine*, or

*It's nine-oh-five*, you would say *Son las nueve y cinco* (literally, They [the hours] are the nine and five (the word *minutos* is understood, not expressed). See the following examples:

*Es la una y veinte.* (It's twenty after one. [It's one-twenty.])

*Es la una y quince.* (It's fifteen after one. [It's one-fifteen.])

*Son las cinco y cinco.* (It's five after five. [It's five-oh-five.])

*Son las siete y treinta.* (It's seven thirty.)

*Son las tres y treinta y cinco.* (It's three thirty-five.)

In English, in order to speak of the number of minutes before the hour, we say, for example, "It's twenty to three." In Spanish, you would first tell the hour, in the usual manner, *Son las tres* (It's three), then you would add the expression that literally means *minus twenty*. In this way, *It's twenty to three* would translate as *Son las tres menos veinte*. See the following examples:

*Es la una menos veinte.* (It's twenty to one.)

*Es la una menos quince.* (It's fifteen minutes to one.)

*Son las siete menos dos.* (It's two minutes to seven.)

*Son las ocho menos veintidós.* (It's twenty-two to eight.)

There is another way to express minutes before the hour. Instead of "*Es la una menos veinte*," for example, you can say "*Son las veinte para la una*, and so on."

In English, we have an alternative way of expressing 15 minutes before or after the hour. For example, we can say "It's a quarter after (or *past*) ten" and "It's a quarter to ten." In Spanish, too, the equivalent is as commonly used as the English *quarter*. You can say, for example, "*Son las diez y cuarto*" and "*Son las diez menos cuarto*."

**PROCEED WITH CAUTION**

Don't confuse *cuatro* (four) with *cuarto* (quarter, fourth). A timed event set for four minutes after the hour, understood as fifteen minutes after the hour, could be disastrous.

In English, we have an alternative way of expressing 30 minutes after the hour. For example, we can say, "It's half-past seven" instead of "It's seven-thirty." In Spanish, too, the equivalent is as commonly used as the English *half-past*. You can say, for example, "*Son las siete y media*."

The usual way to express A.M. and P.M. in Spanish is, after stating the time, to add a phrase that literally means *of the morning, of the afternoon,* or *of the night.* For example, the English *It's 9:00 A.M.* or *It's nine o'clock in the morning* is *Son las nueve de la mañana.*

The English *It's 9:00 P.M.* or *It's nine o'clock at night* is *Son las nueve de la noche.*

The English *It's 5:00 P.M.* or *It's five o'clock in the afternoon* is *Son las cinco de la tarde.*

Study the following questions and answers. When you understand them fully, practice saying them aloud:

*¿Qué hora es?* (What time is it?)

*Es la una de la mañana.* (It's 1:00 A.M. [It's one in the morning.])

*Son las ocho de la noche.* (It's 8:00 P.M.)

*¿Qué hora era cuando ocurrió?* (What time was it when it happened?)

*Era la una y media de la mañana.* (It was one o'clock in the morning.)

*Eran las cinco y cuarto de la tarde cuando llegué.* (It was a quarter past five P.M. when I arrived.)

In both English and Spanish, *twelve o'clock* can be problematic for many people.

To avoid any possibility of confusion, in English, the least ambiguous method is to speak of *noon* (or *midday*) and *midnight.* In Spanish, noon is *el mediodía* (midday), and midnight is *la medianoche.* Notice that the third person singular form of *ser* is used with these terms.

*Pronto será la medianoche.* (It will soon be midnight.)

*Es el mediodía.* (It is noon.)

You have been studying ways of telling what time it is, or was, or will be, and so on. Before leaving this subject, you will want to know how to express the equivalent of the English expression: *at* plus the time, in order to tell when something occurred, occurs, will occur, and so on. The Spanish way is simply to use the preposition *a* in front of the time. For example, *at two o'clock* in Spanish is *a las dos.* The question *At what time?* is *¿A qué hora?* Practice saying the following sentences aloud:

*Voy a la una.* (I'm going at one [o'clock].)

*Ocurrió a las tres.* (It happened at three [o'clock].)

*¿Cuándo es la fiesta?* (When is the party?)

*Es a las cinco.* (It's at five [o'clock].)

*¿A qué hora es el concierto?* ([At] what time is the concert?)

*El mediodía* is masculine because *el día* is masculine. *La medianoche* is feminine because *la noche* is feminine. This is why the word for *half* or *mid* (*medio*) ends in *-o* in *mediodía* but *media* (ending in *-a*) in *medianoche*.

## EMPLOY *SER* AND *ESTAR* + ADJECTIVES

Both verbs that translate into English as *to be* (*ser* and *estar*) are used with adjectives. This does *not* mean they can be used interchangeably. On the contrary, there are very definite denotations and connotations conveyed when using one of these verbs with adjectives, and another, very different, set of denotations and connotations conveyed when using the other verb. Because we have only one verb to express all these meanings in English, you will need to understand the differences in usage between the two verbs when employed with adjectives. Briefly stated, *ser* is used with adjectives to classify or characterize, whereas *estar* is used with adjectives to speak of the condition they happen to be in.

## USE *SER* FOR CHARACTERISTICS

When the verb *ser* connects the subject to an adjective, it serves to speak of the *characteristics* of the person or thing that is the subject. When you use *ser* plus an adjective, you are characterizing that person or thing; you are classifying that person or thing; you are putting the noun or pronoun in a pigeonhole along with other nouns and pronouns that belong to the same class. See the following examples:

(1) *María es bonita.* (María is pretty.)

(2) *Carlos es alto.* (Carlos is tall.)

(3) *La chica es inteligente.* (The girl is intelligent.)

(4) *Hernando es estúpido.* (Hernando is stupid.)

(5) *Pedro es valiente.* (Pedro is brave.)

(6) *Concha es simpática.* (Concha is nice [likeable, pleasant].)

(7) *Carlos es venezolano.* (Carlos is Venezuelan.)

(8) *La mesa es grande.* (The table is big.)

(9) *El Sr. López es viejo.* (Mr. López is old.)

(10) *La Srta. Pérez es joven.* (Miss Pérez is young.)

In sentence 1, we are saying that one of María's characteristics is that of being pretty. We are classifying her as a pretty person. We are metaphorically branding her forehead with the word *bonita*. We are putting her in the pigeon-hole with the rest of the pretty people. The quality of prettiness is an inalienable part of her being. We are definitely not referring to any condition she may be in. We are referring to one of her physical characteristics.

In sentence 2, we are classifying Carlos as tall. This physical characteristic is an inseparable part of his physical makeup. He is inherently a tall person. We are not saying he's in a tall condition. In sentence 3, we are classifying the girl as intelligent. This is one of her characteristics; in this case, a mental characteristic. In sentence 4, we again speak of a mental characteristic; we're classifying Hernando as stupid. In sentence 5, we're referring to a moral quality when we say Pedro is brave. In sentence 6, we're classifying Concha as being a nice person, a likeable person with whom it is easy to get along. These are all characteristics of the persons mentioned, not just conditions they happen to be in.

**GO TO** ▶
See Hour 7 for an explanation of what kind of nouns, under what conditions, omit the indefinite article when following *ser*.

Nationality is considered a characteristic. It is possible for you to change your citizenship, of course, but nationality is thought of as part of a person's characteristics, part of one's makeup, not just the condition he/she happens to be in. If you were giving his basic characteristics, you could say something like *Es alto y moreno, y es venezolano* (He's tall and dark, and he's Venezuelan.) You would not think of his being in a "Venezuelan condition" any more than you would think of his being in a tall or dark condition. Therefore, sentence 7 employs *ser*.

Note that in sentence 7, the word *venezolano*, which we're interpreting as an adjective, could also be interpreted as a noun. (Carlos is *a* Venezuelan.) This is because certain Spanish nouns do not take the indefinite article when coming after the verb *ser*, depending on specified factors. This close relationship between *ser* used with nouns and *ser* used with adjectives underscores the concept of *characteristic* when adjectives are used with *ser*, as opposed to the idea of *condition* when adjectives are used with *estar*, a verb that never connects the subject with a noun.

In sentence 8, we are describing the size of the table; we classify it as being big. The table doesn't fluctuate in size; it doesn't change from big to small.

In sentences 9 and 10, we are referring to age. Although it is true that all living things pass from being young to being old (and inanimate objects from being new to being old), the process is so gradual that age is not viewed as a condition by speakers of Spanish. Besides, if you were giving a description of someone to the police for identification purposes, you would not tell them he or she is worried or busy, because these are only conditions. However, you would certainly tell them whether the person is young or old; this information would refer to one of this person's characteristics, and would help in his or her apprehension.

### PROCEED WITH CAUTION

Because *ser* + adjective speaks of characteristics, the question *¿Cómo es Juan?* does not inquire about Juan's health (which is a condition), but is equivalent to the English idiom *What's Juan like?* which asks for his characteristics. To ask about health, you would say "*¿Cómo está Juan?*"

## USE *ESTAR* FOR CONDITIONS

When the verb *estar* connects the subject to an adjective, it serves *not* to refer to characteristics, but to describe the condition or state of the person or thing that is the subject. You are *not* classifying that subject; you are merely commenting on your immediate subjective perception of the state in which the subject happens to be. See the following examples:

(1) *María está enferma.* (María is ill.)

(2) *Carlos está preocupado.* (Carlos is worried.)

(3) *Las chicas estaban ocupadas.* (The girls were busy.)

(4) *Estábamos muy cansados.* (We were very tired.)

(5) *Hernando está enojado.* (Hernando is probably angry.)

(6) *Yo estaría contento/a si ....* (I'd be happy [content, satisfied] if ....)

(7) *El carro está descompuesto.* (The car is out of order.)

(8) *Todo está arruinado.* (Everything's ruined.)

(9) *El café no está caliente.* (The coffee isn't hot.)

(10) *La sopa está fría.* (The soup is cold.)

Sentence 1 does not refer to a characteristic of María's; it certainly does not classify her. It only refers to her condition; in this case, to the state of her physical health. It answers the question *¿Cómo está María?* Being sick is not part and parcel of her being; it's merely the condition she happens to be in. Previously, she had been in good health (*estaba bien*), and her condition will probably change for the better soon.

Sentence 2 employs the verb *estar* because we're not classifying Carlos; we're only commenting on his present state of mind. We expect that once he has solved the problem that's worrying him, his mental attitude will shift and he will not be in that worried state of mind.

In the rest of the sample sentences, the same situation applies. We are not classifying people or things as being inherently busy, tired, angry, content, out of commission, ruined, hot, or cold. These qualities are not characteristics of the persons or things they describe.

There is no reason conditions can't become permanent. Notice that if you want to say "He's dead" in Spanish, you say "*Está muerto.*" No one is characteristically deceased; it's a condition all living things enter after having been in the condition of being alive.

### PROCEED WITH CAUTION

Never say "*Es muerto*" to mean someone is deceased. Because *ser* refers to characteristics, you could say "*La fiesta es muerta,*" classifying the party as lacking life or as being dull. Do not use *ser* + *muerto/a* for human beings.

Coffee and soup are not inherently either cold or hot; they can only be in a cold or hot state. Very few things are cold or hot by their nature (ice, fire), rather than by condition.

### TIME SAVER

If you have a sentence in which the subject is connected to a noun that is modified by an adjective, do not ponder over whether the adjective speaks of characteristics or condition; it's beside the point. Because the subject is connected to a noun (with or without an adjective), *estar* is never employed. Use *ser* only.

The following table recapitulates in schematic form the various uses discussed for the verbs *ser* and *estar* in this hour as well as in Hour 7.

| Ser | Estar |
|---|---|
| Existence: *Yo soy.* | Never |
| Connects subject to noun or pronoun: *María es estudiante. ¡Es él!* | Never |
| Material: *El libro es de papel.* | Never |
| Possession: *El libro es de Carlos.* | Never |
| Origin: *El libro es de Madrid.* | Never |
| Location (of activity): *La fiesta es en la casa de María.* | Location (physical): *María está en casa.* |
| With adjectives (characteristics): *¿Cómo es Carlos?* | With adjectives (condition): *¿Cómo está Carlos?* |
| *Carlos es inteligente y alto.* | *Carlos está ocupado.* |
| *Carlos es mexicano.* | *Carlos está muy bien.* |

## USE *SER/ESTAR* FOR NORMAL/ABNORMAL

Both *ser* and *estar* can be used, and often are, with identical adjectives. However, the choice of *ser* or *estar* will make a difference in the connotation and even the denotation of the idea being expressed by the adjective. In explaining these differences, it is only sometimes, but not always, satisfactory to say that *ser* is used with adjectives to speak of characteristics, to classify, to pigeonhole— in opposition to *estar,* which is used with adjectives to speak of the condition or state in which the noun happens to be. Sometimes we have to be more subtle, more imaginative, or more flexible in order to understand the mental processes represented by the choice of *ser* or *estar* plus an adjective.

For example, you can say "*María es bonita.*" It is also perfectly correct to say "*María está bonita.*" However, the two statements do not mean the same thing. It is possible to explain the difference in the following terms: *María es bonita* presents prettiness as one of María's characteristics; she is being classified as pretty. We are saying that María is inherently pretty; it's part of her nature.

**JUST A MINUTE**

It is possible to use *ser* and *estar* with the same subject: *Pedro es un hombre que siempre está ocupado.* (Pedro is a man who is always busy.)

However, when we try to explain *María está bonita,* it seems awkward to say it means *María is in a pretty condition.* This really is a somewhat accurate translation of the Spanish meaning, but sounds ridiculously clumsy in English. Then let's look at the opposition of *ser* plus adjective and *estar* plus adjective from a slightly different, but related, point of view.

If you want to present a particular quality belonging to a noun as being not only inherent in and characteristic of that noun, but as being normal, unchanged, and expected of that person or thing, use *ser* with the adjective. This will present the quality more or less objectively.

For example, *María es bonita.* You're saying that being pretty is normal for María—it's expected of her; there has been no change. After all, you are saying that it's characteristic of her to be pretty; it's an inherent quality in her. And, whoever speaks this sentence assumes that he or she is being objective about María.

On the other hand, if you don't intend to classify something or someone, to refer to his/her/its unchanging basic characteristics or to what is normal and expected for that noun, don't use *ser* with the adjective. If you only want to comment very subjectively on the condition of that noun, or on what you perceive as abnormal for that noun, note a change in that noun or simply comment on the way that noun "strikes" you at the moment of perception, then use *estar* with the adjective.

For example, *María está bonita.* You're not classifying her or characterizing her. You're not speaking of her inherent qualities. This does not mean you're saying she's *not* characteristically pretty, either. You're being noncommittal as to whether prettiness is normal for her or expected of her. You're limiting yourself to commenting on your immediate perception of her at the moment. Therefore, while the sentence could be translated literally as *María is pretty* (making it equivalent to *María es bonita*), this translation would not capture the true deep meaning of the sentence. It would also fail to distinguish this sentence from the one using *ser,* thereby losing the distinction between the two verbs and missing the point.

Because by using *estar* in this sentence you are referring to how María "strikes" you at the moment of perception, and because the perception of beauty is a visual function, the closest English translation would be more like *María's looking pretty.* (*María's in a pretty condition* would be good, but it's not really English.)

**GO TO ▶**
*La sopa* (with the definite article) can be used to mean *soup* in the general sense. See Hour 2 for definite articles used with generic nouns.

A sentence like *La sopa es buena* using *ser* means *Soup is good*. In other words, soup is a good thing in general. You're classifying soup; you're saying soup is inherently and generally a good thing. But if you're eating soup, and while you're eating it you approvingly comment "*La sopa está buena*," then you're talking about your immediate and personal perception of that specific soup that you're eating. Because the perception of soup—unlike beauty, which is visual—is accomplished with the sense of taste, probably the closest English translation would be more like "This soup tastes good."

**PROCEED WITH CAUTION**

The very colloquial expression *Está buena* has more of an impact than you might suspect, considering each word separately. It is street slang, referring to a woman, and expresses a man's appreciation for the purely physical qualities of that woman. Although complimentary, it is not polite.

Study the following table for examples of the different connotations of sentences using the same adjective with *ser* and *estar*.

| Ser Plus Adjective | Estar Plus Adjective |
|---|---|
| *María es bonita.* | *María está bonita.* |
| María is pretty. | María's looking pretty. |
| *La sopa es buena.* | *La sopa está buena.* |
| Soup is good. | The soup (this soup) tastes good. |
| *El chico es listo.* | *El chico está listo.* |
| The boy is clever (mentally alert). | The boy is ready. |
| *José es cansado.* | *José está cansado.* |
| José is tiresome (annoying). | José is tired. |
| *Carmen es aburrida.* | *Carmen está aburrida.* |
| Carmen is boring. | Carmen is bored. |
| *La fiesta es muerta.* | *El hombre está muerto.* |
| The party is dull. | The man is dead. |
| *Ella es buena.* | *Ella está buena.* |
| She is a good person. | She looks sexy. |

The preceding list could be extended greatly. Some of the above expressions reflect completely different meanings, depending on whether *ser* or *estar* is the verb employed with the adjective. However, many adjectives lend themselves to being employed with *ser*, when you want to classify or characterize something or someone, whereas *estar* could be used with the same adjectives to speak of the condition of that noun or the way the noun strikes you at the moment.

## SPEAK OF WEATHER AND TEMPERATURES

The way the weather is spoken of in Spanish is somewhat different from the way it is in English. Temperatures (hot and cold) are handled differently, depending on whether we are referring to weather, to the way people and animals experience these sensations, or to the condition of inanimate objects.

### TALK ABOUT THE WEATHER

The verb *hacer* (to do, make) is used for much of the reporting on weather. This verb, in relation to weather conditions, is used only in the third person singular form, because the unstated *it* is the subject. When you say the Spanish equivalent of *it's sunny*, you will not be using the verbs equivalent to the English *to be*, so neither *ser* nor *estar* will be used. Nor will you use any adjective equivalent to the English *sunny*. Literally, you will say "(It) makes sun." Study the following phrases:

*¿Qué tiempo hace?* (How's the weather? [What weather does it make?])

*Hace sol.* (It's sunny. [It makes sun.])

*Hace viento.* (It's windy. [It makes wind.])

*Hace calor.* (It's hot. [It makes heat.])

*Hace frío.* (It's cold. [It makes cold.])

*Hace fresco.* (It's cool. [It makes coolness.])

*Hace buen tiempo.* (The weather's fine. [It makes good weather.])

*Hace mal tiempo.* (The weather's bad. [It makes bad weather.])

*Hace lluvia.* (It's raining. [It makes rain.])

*Hace nieve.* (It's snowing. [It makes snow.])

There are other ways to speak of rain and snow. The verbs *llover* (*ue*) (to rain) and *nevar* (*ie*) (to snow) can be conjugated in the present tense:

*Llueve.* (It's raining. [It rains.])

*Nieva.* (It's snowing. [It snows.])

GO TO ▶
For the lesson on the present progressive tense, as well as other progressive tenses, see Hour 9.

Yet another way is often used, especially when emphasizing that the rain or snow is ongoing. The present progressive tense, which uses the present tense of *estar* plus the present participle, is employed. See the following examples:

> *Está lloviendo.* (It's raining.)
>
> *Está nevando.* (It's snowing.)

Note that the noun *tiempo* in these expressions means *weather*. However, the same noun also means *time*. It does not, however, mean time on the clock, which, as you know is *la hora*, but *time* in a general sense, or *time* as a commodity, something you can have or not have. See the following examples:

> *Borges tiene interés en el tiempo.* (Borges is interested in time.)
>
> *¿Qué es más precioso que el tiempo?* (What is more precious than time?)
>
> *No tengo tiempo.* (I have no time.)
>
> *Ella tiene mucho tiempo.* (She has a lot of time.)
>
> *Vamos a matar el tiempo.* (Let's kill some time.)

But:

> *¿Qué hora es?* (What time is it?)
>
> *Son las cinco de la tarde.* (It's five P.M.)

(See earlier in this hour for a review of telling time.)

## TALK ABOUT FEELING TEMPERATURES

Even though the English *It's cold* comes out as *Hace frío* in Spanish, keep in mind that this is the structure used only in speaking of the weather. The weather is what is "making cold." In English, we say things like I'm warm, She's cold, and so on to speak of how people and animals experience temperatures. In Spanish, a different structure is used for this purpose. For example, to say I'm cold or I'm hot, which talks about the way I feel or the way I am experiencing temperatures, Spanish uses the verb *tener* (to have) plus the noun that means *cold* or *heat*. See the following examples, and practice the expressions until you know them automatically:

> *Tengo frío.* (I'm cold. [I have cold.])
>
> *¿Tienes calor?* (Are you hot? [Do you have heat?])

## TALK ABOUT TEMPERATURE OF THINGS

Whereas *hacer* plus the nouns *frío* or *calor* are used to speak of the atmospheric temperature, and *tener* plus one of the two temperature nouns are used to refer to a sentient being's experience of temperature, the temperature of all other things will use either *ser* or *estar* plus an adjective.

Very few things are inherently hot or cold; this means, of course, that the verb *ser* has an extremely limited use for speaking of temperature. Not many things are hot or cold by nature other than fire and ice:

> *El fuego es caliente.* (Fire is hot. [characteristically])
>
> *El hielo es frío.* (Ice is cold. [characteristically])

In most other situations, you will use the verb *estar* to speak of the *condition* of inanimate objects. Practice with the following sample sentences:

> *La sopa está caliente.* (The soup is hot.)
>
> *La sopa está fría.* (The soup is cold.)
>
> *El café está caliente.* (The coffee is hot.)
>
> *El café está frío.* (The coffee is cold.)
>
> *Las papas están calientes.* (The potatoes are hot.)
>
> *Las papas están frías.* (The potatoes are cold.)

Note that the word *frío* is both a noun and an adjective. Used in the expression *Hace frío*, or with *tener*, it's a noun and has only one form. As an adjective (as in the preceding sentences), it has four forms: *frío; fríos; fría; frías*.

### PROCEED WITH CAUTION

If you mean someone is suffering from the heat, be careful not to say "*Está caliente.*" This has strong sexual implications. Say "*Tiene calor.*"

# THE 30-SECOND RECAP

In this hour, you've learned how to count in Spanish through 1,000,000. You've continued to learn about the different uses of the two verbs that translate into English as *to be* (*ser* and *estar*), specifically, using *ser* to speak of time, and using both *ser* and *estar* with adjectives. *Ser* is used with adjectives to speak of inherent characteristics, whereas *estar* is used with adjectives to speak of conditions or states, and to express subjective impressions or register departures from what you consider the norm for the noun in question. In this hour, you have also learned to speak of the weather and temperatures.

## QUIZ

# HOUR'S UP!

Review this hour, and then test yourself by answering the following questions. For best results, do not consult this hour for the answers while actually taking the test.

1. Choose the correct Spanish sentence relating to time: It is 8:10 A.M.

    a. Es la ocho y diez de la mañana.

    b. Son las ocho para los diez de la mañana.

    c. Es ocho horas y diez minutos de la mañana.

    d. Son las ocho y diez de la mañana.

2. Choose the correct Spanish sentence relating to time: It's at 8:45 P.M.

    a. Es a las nueve menos cuarto de la noche.

    b. Es a las veinte horas y cuarenta y cinco minutos.

    c. Es a los quince para las nueve de la noche.

    d. All of the above.

3. Choose the most accurate translation: How is Carlos?

    a. ¿Cómo está Carlos?

    b. ¿Cómo es Carlos?

    c. ¿Cómo estás, Carlos?

    d. All of the above.

4. Choose the most accurate translation: What is María like?

    a. ¿Cómo está María?

    b. ¿Qué es María?

    c. ¿Qué está María?

    d. ¿Cómo es María?

5. Choose the most accurate translation: I'm ready.

    a. Soy lista.

    b. Estoy lista.

    c. Soy listo.

    d. None of the above.

6. Choose the most accurate translation: I'm warm.

    a. Soy caliente.

    b. Hace calor.

    c. Tengo calor.

    d. Estoy caliente.

# HOUR 9

# Progressive Tenses; Past Participles

## CHAPTER SUMMARY

**LESSON PLAN:**

In this hour, you'll learn ...

- How to count in the millions.
- How to form the present participle.
- How to use the present participle in isolation as well as with *estar* to form the progressive tenses.
- How to form the past participle, and to use it as an adjective.

Study the following representative numbers in the millions:

1.000.000 un millón

2.000.000 dos millones

3.000.000 tres millones

5.150.002 cinco millones ciento cincuenta mil dos

10.000.001 diez millones uno

15.000.015 quince millones quince

33.000.124 treinta y tres millones ciento veinticuatro

98.000.199 noventa y ocho millones ciento noventa y nueve

100.000.100 cien millones cien

211.156.319 doscientos once millones ciento cincuenta y seis mil trescientos diecinueve

555.555.555 quinientos cincuenta y cinco millones quinientos cincuenta y cinco mil quinientos cincuenta y cinco

600.000.000 seiscientos millones

800.000.000 ochocientos millones

987.825.123 novecientos ochenta y siete millones ochocientos veinticinco mil ciento veintitrés

**JUST A MINUTE**

Whereas all the numbers from one through the thousands are adjectives, the word *millón* and its plurals are *nouns*. Saying *a million boxes* (*un millón de cajas*) is handled something like saying *a pile of boxes*: *un montón de cajas*.

Notice that, unlike *mil* (one thousand), *millón* (one million) carries the article *un*. Furthermore, when you're dealing with 2.000.000 and beyond, *millón* is pluralized by adding -*es*. The period is still used instead of the comma in these numbers.

In addition, the preposition *de* is used after the word *millón* or *millones* before the noun that is being counted. See the following examples:

*un millón de cajas* (a [one] million boxes)

*un millón de libros* (a [one] million books)

*dos millones de personas* (2.000.000 people)

*quinientos millones de lápices* (500.000.000 pencils)

*cincuenta millones de cartas* (50.000.000 letters)

*cien millones de hombres* (100.000.000 men)

*ciento diez millones de mujeres* (110.000.000 women)

Notice that 100 is written as *cien* when it is found directly in front of numbers of larger denomination such as *cien millones* for 100.000.000, but it is written as *ciento* before numbers of smaller denominations, as in *ciento veinticuatro millones* for 124.000.000.

The English word *percent* in Spanish is *por ciento*. The expression *100 percent* can be expressed as either *cien por ciento* or *cien por cien*. The noun percentage is the masculine noun *el porcentaje*.

## FORM THE PRESENT PARTICIPLE

In English and in Spanish, the present participle has many uses. It can be used independently or in conjunction with other verbs and phrases to form the progressive tenses. In English, the present participle is the form of the verb that ends in -*ing*. For example, the present participle of the verb *to speak* is *speaking*.

To form the Spanish present participle, remove the infinitive ending from the verb and add -*ando* to -*ar* verbs, and -*iendo* to -*er* and -*ir* verbs.

For *-ar* verbs, add *-ando* to the verb stem:

- hablar
- habl – *-ar*
- habl
- habl+ *-ando*
- hablando

For *-er* verbs, attach *-iendo* to the verb stem:

- comer
- com – *-er*
- com
- com + *-iendo*
- comiendo

The very short verb *ver* (to see) is no exception; it is completely regular in the present participle:

- ver
- v – *-er*
- v
- v + *-iendo*
- viendo

For *-ir* verbs, attach the *-iendo* ending to the verb stem:

- vivir
- viv – *-ir*
- viv
- viv + *-iendo*
- viviendo

There are some irregular present participles. One type of irregular present participle is confined to the *-ir* verbs with a stem change in the present tense. All *-ir* verbs with a stem change from *-o-* to *-ue-* in the present tense have a stem change from *-o-* to *-u-* in the present participle. See the following examples:

- dormir (*ue*) – durmiendo
- morir (*ue*) – muriendo
- poder (*ue*) – pudiendo

**JUST A MINUTE**

Even though *poder* is an *-er* verb rather than an *-ir* verb, it, too, has a stem change from *-o-* to *-u-* in the present participle.

*-ir* verbs that have a stem change in the present tense from *-e-* to either *-ie-* or *-i-* have a stem change from *-e-* to *-i-* in the present participle. See the following examples:

- venir (*ie; i*) – viniendo
- decir (*i; i*) – diciendo
- reír (*i; i*) – riendo
- pedir (*i; i*) – pidiendo

Note that *-ar* and *-er* verbs with stem changes in the present tense (except for *poder*) are *not* affected:

- costar (*ue*) – costando
- mostrar (*ue*) – mostrando
- oler (*ue*) – oliendo
- perder (*ie*) – perdiendo

There is another kind of irregularity in the formation of the present participle. *-er* and *-ir* verbs whose stem ends with a *vowel* add *-yendo* instead of *-iendo*. (*-ar* verbs, of course, are not affected by this.) See the following process with the verb *caer* (to fall):

- caer
- ca – *-er*
- ca
- ca + *-yendo*
- cayendo

Notice that the extremely short verb *ir*, which looks as though it is formed of the infinitive ending alone, falls into this pattern:

- ir
- o – *-ir*
- o
- o + *-yendo*
- oyendo

Other verbs of this type follow:

- oír – oyendo
- traer – trayendo
- distraer – distrayendo
- contraer – contrayendo
- leer – leyendo
- creer – creyendo
- construir – construyendo
- destruir – destruyendo
- constituir – constituyendo
- instruir – instruyendo
- huir – huyendo

**GO TO ▶**
The verb *oír* and verbs that end in *-uir* contain the letter *y* in some of their forms in the present tense. See Hour 4 to review.

## USE THE PRESENT PARTICIPLE INDEPENDENTLY

The present participle can be used independently to show instrumentality or perceived action.

To show instrumentality—that is, in order to state that a goal is accomplished by doing something—we represent that *doing something* with the present participle. In other words, to show that by doing one thing something else results, the present participle is used to express the action that is taken to make the other event happen. See the following examples:

*Estudiando, uno aprende.* (By studying, one learns.)

*Leyendo mucho, comprendo más.* (By reading a great deal, I understand more.)

*Trabajando, ganan la vida.* (By working, they earn a living.)

**JUST A MINUTE**

Do not use any preposition, or any other word, to translate the English word *by* in these constructions of instrumentality. The present participle alone expresses the idea.

Note that you can reverse the sentence order, just as you can in English:

*Uno aprende estudiando.* (One learns by studying.)

*Comprendo más leyendo mucho.* (I understand more by reading a great deal.)

*Ganan la vida trabajando.* (They earn a living by working.)

## USE THE PRESENT PARTICIPLE FOR PERCEIVED ACTIONS

The present participle can also be used after a verb of perception (to see, to hear, to smell, to listen to, to watch, to feel, and so on) to report the activity one person was engaging in while another person perceived it:

*Yo vi a Carlos leyendo.* (I saw Carlos reading.)

*¿Oíste a María cantando?* (Did you hear María singing?)

*Miraron al profesor escribiendo en la pizarra.* (They watched [looked at] the professor writing on the chalkboard.)

Caution: The previous sentence types are susceptible to misinterpretation because they could be construed as ambiguous. For example, *Vi a María mirando por la ventana* could mean either *I saw María looking out the window* or *I saw María **by** looking out the window.* Was María looking out the window, or was I? Am I reporting what I saw her doing, or the method I used to see her? There are ways to clarify the matter.

If you want to state unambiguously that you were able to see María by looking out the window, you can place the present participle at the beginning of the sentence: *Mirando por la ventana, vi a María.*

### PROCEED WITH CAUTION

Do not use the present participle as a noun (subject or object) as we do in English; use the infinitive: Studying is important = (*El*) *estudiar es importante.*

To avoid ambiguity when you are reporting the perception of someone engaging in an activity (rather than speaking of instrumentality), use the infinitive verb instead of the present participle. To say unambiguously that you saw María looking out the window (she was the one looking out the window), you could use the infinitive form of the verb rather than the present participle. You could say "*Vi a María mirar por la ventana.*" The order of the sentence could also be *Vi mirar por la ventana a María.* Because ambiguity is eliminated by this method, it is to be preferred. In this same way, the following sentences would become …

| | |
|---|---|
| Yo vi a Carlos leer. | Yo vi leer a Carlos. |
| ¿Oíste a María cantar? | ¿Oíste cantar a María? |
| Miraron al profesor escribir en la pizarra. | Miraron escribir en la pizarra al profesor. |

**JUST A MINUTE**

The verb *tomar* literally means *to take*. It is also used as a more genteel synonym for *beber* (to drink).

## USE THE PRESENT PROGRESSIVE TENSE

You learned in Hour 3 that unlike its English counterpart, the Spanish present tense has many uses. You learned that you can say *yo hablo* to indicate the action of speaking as it is happening right now: I am speaking (right now). This use of the Spanish present tense is perfectly acceptable and common; however, if you want to *emphasize* the fact that the action or situation is happening right now or is in progress, then you should use the present progressive tense. In English, we use the present progressive tense to talk about an act in progress, too. Before proceeding to the Spanish present progressive tense, let's look at the English tense of the same name.

**GO TO ▶**
For a review of the uses of the present tense, see Hour 3.

The present progressive tense in English is composed of two parts: the present tense of the verb *to be* plus the present participle of the main verb. To form the present progressive of the verb *to speak*, conjugate the auxiliary verb *to be* in the present tense and add the present participle to form *I am speaking*. This tense, of course, refers to what is happening at the present moment.

The Spanish present progressive tense is very similar in structure. We use *estar* (never *ser*) as the auxiliary verb, conjugated in the present tense, and add the present participle of the main verb.

Study and then say aloud the following examples:

*¿Qué estás haciendo?* (What are you [in the middle of] doing?)

*Estoy escribiendo.* (I am writing.)

*¿Qué estás mirando?* (What are you [in the middle of] looking at?)

*Estoy mirando las fotos.* (I am looking at photographs.)

Because *estar* is the verb used to speak of physical location, you could think of the meaning of the second sentence as something like *Here I am, writing*.

## USE OTHER PROGRESSIVE TENSES

In English, the progressive tenses (*to be* plus the present participle) are not limited to the present. We can use any tense of *to be* we want, including the infinitive, and then add the present participle in order to describe ongoing actions or situations. See the following English examples:

- We are speaking. (present progressive)
- We were speaking. (past progressive)
- We shall (We'll) be speaking. (future progressive)
- We would be speaking. (conditional progressive)
- We have been speaking. (present perfect progressive)
- We had been speaking. (past perfect progressive)
- We will have been speaking. (future perfect progressive)
- To be speaking. (infinitive progressive)
- We would have been speaking. (conditional perfect progressive)

The same is true in Spanish. Whereas the present participle is unchanging, the auxiliary verb *estar* is conjugated in whatever tense is required to express the message. It can be left unconjugated (infinitive) as well, as in the next-to-last of the previous sentences.

### USE THE PRETERIT PROGRESSIVE TENSE

You can use the preterit tense of *estar* plus the present participle to form the preterit progressive tense. See the following examples:

*Ayer estuve hablando mucho.* (Yesterday I was talking a lot.)

*La semana pasada estuvimos comiendo tomates.* (Last week we were eating tomatoes.)

*Estuvieron viendo la televisión todo el día.* (They were watching television all day long.)

The preterit progressive tense is employed to sum up (preterit) an ongoing action in the past. It is not used as much as the simple preterit tense for summing up an action or situation, on one hand, or as much as the imperfect progressive tense for seeing the middle of the ongoing situation on the other hand.

## USE THE IMPERFECT PROGRESSIVE TENSE

The imperfect progressive tense is commonly used to emphasize the ongoing quality of an action or situation in the past. To form this tense, you use the imperfect tense of *estar* plus the present participle. See the following examples:

> *¿Qué estabas haciendo hace unas horas?* (What were you [in the middle of] doing a couple of hours ago?)
>
> *Yo estaba escribiendo.* (I was writing.)
>
> *¿Qué estabas mirando hace un momento?* (What were you looking at a moment ago?)
>
> Estaba leyendo cuando ella vino. (I was reading when she came.)

All the preceding sentences provide a mental image of the subject in the midst of an action or situation in the past. The use of the participle makes the listener visualize the subject as he or she was engaged in these activities, thus stretching out the action. There is no question of seeing either the beginning or the end of the action or situation.

The fact that the first and third sentences mention a time period that ended some time ago changes nothing; we see the time period as having an end, but during that time period we see the subjects in the middle of what they were doing. We don't see the end of their action.

In the fourth sentence, a verb in the preterit tense (*vino*) is used in addition to the verb in the imperfect progressive (*estaba leyendo*). The subject was in the middle of reading (which serves as the background) when somebody arrived.

## USE THE FUTURE PROGRESSIVE TENSE

In English, we use the future tense of the auxiliary verb *to be* before the present participle to form the future progressive tense, the purpose of which is to state that something will be in progress, or will be (in the middle of) happening in the future. We refer to the middle of ongoing actions or situations in the

**GO TO** ▶
The imperfect progressive accomplishes very much what the straight imperfect tense does; it just insists a bit more on stretching things out, on the ongoing nature of the action. For a review of the imperfect tense use, see Hour 6.

future. Spanish does the same. Simply use the future tense of *estar* plus the present participle. See the following examples:

> *¿Qué estarás haciendo mañana por la mañana?* (What will you be [in the middle of] doing tomorrow morning?)
>
> *Estaré escribiendo.* (I'll be writing.)
>
> *¿Qué estarás mirando esta noche?* (What will you be watching tonight?)
>
> *Estaré leyendo.* (I'll be reading.)

The second of these sample sentences could be thought of as *I'll be here* (or *there*), (*in the middle of*) *writing*.

## USE THE CONDITIONAL PROGRESSIVE TENSE

The conditional progressive tense represents what we *would be* in the middle of doing, if certain conditions were to prevail. To form the conditional progressive tense in English, we use the conditional tense of the auxiliary verb *to be* plus the present participle. In Spanish we use the conditional tense of the auxiliary verb *estar* plus the present participle. See the following examples:

> *¿Qué estarías haciendo mañana por la mañana si …?* (What would you be [in the middle of] doing tomorrow morning if …?)
>
> *Estaría escribiendo.* (I'd be writing.)
>
> *¿Qué estarías mirando esta noche si …?* (What would you be watching tonight if …?)
>
> *Estaría leyendo.* (I'd be reading.)

GO TO ▶
For a review of the conditional tense, see Hour 7.

You will remember from the lesson on the conditional tense that this tense, in addition to being used for truly conditional situations, is also used as the future of the past in both English and Spanish. For example, we say, "I tell you I'll be leaving," but "I told you I'd be leaving." See the following sentences for examples of the conditional progressive tense used to represent the future of the past:

> *(Él) dijo que estaría escribiendo.* (He said [that] he'd be writing.)
>
> *Dijimos que estaríamos almorzando.* (We said [that] we'd be having lunch.)
>
> *Ud. informó que ellos no estarían hablando.* (You reported [that] they would not be talking.)

**JUST A MINUTE**

In English, we often omit the relative pronoun *that,* as in all the preceding sentences. The Spanish equivalent (*que*) is not normally omitted.

### English Verb Forms

| Base Form | Preterit Tense | Past Participle |
| --- | --- | --- |
| go | went | gone |
| do | did | done |
| eat | ate | eaten |
| see | saw | seen |
| talk | talked | talked |
| arrive | arrived | arrived |
| leave | left | left |

## USE THE PAST PARTICIPLE

The Spanish past participle is used …

- As an adjective, to describe the condition of something or someone as the result of a past action.
- To accompany the verb *ser* (to be) to form the passive voice.
- To accompany the auxiliary verb *haber* in the compound (or perfect) tenses to state that something has been done, had been done, will have been done, or would have been done.

Only the first bullet, the past participle used as an adjective, will be treated in this hour.

**GO TO** ▶
The lesson on the passive voice referred to in the second bullet can be found in Hour 10. The lessons on the compound (perfect) tenses (referred to in the third bullet) are found in Hours 15, 16, 17, 18, 20, and 24.

## FORM THE PAST PARTICIPLE

In Spanish, the regular past participles (the overwhelming majority) of *-ar* verbs are formed by …

- Removing the infinitive ending of the verb.
- Adding *-ado* to the stem.

Let's look at the formation of the past participle of *hablar:*

- hablar
- habl – -*ar*
- habl + -*ado*
- hablado

To form the regular past participles (the overwhelming majority) of -*er* and -*ir* verbs …

- Remove the infinitive ending of the verb.
- Add -*ido* to the stem.

Study the formation of the past participle of *comer:*

- comer
- com – -*er*
- com + -*ido*
- comido

The following is the method of forming the past participle of *vivir:*

- vivir
- viv – -*ir*
- viv + -*ido*
- vivido

See the following table for the past participles of regular verbs.

**Past Participles of Regular Verbs of All Three Conjugations**

| | | |
|---|---|---|
| combinar – combinado | coger – cogido | salir – salido |
| cantar – cantado | comer – comido | dormir – dormido |
| llevar – llevado | leer – leído | recibir – recibido |
| llamar – llamado | creer – creído | concebir – concebido |
| viajar – viajado | correr– corrido | elegir – elegido |

There is a small number of irregular past participles you should know. Study the following list of verbs with their irregularly formed past participles:

*abrir* (to open)        *abierto* (open, opened)

*cubrir* (to cover)        *cubierto* (covered)

| | |
|---|---|
| *decir* (to say, tell) | *dicho* (said, told) |
| *escribir* (to write) | *escrito* (written) |
| *hacer* (to do, make) | *hecho* (done, made) |
| *morir* (to die) | *muerto* (dead, died) |
| *poner* (to put, place) | *puesto* (put, placed) |
| *exponer* (to expose, display) | *expuesto* (exposed, displayed) |
| *romper* (to break) | *roto* (broken) |
| *(de)volver* (to return) | *(de)vuelto* (returned) |
| *ver* (to see) | *visto* (seen) |

Note that the irregular past participles all end in either -*to* (the majority) or -*cho*.

**JUST A MINUTE**

*Volver* means *to return* in the sense of *to go back, to come back.* The verb *devolver* means *to return* in the sense of *to give (something) back.*

## USE THE PAST PARTICIPLE AS ADJECTIVE

Many past participles are used in English as adjectives to describe the condition of something or someone as the result of a past action. For example, we say, "The door is closed." The condition of the door, which could be either open or closed, is in this case closed. This is the result of an action performed in the past: Someone closed it. Its condition now is *closed*.

In Spanish, if you want to speak of the condition of someone or something, use the verb *estar* plus the past participle. Keep in mind that if you use the past participle to describe a condition, even though it is a form stemming from a verb, you are using it as an adjective. Like all adjectives in Spanish, it will have to agree in number and gender with the noun it modifies. Study the following examples and practice saying them aloud:

*La puerta está cerrada.* (The door is closed.)

*Las puertas están cerradas.* (The doors are closed.)

*El libro está cerrado.* (The book is closed.)

*Los libros están cerrados.* (The books are closed.)

*La mesa está rota.* (The table is broken.)

**GO TO ▶**
For the passive voice, which uses *ser* plus the past participle, see Hour 10.

Note that the past participle used as an adjective, like any other adjective, does not have to be used in a phrase that connects the subject to the adjective by means of a verb; it can directly modify the noun. See the following phrases:

*Veo la puerta cerrada.* (I see the closed door.)

*Veo las puertas cerradas.* (I see the closed doors.)

*Veo el libro cerrado.* (I see the closed book.)

*Veo los libros cerrados.* (I see the closed books.)

*Tengo la mesa rota.* (I have the broken table.)

Note: When the meaning of the past participle of *decir* (*dicho*) is equivalent to the English *the aforesaid*, the adjective always precedes the noun it modifies and omits the article:

| | |
|---|---|
| *dicho trabajo* | the aforesaid work |
| *dichas regiones* | the aforementioned regions |

## The 30-Second Recap

In this hour, you have learned to count in Spanish through the millions. You have learned to form and use the present participle to show instrumentality, and to form the progressive tenses by combining the present participle with the auxiliary verb *estar*. You have also learned to form the past participle and to use it as an adjective.

## Hour's Up!

Review the hour, and then test your progress by answering the following questions. Try to answer the questions without referring back to the pertinent pages.

1. Choose the correct translation: 5,000,000 chairs.

   **a.** quinientos mil sillas

   **b.** quinientas mil sillas

   **c.** cinco millón sillas

   **d.** cinco millones de sillas

   **e.** cinco millonas sillas

**2.** The present participle …

    **a.** Is usually equivalent to English verbs that end with *-ing*.

    **b.** Is used with *estar* to emphasize the ongoing nature of an action or situation.

    **c.** Is used to show cause and effect.

    **d.** Is used to show what someone sees, hears, smells, or otherwise perceives someone else doing.

    **e.** All of the above.

**3.** The past participle …

    **a.** Can be used to describe a condition.

    **b.** Can be used instead of the preterit tense.

    **c.** Is always used with the verb *estar*.

    **d.** Can be used to substitute for the present participle.

    **e.** All of the above.

**4.** Choose the correct translation: We are eating.

    **a.** Nosotros comiendo.

    **b.** Estamos comando.

    **c.** Nosotros comando.

    **d.** Estamos comiendo.

    **e.** Nosotros somos comiendo.

**5.** Choose the correct translation: You are singing.

    **a.** Tú estás cantiendo.

    **b.** Estáis cantando.

    **c.** Ud. está cantado.

    **d.** Uds. están cantados.

    **e.** Vosotros cantando.

**6.** Choose the correct translation: They are building.

    **a.** Están construyendo.

    **b.** Están construando.

    **c.** Están construendo.

    **d.** Ellos construendo.

    **e.** Ellas construyendo.

**7.** Choose the correct translation: The open window is broken.

    **a.** La ventana cerrada está rompida.

    **b.** La ventana abierta es rota.

    **c.** La ventana abrida está rota.

    **d.** La ventana cerrada es rompida.

    **e.** La ventana abierta está rota.

**8.** Choose the correct translation: I'll be reading the magazine.

    **a.** Estoy leendo la revista.

    **b.** Estoy leyendo la revista.

    **c.** Yo estaré leiendo la revista.

    **d.** Estaré leíndo la revista.

    **e.** Estaré leyendo la revista.

**9.** Choose the correct translation: I earn a living by working.

    **a.** Trabajando, gano la vida.

    **b.** Gano la vida de trabajando.

    **c.** De trabajar, gano la vida.

    **d.** Gano la vida por trabajar.

    **e.** Gano la vida por trabajando.

**10.** Choose the correct translation: Studying is good.

    **a.** Estudiando es bueno.

    **b.** Estudiar es bueno.

    **c.** El estudiando es bueno.

    **d.** Estudiado es bueno.

**QUIZ**

# PART III
# Interpersonal Activities

# Hour 10
# Meeting People

CHAPTER SUMMARY

**LESSON PLAN:**
In this hour, you'll learn ...

- The passive voice.
- How to make new friends.
- How to greet people.
- How to ask about their names, health, and age.

In Hour 9, you learned how to form the past participle, and how to use it as an adjective, either directly modifying the noun or connected to the subject by the verb *estar*. In this lesson, you'll learn how to use the past participle with *ser* to form the passive voice. Then you'll learn to distinguish the passive voice from the active voice, and more descriptions of conditions.

## LEARN TO FORM THE PASSIVE VOICE

To form the passive voice in Spanish, use *ser* in conjunction with the past participle. The passive voice in Spanish provides a narration of an action. It focuses on the action itself rather than the person or thing that performs the action. Sentences in the passive voice always concern an action being performed. This is in direct contrast to sentences that merely describe existing conditions, which employ the verb *estar* instead of *ser*. Let's look at some examples of sentences in the passive voice:

Cuando llegué, las puertas *fueron cerradas* por el portero.

Mañana las tiendas *serán cerradas* por el Ayuntamiento.

Cuando llegué, las ventanas *fueron rotas* por maleantes.

El soldado *fue* gravemente *herido* por el enemigo (en ese momento).

La comida *fue preparada* por el jefe de cocina cuando llegué.

Notice the combination of the verb *ser* and the past participle to form the passive voice.

In the passive voice, the past participle agrees in number and gender with the noun to which it refers.

## DISTINGUISH BETWEEN THE PASSIVE AND ACTIVE VOICES

Both the passive and active voices present *action*, not the description of a condition. A sentence can be changed from active to passive and vice versa without changing the meaning of the sentence. The difference between the voices is that the active voice revolves around the person or thing that performs the action of the verb, whereas the passive voice focuses on the action itself. Look at the following examples.

| Active Voice Sentence | Passive Voice Sentence |
| --- | --- |
| The man closes the door. | The door is closed (by the man). |
| Mary drove the car. | The car was driven (by Mary). |
| Steve will study the lesson. | The lesson will be studied (by Steve). |
| I'd wash the dishes if …. | The dishes would be washed (by me) if …. |
| I'm drying the dishes. | The dishes are being dried (by me). |

Note that the passive voice can be used in any tense. In the preceding table, the sentences, in order, happen to be in the present, the preterit, the future, the conditional, and the present progressive.

You will notice that all of the preceding sentences (whether employing the active or passive voice) concern action. In each of them, some action is being carried out by someone. A door is closed, a car was driven, a lesson will be studied, dishes would be washed, dishes are being dried. Notice that the performer of the action in the passive voice sentences is given in parentheses. This is to stress that passive sentences are complete with or without indicating who the performer of the action is. The important matter in a passive sentence is the action, not the performer of the action.

The active voice sentences, on the other hand, are not complete without indicating who performed the action. This fact underscores the importance of the performer of the action in active sentences, and the lack of importance assigned to the performer in the passive sentences. In an active voice sentence, the actor is just as important as the action; perhaps more important at times.

The following list details the structural differences between the active and passive voices.

- **Active voice.** The subject of the verb is the person or thing that performs the action of the verb, while the direct object is the thing acted upon.

- **Passive voice.** The subject of the verb is the thing acted upon, while the performer of the action—if mentioned at all—is preceded by the preposition *by*.

**GO TO** ▶
For a review of *estar* plus the past participle to indicate description of conditions, see Hour 9.

## DIFFERENTIATE BETWEEN THE PASSIVE VOICE AND DESCRIPTIONS OF CONDITIONS

You must be absolutely clear about the difference between a description of conditions and the passive voice. Bear in mind that the passive voice is always used to narrate action, whereas a description of conditions merely tells you about an existing condition. Also, a description of conditions has no agent performing the action described. Furthermore, what is described is not taking place at whatever time you are describing. Look at the following English sentences:

When I arrived, the doors were closed.

Tomorrow the stores will be closed.

When I arrived, the windows were broken.

The soldier was badly wounded.

The food was prepared when I got there.

**JUST A MINUTE**

Notice that we very often would colloquially say "when I got there" rather than the more formal "when I arrived." In both cases, the Spanish is *cuando llegué.*

In the absence of context, we can't tell if the preceding sentences are in the passive voice (signifying action), or merely represent the description of a condition resulting from action taken earlier. They could represent either case. If we were to express those thoughts in Spanish, however, you would know which the case would be.

If you were to tell me that you wanted to work at your office late last night, and then you told me "When I arrived, the doors were closed," it would be perfectly natural for me to respond, "You mean they were already closed, or someone closed them right in your face?" In Spanish, as you'll see, there would be no need to ask that question.

Does the second of the previous sample sentences mean that tomorrow the stores will be in a closed condition because, perhaps, someone closed them tonight? Or does it mean they will be closed *by someone* tomorrow, indicating action? The same problem exists with the rest of the sentences listed above.

If those five sentences were meant to describe conditions, then the Spanish equivalents would be the following:

> Cuando llegué, las puertas estaban cerradas.
>
> Mañana las tiendas estarán cerradas.
>
> Cuando llegué, las ventanas estaban rotas.
>
> El soldado estaba gravemente herido.
>
> La comida estaba preparada cuando llegué.

On the other hand, if those five English sentences were meant to refer to action, the Spanish versions would not use the verb *estar*. The English sentences would be in the passive voice. This means you could add to each one a phrase beginning with the preposition *by*, thereby informing your listener who the agent of the action is. For example:

> When I arrived, the doors were closed by the janitor.
>
> Tomorrow the stores will be closed by the municipality.
>
> When I arrived, the windows were broken by hoodlums.
>
> The soldier was badly wounded by the enemy at that moment.
>
> The food was prepared by the chef when (as soon as) I got there.

If these sentences were in the passive voice, it also means you could just as well state the facts in the active voice, without changing the basic meaning, as in the following sentences:

> When I arrived, the janitor closed the doors.
>
> Tomorrow the municipality will close the stores.
>
> When I arrived, hoodlums broke the windows.
>
> The enemy badly wounded the soldier at that moment.
>
> The chef prepared the food when I got there.

In a passive voice sentence, it's understood that there is an agent, whether specifically mentioned or not.

## Learn to Form the Passive Voice

Now that you understand the difference in function and meaning between the description of conditions and the passive voice, let's move on to how the passive voice is formed in Spanish.

*Ser* + past participle = passive voice

The passive voice in Spanish (unlike in English) is clearly distinguishable from a sentence in which conditions are being described. Instead of using *estar* plus the past participle, you would employ the verb *ser* plus the past participle.

In the passive voice, the past participle still agrees in number and gender with the noun to which it relates.

If the preceding five English sentences given as passive voice sentences (the sentences including the preposition *by* plus the agent) were spoken in Spanish, they would be the following:

Cuando llegué, las puertas fueron cerradas por el portero.

Mañana las tiendas serán cerradas por el Ayuntamiento.

Cuando llegué, las ventanas fueron rotas por maleantes.

El soldado fue gravemente herido por el enemigo (en ese momento).

La comida fue preparada por el jefe de cocina cuando llegué.

Notice that in the fourth sentence, you don't have to add *en ese momento* to make clear the action (wounding) rather than the description of condition, because the use of *ser* plus the past participle makes it clear. This clarity is absent in the English sentences without the addition of *at that moment*.

As in English, Spanish sentences in the passive voice, because they represent action, can be stated just as well as active voice sentences, as in the following sentences:

Cuando llegué, el portero cerró las ventanas.

Mañana el Ayuntamiento cerrará las tiendas.

GO TO ▶
For a review of the preterit tense (used in the five preceding sentences), see Hour 5.

Cuando llegué, los maleantes rompieron las ventanas.

El enemigo hirió gravemente al soldado.

El jefe de cocina preparó la comida cuando llegué.

## Learn to Interact with People

At this point, you have mastered the nuts and bolts of the Spanish language. That is, you have learned to use the basic tenses: present, preterit, imperfect, future, future substitute, conditional, progressive tenses, *estar* plus past participle, and the passive voice. You have also learned to differentiate between the two *to be* verbs, *ser* and *estar,* and you have picked up an incidental but notable lexical battery. There are still other tenses to learn, but you can communicate without much difficulty on basic matters with speakers of Spanish.

Grammar is a closed system; it has definite limits. It is possible to master the grammatical system of a language. It is an achievable goal, and you are well on your way to mastering the entire grammatical system of Spanish.

GO TO ▶
For a review of the present tense to express the immediate future (as in *Nos vemos* and *Te veo*), see Hour 3.

Vocabulary is an open system. No one ever finishes learning the entire vocabulary of any language; this includes his or her own native language. You have not learned the entire vocabulary of the English language; this is actually impossible. We all keep adding vocabulary in our native language as we go about our business every day. We even forget some lexical items we used to know if we don't use them. Furthermore, life is so complicated in today's world that specialists in different fields (medicine, architecture, computer technology, literature, and so on) practically speak different languages from those who are not specialists in the same field.

Because no one ever learns the entire vocabulary of his or her native language, no one can expect to learn the entire vocabulary of a second language either. It is possible, however, to master the most essential vocabulary needed for survival. You are already on your way to doing this. It is equally feasible to learn the vocabulary necessary for dealing with specific situations (see Parts 4 and 5).

GO TO ▶
See Hour 9 for a review of past participles.

In this lesson, you will concentrate on interacting with other people in social situations.

### Greet and Be Courteous

The following are common greetings and expressions of courtesy and related vocabulary. Practice saying them aloud:

| | |
|---|---|
| Hola. | Hello. |
| Buenos días. | Good day; Good morning. |
| Buenas tardes. | Good afternoon. |
| Buenas noches. | Good evening; Good night. |
| Adiós. | Goodbye. |
| Hasta luego. | See you later. (Until later.) |
| Hasta pronto. | See you soon. (Until soon.) |
| Hasta mañana. | See you tomorrow. (Until tomorrow.) |
| Hasta la vista. | Be seeing you. (Until the sight.) |
| Hasta la próxima (vez). | Until next time. |
| Hasta la próxima semana. | Until next week. |
| Hasta el próximo mes. | Until next month. |
| Hasta el próximo año. | Until next year. |
| Nos vemos. | Be seeing you. (We [will] see each other.) |
| Te veo. | Be seeing you. (I [will] see you.) |
| Chau. | Ciao. |
| saludar. | to greet |
| el saludo (m.): | greeting |
| ¿Cómo está(s)? | How are you? |
| ¿Qué tal? | How's it going? |

*Buenas noches* covers both the English phrases *Good evening*, when used to greet someone at a time we consider to be the beginning of activities, and *Good night*, when we take our leave of someone at the end of our activities, or when we're actually about to go to bed.

GO TO ▶
For a review of clock time, see Hour 8.

## LEARN ABOUT TIME

There are several words in Spanish that translate as *time*. They are not, however, synonymous or interchangeable. See the following list, which explains the various kinds of time indicated by several Spanish words.

- *El tiempo* (which also means weather) refers to time in a general sense, and to time as a commodity that one can have or not have.

- *La hora* is time on the clock, and even time for something to happen or to be done.

- *La vez* is time in the sense of an occasion, a moment.

Study the following examples of the use of the various words for time in Spanish:

*El problema del tiempo preocupa al escritor, Jorge Luis Borges.* (The problem of time worries [preoccupies] the writer, Jorge Luis Borges.)

*Podemos viajar por el espacio, pero, ¿podemos viajar por el tiempo?* (We can travel through space, but can we travel through time?)

*Tengo mucho tiempo ahora.* (I have a lot of time now.)

*¿Qué hora es?* (What time is it?)

*No sé la hora.* (I don't know the time./I don't know what time it is.)

*Es la hora de comer.* (It's time to eat.)

*Fui una vez.* (I went once [one time].)

*María comió dos veces.* (María ate twice [two times].)

*Es la última vez.* (It's the last time.)

*La próxima vez comeremos.* (Next time we'll eat.)

## GET ACQUAINTED AND INTRODUCE PEOPLE

If you want to introduce one person to another, use the verb *presentar* (literally, to present) and say, for example, "*María, quiero presentarte a mi amigo Víctor González.*" ("María, I want to introduce you to my friend Víctor González.") When you are introduced to someone, a polite response would be *mucho gusto*. This literally means *much pleasure*, standing for the idea *It gives me great pleasure to make your acquaintance*.

Another, perhaps even more courteous, response is *encantado/a*, meaning *enchanted*, or *charmed*. (We might say "delighted.") After you've responded with *mucho gusto* or *encantado/a*, the other person should respond with equal courtesy with *el gusto es mío* (the pleasure is mine) or *igualmente*, which literally means *equally*, and is used the way English uses *same here*. Study the following sample conversations in which people are introduced, and practice saying these sentences aloud, picturing the meaning and the circumstances:

*Juan Vallejo: María*, quiero presentarte a mi amigo, Víctor González.

*María Duarte:* Mucho gusto, Víctor.

*Víctor González:* El gusto es mío, María.

GO TO ▶
You might have noticed the words *te* and *le* attached to the verb *presentar* in the preceding examples. These words are indirect object pronouns, discussed in Hour 11.

**PROCEED WITH CAUTION**

Never use the verb *introducir* for introducing people. This verb means to introduce only in the very literal meaning of *to insert* or *to bring into*.

*La Sra. Cruz:* Señorita Herrera, quiero presentarle al Doctor Rivera.

*La. Srta. Herrera:* Encantada, Doctor.

*El Dr. Rivera:* Igualmente, Señorita.

## TALK ABOUT GENERAL HEALTH

Part of polite conversation in Spanish as well as in English, and probably in any language, is asking about someone's health and commenting on the weather. The following list shows some common expressions relating to health.

| | |
|---|---|
| ¿Cómo está Ud.? (¿Cómo estás?) | How are you? |
| Estoy (muy) bien. | I'm (very) well. (I'm fine.) |
| Estoy enfermo/a. | I'm ill. |
| Estoy mal. | I'm ill. |
| No estoy (muy) bien. | I'm not (very) well. |
| ¿Qué tal? | How are you? How's it going? How are things? |
| (Muy) bien. | (Very) Fine. |
| ¿Qué tal la familia? | How's the family? |
| ¿Cómo está la familia? | How's the family? |
| ¿Cómo andas? (¿Cómo anda Ud.?) | How're you doing? |
| ¿Cómo te va? (¿Cómo le va?) | How's it going (for you)? |
| Así así. | Not bad. (So so.) |
| Regular. | Not bad. (So so.) |

You will remember that the first sentence is formal (it uses *usted*), whereas the sentence in parentheses is familiar (it uses *tú*). *¿Qué tal?* is a slang (and common) expression, which literally means *What such?* Naturally, no one thinks of it in the literal sense. *¿Cómo andas?* and *¿Cómo te va?* are very idiomatic and colloquial, too. (*¿Cómo andas?* literally means *How do you walk?* or *How do you go?*)

Following are some model conversations using greetings and expressions of courtesy as well as of health. Study them for understanding; then practice saying them aloud, feeling what they mean.

### Conversation I

*Carlos:* ¡Hola, María! Buenos días.

*María:* Muy buenos, Carlos.

*Carlos:* ¿Qué tal hoy?

*María:* Muy bien, gracias, Carlos. ¿Y tú?

*Carlos:* Bastante bien. ¿Adónde vas ahora?

*María:* Voy a la tienda. Bueno, hasta la próxima, Carlos.

*Carlos:* Hasta luego, María.

Rough translation of preceding conversation into normal, colloquial English:

*Carlos:* Hi, María! Good morning.

*María:* Good morning.

*Carlos:* How's it going today?

*María:* Fine, thanks, Carlos. How about you?

*Carlos:* Pretty good. Where are you going now?

*María:* I'm going to the store. Well, see you around, Carlos.

*Carlos:* See you later, María.

### Conversation II

*El Sr. Pérez:* Buenas tardes, Señor Rodríguez.

*El. Sr. Rodríguez:* Buenas. ¿Cómo está Ud. hoy?

*El Sr. Pérez:* Muy bien. ¿Y Ud.?

*El Sr. Rodríguez:* Excelente. ¿Va a casa ahora?

*El Sr. Pérez:* No, no. Voy al parque.

*El Sr. Rodríguez:* ¡Ajá! Claro, hace muy buen tiempo.

*El Sr. Pérez:* Y, ¿Adónde va Ud.?

*El Sr. Rodríguez:* ¿Yo? Y, qué cree Ud.? Voy a la oficina.

*El Sr. Pérez:* Ah, sí. Ya terminó la siesta. Bueno, adiós.

*El Sr. Rodríguez:* Hasta mañana.

Translation of the preceding conversation:

GO TO ▶
For a review of the expressions related to weather, see Hour 8.

*Mr. Pérez:* Good morning, Mr. Rodríguez.

*Mr. Rodríguez:* You too. How are you today?

*Mr. Pérez:* Fine. And you?

*Mr. Rodríguez:* Terrific. Are you going home now?

*Mr. Pérez:* No, no. I'm going to the park.

*Mr. Rodríguez:* Aha! Of course, the weather's great.

*Mr. Pérez:* And where are you off to?

*Mr. Rodríguez:* Me? What do you think? I'm going to the office.

*Mr. Pérez:* Oh, yes. The siesta's over. Well, 'bye.

*Mr. Rodríguez:* See you tomorrow.

## TELL/ASK PEOPLE'S NAMES

You are already familiar with the verb *llamar* (to call), as in *Llamé a Elena por teléfono.* (I called Elena on the phone.) It is also used to ask what someone's name is and to tell your own. See the following examples and practice saying them:

*¿Cómo té llamas (tú)?* (What's your name? [familiar])

*¿Cómo se llama Ud.?* (What's your name? [formal])

*(Yo) me llamo Robert.* (My name is Roberto.)

*(Yo) me llamo Elena.* (My name is Elena.)

*¿Cómo se llama ella?* (What's her name?)

*(Ella) se llama Carlota.* (Her name is Carlota.)

*¿Cómo se llama el muchacho?* (What's the boy's name?)

*(Él) se llama Pedro.* (His name is Pedro.)

*¿Cómo se llaman ellos?* (What are their names?)

*(Ellos) se llaman Juan y María.* (Their names are Juan and María.)

**JUST A MINUTE**

In the preceding expressions, you are literally saying *How do you call yourself? I call myself Roberto,* and so on.

**GO TO ▶**

The sentences in the preceding list involve the use of the possessive adjectives. For the lesson on possessive adjectives, see Hour 13.

There is another way to talk about names. The construction is very similar to English. See the following examples:

*¿Cuál es tu nombre?* (What is your name? [familiar])

*¿Cuál es su nombre?* (What is your name? [formal])

*Mi nombre es Roberto.* (My name is Roberto.)

*Mi nombre es Elena.* (My name is Elena.)

---

**JUST A MINUTE**

It's a good idea to practice more with sentences using the verb *llamar* to talk about names.

---

Practice with the following conversation at a party:

*Víctor:* Hola. Ah … No te conozco.

*María:* Es verdad.

*Víctor:* ¡Pero … eres de aquí?

*María:* Ahora, sí.

*Víctor:* ¿Cómo?

*María:* Soy de Guatemala, pero ahora vivo aquí.

*Víctor:* Ajá. ¡Y, cómo te llamas?

*María:* Me llamo María Balseca. ¿Y tú, cómo te llamas?

*Víctor:* Yo me llamo Víctor González, para servirte.

*María:* Mucho gusto, Víctor.

*Víctor:* El gusto es mío.

Translation of the preceding conversation:

*Víctor:* Hi. Uh … I don't know you.

*María:* That's true.

*Víctor:* But … are you from around here?

*María:* I am now. (Now, yes.)

*Víctor:* How's that?

*María:* I'm from Guatemala, but I live here now.

*Víctor:* Aha. And, what's your name?

*María:* My name is María Balseca. What's *your* name?

*Víctor:* My name is Víctor González, at your service.

*María:* Glad to know you, Víctor.

*Víctor:* The pleasure's all mine.

**JUST A MINUTE**

Although *at your service* isn't used much anymore in English, Víctor's *para servirte* (literally, to serve you) or *a sus órdenes* (at your command) is still a polite phrase to use when introducing yourself in Spanish.

## TALK ABOUT AGE

You have already learned to use the verb *tener* in idioms referring to the way a person feels with regard to temperature. This verb is also used in place of the English *to be* when speaking of age. Instead of saying "He is 20 years old," we use *tener* plus the number of years to say "He has 20 years." *Él tiene veinte años.*

When you want to ask how old someone is, you ask literally, "How many years do you have?" Practice saying the following sentences:

*¿Cuántos años tiene Ud., señor?* (How old are you, sir?)

*Yo tengo ochenta y tres años, señorita.* (I'm 83 years old, Miss.)

*¿Cuántos años tienes (tú)?* (How old are you?)

*Tengo siete años.* (I'm seven years old.)

Víctor continues speaking with María. Practice orally with the following conversation:

*Víctor:* Bueno, María, y ¿qué haces?

*María:* ¿Que qué hago? Pues, estoy hablando y comiendo.

*Víctor:* ¡Ja ja! No. ¿Quiero decir, cómo ocupas tu tiempo?

*María:* Ah! Sí. Trabajo por horas, pero también asisto a la universidad.

*Víctor:* Yo también. Es decir, asisto a la universidad.

*María:* ¿Entonces, no trabajas?

*Víctor:* También. Trabajo los fines de semana.

*María:* ¿Víctor, cuántos años tienes?

*Víctor:* Tengo veinte años. ¿Y tú?

*María:* ¡Hombre! ¿No sabes que no es cortés …?

*Víctor:* ¿Porque eres mujer?

*María:* Claro.

**GO TO ▶**
María pretends not to realize that Víctor is asking what she usually does, rather than what she is doing now. The present tense can be used both ways. For a review of the uses of the present tense, see Hour 3.

Translation of the preceding conversation:

*Víctor:* Well, María, and what do you do?

*María:* What am I doing? Well, I'm talking and eating.

*Víctor:* Ha ha! No. I mean (want to say), how do you occupy your time?
Do you work?

*María:* Oh! Yes. I work part-time, but I attend college, too.

*Víctor:* So do I. That is to say, I go to college.

*María:* Then, you don't work?

*Víctor:* That, too. I work on weekends.

*María:* Víctor, how old are you?

*Víctor:* I'm 20 (years old). What about you?

*María:* Hey, c'mon! Don't you know it's not polite …?

*Víctor:* Because you're a woman?

*María:* Of course.

## NEW VOCABULARY

The following list introduces a few more treasures for your vocabulary chest:

- **Asistir.** The verb *asistir* means *to attend* (school, a concert, a play, and
  so on). When you tell exactly what you're attending, you place the
  preposition *a* after the verb and before the noun. For example, *Asisto a
  la Universidad.*

- **Claro.** The adjective *claro/a* literally means *clear,* or in speaking of colors, *light* (*gris claro* = light gray). The masculine form is also commonly
  used, as María does, to mean *of course.* You can be more emphatic by
  using the expression *claro que sí* (of course it is; of course I [you, he,
  and so on] do [does]). A synonym is *naturalmente* (naturally).

- **Entonces.** *Then* or *so.*
- **Fin de semana.** *El fin de semana* is *the weekend.* The plural *weekends* is
  *los fines de semana.*

- **Hombre.** As you know, *hombre* means *man*, but it's very frequently used in Spanish as an exclamation of surprise, wonderment, or to mildly chide. María's use of it as an exclamation prompts the English that might be used in the same vein in this particular case: Hey, c'mon!

- **¿Que qué hago?** Idiomatic usage short for an underlying thought standing for something roughly like *¿Dices que qué hago?* (You're saying "what do I do?") Note: When you report what someone says, you always use *Dice que ...* (He/she says that ...). We can omit the relative pronoun in English, but Spanish does not.

## LEARN OTHER *TENER* IDIOMS

You have been using *tener* (to have) plus nouns in idioms having to do with temperatures felt by people, and to speak of people's ages. Now you will learn many other *tener* idioms that deal with the way people feel. See the following table.

**More Idioms of Feeling with the Verb *tener* Plus Noun(s)**

| Idiom | Literal Meaning | English Equivalent |
| --- | --- | --- |
| tener hambre | to have hunger | to be hungry |
| tener sed | to have thirst | to be thirsty |
| tener sueño | to have sleepiness | to be sleepy |
| tener miedo | to have fear | to be afraid |
| tener prisa | to have haste | to be in a hurry |

## LEARN THE *A* AND *HA* FEMININE NOUNS WITH MASCULINE ARTICLES

An interesting condition exists with words like *hambre*. A singular noun, even though *feminine*, employs the definite article *el* and the indefinite article *un* under two conditions:

- The noun begins with the letter *a* or the letters *ha*.
- The noun is stressed on that first syllable.

**PROCEED WITH CAUTION**

Don't overgeneralize. Feminine words like *la actriz* do not use *el* or *un*, even though they begin with *a* or *ha*, because they are not stressed on the first syllable.

See the follow examples of feminine nouns that begin with *a* or *ha* and are stressed on the first syllable:

*El hambre; un hambre* (hunger)

*El agua; un agua* (water)

*El águila; un águila* (eagle)

*El arma; un arma* (weapon)

*El alma; un alma* (soul)

Keep in mind that these nouns are feminine. This means that any adjectives that are used to modify them must also be in the feminine form:

*Tengo mucha hambre.* (I'm very hungry. [I have much hunger.])

*Lola tenía mucha sed.* (Lola was very thirsty. [Lola had much thirst.])

*Es agua clara.* (It's clear water.)

*El águila americana …* (The American eagle …)

*Un arma fina …* (A fine weapon …)

Note, too, that because these nouns are feminine, their plural definite article is *las* and their plural indefinite article is *unas*:

*las aguas; unas aguas* (the waters; some waters)

*las águilas; unas águilas* (the eagles; some eagles)

*las armas; unas armas* (the weapons; some weapons)

## THE 30-SECOND RECAP

In this hour, you've learned to use the passive voice as well as how to take part in social situations (make new friends, greet people, introduce people, and ask about their names, health, and age). All this has involved …

- *Ser* plus the past participle.
- An idiom using the verb *llamar*.
- Additional idioms using the verb *tener*.
- Different concepts of "time."
- Specialized vocabulary.
- Feminine nouns with masculine-appearing articles.

## HOUR'S UP!

Review the lessons of this hour, and then test your progress by answering the following questions. Don't consult with the lessons themselves while doing the exam.

1. Change the infinitive verb in parentheses to the correct form, according to the rest of the sentence: *María fue (aceptar):*

    **a.** aceptó

    **b.** acepta

    **c.** aceptada

    **d.** aceptado

    **e.** aceptida

2. Change the infinitive verb in parenthesis to the correct form, according to the rest of the sentence: *Los soldados fueron (atacar):*

    **a.** atacado

    **b.** atacaron

    **c.** atacó

    **d.** atacan

    **e.** atacados

3. Change the infinitive verb in parenthesis to the correct form, according to the rest of the sentence: *Fuimos (saludar):*

    **a.** saludados

    **b.** saludamos

    **c.** saludimos

    **d.** saludidos

    **e.** saludaron

4. Change the infinitive verb in parenthesis to the correct form, according to the rest of the sentence: *¿Cuándo fueron (ver) las chicas?*

    **a.** veídas

    **b.** vidas

    **c.** vio

    **d.** vistas

    **e.** visto

5. Change the infinitive verb in parenthesis to the correct form, according to the rest of the sentence: *La ventana fue (romper):*

   **a.** rompido

   **b.** rota

   **c.** rompida

   **d.** rompió

   **e.** rompada

6. Choose the most appropriate response: *¿Qué tal?*

   **a.** No sé.

   **b.** Bien, gracias.

   **c.** Me llamo María.

   **d.** Tengo dieciocho años.

7. Choose the most appropriate response: *Quiero presentarte a Carlos Silveira.*

   **a.** Encantada.

   **b.** ¿Cómo te llamas?

   **c.** Bien, gracias.

   **d.** Tengo que salir.

8. Choose the most appropriate response: Mucho gusto.

   **a.** ¿Cómo te llamas?

   **b.** Me gustan las chicas.

   **c.** ¿No trabaja Ud.?

   **d.** El gusto es mío.

9. Choose the most appropriate response: ¿Cómo te va?

   **a.** Voy en coche.

   **b.** Me llamo Roberto.

   **c.** Voy mañana.

   **d.** Bien, gracias.

10. Choose the most appropriate response: ¿Cuál es tu nombre?

    **a.** Me llamo Carlos.

    **b.** ¿Estoy bien, y tú?

    **c.** Tengo veinte años.

    **d.** Soy de Guatemala.

QUIZ

# HOUR 11

# Having Fun

## CHAPTER SUMMARY

**LESSON PLAN:**

In this hour, you'll learn …

- How to use indirect object pronouns.
- How to talk about wishes, desires, and preferences.
- How to talk about entertainment, sports, and other pastimes.

It's essential to know how to use the indirect object pronoun in Spanish. It is necessary in statements as simple as *I like it*.

You were exposed to a few sentences that use indirect object pronouns in Hour 10, but without any significant explanation. In this hour, you will learn how to use the Spanish indirect object pronouns.

## KNOW DIRECT FROM INDIRECT OBJECTS

Remember that all pronouns are used to take the place of nouns. Unlike subject pronouns, which take the place of nouns that *perform* the action of the verb, object pronouns take the place of nouns that *receive* the action of the verb. There are two types of object pronouns: direct and indirect. How do we know which is the direct object and which is the indirect object? The technical explanation is that the direct object receives the action of the verb directly, whereas the indirect object receives the action of the verb indirectly.

Look at the following English sentence:

Roberto gave the book to Elena.

In this sentence you have two object nouns: *the book* and *Elena*. Which of these directly received the action of the verb *gave?* At first glance someone might say *Elena* because she received the book. However, the thing Roberto actually gave is *the book*. So, the book receives the action of

**GO TO ▶**
To review the subject pronouns, see Hour 3.

the verb directly; it is what was given. Therefore, *the book* is the direct object. To find out what received the action of the verb indirectly, ask yourself, "To whom, or for whom, was the action of the verb performed?" Or even, "Who was affected by the action of the verb?" In this example, of course, it is *Elena*. She is the indirect object.

Keep in mind that the sample sentence could have been written:

> Roberto gave Elena the book.

Do not be misled by the placement of the indirect object immediately after the verb. The book still receives the action of the verb, and Elena is still the noun for whom the action takes place.

If we changed that sentence so that there were no nouns in it, only pronouns (both the subject and the two objects), the sentence would read as follows:

> He gave it to her.

The third person singular masculine subject pronoun *He* takes the place of the proper noun *Roberto*, while the third person singular neuter object pronoun *it* takes the place of the noun *the book*, and the third person singular feminine object pronoun *her* takes the place of the proper noun *Elena*. (Remember, Spanish has no neuter nouns; all nouns are either masculine or feminine.)

**JUST A MINUTE**

We only substitute pronouns for nouns, in any language, if we already know what or who the nouns are.

## FORM INDIRECT OBJECT PRONOUNS

Now that you're clear on how the system operates in English, you are ready to learn how it operates in Spanish. The following table shows the subject pronouns in both Spanish and English. In the rightmost columns, you'll find the Spanish indirect object pronouns and their English equivalents. Study the table in order to learn the indirect object pronouns of Spanish.

**Spanish Subject Pronouns and Indirect Object Pronouns**

| Subject Pronouns | | Indirect Object Pronouns | |
|---|---|---|---|
| **Spanish** | **English** | **Spanish** | **English** |
| yo | I | me | me |
| tú | you | te | you |

| Subject Pronouns | | Indirect Object Pronouns | |
| --- | --- | --- | --- |
| **Spanish** | **English** | **Spanish** | **English** |
| él | he | le | him |
| ella | she | le | her |
| usted | you | le | you |
| nosotros/as | we | nos | us |
| vosotros/as | you | os | you |
| ellos | they | les | them |
| ellas | they | les | them |
| ustedes | you | les | you |

**PROCEED WITH CAUTION**

Translation is not always helpful; the English pronoun *you* is both the subject pronoun and the object pronoun, and is plural as well as singular.

Indirect object pronouns do not show a gender difference. The only difference is for number: *le* (singular) and *les* (plural).

Notice, too, that *le*—the indirect object pronoun equivalent of *él*, *ella*, and *Ud.*—could be translated into English as meaning to or for *him*, *her*, or *you* (formal, singular). In the same way, *les*—the indirect object pronoun standing for the subject pronouns *ellos*, *ellas*, or *Uds.*—could be translated into English as signifying to or for *them* or *you* (plural). This is not a problem. The persons intended as the indirect objects are usually clear because of context.

## SITUATE INDIRECT OBJECT PRONOUNS

In English, we situate the indirect object, whether noun or pronoun, somewhere after the verb: He gave *Elena* the book. He gave the book to *Elena*. He gave it *to her*. In most cases, this is not true of Spanish.

In Spanish, we place the object pronouns in front of conjugated verbs. The operative word here is *conjugated*. Study the sentences in the following table in which the indirect object nouns are converted into indirect object pronouns.

### Converting Indirect Object Nouns to Indirect Object Pronouns

| Indirect Object Nouns | Indirect Object Pronouns |
| --- | --- |
| *Roberto dio el libro a **Elena.*** | *Roberto **le** dio el libro.* |
| Roberto gave the book to *Elena*. | Roberto gave the book to *her*. |
| Roberto gave *Elena* the book. | Roberto gave *her* the book. |
| *María dio la revista al **hombre.*** | *María **le** dio la revista.* |
| María gave the magazine to *the man*. | María gave the magazine to *him*. |
| María gave *the man* the magazine. | María gave *him* the magazine. |

Because the object of the verb in the first sentence, *Elena*, is a third person proper noun, you use *le*, the third person indirect object pronoun, to take its place. Because the object of the verb in the second sentence, *the man*, is also a third person noun, you again use *le* to take its place.

The Spanish sentences in the left-hand column of the preceding table are technically correct. However, because Spanish-speakers normally insert the indirect object pronoun into the sentence, even though the specific noun is present, those two sentences will read:

Roberto *le* dio el libro a Elena.

María *le* dio la revista al *hombre*.

Study the following sample sentences using indirect object pronouns, with their English translations, and then practice saying them aloud:

*Carlos me dijo la verdad*. (Carlos told me the truth.)

*Yo le dije la verdad (a él)*. (I told him the truth.)

*(A ella) siempre le digo la verdad*. (I always tell her the truth.)

*Nos dieron la pelota*. (They gave us the ball.)

*Pero no nos dieron el bate*. (But they didn't give us the bat.)

*Sara os habló ayer*. (Sara spoke to all of you yesterday.)

*A Ud. yo le dije la verdad*. (I told you the truth.)

*Te dije la verdad*. (I told you the truth.)

*Les di los patines (a ellos)*. (I gave them the skates.)

*Les di los patines (a Uds.)*. (I gave you the skates.)

*(Les) hablé a María y a Elena en español*. (I spoke to María and Elena in Spanish.)

You could think of a sentence like *Le hablé a María* as though you were saying *Le hablé*, and then realize that the *le* might not be clear, so you add as an afterthought *a María*.

## PLACE THE INDIRECT OBJECT PRONOUNS WITH INFINITIVE VERBS

When you use an indirect object pronoun with a verb in the infinitive form, you attach the pronoun to the end of the verb so that it is written as one single word:

| | |
|---|---|
| decirle | to tell him (her, you) |
| decirme | to tell me |
| decirte | to tell you |
| hablarnos | to speak to us |
| hablaros | to speak to all of you |
| hablarles | to speak to them (you) |

Look at the following sentences, which use an infinitive verb plus the indirect object pronoun:

*Decirme la verdad es importante.* (Telling me the truth is important.)

*Es importante decirme la verdad.* (It's important to tell me the truth.)

*Hablarnos será imposible.* (Speaking to us will be impossible.)

*Será imposible hablarnos.* (It will be impossible to speak to us.)

*Darte el libro sería preferible.* (Giving you the book would be preferable.)

*Sería preferible darte el libro.* (It would be preferable to give you the book.)

## USE INDIRECT OBJECT PRONOUNS WITH A CONJUGATED VERB PLUS AN INFINITIVE VERB

More often, you will find occasion to use an infinitive verb in conjunction with a conjugated verb.

When you have a conjugated verb working together with an infinitive verb, you have a choice: You can either place the object pronoun in its normal position in front of the conjugated verb, or you can attach it to the infinitive. There is no difference in meaning. See the following sentences, and practice saying them aloud.

**PROCEED WITH CAUTION**

Never place the object pronoun between the conjugated verb and the infinitive verb.

### Sentences with Pronoun as Object of Conjugated Verb Plus Infinitive Verb

| Attached | Preceding | English |
|---|---|---|
| Quiero hablarte. | Te quiero hablar. | I want to speak to you. |
| Voy a hablarles. | Les voy a hablar. | I'm going to speak to them. |
| Desean decirnos … | Nos desean decir …. | They wish to tell us …. |
| Prefiero decirle que … | Le prefiero decir que …. | I prefer to tell her that …. |

## USE INDIRECT OBJECT PRONOUNS WITH PRESENT PARTICIPLES

If the verb you want to use with an indirect object pronoun is in the form of the present participle, attach the object pronoun to the end of the participle, forming one word. See the following examples:

| diciéndole | (by) telling him (her, you) |
| diciéndome | (by) telling me |
| diciéndote | (by) telling you |
| hablándonos | (by) speaking to us |
| hablándoos | (by) speaking to all of you |
| hablándoles | (by) speaking to them (you) |

(You might want to review the rules of accentuation in Hour 1 to understand why the written accent mark has been inserted in the preceding present participles.)

**GO TO** ▶
For a review of the present participle, see Hour 9.

Look at the following sentences, which use a present participle plus the indirect object pronoun:

*Diciéndole todo, gané respeto.* (By telling him everything, I earned respect.)

*Dándome el arma, obtuvo la libertad.* (By giving me the weapon, he obtained freedom.)

*Aprendí mucho hablándoles.* (I learned a great deal by talking to them.)

*Sabrán algo escuchándote.* (They will know something by listening to you.)

*Prestándonos atención, ganaron.* (By paying attention to us, they won.)

Even more often, you will find yourself using a conjugated verb working with the present participle, as, for example, in the progressive tenses. In that case, you have a choice: Either place the object pronoun directly before the conjugated verb, or attach it to the end of the present participle to form one word. There is no difference in meaning. Study the following examples, and then practice saying them aloud.

**Sentences with Pronoun as Indirect Object of Conjugated Verb Plus Present Participle**

| Attached | Preceding | English |
| --- | --- | --- |
| Estoy hablándote. | Te estoy hablando. | I'm talking to you. |
| Estaban hablándonos. | Nos estaban hablando. | They were talking to us. |
| Estabas diciéndome .... | Me estabas diciendo .... | You were telling me .... |
| Estamos diciéndoles .... | Les estamos diciendo .... | We're telling them .... |

**PROCEED WITH CAUTION**

Never place the object pronoun between the conjugated verb and the present participle.

## SPEAK OF WISHES, DESIRES, PREFERENCES

Spanish has many ways of expressing what one wants, wishes, desires, prefers, and likes. The structure of sentences that convey these ideas often is not very different from that of the English equivalents; however, some of these structures are different from what you might expect. You'll need to spend a bit more time thinking about the structures that differ from those of English than about those that are more like the English ones.

### TALK OF LIKING

There is no Spanish verb that has the same meaning and function as the English *to like*. The Spanish direct equivalent of *to like* does not exist. Instead, the Spanish verb *gustar* (to please) is used.

When we use *to like* in English, the one who is experiencing the enjoyment is the subject, while the provider of the enjoyment is the object. Yet in Spanish with the verb *gustar*, the subject is the thing or person that provides the enjoyment, while the one who experiences it is the object. This is the opposite of the way *to like* functions in English. To avoid confusion, think only of *to please, to be pleasing,* or *to give pleasure*.

Suppose you want to say the equivalent of the English sentence, I like baseball. The person uttering this sentence is the one experiencing enjoyment, and is the subject of the verb. Baseball is the entity providing the enjoyment, and is the direct object.

This order is completely reversed in Spanish when you use the verb *gustar*. You would say, "*Me gusta el béisbol.*" This sentence means, *Baseball pleasures me* (or *Baseball is pleasing to me* or *Baseball gives me pleasure*). The provider of the enjoyment, *el béisbol*, is the subject, while the one who experiences the enjoyment, me, as represented by the direct object pronoun *me*, is the object. Notice that the verb ending *-a* corresponds to the subject *el béisbol*, not *yo*.

### PROCEED WITH CAUTION

 Because of thinking of *I like,* many English speakers are prone to saying things like (*Yo*) *me gusto*. This, of course, means, *I like myself* (I am pleasing to me).

In English, when you use the verb *to like*, and want to show changes in the identity of the one who is experiencing pleasure, you change the subject:

> I like baseball.
> You like baseball.
> Bob likes baseball.
> We like baseball.

In English, when you use the verb *to please* and wish to show changes in the identity of the one who is experiencing pleasure, you change the object:

> Baseball pleases me.
> Baseball pleases you.
> Baseball pleases Bob.
> Baseball pleases us.

The Spanish *gustar* pattern is like that of the English *to please*. The preceding five sentences, whether you think of them as using *to like* or *to please*, will involve a change—not of subject, but of object:

> Me gusta el béisbol.
>
> Te gusta el béisbol.
>
> A Bob le gusta el béisbol.
>
> Nos gusta el béisbol.

Baseball is the subject of the verb *gustar* in all the preceding sentences. The only element that changes is the indirect object, the one who experiences the enjoyment. Think of the process in this way: The important thing is that baseball is pleasing. Secondarily, you tell *who* is being pleased by the sport. Schematically, it would be as follows:

*Gusta el béisbol.* (Baseball is pleasing.)

*Me gusta el béisbol.* (Baseball is pleasing to me.)

*Te gusta el béisbol.* (Baseball is pleasing to you.)

*Nos gusta el béisbol.* (Baseball is pleasing to us.)

No matter who is being pleased by baseball, the verb form does not change because the subject has not changed; it's still baseball. Baseball is third person singular, so this regular *-ar* verb ends with the vowel *a*. The object does not make the verb form change; only the subject does.

When the subject changes, then, as with all Spanish verbs, the verb is affected. So if you want to say you like sports, which is third person plural, the verb will end with the letter *-n: Me gustan los deportes.* Again, the essential message is that sports are pleasing, and secondarily, *who* is being pleased by sports. For example …

*Gustan los deportes.* (Sports are pleasing.)

*Me gustan los deportes.* (Sports are pleasing to me.)

*Te gustan los deportes.* (Sports are pleasing to you.)

*Nos gustan los deportes.* (Sports are pleasing to us.)

**JUST A MINUTE**

Habitually, *gustar* expressions place the verb before the subject. But it's perfectly correct, if slightly unusual, to place the subject first: *Los deportes me gustan.*

If you say you like several different things (that is, several different things are pleasing to you), the subject is third person plural once more, and the verb will end with the letter *-n.*

*Gustan el béisbol, el golf, y el fútbol.*
Baseball, golf, and soccer are pleasing.

*Me gustan el béisbol, el golf, y el fútbol.*
Baseball, golf, and soccer are pleasing to me.

*Te gustan el béisbol, el golf, y el fútbol.*
Baseball, golf, and soccer are pleasing to you.

*Nos gustan el béisbol, el golf, y el fútbol.*
Baseball, golf, and soccer are pleasing to us.

The verb *gustar* is most commonly used in the third person (singular or plural), as shown in the preceding examples. But it can be used in the first and second persons as well; it just isn't done as frequently. It's considered a bit forward, for example, to ask someone "*¿Te gusto?*" ("Do I please you?" that is, "Do you like me?")

### PROCEED WITH CAUTION

It's considered somewhat daring for a man to tell a woman, *Me gustas.* (You are pleasing to me; that is, I like you.) On the other hand, *Te quiero* (I love you, I want you) is welcome if thought to be sincere; it's also more serious.

Practice saying the following sentences aloud, picturing their meaning:

*Me gustó la comida.* (I liked the food.)

*Me gustaron los partidos.* (I liked the games [sporting events, matches].)

*¿Te gustan los deportes?* (Do you like sports?)

*Sí. Me gustan mucho.* (Yes. I like them a lot.)

*¿Os gustan jugar o mirar?* (Do all of you like to play or watch?)

The preceding translations use the most common English verb for the idea of *gustar: to like*. This makes it look as though subject and object are reversed from the English point of view. But you know that the first of these sample sentences, for instance, more literally is like the English *The food pleased me* (To me pleased the food).

Compare the following two sentences:

*Me gustan los dulces.* (I like candy.)

*Me gusta comer dulces.* (I like to eat candy.)

The subject of the first sentence is the plural *los dulces*, so the verb ends with *-n*. The subject of the second sentence is the singular activity of eating candy, not the sweets themselves, so the verb ends with *-a*.

## USE VERBS LIKE *GUSTAR*

Other verbs function the way *gustar* does. For example, the English idiom that uses *to love* when talking about inanimate objects does not translate into Spanish by verbs that really mean *to love*. Spanish-speakers think a sentence like *I love ice cream* is hilarious. Spanish usually uses two verbs to express this idea: *fascinar* (to fascinate) and *encantar* (to enchant, charm, bewitch).

In Spanish, you can't love it if it's something that can't love you back.

When thinking of the English *I love ice cream* and going to Spanish, the same type of problem that is present with *to like* and *gustar* arises. The subject and object seem to be reversed going from English to Spanish. This is because you're not really saying "I love ice cream"; the ice cream is the subject, and you are the object. But this is what happens if we use English verbs like *fascinate* or *enchant*, anyway. See the following sentences:

*Fascina el helado.*
Ice cream fascinates (is fascinating).

*Me fascina el helado.*
To me ice cream is fascinating.

*Te fascina el helado.*
To you ice cream is fascinating.

*A María le fascina el helado.*
To María ice cream is fascinating.

*Nos fascina el helado.*
To us ice cream is fascinating.

Naturally, the normal English for the above sentences would be as follows:

*Fascina el helado.* (Ice cream is terrific.)

*Me fascina el helado.* (I love ice cream.)

*Te fascina el helado.* (You love ice cream.)

The same feelings can be expressed with the verb *encantar*:

Encanta el helado.

Me encanta el helado.

Even though it's more common to place the subject after these verbs, it is also correct to place the subject before them, as in the following:

El helado me encanta.

El helado me fascina.

The verb *importar*, in addition to its meaning of *to import* (as in import/export), means *to be of importance*, or *to matter*. Study the following sentences:

*Ella me importa mucho.*
She matters to me a great deal.

*Está bien; no me importa.*
It's all right; it doesn't matter to me (I don't care).

The structure of sentences with *importar* is very much like that of English sentences with *to matter*. Just don't be taken aback if you're thinking in English, and want to say, "I don't care!" (in the sense of I don't give a hoot), because that's idiomatic English for *It doesn't matter to me* or *It isn't important to me*.

**PROCEED WITH CAUTION**

*Importar* does not mean *to take care of;* that's the verb *cuidar* with which the subject is the one who takes care of the object.

Practice saying the following sentences aloud:

*¿Te importa si voy?*
Do you care if I go?

*Me importa mucho.*
It matters a great deal to me.

*No me importa nada.*
I don't care at all.

*La verdad importa.*
The truth matters. (The truth is important.)

*Nos importa la verdad.*
We care about the truth. (The truth matters to us.)

*(A ella) no le importan las noticias.*
She doesn't care about the news.

*Antes me importaba la cosa, ahora no me importa.*
The thing mattered to me before, now I don't care (about it).

Notice that in the fourth sentence, the verb is in third person plural and, therefore, ends with *-n*, because the subject is plural.

The last of the previous sample sentences has no indirect object pronoun; it doesn't tell who is affected. It just indicates that the matter (whatever it may be) is an important one, one that matters.

The verb *interesar* works the same way as *gustar, fascinar, encantar,* and *importar.* But so does the English verb *to interest.* It's just that one way of saying you're interested in something is to say that it interests you:

*Me interesa el caso.*
The case interests me. (I'm interested in the case.)

*No me interesa el caso.*
The case doesn't interest me (I'm not interested in the case.)

*¿Te interesan las noticias?*
Are you interested in the news?

*No les interesa el fútbol.*
They're not interested in soccer.

There are two other ways to show interest: *tener interés en* …; *estar interesado/a en* …. The first two preceding sentences could be expressed as follows:

Tengo interés en el caso.

No tengo interés en el caso.

Estoy interesado/a en el caso.

No estoy interesado/a en el caso.

## TALK ABOUT ENTERTAINMENT AND SPORTS

The following list contains vocabulary you need if you want to talk about entertainment and sports.

*El cine* is the film industry or the movie house in which you see a *película* or its synonym, a *film. Película* also means *film* for a camera.

| | |
|---|---|
| acampar | to go camping |
| alquilar | to rent |
| el ajedrez (m.) | chess |
| andar en bicicleta | to go bicycle riding |
| bailar | to dance |
| el baile (m.) | dance |
| el baloncesto (m.) | basketball |
| el básquetbol (m.) | basketball |
| el bate | bat (used in baseball) |
| el béisbol (m.) | baseball |
| el bosque (m.) | woods, forest |
| el caballo (m.) | horse |
| el campo (m.) | the country; field |
| las cartas (f. pl.) | cards (the game) |
| cazar | to hunt |
| el cine (m.) | the movies (movie house; film industry) |
| comprar | to buy |
| las damas (f. pl.) | checkers |
| el deporte (m.) | (the) sport |
| el (la) deportista (m., f.) | sportsman, sportswoman |
| desear | to wish, want, desire |
| el disco compacto (m.) | compact disc (CD) |
| el ejercicio (físico) (m.) | (physical) exercise |
| el equipo | the team |
| escuchar discos | to listen to records |
| el esquí (m.) | ski; skiing |
| el estadio (m.) | stadium |
| el film (m.) | movie, motion picture |
| el fútbol (m.) | soccer |
| el fútbol americano | football |
| el jaque (m.) | check (in chess) |
| el jaque mate (m.) | checkmate |
| el juego (m.) | game |

| | |
|---|---|
| jugar (ue) | to play (games or sports) |
| el lago (m.) | lake |
| leer | to read |
| la montaña (f.) | mountain |
| montar a caballo | to ride a horse (to go horseback riding) |
| nadar | to swim |
| los naipes (m. pl.) | cards (the game) |
| la novela (f.) | novel |
| la partida (f.) | game, round, hand (cards, table games; not sports) |
| el partido (m.) | game (in sports), match |
| patinar | to skate |
| patinar en el hielo | to ice skate |
| la película (f.) | film; movie, motion picture |
| la pesca (f.) | fishing |
| pescar | to fish |
| querer | to want; to love (a living being) |
| la telenovela (f.) | soap opera |
| la televisión (f.) | television |
| el voleibol (m.) | volleyball |

You have learned enough grammar to create your own sentences, using any of the vocabulary that interests you. Form sentences in various tenses and practice using them.

To start off, practice saying the following sentences:

*Prefiero jugar al ajedrez o ver la televisión.*
I'd rather play chess or watch television.

*Cazaremos en el bosque y pescaremos en el lago.*
We'll hunt in the woods and fish in the lake.

*Siempre patinábamos en el hielo cuando hacía frío y jugábamos en la nieve.*
We always used to ice skate when it was cold and we'd play in the snow.

*Nos gusta jugar al ajedrez o a las damas o a los naipes cuando llueve.*
We like to play chess or checkers or cards when it rains.

*Anoche fui a un club donde bailamos, comimos, y tomamos.*
Last night I went to a club where we danced, ate, and drank.

*Preferir* plus an infinitive verb, as in the first sample sentence, often comes out in English as *I'd rather ....*

Note that in most Spanish-speaking countries (though not all), to talk about playing a game, you use *jugar* plus the preposition *a* before naming the game. All Spanish-speakers use the definite article with the name of the game.

## THE 30-SECOND RECAP

In this hour, you've learned the difference between direct and indirect objects, and to form and use indirect object pronouns with conjugated verbs, with infinitive verbs, and with present participles. You've also learned to use verbs that speak of liking, "loving" (things), mattering, and being interested. And you've developed a vocabulary dealing with sports, entertainment, and other pastimes.

## HOUR'S UP!

Review the hour, and then test yourself by answering the following questions.

1. The object pronoun should *not* be placed …

    **a.** Before a conjugated verb.

    **b.** After an infinitive verb.

    **c.** After a present participle.

    **d.** Between a conjugated verb and an infinitive verb.

2. In the sentence *Stacey gave the boys some candy*, there is (are) …

    **a.** One object.

    **b.** Two objects.

    **c.** No objects.

    **d.** Three objects.

3. In the sentence in question 2, which noun will become the pronoun *les?*

    **a.** Some candy

    **b.** Stacey

    **c.** The boys

    **d.** None of the above

**4.** *We like candy* in Spanish is ...

   **a.** Nosotros gustamos los dulces.

   **b.** Nos gustamos los dulces.

   **c.** Nos gustan los dulces.

   **d.** Nos gusta los dulces.

**5.** *Do you like yourself?* in Spanish is ...

   **a.** ¿Te gusto?

   **b.** ¿Me gustas?

   **c.** ¿Le gustas tú?

   **d.** ¿Te gustas?

**6.** *I'm not interested* in Spanish is ...

   **a.** No tengo interés.

   **b.** No estoy interesada.

   **c.** No me interesa.

   **d.** All of the above.

**7.** She used to love soccer in Spanish is ...

   **a.** Le gustaba el fútbol.

   **b.** Ella quería al fútbol.

   **c.** Le fascinaba el fútbol.

   **d.** Ella amaba al fútbol.

**8.** I'd rather fish in Spanish is ...

   **a.** Me gustaría pescar.

   **b.** Me gusta pescar.

   **c.** Deseo pescar.

   **d.** Prefiero pescar.

**9.** No me importa in English is ...

   **a.** I'm not an importer.

   **b.** I don't care.

   **c.** I'm not important.

   **d.** She doesn't accept me.

QUIZ

**10.** Le canté una canción in English is …

    **a.** I sang a song to her.

    **b.** I sang him a song.

    **c.** I sang a song for you.

    **d.** All of the above.

## CHAPTER SUMMARY

**LESSON PLAN:**
In this hour, you'll learn ...

- How to use the subjunctive mood to state what you want others to do.

- How to advise, command, and forbid certain kinds of behavior.

- How to use the direct object pronouns and some idioms dealing with urges and obligations.

All the Spanish verb tenses you have learned up until now are in the indicative mood. Now you will begin to learn how to use the subjunctive mood. Translation is of less value in working with the subjunctive mood because the English subjunctive is now close to extinction.

There are traces of the English subjunctive in certain practically fossilized expressions, such as *be that as it may; the powers that be; be he alive or be he dead/I'll grind his bones to make my bread*, and *as it were*. In legal parlance or extremely formal English, we find it in expressions such as *in order that he go ...*. In most cases, the English subjunctive mood is dead or dying. In Spanish, however, the subjunctive mood is alive and well. For that reason, you need to know how to handle it in order not to be misunderstood.

## FORM THE REGULAR PRESENT SUBJUNCTIVE

To be able to understand examples that illustrate the use of the present subjunctive, you'll want to learn how to form the present tense of the subjunctive mood first. If you remember the present indicative tense, you'll have no trouble. The way to form the present subjunctive is as follows:

1. Think of the *yo* form of the verb in the present indicative.

2. Remove the ending that shows it to correspond to *yo*.

3. Place the "opposite" vowel on the end.

**GO TO** ▶

For a review of the regular present indicative, see Hour 3.

What is meant by "opposite" vowel? If you're dealing with an -*ar* verb, use the vowel -*e* as an ending. If it's an -*er* or -*ir* verb, use the vowel -*a* as the ending.

The following list illustrates the process with the verb *hablar*:

- **Infinitive.** Hablar
- **Present indicative, *yo* form.** Hablo
- **Remove *yo* ending.** Habl – *o*
- **The stem remains.** Habl
- **Add "opposite" ending.** Habl + *e*
- **Present subjunctive, *yo* form.** Hable

The next step is, as it was in the present indicative, to attach to the stem (the syllable right before the infinitive ending) the ending that shows the person, number, and tense.

**Present Subjunctive of -*ar* Verbs: *Hablar***

| Subject Pronoun | Verb Stem | Ending | Conjugated Verb |
|---|---|---|---|
| **Singular** | | | |
| yo | habl- | -*e* | hable |
| tú | habl- | -*es* | hables |
| él | habl- | -*e* | hable |
| ella | habl- | -*e* | hable |
| usted | habl- | -*e* | hable |
| **Plural** | | | |
| nosotros/as | habl- | -*emos* | hablemos |
| vosotros/as | habl- | -*éis* | habléis |
| ellos | habl- | -*en* | hablen |
| ellas | habl- | -*en* | hablen |
| ustedes | habl- | -*en* | hablen |

Practice conjugating the following -*ar* verbs in the present subjunctive, using the same method as employed for *hablar*:

- *cantar* (to sing)
- *llevar* (to bring, to carry)
- *llamar* (to name, to attract)

- *viajar* (to travel)
- *usar* (to use)

Most (perhaps all other) Spanish textbooks present the verbs *dar* and *estar* as irregular present subjunctive. They're not. They're regular; they follow the rules previously given.

- **Infinitive.** Dar
- **Present indicative, yo form.** Doy
- **Remove yo ending.** D – *oy*
- **Stem.** D
- **Add "opposite" ending.** D + *é*
- **Present subjunctive, yo.** Dé

The full conjugation is what you would expect: *dé, des, dé, demos, deis, den.*

**JUST A MINUTE**

The written accent mark on *dé* is there merely to distinguish this verb form from the preposition *de* (of, from).

What was said about *dar* is true for *estar*, too:

- estar
- estoy
- est – *oy*
- est
- est + *é*
- esté

The full conjugation is again what you would expect: *esté, estés, esté, estemos, estéis, estén.* (*Estar* is irregular in the present indicative tense, being accented on the last syllable, except with *nosotros*, but follows the rules for the present subjunctive.)

The following list illustrates the process for regular *-er* verb *comer*:

- **Infinitive.** Comer
- **Present indicative, yo form.** Como
- **Remove yo ending.** Com – *o*
- **The stem remains.** Com
- **Add "opposite" ending.** Com + *a*
- **Present subjunctive, yo.** Coma

The next step is to attach to the stem the ending that shows the person, number, and tense.

**Present Subjunctive of -er Verbs: *Comer***

| Subject Pronoun | Verb Stem | Ending | Conjugated Verb |
|---|---|---|---|
| **Singular** | | | |
| yo | com- | -a | coma |
| tú | com- | -as | comas |
| él | com- | -a | coma |
| ella | com- | -a | coma |
| usted | com- | -a | coma |
| **Plural** | | | |
| nosotros/as | com- | -amos | comamos |
| vosotros/as | com- | -áis | comáis |
| ellos | com- | -an | coman |
| ellas | com- | -an | coman |
| ustedes | com- | -an | coman |

**PROCEED WITH CAUTION**

Don't be tempted to use an -o ending for *yo*.

Practice conjugating the following -er verbs in the present subjunctive, using the same method employed for *comer*.

- *romper* (to break)
- *leer* (to read)
- *creer* (to believe)

The following illustrates the process for the regular -ir verb *vivir*:

- **Infinitive.** Vivir
- **Present indicative, yo form.** Vivo
- **Remove yo ending.** Viv – o
- **The stem remains.** Viv
- **Add "opposite" ending.** Viv + a
- **Present subjunctive, yo.** Viva

The next step is to attach to the stem the ending that shows the person, number, and tense.

### Present Subjunctive of *-ir* Verbs: *Vivir*

| Subject Pronoun | Verb Stem | Ending | Conjugated Verb |
|---|---|---|---|
| **Singular** | | | |
| yo | viv- | -a | viva |
| tú | viv- | -as | vivas |
| él | viv- | -a | viva |
| ella | viv- | -a | viva |
| usted | viv- | -a | viva |
| **Plural** | | | |
| nosotros/as | viv- | -amos | vivamos |
| vosotros/as | viv- | -áis | viváis |
| ellos | viv- | -an | vivan |
| ellas | viv- | -an | vivan |
| ustedes | viv- | -an | vivan |

**JUST A MINUTE**

You've heard expressions like *¡Viva el Presidente!* This use of the subjunctive doesn't state that the President lives, rather a *wish* that the President live.

The following are *-ir* verbs you already know. Practice conjugating them in the present subjunctive in the same manner shown for *vivir*:

- *escribir* (to write)
- *describir* (to describe)
- *recibir* (to receive)

At this point you might well ask why you're bothering to go back to the yo form of the present indicative tense to start the process of forming the present subjunctive. Why can't you simply go to the infinitive? In the case of verbs that are completely regular, you could just as well do that. Nevertheless, there are many irregular verbs in the present indicative tense, including many that are irregular only in the yo form; it is precisely this yo form that shapes the present subjunctive. For example, in the case of the verb *tener*,

**GO TO** ▶

For a review of the irregular present indicative verbs, see Hour 4.

you don't start with the infinitive stem, *ten-* (or with the stem of the *tú* form, *tien-*), you start with the stem of the *yo* form: *teng-*.

Let's take examples of present subjunctive conjugations of sample verbs that have irregularities in the present indicative which affect the *yo* form and, because of this, have a bearing on the present subjunctive.

### CHANGE THE *-E-* OF THE STEM

Verbs in the present indicative tense with a stem change in the *yo* form will, because the present subjunctive is based on the *yo* form of the present indicative, have that same stem change in the present subjunctive. See the following table for a sampling of verbs in all three conjugations with a stem change of *e* to *ie* or *i* in the *yo* form of the present indicative.

**Present Subjunctive of *-e-* Stem-Change Verbs**

| Cerrar (To Close) | Perder (To Lose) | Pedir (To Ask For) |
| --- | --- | --- |
| cierre | pierda | pida |
| cierres | pierdas | pidas |
| cierre | pierda | pida |
| cerremos | perdamos | pidamos |
| cerréis | perdáis | pidáis |
| cierren | pierdan | pidan |

**GO TO** ▶

For a review of stem-changing *-ir* verbs in the preterit tense, see Hour 5.

Notice that *-ar* verbs and *-er* verbs in the present subjunctive do not have a stem change in the *nosotros* and *vosotros* forms. This reflects what happens in the present indicative tense, too.

Caution: In the present subjunctive, the *-ir* verbs *do* share the stem change in the *nosotros* and *vosotros* forms. The stem change for *-ir* verbs in the *nosotros* and *vosotros* forms of the present subjunctive will always be from *-e-* to *-i-*, even if the present indicative stem change was from *-e-* to *-ie-*. For example, take the verb *mentir* (to lie, tell untruths), shown in the following table.

**Conjugation of Present Indicative and Present Subjunctive for *Mentir***

| Present Indicative | Present Subjunctive |
| --- | --- |
| miento | mienta |
| mientes | mientas |
| miente | mienta |

| Present Indicative | Present Subjunctive |
|---|---|
| mentimos | mintamos |
| mentís | mintáis |
| mienten | mientan |

## CHANGE THE -o- OF THE STEM

Verbs that have a stem change of -o- to -ue- in the yo form of the present indicative will have the same stem change in the present subjunctive for -ar and -er verbs. But, just as in the present indicative, the nosotros and vosotros forms will not have a stem change.

This same type of stem-changing verb in -ir verbs, however, will have a stem change in the nosotros and vosotros forms, but that change will be only to letter -u-. (This reflects the third person stem changes of the preterit tense.)

Study the following table for verbs that had a -ue- stem change in the yo form of the present indicative, to learn what occurs in the present subjunctive.

**GO TO ▶**
The gue in the jugar endings is a spelling convention for maintaining the sound of g, as in English go. The -u- after the g- is silent. To review the pronunciation and spelling rules, see Hour 1.

**Present Subjunctive of Jugar and -o- Stem-Change Verbs**

| jugar | volver | dormir | morir |
|---|---|---|---|
| juegue | vuelva | duerma | muera |
| juegues | vuelvas | duermas | mueras |
| juegue | vuelva | duerma | muera |
| juguemos | volvamos | durmamos | muramos |
| juguéis | volváis | durmáis | muráis |
| jueguen | vuelvan | duerman | mueran |

## REMEMBER OTHER Yo CHANGES

Remember that there are many verbs in the present indicative tense with irregularities in the yo form. Because you start with that form to conjugate the present subjunctive, they will affect this mood. Following is a sampling:

- **tener/tengo.** tenga, tengas, tenga, tengamos, tengáis, tengan
- **caer/caigo.** caiga, caigas, caiga, caigamos, caigáis, caigan
- **hacer/hago.** haga, hagas, haga, hagamos, hagáis, hagan
- **decir/digo.** diga, digas, diga, digamos, digáis, digan

- **conocer/conozco.** conozca, conozcas, conozca, conozcamos, conozcáis, conozcan

- **reducir/reduzco.** reduzca, reduzcas, reduzca, reduzcamos, reduzcáis, reduzcan

- **oír/oigo.** oiga, oigas, oiga, oigamos, oigáis, oigan

These other verbs follow this pattern:

poner-pongo-ponga
salir-salgo-salga
traducir-traduzco-traduzca
traer-traigo-traiga
venir-vengo-venga

## KNOW SPELL-CHANGE SUBJUNCTIVE

Some verbs in the present subjunctive are perfectly regular in the spoken language, but appear irregular in writing. Verbs that end in -car substitute -qu- for -c- before e or i. Verbs that end in -gar substitute -gu- for -g- before e or i. This is to prevent their sounds from changing (for example, *notificar-notifique; castigar-castigue*). This occurs in the preterit tense as well (for example, *notificar-notifiqué; castigar-castigué*). (You can review the sounds of Spanish and the spelling system in Hour 1.)

## FORM IRREGULAR SUBJUNCTIVE VERBS

There actually are irregular present subjunctive verbs—that is, verbs that depart from the rules you have just learned in this lesson for forming the present subjunctive.

| Infinitive | Present Indicative Yo | Subjunctive Yo |
| --- | --- | --- |
| haber | he | haya |
| ir | voy | vaya |
| saber | sé | sepa |
| ser | soy | sea |

**GO TO ▶**
The many uses of the verb *haber* will be discussed in this hour and in Hours 15 though 18, 20, and 24.

See the following full conjugation of the above four verbs in the present subjunctive:

- **haber.** haya, hayas, haya, hayamos, hayáis, hayan.

- **ir.** vaya, vayas, vaya, vayamos, vayáis, vayan.

- **saber.** sepa, sepas, sepa, sepamos, sepáis, sepan.
- **ser.** sea, seas, sea, seamos, seáis, sean.

## EXPRESS DESIRES FOR OTHERS' BEHAVIOR

Now that you know how to form the present subjunctive, we can use those forms for illustrative purposes. You can now begin to learn some of the uses of the subjunctive mood.

All the indicative mood tenses you have learned in previous hours serve the purpose of reporting an action, an event, a situation, or a state. Reporting those matters is *not* the function of the subjunctive mood. This is an important distinction.

One of the main functions of the subjunctive mood is to tell how someone feels about the action, event, situation, or state. This general idea of how one feels about an action can be further broken down into subheadings.

## EXPRESS YOUR WISHES

One of the specific uses of the subjunctive is for expressing wishes or desires. Think of the following English sentence:

I want him to go.

That sentence expresses a wish on the part of the speaker that someone else do something: go. The structure of the sentence makes it appear as though *him* is the direct object, and the verb *to go* must be in the infinitive form.

### PROCEED WITH CAUTION

If you were to use *quiero* with the direct object equivalent to *him* in Spanish, it would be understood to mean *I love him*.

The sentence structure in Spanish is very different. Translated directly to English, the proper Spanish structure reads as follows:

I want that he go.

This is where the subjunctive mood enters. The Spanish verb for the English *go* must be in the present subjunctive:

(Yo) quiero que él vaya.

To sum up, after verbs of wishing, wanting, and desiring—when there is a change of subject—you need to use the subjunctive mood. In the preceding example, the speaker (I) wants that another person (he) go.

If there is no change of subject (the same person is the subject of both wanting and the other verb), conjugate the verb showing desire, and follow it with the infinitive. For example, *I want to go* would be *Quiero ir* in Spanish. This is because the subject of *ir* is the same as the (understood) subject of *Quiero: yo.*

### PROCEED WITH CAUTION

 The verb *esperar* can mean *to hope, to expect,* and *to wait* (*for*). With the subjunctive following it in a sentence like the last sentence in the following list, it means *to hope.* Otherwise, it means *to expect.*

Practice saying the following sentences aloud, while "feeling" what they mean:

*María desea que yo vaya.* (María wants me to go.)

*Yo deseo que María vaya.* (I want María to go.)

*Quieren que vayamos.* (They want us to go.)

*Queremos que ellos vayan.* (We want them to go.)

*Carlos no quiere que Roberto venga.* (Carlos doesn't want Roberto to come.)

*Carlos quiere que Roberto no venga.* (Carlos wants Roberto not to come.)

*Mamá quiere que comamos.* (Mom wants us to eat.)

*Espero que me digas la verdad.* (I hope you tell me the truth.)

Examples of wishing without a change in subject from one verb to the other:

*María desea ir.* (María wishes to go.)

*Quieren venir.* (They want to come.)

*Mamá quiere comer.* (Mom wants to eat.)

### GIVE ADVICE AND RECOMMENDATIONS

When someone advises another person to do something, the subjunctive is used. In English, we can say either *I advise you to study* or *I advise that you study*. As you might guess from what you've already learned, the normal Spanish structure is like the English formal: (*Te*) *Aconsejo que* (*tú*) *estudies*. Practice saying the following sentences aloud:

*Me aconsejan que yo estudie.*
They advise me to study.

*Les recomiendo que no vayan al centro esta noche.*
I recommend you don't go downtown tonight.

*A ella le recomendaré que compre otra cosa.*
I'll recommend that she buy something else (another thing).

*¿(Me) Aconseja Ud. que (yo) diga que no?*
Are you advising me to say no?

Once again, my advising you to study does not allow me to report that you actually do study, or will study. Because I'm only stating my feelings about the matter, *estudie* is in the subjunctive.

### TIME SAVER

In the last of the previous sentences, either the *Me* or the *yo* could be omitted. Whichever one is left would tell you who's being advised to study.

### COMMAND, FORBID, AND PERMIT

When you command or order someone to do something, you're demonstrating, in a forceful way, your feelings about what that person should do. The subjunctive is used after verbs of commanding and forbidding. Practice saying the following examples:

*¡(Te) Mando que salgas inmediatamente!* (I command you to leave immediately!)

*El jefe (nos) manda que trabajemos.* (The boss orders us to work.)

*(Les) Prohíbo que entren.* (I forbid them to enter.)

*(Me) Prohíben que yo le hable a ella.* (They forbid me to speak to her.)

*¿(Nos) Permitirá Ud. que hablemos?* (Will you allow us to speak?)

*Sí, (les) permitiré que (Uds.) hablen.* (Yes, I'll permit you to speak.)

*Siempre hacen que yo estudie.* (They always make me study.)

*Haré que salgas.* (I'll make you leave.)

Where both the indirect object pronoun and the subject pronoun are in parentheses (as in the sixth sample sentence), it would not be incorrect to use both; however, it would be overkill and sound somewhat pompous.

The verb *decir* can be used in two different ways. It can be used simply to report events (He told me they left), or as the equivalent of a command: He told me to leave = He commanded me to leave. If it's used simply to report events, use the indicative. But if it's used as a command, use the subjunctive.

> *Me dicen que está lloviendo.*
> They tell (inform) me it's raining. (report)

> *Me dicen que yo coma.*
> They tell (order) me to eat. (command)

What is true for *decir* is also true for *insistir en*. You can insist that something did happen, in which case the verb is being employed merely to report facts and you would use the indicative. On the other hand, if *insistir en* is used to command or demand, then we use the subjunctive. See the following examples:

> *Insisto en que ellos no hacen nada.*
> I insist (on the fact) that they don't do anything.

> *Insisto en que ellos no hagan nada.*
> I insist (command) that they do nothing.

> *Insistimos en que dicen la verdad.*
> We insist (emphatically report) that they're telling the truth.

> *Insistimos en que digan la verdad.*
> We insist (demand) that they tell the truth.

## Use Direct Object Pronouns

In Hour 11, you learned to distinguish direct objects from indirect objects; you also learned how to form the indirect object pronouns. In this lesson, you will learn how to form and use the direct object pronouns.

The following table is set up so that in the left column you'll see the Spanish subject pronouns you already know. In the middle column, you'll find the Spanish indirect object pronouns that you learned in Hour 11. In the right column, you'll see the new material: the direct object pronouns.

**Spanish Pronouns**

| Subject | Indirect Object | Direct Object |
|---------|-----------------|---------------|
| yo | me | me |
| tú | te | te |
| él | le | lo |
| ella | le | la |
| usted | le | la, lo |
| nosotros/as | nos | nos |
| vosotros/as | os | os |
| ellos | les | los |
| ellas | les | las |
| ustedes | les | las, los |

You will be pleased to see that four of the direct object pronouns are exactly the same as the indirect object pronouns (*me, te, nos, os*). The only ones that differ are *lo* and *la* instead of *le*, and the plural *los* and *las* instead of *les*.

**PROCEED WITH CAUTION**

Indirect object pronouns ignore gender; direct object pronouns take it into account for the third person.

The direct object pronouns for *usted* and *ustedes* show that either the feminine or the masculine can be used. If the person you're talking to is a man, use the masculine direct object *lo*, and if it is a woman, use the feminine direct object *la*. If the people you are addressing as the subject pronoun *ustedes* are all men, or mixed men and women, use the direct object pronoun *los*; if they are exclusively women, you use *las*.

You've learned where to place the indirect object pronoun in relation to the verb; the rule is exactly the same for the direct object pronoun. See the following table for examples of the conversion of direct object nouns to direct object pronouns. The sentences in the left column have direct objects in the form of nouns, whereas the sentences in the right column have the object nouns changed into object pronouns.

**Conversion of Direct Object Nouns to Direct Object Pronouns**

| Direct Object Nouns | Direct Object Pronouns |
|---|---|
| *Roberto dio el libro a Elena.* <br> Roberto gave the book to Elena. <br> (Roberto gave Elena the book.) | *Roberto lo dio a Elena.* <br> Roberto gave it to Elena. |
| *María dio la revista al hombre.* <br> María gave the magazine to the man. <br> (María gave the man the magazine.) | *María la dio al hombre.* <br> María gave it to the man. |
| *(Yo) veo a Roberto.* <br> I see Roberto. | *(Yo) lo veo.* <br> I see him. |
| *¿Estás mirando a las chicas?* <br> Are you looking at the girls? | *¿Estás mirándolas?* <br> *(¿Las estás mirando?)* <br> Are you looking at them? |
| *Quiero encontrar a Carlos.* <br> I want to find Carlos. | *Quiero encontrarlo.* <br> *(Lo quiero encontrar.)* <br> I want to find him. |

**GO TO ▶** <br> To review the position of object pronouns with relation to the verb, see Hour 11.

The third person direct object pronouns do not have to refer to people (him or her), but can refer to any third person noun, including *it*.

Study the following sample sentences that convert direct object nouns into direct object pronouns, saying them aloud:

Yo tengo el libro. (I have the book.)

Yo lo tengo. (I have it.)

¿Tienes los libros? (Do you have the books?)

¿Los tienes? (Do you have them?)

Tomamos una cerveza. (We're having [drinking] a beer.)

La tomamos. (We're having [drinking] it.)

¿Viste las revistas? (Did you see the magazines?)

¿Las viste? (Did you see them?)

¿Quieres tener el libro? (Do you want to have the book?)

¿Quieres tenerlo? (¿Lo quieres tener?) (Do you want to have it?)

## TALK OF EXISTENCE WITH *HABER*

The verb *haber* has several different uses. For now, you'll learn how to use it to comment on the existence of someone or something. To show existence, it is conjugated only in the third person singular form. In the present tense, this form is a bit different from the form it takes for other functions: *hay*. It is equivalent in meaning to the English idioms *there is* and *there are*, or in a question, *is there?* and *are there?* Practice with the following sentences:

**GO TO** ▶

To learn how to use a direct object pronoun and an indirect object pronoun together (that is, with the same verb), see Hour 15.

> *¿Hay un libro aquí?* (Is there a book here?)
>
> *Sí, hay un libro aqí.* (Yes, there's a book here.)
>
> *¿Hay muchas personas en la casa?* (Are there many people in the house?)
>
> *Sí, hay muchas personas en la casa.* (Yes, there are a lot of people in the house.)
>
> *¿Qué hay hoy?* (What is there today?)
>
> *Hoy hay muchas actividades.* (Today there are a lot of activities.)

Note: The expression in the fifth sentence, *¿Qué hay?*, is often used colloquially to mean *What's up?* or *What's happening?* The preterit *¿Qué hubo?* is used in the same way.

Practice the idiom *haber* to express existence in other tenses:

- **Preterit.** *Hubo un accidente.* (There was an accident.)
- **Imperfect.** *Había cinco personas.* (There were five people.)
- **Future.** *¿Habrá guerra?* (Will there be war?)
- **Conditional.** *No habría problema si ….* (There wouldn't be a problem if ….)
- **Infinitive.** *Va a haber guerra.* (There's going to be [a] war.)

## THE 30-SECOND RECAP

In this hour, you have learned to form the present subjunctive, and to use it for expressing wishes and desires and trying to influence the behavior of others (advising, commanding, forbidding, or permitting). You have also learned the direct object pronouns and how to use them. In addition, you've added to your vocabulary an idiom that refers to existence.

## HOUR'S UP!

This would be a good time to review this hour's lessons. Then, test yourself on the following questions.

1. Choose the correct object pronoun and its position to replace the noun: *Veo las casas*.

   **a.** Les veo.

   **b.** La veo.

   **c.** Las veo.

   **d.** Véolas.

2. Choose the correct object pronoun and its position to replace the noun: *Tengo el libro*.

   **a.** Lo tengo.

   **b.** Téngole.

   **c.** Le tengo.

   **d.** Téngolo.

3. Choose the correct object pronoun and its position to replace the noun: *Quieren decir la verdad*.

   **a.** Quieren la decir.

   **b.** La quieren decir la verdad.

   **c.** Quieren decirle la verdad.

   **d.** La quieren decir.

4. Complete the sentence: *Les mando que (salir)* …

   **a.** salen.

   **b.** salgan.

   **c.** salan.

   **d.** salgen.

5. Complete the sentence: *No quiero que Marta (ir)* …

   **a.** ía.

   **b.** voya.

   **c.** va.

   **d.** vaya.

**6.** Complete the sentence: *Recomendamos que Ud. no (hacer)* …

   **a.** lo hace.

   **b.** lo haga.

   **c.** lo haya.

   **d.** lo haiga.

**7.** True or false: The subjunctive mood is used to report actions and situations.

**8.** True or false: The subjunctive mood is used to express the subject's feelings.

**9.** Choose the correct alternate way to say the following: No permito que coma.

   **a.** No le permito comer.

   **b.** No lo permito comer.

   **c.** No permítole comer.

   **d.** No permito que come.

**10.** Choose the correct alternative way to say the following: Me dice que está ocupado.

   **a.** Me dice que él esté ocupado.

   **b.** Dice que yo esté ocupado.

   **c.** Me dice estar él ocupado.

   **d.** None of the above.

# HOUR 13

## Possession; More Subjunctive

## CHAPTER SUMMARY

**LESSON PLAN:**

In this hour, you'll learn ...

- How to use possessive adjectives.

- How to use the subjunctive mood with verbs of doubting, denying, expressing emotion, and impersonal expressions.

- Idioms expressing urges, desires, and obligations.

In Hour 12, you learned to form the present subjunctive, and to use it when trying to influence the behavior of others. In this hour, you'll be using the present subjunctive to show doubt, disbelief, and denial, and to express emotion about actions, events, and situations.

### SHOW DOUBT AND DISBELIEF

The indicative mood is used to report events, but the subjunctive mood cannot do this. Instead, it is used to comment on the way the subject feels about the events. Doubting, not believing, and denying events fit into this category as well. These feelings relegate the events mentioned in the subjunctive mood to the world of unreality. Learn the following relevant verbs:

- *dudar* (to doubt)
- *creer* (to believe, think)
- *negar* (ie) (to deny)
- *parecerle a uno* (to seem/appear/look like to one)

To believe (*creer*) does not take the subjunctive, because what one believes belongs in the real world; it's considered on a par with knowing a fact. However, *not to believe* (*no creer*) does take the subjunctive, because it's equivalent to denying or doubting, and puts the event commented on in that world of unreality that can't be reported. Denial (*negar*) works the other way. It does take the subjunctive, because the subject of *negar* says the event is unreal. However, *not* denying usually takes the indicative, because not denying something tends to allow the event to exist in the real, reportable world.

### PROCEED WITH CAUTION

You can be subtly ironic if you use the subjunctive with *not* denying. *No niego que él lo sepa* means *I don't deny that he may know it.* You don't deny it, but you show some doubt.

Study the following sentences contrasting indicative and subjunctive, and then practice saying them aloud:

(1) *Yo sé que Elena sabe mucho.* (I know [that] Elena knows a lot.)

(2) *Yo dudo que Elena sepa mucho.* (I doubt [that] Elena knows a lot.)

(3) *Elena dice que yo trabajo muy poco.* (Elena says [that] I work very little.)

(4) *Ella niega que yo trabaje mucho.* (She denies [that] I work a lot.)

(5) *Creen que el mundo es redondo.* (They think the world is round.)

(6) *No creen que el mundo sea plano.* (They don't think the world is flat.)

(7) *¿Cree Ud. que Antonio vendrá?* (Do you think Antonio will come?)

(8) *¿Cree Ud. que Antonio venga?* (Do you think Antonio will come?)

(9) *¿No cree Ud. que Antonio vendrá?* (Don't you think Antonio will come?)

(10) *¿No cree Ud. que Antonio venga?* (Don't you think Antonio will come?)

**GO TO ▶**
For a review of the present indicative tense, used in sentences 1, 3, and 5, see Hours 3 and 4. For a review of the future indicative, used in sentences 7 and 9, see Hour 6.

Sentences 1 and 3 would never take the subjunctive; they would always take the indicative because if you say you know something or say that something is true, that action or situation is considered (by the one doing the knowing) a fact, a part of the real world.

Sentences 2, 4, and 6 take the subjunctive because in 2, Elena's knowing is doubted; in 4, my working a lot is flatly denied; and in 6, the world's being flat is not believed. All these things, then, cannot be reported, and are not thought of as being in the real world.

Sentence 5 takes the indicative rather than the subjunctive because it tells what they believe—which, in Spanish, is usually considered as good as knowing. Nevertheless, it is possible for the speaker of this sentence to show that, although *they* believe the world is round, he or she has some reservations about the matter. In that case, the sentence would be *Creen que el mundo sea plano.* This would show doubt on the part of the speaker. However, the norm would be to use the indicative.

In sentence 7, the indicative is used (future tense) because it's a straight-forward question about what the other person believes. The speaker doesn't show any doubt about Antonio's coming; he just wants to know the other person's opinion. Number 8 is practically the same question, but the use of the subjunctive betrays doubt on the part of the person asking the question.

Sentence 9 is the most normal form of a belief-question phrased negatively. Just as in the English *Don't you think Antonio will come?*, a negative belief-question strongly suggests the one asking the question expects the answer to be yes. But it is possible to ask that question and show your own doubt, by using the subjunctive, as in sentence 10.

Synonymous with sentences 5, 6, 7, 8, 9, and 10 are the following:

> *Les parece que el mundo es redondo.* (It seems to them ....)
>
> *No les parece que el mundo sea plano.* (It doesn't seem to them ....)
>
> *¿Le parece (a Ud.) que Antonio vendrá?* (Does it seem to you ...?)
>
> *¿Le parece (a Ud.) que Antonio venga?* (Does it seem to you ...?)
>
> *¿No le parece (a Ud.) que Antonio vendrá?* (Doesn't it seem to you ...?)
>
> *¿No le parece (a Ud.) que Antonio venga?* (Doesn't it seem to you ...?)

## SHOW EMOTION CONCERNING EVENTS

When you comment on your emotions concerning events, the primary function of your message is not to report the events, but to tell how you feel about them. Use the subjunctive for these events. Learn the following verbs of emotion:

- *estar contento/a de que* ... (to be happy that ...)
- *estar triste de que* ... (to be sad that ...)
- *tener miedo de que* ... (to be afraid that ...)
- *temer* (to fear)
- *sorprender* (to surprise)
- *gustar* (to please [like])
- *entristecer* (to sadden)
- *sentir (ie, i)* (to feel [regret, be sorry])

Note that *sentir* literally means *to feel*. It can also be used to mean *to hear* or *to smell*, or in its most general meaning, *to sense*. However, it is also used idiomatically in Spanish to mean *to regret* or *to be sorry*. Study the following sentences, and then practice saying them aloud, feeling their meaning:

(1) *María está contenta de que estemos aquí.* (María's glad we're here.)

(2) *Estoy triste de que Ud. no pueda venir.* (I'm sad you can't come.)

(3) *Tenemos miedo de que sea verdad.* (We're afraid it may be true.)

(4) *Temo que pueda pasar.* (I'm afraid [I fear] it may happen.)

(5) *Temo que puede pasar.* (I'm afraid [I fear] it can happen.)

(6) *Temo que él no venga.* (I'm afraid he won't come.)

(7) *Temo que él no vendrá.* (I'm afraid he won't come.)

(8) *¿Te sorprende que ella hable español?* (Does it surprise you that she speaks Spanish?)

**GO TO** ▶
For a review of the formation of the present subjunctive, see Hour 12.

There are different connotations in the *Temo* … sentences (4, 5, 6, 7). In sentences 4 and 6, the speaker doesn't know for a fact that what he or she fears will or will not take place; he or she can't report on it happening or not happening. He or she is just afraid it might possibly happen (4), or not happen (6). In sentences 5 and 7, he or she considers the event he or she fears to be pretty certain; he or she is reporting it, and he or she is afraid because of it. Because of the feeling of certainty, the indicative is used.

When there is one subject for the verb of emotion and a different one for the following verb (as in the preceding sentences), you must use the subjunctive. If the subject of both verbs is the same, simply use the infinitive of the second verb:

*María está contenta de estar aquí.* (María is glad to be here.)

*Me gusta hablar español.* (I like to speak Spanish.)

*Nos entristece decirlo.* (It saddens us to say it.)

**JUST A MINUTE**

In the second sentence, technically, the object of *gusta* is the same person as the subject of *hablar*. The same is true of the third sentence with regard to *entristece* and *decirlo*. The point is, there is only one person involved in each sentence.

## USE SUBJUNCTIVE WITH IMPERSONAL EXPRESSIONS

It might be easy to remember that an impersonal expression is an expression in which no person is the subject. In English, the subject is always *it*: It's impossible for him to go; it's probable he'll do it; and so on. In Spanish, the idea of *it*, when it's the subject, is not expressed. You merely use the third person singular verb form: *Es imposible que …; es probable que …*.

Most impersonal expressions are followed by the subjunctive. The reason is that most impersonal expressions demonstrate all the reasons you've studied in this hour and in Hour 12 for using the subjunctive: attempting to influence someone else's behavior (wishing, wanting, advising, recommending, commanding, or forbidding), showing doubt or disbelief, or denying an event, or simply demonstrating emotion over an event. Study the following sentences, and then practice saying them aloud:

>*Es posible que ella venga.* (It's possible she'll come.)
>
>*Es imposible que ella venga.* (It's impossible that she'll come.)
>
>*Es probable que yo lo lea.* (It's probable that I'll read it.)
>
>*Es improbable que yo lo lea.* (It's improbable that I'll read it.)
>
>*Es bueno que lo estés haciendo.* (It's good that you're doing it.)
>
>*Es malo que lo estés haciendo.* (It's bad that you're doing it.)
>
>*Será preferible que lo hagan.* (It will be preferable for them to do it.)

In the Spanish psyche, if something is only possible, it's not an absolute certainty; therefore, there's doubt (*Es posible*). If it's impossible (*Es imposible*), then you're denying the truth of the event. *Es probable* still is not an absolute certainty, so there's room for doubt. *Es improbable* actually declares the doubt; it borders on denial. *Es bueno* and *Es malo* can be forms of advice, of recommending for or against an action, or simply of showing emotion about the goodness or badness of the action. *Será preferible* is an extremely mild way of giving an order.

Note: The few impersonal expressions that do not fall into the categories requiring the subjunctive, as explained in this hour and Hour 12, and previously summarized, do not use the subjunctive. Impersonal expressions that take the event referred to as true or factual use the indicative because they are reporting the action, event, or situation:

>*Es verdad que está aquí.* (It's true he's here.)
>
>*Es cierto que trabajo mucho.* (It's true that I work hard.)
>
>*Es obvio que lo saben.* (It's obvious that they know it.)

It's as if the first sentence said *Está aquí*, a straight factual report, and then added *Es verdad*. The same situation applies to the other two sentences: *Trabajo mucho; es cierto; lo saben; es obvio.* And, of course, you could actually say it that way.

Note: Examine the previous three impersonal expression sentences, which use the indicative, and the preceding seven impersonal expression sentences, which use the subjunctive. They all refer to some person: It's possible she'll come. It's probable I'll read it. … If no person (or animal, or thing) is mentioned, then neither the subjunctive nor the indicative is used; just as in English, the infinitive is used. For example:

*Es posible ir.* (It's possible to go.)

*Es imposible salir.* (It's impossible to leave.)

*Es bueno hacerlo.* (It's good to do it.)

*Es aconsejable estudiar.* (It's advisable to study.)

*Es terrible tener que trabajar de noche.* (It's terrible having to work at night.)

**JUST A MINUTE**

Notice the impossibility of *not* referring to a specific person, and therefore, the impossibility of using the infinitive with the impersonal expressions that are factual, in English as well as in Spanish. You can't say, "It's true to be here," or, "It's obvious to know it." They have no meaning.

## SHOW POSSESSION WITH *DE*

Spanish does not use the apostrophe to show possession. If you want to say María's raincoat, you say "the raincoat of María": *El impermeable de María.* Study the following examples:

*el coche de Juan* (Juan's car)

*el libro de María* (María's book)

*la casa de Alberto* (Alberto's house)

*las clases de mi amigo* (my friend's classes)

*los amigos de Elena* (Elena's friends)

**GO TO** ▶
For a review of *ser* plus *de* to show possession, see Hour 7.

In English, if we already know what the possessed noun is, we leave it out. Spanish does the same. Understand the mental process involved in this noun suppression by looking at the step-by-step depiction of it in both languages:

> *el coche de Juan* (Juan's car)
>
> *el [coche] de Juan* (Juan's [car])
>
> *el de Juan* (Juan's)
>
> *la casa de los cubanos* (the Cubans' house)
>
> *la [casa] de los cubanos* (the Cubans' [house])
>
> *la de los cubanos* (the Cubans')

Assume that you're referring to the people and possessions of the first and fifth sample sentences above, and that you and the person to whom you're talking know what those nouns are. The following illustrates what happens:

> *¿El coche de quién?* (Whose car?)
>
> *El de Juan* (Juan's)
>
> *¿La casa de quién?* (Whose house?)
>
> *La de mis amigos* (My friends')
>
> *¿Los libros de quién?* (Whose books?)
>
> *Los de mi amigo Miguel* (My friend Miguel's)

## USE POSSESSIVE ADJECTIVES

Possessive adjectives are adjectives that indicate to whom a noun belongs. The English equivalents are my, your, his, her, our, and their. The following table contains two columns. The left column shows the subject pronouns with which you are already familiar. The right column shows the possessive adjectives that apply to the person indicated by the subject pronouns. (English translations are in parentheses.)

**Possessive Adjectives**

| Subject Pronouns | Corresponding Possessive Adjectives |
|---|---|
| **Singular** | |
| *Yo* (I) | *mi, mis* (my) |
| *tú* (you) | *tu, tus* (your) |
| **Plural** | |
| *nosotros/as* (we) | *nuestro, nuestros, nuestra, nuestras* (our) |
| *vosotros/as* (you, pl.) | *vuestro, vuestras, vuestra, vuestras* (your) |

**GO TO** ▶

For a review of the agreement between nouns and adjectives, see Hour 2.

The possessive adjectives for *él, ella, usted, ellos, ellas,* and *ustedes* have purposely been left out of the preceding table. They will be treated separately.

You remember that adjectives must agree in number and gender with the nouns they modify. This is why *mi* and *tu* have plural forms. They do not have feminine forms because they already are both masculine and feminine at the same time. *Nuestro* and *vuestro* do have four different forms, because the masculine singular forms end with *-o*.

Study the following sentences, and practice saying them aloud:

*Tengo mi libro.* (I have my book.)

*Tengo mis libros.* (I have my books.)

*¿Tienes mi silla?* (Do you have my chair?)

*¿Tienes mis sillas?* (Do you have my chairs?)

*Sí, tengo tu silla.* (Yes, I have your chair.)

*No, no tengo tus sillas.* (No, I don't have your chairs.)

*¿Quiénes tienen nuestro carro?* (Who [pl.] have our car?)

*Nosotros tenemos vuestro carro.* (We have your car.)

*¿Quién robó nuestras cosas?* (Who stole our things?)

**PROCEED WITH CAUTION**

In written Spanish, the subject pronoun *tú* is distinguished from the possessive adjective *tu* by means of the written accent mark.

Notice that the possessive adjective does not agree in number and gender with the owner of the noun being possessed. Like any other adjective in Spanish, it agrees in number and gender with the noun it modifies.

Let's examine the possessive adjectives for the remaining subject pronouns. Study the following table.

**Possessive Adjectives**

| Subject Pronoun | Corresponding Possessive Adjective |
|---|---|
| **Singular** | |
| *él* (he) | *su, sus* (his) |
| *ella* (she) | *su, sus* (her) |
| *usted* (you) | *su, sus* (your) |
| **Plural** | |
| *ellos* (they, m.) | *su, sus* (their, m.) |
| *ellas* (they, f.) | *su, sus* (their, f.) |
| *ustedes* (your) | *su, sus* (your) |

Examine the following sentences:

*María busca su impermeable.*
María's looking for her raincoat.

*Ella tiene sus guantes.*
She has her gloves.

*Carlos busca su coche.*
Carlos is searching for his car.

*Él tiene sus lápices.*
He has his pencils.

*¿Busca Ud. su coche?*
Are you looking for your car?

*¿Tiene Ud. sus guantes?*
Do you have your gloves?

*Los chicos van a ir a la casa de su amigo.*
The boys are going to go to their friend's house (the house of their friend).

*Ellos van a ir a la casa de sus amigos.*
They're going to go to their friends' house (the house of their friends).

Because the possessive adjective is the same for all six subject pronouns, how do we determine who or what the subject is?

Usually context clues resolve the ambiguity of the possessive pronouns. In the previous sentences, it is assumed from context that the possessor is clear. In the first sentence, María is looking for someone's raincoat. We might assume that María is looking for her own raincoat; however, the possessive pronoun *su* leaves the matter open to many more possibilities.

**JUST A MINUTE**

In the absence of any indications to the contrary, it will be assumed by anyone listening to this sentence—which has no context—that María is looking for her own coat.

Let's take a scenario that would change your interpretation of the possessive *su* in this sentence: María's date has misplaced his raincoat and has been searching high and low for it. You know this. After half an hour, he comes back to the living room and excitedly asks you where María is. You say, "*María busca su impermeable*." Knowing the circumstances (context), there is no doubt in your mind that María is looking for *his* raincoat.

A similar change of circumstances could be performed on any of the above sentences. Context, then, is one way of being certain about the meaning of the possessive adjective *su* and its plural *sus*.

## Use Specific Indicators

If you think that context will not make the possessor clear, or you want to place heavy emphasis on the possessor, then you can use an alternative method. Instead of using *su/sus*, you can employ an entire phrase using the following formula:

> Definite article + noun + the preposition *de* + one of the six prepositional object pronouns

**JUST A MINUTE**

The noun of the formula is the thing possessed.

Study the following table for a presentation of the longer, more specific (or emphatic) alternative method of showing possession for the six pronouns: *él, ella, usted, ellos, ellas, ustedes*.

**More Specific Indicators of Ownership**

| Short Form | More Specific Form | English |
|---|---|---|
| su coche | el coche de él | his car |
| su coche | el coche de ella | her car |
| su coche | el coche de usted | your car |
| su coche | el coche de ellos | their car |
| su coche | el coche de ellas | their car |
| su coche | el coche de ustedes | your car |
| sus coches | los coches de él | his cars |
| sus coches | los coches de ella | her cars |

The definite articles of this formula, as in any other case, must agree in number and gender with the nouns they modify; because we're dealing with possession, the nouns they modify are the things possessed.

**TIME SAVER**

If context makes the possessor clear, use *su/sus;* it's shorter and saves time and breath.

## STATE YOUR URGES AND OBLIGATIONS

In Hour 11, you learned to speak of liking and "loving" inanimate objects. You have, in past lessons, learned several idioms that use the verb *tener*. This verb is also used to speak of urges and obligations.

### USE *TENER GANAS DE* + INFINITIVE

The verb *tener* plus the plural feminine noun *ganas* plus the preposition *de* plus the infinitive verb is used to speak of urges. *Tengo ganas de comer* means that the subject of the verb *has a desire, an urge, to eat*. The best translation of this sentence would be with the idiomatic English, *I feel like eating*. Practice the following sentences:

*¿Tienen Uds. ganas de comer?*
Do you feel like eating?

*Sí, tenemos ganas de comer.*
Yes, we feel like eating.

*No tuve ganas de ir.*
I didn't feel like going.

*¿La semana que viene, tendrás ganas de nadar?*
Next week, will you feel like swimming?

*No vamos, porque no tenemos ganas.*
We're not going, because we don't feel like it.

---

**JUST A MINUTE**

The infinitive verb follows *tener ganas de* because in Spanish, the *only* form of the verb that comes after any preposition is the infinitive; for example, *antes de ir = before going.*

## USE *DAN GANAS DE* + INFINITIVE

An expression related to *tener ganas de* is the very idiomatic expression *dan ganas* plus *de* plus the infinitive verb. The *dan* is always in the third person plural. You know who the person is who has the urge or desire by the indirect object pronoun used with it. Study the following sentences, and practice saying them aloud:

*Me dan ganas de tomar café.*
I feel like having coffee.

*¿Te dan ganas de comer?*
Do you feel like eating?

*Nos daban ganas de salir.*
We were in the mood to leave.

*A ellos les dan ganas de hacer algo interesante.*
They're in the mood to do something interesting.

## USE *DAR LA GANA*

The singular *dar la gana* is also used with the same feeling, usually as a self-contained phrase:

*¿Por qué lo hiciste?*
Why did you do it?

*Porque me dio la gana.*
Because I felt like it.

*¿Por qué no fuiste a la fiesta?*
Why didn't you go to the party?

*No fui porque no me dio la gana.*
I didn't go because I didn't feel like it.

You might hear the above expression with the adjective *real* in front of *gana*. These expressions are a very rude and arrogant way of saying you did something (or didn't do it) because you felt like it (or didn't feel like it). (The literal meaning of *real* is either *real* or *royal*; in this idiom it means *royal*.) It projects a feeling of *to hell with everyone else; I do or don't do what I want.* The English translations given alongside the sentences don't do justice to the feeling of self-assertion implied. See the following examples:

**PROCEED WITH CAUTION**

You would do best in social and business situations to steer clear of the *real gana* idiom. It leaves a negative impression.

*¿Por qué lo hiciste?* (Why did you do it?)

*Porque me dio la real gana.* (Just because I felt like it.)

*¿Por qué no fuiste a la fiesta?* (Why didn't you go to the party?)

*No fui porque no me dio la real gana.* (I didn't go because I just didn't feel like it.)

## USE *TENER* + *QUE* + INFINITIVE

The verb *tener* plus the relative pronoun *que* plus an infinitive verb is used to talk of obligation. It is very much like the English idiom *to have to* plus a verb. Practice the following sentences:

*¿Qué tienes que hacer?* (What do you have to do?)

*Tengo que salir.* (I have to leave.)

*¿Qué tuvieron Uds. que hacer ayer?* (What did you have to do yesterday?)

*Ayer tuvimos que trabajar.* (Yesterday we had to work.)

*Mañana tendré que estudiar.* (Tomorrow I'll have to study.)

## USE *HABER* + *QUE* + INFINITIVE

The verb *haber* plus the relative pronoun *que* plus the infinitive verb shows obligation or necessity. With this meaning, it is always conjugated in the third person singular. The English equivalent idioms would be *It's necessary to …*, *One has to …*, *One must …*, or *One needs to …*, and so on. Practice with the following sentences:

*Hay que trabajar.* (One must work. [It's necessary to work.])

*Había que hacerlo.* (One had to do it. [It was necessary to do it.])

*Hubo que salir.* (It was necessary to leave.)

*¿Habrá que asistir?* (Will it be necessary to attend?)

*Habría que asistir si …* (It would be necessary to attend if …)

*No va a haber que hacerlo.* (It's not going to be necessary to do it.)

Note: *Haber que* (unlike *tener que*) is general and impersonal. It doesn't specify *who* has to do something.

## USE THE *DEBER* IDIOMS

The verb *deber* plus an infinitive verb is also used to show obligation, usually of the moral, ethical kind. It usually has the same feeling as *ought to* or *should* do something. Sometimes it has the force of *must* or *to have to*. Practice saying the following sentences:

*Debemos pensar en el futuro.* (We should think about the future.)

*Deben salir ahora.* (They ought to leave now.)

*Yo debía hacerlo.* (I had to do it.)

*Ahora debo trabajar.* (Now I must work.)

*No debías decirlo.* (You shouldn't have said it.)

Very often, people will use the conditional tense of *deber*. The meaning is not changed, but the tone is less strong, less definite, more polite, more diplomatic, and more diffident. The English translations don't reflect the difference very well:

*Deberíamos pensar en el futuro.* (We ought to think about the future.)

*Deberían salir ahora.* (They ought to leave now.)

*Ahora yo debería trabajar.* (Now I ought to work.)

*No deberías decirlo.* (You shouldn't say it.)

*Ella debería estudiar.* (She ought to study.)

The imperfect subjunctive of *deber* is also used for acquiring the same diffident tone as the conditional indicative tense. The following sentences use the imperfect subjunctive of *deber* and have the same meaning and tone as the five previous sentences:

**GO TO ▶**
Lessons on the imperfect subjunctive will begin in Hour 21.

> Debiéramos pensar en el futuro.
>
> Debieran salir ahora.
>
> Ahora yo debiera trabajar.
>
> No debieras decirlo.
>
> Ella debiera estudiar.

*Deber* + *de* + infinitive: The verb *deber* plus the preposition *de* is used with the meaning of *must* in the sense of *probably*. See the following examples:

> *Roberto debe de estar en casa.*
> Roberto must be (probably is) home.
>
> *Yo debía de estar comiendo.*
> I must've been (probably was) eating.
>
> *Deben de ser españoles.*
> They must be (probably are) Spaniards.

*Deber* also means *to owe*:

> *Paco me debe cien dólares.* (Paco owes me a hundred dollars.)
>
> *Tú me debes la vida.* (You owe me your life.)
>
> *Me vas a deber un favor.* (You're going to owe me a favor.)

The noun *el deber* means *duty* or *obligation*. See the following examples:

> *Es mi deber trabajar.* (It's my duty to work.)
>
> *Fue tu deber luchar.* (It was your duty to fight.)
>
> *Será nuestro deber irnos.* (It will be our duty to go away.)

## THE 30-SECOND RECAP

In this hour, you've learned to show ownership through use of the preposition *de*, and through possessive adjectives, and to use the subjunctive mood with verbs of doubting, denying, and expressing emotion, and impersonal expressions. You've also learned idioms expressing urges, desires, and obligations.

## HOUR'S UP!

This would be a good time to review this hour. Then, when you feel ready, test yourself by answering the following questions, without, of course, referring back to the pages of the lessons in this hour.

1. Choose the correct form of the verb in parentheses: *Siento mucho que ella no (poder) ____ venir.*

   **a.** pode

   **b.** puede

   **c.** pueda

   **d.** poda

2. Choose the correct form of the verb in parentheses: *Sé que ella (estudiar) ____ mucho.*

   **a.** estudia

   **b.** estudió

   **c.** estudiará

   **d.** All of the above

3. Choose the correct form of the verb in parentheses: *No creen que José (hacer) ____ mucho.*

   **a.** haga

   **b.** hace

   **c.** hizo

   **d.** hará

4. Use the possessive adjective in a way that the subject of the verb will be the owner of the item possessed: *Yo busco ____ libros.*

   **a.** mi

   **b.** su

   **c.** sus

   **d.** mis

   **e.** mes

**5.** Use the possessive adjective in a way that the subject of the verb will be the owner of the item possessed: *¿Ven ellos _____ coche?*

    **a.** tu

    **b.** tus

    **c.** su

    **d.** sus

    **e.** tú

**6.** Use the possessive adjective in a way that the subject of the verb will be the owner of the item possessed: *Estudiamos _____ lección.*

    **a.** nosotras

    **b.** nuestra

    **c.** nuestras

    **d.** nuestro

    **e.** nosotros

**7.** Choose the correct form of the verb in parentheses: Es lástima que yo no (tener) _____ tiempo.

    **a.** tiena

    **b.** tengo

    **c.** tena

    **d.** tenga

**8.** Choose the correct alternative way of saying the following: Me gusta la casa de ellas.

    **a.** Me gusta su casa.

    **b.** Me gustan sus casas.

    **c.** Me gusta ella's casa.

    **d.** None of the above.

**9.** Translate: One must eat.

    **a.** Tengo que comer.

    **b.** Debemos comer.

    **c.** Tengo comer.

    **d.** Hay que comer.

**10.** Translate: I feel like seeing her.

    **a.** Tengo que verla.

    **b.** La tengo que ver.

    **c.** Tengo ganas de verla.

    **d.** Hay que verla.

# PART IV
## Daily Routine

# HOUR 14

# At Home

**CHAPTER SUMMARY**

**LESSON PLAN:**

In this hour, you'll learn ...

- How to use possessive pronouns as well as another kind of possessive adjectives.
- How to talk about your home (rooms, furniture, and activities in the home) and family.
- About some cultural differences between the United States and the Hispanic world.

This hour will be divided between nomenclature for parts of the house and items in the house on one hand, and vocabulary concerning activities in the house on the other.

## LEARN NOUNS DEALING WITH HOUSES

The following table lists useful vocabulary for speaking about the home.

### Vocabulario para la Casa

| Spanish | English |
| --- | --- |
| la alacena (f.) | cupboard |
| la alfombra (f.) | rug |
| la almohada (f.) | pillow |
| el almuerzo (m.) | lunch |
| el apartamento (m.) | apartment |
| la araña (f.) | chandelier; spider |
| el ascensor (f.) | elevator |
| la aspiradora (f.) | vacuum cleaner |
| la azotea (f.) | (flat) roof |
| la bañera (f.) | bathtub |
| el baño (m.) | bath; bathroom |
| la basura (f.) | garbage |
| el cajón (m.) | drawer |
| la cama (f.) | bed |
| la casa (f.) | house |
| la casa particular (f.) | private house |

*continues*

**Vocabulario para la Casa** (continued)

| Spanish | English |
| --- | --- |
| la cena (f.) | supper |
| el césped (m.) | lawn, grass (of a lawn) |
| la cerca (f.) | fence |
| el cielo raso (m.) | ceiling |
| la cocina (f.) | kitchen |
| el comedor (m.) | dining room |
| la congeladora (f.) | freezer |
| la comida (f.) | meal; food; lunch |
| la cómoda (f.) | chest of drawers |
| la cortina (f.) | curtain |
| el cuadro (m.) | picture |
| el cuarto (m.) | room; bedroom |
| la chimenea (f.) | fireplace |
| el desayuno (m.) | breakfast |
| el dormitorio (m.) | bedroom |
| la ducha (f.) | shower |
| el edificio (m.) | building |
| el edificio de apartamentos (m.) | apartment building |
| la escoba (f.) | broom |
| la escalera (f.) | stairway, stairs |
| la esquina (f.) | corner (outside angle) |
| el estropajo (m.) | mop |
| la estufa (f.) | stove |
| el estante (m.) | shelf; bookcase |
| el fregadero (m.) | kitchen sink |
| el hogar (m.) | hearth; home |
| el horno (m.) | oven |
| el horno de microondas (m.) | microwave oven |
| el inodoro (m.) | toilet |
| el jardín (m.) | flower garden; yard |
| el lavabo (m.) | bathroom sink |
| la lavadora (f.) | washing machine |

| Spanish | English |
| --- | --- |
| el lavaplatos (m.) | dishwasher |
| la luz (f.) | light |
| la mesa (f.) | table |
| la mesita (f.) | coffee table |
| el mueble (m.) | piece of furniture |
| los muebles (m. pl.) | the furniture (as a whole) |
| la pared (f.) | wall |
| el patio (m.) | courtyard |
| el piso (m.) | floor |
| la puerta (f.) | door |
| el rincón (m.) | corner (inside angle) |
| la ropa (f.) | clothes, clothing |
| la sala (f.) | living room |
| la silla (f.) | chair |
| el sillón (m.) | easy chair |
| la secadora (f.) | clothes dryer |
| el tejado (m.) | tile roof |
| el techo (m.) | roof; ceiling |
| el tocador (m.) | dresser |
| la torre (f.) | tower; high-rise |
| la ventana (f.) | window |
| el zaguán (m.) | front hall; vestibule |

**PROCEED WITH CAUTION**

Don't raise eyebrows by saying "*Trabajo en el dormitorio*" when you want to say you work in the dorm; that sentence means *I work in the bedroom*. The dorm is *la residencia* (*estudiantil*).

*La cama* is used everywhere to mean *bed,* but a more elegant or literary word for the same piece of furniture is *el lecho*.

*El patio* doesn't have the same meaning that it does in our English borrowing; it is a courtyard. In traditional or Spanish colonial-style houses, the *patio* is a roofless area, paved with flagstones or left with its natural dirt floor, entirely enclosed by the house itself. Usually they are gardens and have some outdoor furniture. In this way, it is like a backyard, but much more private.

There are two words for *corner* in Spanish, and each one has a distinct meaning. *La esquina* refers to the outside angle of any corner, whether of the outside of a house, of a table, or of a box. Because it is the outside angle, it is also the street corner. *El rincón* is the inside angle of a corner. You can stand in a *rincón* or sit in a *rincón,* but you can't do those things in an *esquina.* You can't get into an *esquina.* You can hurt yourself on the *rincón* of a desk if you back up against it, and if you're standing on the (street) corner, you're referring to the *esquina.*

**JUST A MINUTE**

*El lavaplatos* also means *dishwasher* in the sense of a man who washes dishes for a living. The woman would be *la lavaplatos.*

In Spanish-speaking countries, breakfast (*el desayuno*) is usually toast, bread, or rolls, with butter and/or jelly, accompanied by coffee, tea, or hot chocolate. Lunch (*el almuerzo*) tends to be a heavy meal eaten about 1:00 or 2:00. Traditionally, people take their *siesta* (a nap, or just relaxing with family and friends), until about 4:00; then shops re-open, and people return to work until the evening. The evening meal (*la cena*) habitually starts anywhere from 10:00 P.M. to midnight. Eleven o'clock is very common.

## LEARN ACTIVITIES PERFORMED AT HOME

The following vocabulary list deals with activities commonly performed at home.

### Vocabulario para las Actividades del Hogar

| Spanish | English |
| --- | --- |
| almorzar (ue) | to have lunch |
| apagar | to turn off (electrical appliances); to extinguish |
| barrer | to sweep |
| sacar | to take out |
| bonito/a | pretty |
| cenar | to have dinner, dine |
| cocinar | to cook |
| comer | to eat |
| cortar | to cut |
| cortar el césped | to mow the lawn |
| chico/a | small, little |

| Spanish | English |
| --- | --- |
| desayunar | to have breakfast |
| desempolvar | to dust |
| encender (ie) | to light; to turn on (an electrical appliance) |
| feo/a | ugly |
| grande | big, large |
| lavar | to wash |
| lavar los platos | to wash the dishes |
| limpiar | to clean |
| pequeño/a | small, little |
| prender | to turn on (an electrical appliance) |
| preparar la comida | to prepare a meal; "fix" dinner |
| regar (ie) | to water, sprinkle |
| sacar | to take out |
| secar | to dry |

**JUST A MINUTE**

As an adjective, *chico/a* means *little*. Used as nouns, *chico* and *chica* mean *boy* and *girl* (little ones), respectively.

The verbs *apagar* and *encender* respectively mean *to extinguish* and *to light* a fire. In our modern, electrified world, they also mean to *turn off* and to *turn on* an electrical appliance, respectively. The verb *prender*, in addition to the idea of switching on an electrical appliance, also means *to seize, to grasp, to capture, to apprehend,* and *to fasten*. It also refers to lighting a fire, as in *prender un cigarro* (to light a cigar).

Study the following sentences for meaning, and then practice saying them aloud:

María lavó los platos. (María washed the dishes.)

Mamá prepara el almuerzo. (Mom fixes lunch.)

Pepe limpiará el piso. (Pepe will clean the floor.)

Papá está sacando la basura. (Dad is taking out the garbage.)

Luis lava la ropa. (Luis washes the clothes.)

Usa la lavadora. (He uses the washing machine.)

*Luego, seca la ropa en la secadora.* (Later, he dries the clothes in the dryer.)

*Marta barría el piso los lunes.* (Marta used to sweep the floor on Mondays.)

*Esta noche, Mamá no va a cocinar.* (Tonight, Mom isn't going to cook.)

## USE THE EMPHATIC POSSESSIVE ADJECTIVE

You've already learned to use possessive adjectives. In this lesson, you'll learn to use another form of them, as well as possessive pronouns.

Sometimes you may want to emphasize the owner of the thing possessed. In English, we do this by pronouncing the possessive adjective louder: It's *my* house! (Not anyone else's) The possessive adjectives you have learned are not pronounced in this emphatic way in Spanish. Instead, a different form of the possessive adjective, the emphatic (or the "long form") is used. This "long form" is placed *after* the noun possessed. As you will remember, the nearer the end of a sentence or expression a word is placed in Spanish, the more emphasis it has. In this construction, the definite article is used and is placed before the noun possessed. Study the following table.

**Possessive Adjectives: Short Form Compared to Emphatic Long Form**

| Short Form | Long Form | English |
| --- | --- | --- |
| mi comedor | el comedor mío | my dining room |
| mis cuadros | los cuadros míos | my pictures |
| mi cocina | la cocina mía | my kitchen |
| mis toallas | las toallas mías | my towels |
| tu garaje | el garaje tuyo | your garage |
| tus armarios | los armarios tuyos | your closets |
| tu mesa | la mesa tuya | your table |
| tus sillas | las sillas tuyas | your chairs |
| su sofá | el sofá suyo | (see footnote) |
| sus muebles | los muebles suyos | (see footnote) |
| su chimenea | la chimenea suya | (see footnote) |
| sus lámparas | las lámparas suyas | (see footnote) |
| nuestro baño | el baño nuestro | our bathroom |
| nuestra estufa | la estufa nuestra | our stove |
| nuestros espejos | los espejos nuestros | our mirrors |
| nuestras cortinas | las cortinas nuestras | our curtains |

| Short Form | Long Form | English |
|---|---|---|
| vuestro sillón | el sillón vuestro | your easy chair |
| vuestra sala | la sala vuestra | your living room |
| vuestros platos | los platos vuestros | your dishes |
| vuestras alfombras | las alfombras vuestras | your rugs |

*You already know that su and sus can stand for his, her, your, and their. The same is true of suyo(s) and suya(s).*

Study the following sentences:

*No son tus toallas; son las toallas mías.*
They're not your towels; they're *my* towels.

*No es vuestra casa; es la casa nuestra.*
It's not your house; it's *our* house.

*No me gustan mis platos; prefiero los platos tuyos.*
I don't like my dishes; I prefer *your* dishes.

*¿Mis cuadros están aquí; dónde están los cuadros tuyos?*
My pictures are here; where are *your* pictures?

*Tu alfombra es bonita; la alfombra nuestra es fea.*
Your rug is pretty; our rug is ugly.

## Use Possessive Pronouns

No doubt the English sentences in the previous exercise sound childishly repetitive. This is because each sentence has the same noun twice (pictures/ pictures; couch/couch, and so on). When we know what the noun is in English, we don't repeat it. We don't use possessive adjectives when we omit the noun; we use the possessive pronoun (*mine* instead of *my*; *yours* instead of *your*; *hers* instead of *her*; *ours* instead of *our*; *theirs* instead of *their*).

The Spanish sentences sound just as childishly repetitive as the English ones, for the same reason. In Spanish, too, you omit the noun if you know what it is, especially if you've just mentioned it. This corresponds to English usage. And, as in English, you employ not the possessive adjective, but the possessive pronoun instead.

Remember: The purpose of a pronoun is to take the place of a noun. If the possessive word doesn't modify a noun (because the noun has been omitted), it's taking the place of the noun; therefore, it's a possessive pronoun.

To form the possessive pronoun in Spanish, start with the emphatic (or "long") form, which uses the definite article, the noun, and the possessive adjective, as you've just learned, and as is illustrated in the preceding table. Then simply drop the noun. The process follows:

el comedor mío
el [comedor] mío
el mío

los cuadros míos
los [cuadros] míos
los míos

la chimenea suya
la [chimenea] suya
la suya

las lámparas suyas
las [lámparas] suyas
las suyas

Doing it this way, you see that the definite articles and the possessive pronouns agree in number and gender with the nouns whose place they're taking. You can take the same sentences we had earlier and drop the second mention of the noun in question. Let's see the process first:

*No son tus toallas; son las [toallas] mías.*
They're not your towels; they're [my towels] mine.

*No es vuestra casa; es la [casa] nuestra.*
It's not your house; it's *our+s* [house].

*No me gustan mis platos; prefiero los [platos] tuyos.*
I don't like my dishes; I prefer *your+s* [dishes].

*Mis cuadros están aquí; ¿dónde están los [cuadros] tuyos?*
My pictures are here; where are *your+s* [pictures]?

*Tu alfombra es bonita; la [alfombra] nuestra es fea.*
Your rug is pretty; *our+s* [rug] is ugly.

Study the finished product, and then practice saying the following sentences aloud:

*No son tus toallas; son las mías.*
They're not your towels; they're mine.

*No es vuestra casa; es la nuestra.*
It's not your house; it's ours.

*No me gustan mis platos; prefiero los tuyos.*
I don't like my dishes; I prefer yours.

*¿Mis cuadros están aquí; dónde están los tuyos?*
My pictures are here; where are yours?

*Tu alfombra es bonita; la nuestra es fea.*
Your rug is pretty; ours is ugly.

## USE SPECIFIC EMPHATIC POSSESSIVE ADJECTIVES

None of the sentences you've been practicing with so far have included the possessive adjectives of the third person. They are the ones that can sometimes be vague, if context or pointing doesn't clarify them. Those adjectives can, out of context, represent the persons you would call *él*, *ella*, *usted*, *ellos*, *ellas*, and *ustedes*. In other words, a sentence like *Yo tengo la alfombra suya*, out of context, could mean *I have **his** rug, I have **her** rug, I have **your** (one person) rug, I have **their** rug*, or *I have **your*** (more than one person) *rug*. You've already learned the alternate possessive adjectives for the third person. It comes out exactly the same as the alternate emphatic (or "long-form") possessive adjectives.

Because you've already learned how to do this, let's just look at several sentences using this form. This time, however, you'll see the alternate form alongside the emphatic ("long") form. Study the following sentences.

**GO TO** ▶
For a review of the nonemphatic possessive adjectives (both regular and alternate), see Hour 13.

**Third Person Possessive Adjectives: Specific and Regular Emphatic Form**

| Regular Emphatic | Alternate Emphatic | English |
| --- | --- | --- |
| ¿Ven las cercas suyas? | ¿Ven las cercas de él? | Do you see *his* fences? |
| Uso el ascensor suyo. | Uso el ascensor de ella. | I use *her* elevator. |
| Tengo los platos suyos. | Tengo los platos de Ud. | I have *your* dishes. |
| Es la casa suya. | Es la casa de ellos. | It's *their* house. |
| Apagó la radio. | Apagó la radio de ellas. | He turned off *their* radio. |
| Es la aspiradora suya. | Es la aspiradora de Uds. | It's *your* vacuum cleaner. |

If the context (or pointing) made it clear who the owners of the fences, elevator, dishes, house, radio, and vacuum cleaner are, there would be no need to use the middle column. Nevertheless, there is nothing wrong with using it if you want to. Just be familiar with both forms, because you're sure to hear them both.

Meanwhile, let's look at some situations in which you could use the sentences in the left column and the listener would find the meaning absolutely clear.

You're talking to several neighboring ranchers about the type of fencing you're using to separate your properties. You all agree that barbed wire is acceptable, but that razor wire is not. All the ranchers present, including yourself, say they have barbed wire fencing, and that not one of them has razor fencing. However, you know that Jones, who is not present, has razor fencing, because you've seen it. You say to the others, "*Sí, pero Jones … ¿Ven (Uds.) las cercas suyas?*" There is no doubt in anyone's mind that you're referring to Jones's fences. The English would be *Yes, but Jones … Do you see **his** fences?*

Here's another scenario: You're talking to a friend on the phone, and you've complained that the elevator on your side of a high-rise apartment building is out of commission. (You live on the twentieth floor.) You also mention that the elevator on the other side of the building, in which your cousin Marta lives, is in perfect working order. Your friend asks how you manage. You say, "*Uso el ascensor suyo.*" There is not the shadow of a doubt that you mean you use her (Marta's) elevator.

GO TO ▶
For a review of *de* taking the place of English apostrophe + *s*, see Hour 13.

Context, then, makes it possible to use the forms in the left column with no reasonable possibility of confusion. Still, you can use the type of sentences you see in the middle column.

**JUST A MINUTE**

There is absolutely no reason why the first sentence in the table has to refer to *él*, the second one to *ella*, etc. Any of the possessive adjectives in the left column could refer to any of the third person pronouns in the middle column.

## LEARN TO SPEAK OF FAMILY

In traditional Hispanic society, the family is very important. The extended family exhibits more solidarity than the typical modern American family. You will see, as well, that "dating," in traditional Hispanic society is not the same as it is in the United States. Study the terminology in the following table dealing with family relationships.

**PROCEED WITH CAUTION**

In addition to the primary meaning of *comadre,* the word is used colloquially to mean a *gossip* in some regions, and a *go-between* or a *procuress* in other regions.

### Vocabulario de la Familia

| Spanish | English |
| --- | --- |
| el/la abuelo/a (m./f.) | grandfather/mother |
| el/la bisabuelo/a (m./f.) | great-grandfather/mother |
| la comadre (f.) | "co-mother"; midwife |
| el compadre (m.) | "co-father" |
| el/la cuñado/a (m./f.) | brother-in-law/sister-in-law |
| el/la esposo/a (m./f.) | husband/wife; spouse |
| el/la hermanastro (m./f.) | step-brother/sister |
| el/la hermano/a (m./f.) | brother/sister |
| el/la hijastro/a (m./f.) | stepson/stepdaughter |
| el/la hijo/a (m./f.) | son/daughter |
| la madrastra (f.) | stepmother |
| la madre (f.) | mother |
| la madrina (f.) | godmother |
| la mamá (f.) | mother, "mom" |
| el marido (m.) | husband |
| la mujer (f.) | woman; wife |
| la novia (f.) | girlfriend; sweetheart; fiancée; bride |
| el novio (m.) | boyfriend; sweetheart; fiancé; bridegroom |
| la nuera (f.) | daughter-in-law |
| el padrastro (m.) | stepfather |
| el padre (m.) | father |
| el padrino (m.) | godfather |
| el papá (m.) | father, "dad" |
| el/la pariente/a (m./f.) | relative, relation, kin |
| el/la primo/a (m./f.) | cousin |
| el/la sobrino/a (m./f.) | nephew/niece |
| el/la suegro/a (m./f.) | father-in-law/father-in-law |
| el/la tatarabuelo/a (m./f.) | great-great-grandfather/mother |
| el/la tío/a (m./f.) | uncle/aunt |
| el yerno (m.) | son-in-law |

In many regions, it would be considered an intentional and grave insult for you to call a man who is not truly your brother-in-law *cuñado*. You'd be implying that you have sexual relations with his unmarried sister.

Spanish is an extremely male-oriented language; it is *macho*. Although *padre* means *father* and *madre* means *mother*, the masculine plural *los padres* could mean either *the fathers* or *the parents* (mother and father; mothers and fathers), depending on context. *Los hijos* can mean either *the sons* or *the sons and daughters, the children* in the sense of offspring rather than simply very young people. *Los primos* can mean either *male cousins* or *cousins* in general, male and female. *Los tíos* can mean either *the uncles* or *the aunt and uncle* or *the aunts and uncles*. *Los abuelos* can mean either *the grandfathers* or *the grandparents*, and so on.

**JUST A MINUTE**

Thinking of *yerno,* some Spanish speakers use *\*yerna* to mean *daughter-in-law,* forgetting the word *nuera*. Dictionaries do not register *\*yerna*.

The words for *son-in-law* and *daughter-in-law* are peculiar in that, unlike most of the other kinship terms, the masculine and feminine words don't resemble each other at all (*el yerno* and *la nuera*).

Notice the cultural implications of the following: The word *novio* is translated into English variously as *boyfriend, sweetheart, fiancé,* and *bridegroom*. Similarly, *novia* comes out in English as *girlfriend, sweetheart, fiancée,* and *bride*. In traditional middle- and upper-class Hispanic society, "dating," in the North American sense of the word, is not acceptable. Teenagers go places (dances, parties, movies, concerts, walks, and so on) in groups, and often with chaperones. When they start to pair off, this is considered a serious step that will ultimately lead to marriage. For this reason, *novio* and *novia* have no single acceptable translations in English. North American influence may be making inroads in some sectors of some Spanish-speaking countries, but in general, the situation as described still holds true in most of the countries among the middle and upper classes.

Indicating another sharp difference between Anglo culture and Hispanic culture, English has no equivalents for the Spanish terms *compadre* and *comadre*.

The primary meaning of *compadre* is as a term that the father of a child and the child's godfather call each other. It's a mutual term just as *brother* is. The relationship between the *padre* and the *padrino* is a very special, very strong one that is lifelong. It implies obligations and privileges, and a very close friendship. The two "co-fathers" become almost blood brothers.

In almost all Spanish-speaking regions, the word *compadre* has also become, by extension, a colloquial term for a close friend of long standing, like *buddy* or *pal*, or in British slang, *mate*.

Practice saying the following sentences:

*Mis tíos me esperan en la sala.*
My aunt and uncle are waiting for me in the living room.

*¿Están en casa tus padres?*
Are your parents home?

*Los míos, no, pero los tuyos están en nuestro comedor, comiendo.*
Mine, no, but yours are in the dining room, eating.

*Mi suegra va a venir de visita mañana.*
My mother-in-law's going to come on a visit tomorrow.

*Dudo que mi suegra esté en nuestra casa por mucho tiempo.*
I doubt my mother-in-law will be at our house for long ("much time").

*¿Es que lo dudas, o que esperas que no esté en vuestra casa por mucho tiempo.*
(Is it that) you doubt it, or that you hope she won't be in your house for long?

*Me gusta estar junto a la chimenea, con un buen libro, y una cerveza.*
I like to be next to the fireplace, with a good book, and a beer.

*¿En qué cuarto tienen Uds. el televisor?*
In what room do you have the TV set?

*Lo tenemos en el dormitorio, porque nos gusta ver la televisión cuando estamos en la cama.*
We have it in the bedroom, because we like to watch TV when we're in bed.

**JUST A MINUTE**

*La televisión* refers to the electronic process, and to what you watch. *El televisor* is the television set; it's what you buy and what stands in your living room.

## THE 30-SECOND RECAP

In this hour, you've learned more about possessive adjectives and possessive pronouns. You've also learned to talk about your home (rooms, furniture, and activities in the home) and your family, as well as certain cultural differences between the United States and the Spanish-speaking world.

## QUIZ

## HOUR'S UP!

Review this hour, and then test your progress by taking the following quiz. Naturally, try to do this without consulting the lessons in this hour while actually quizzing yourself.

1. Fill in the blank with the most appropriate word: *El papá de mi madre es mi _____.*

   **a.** tío

   **b.** abuelo

   **c.** primo

   **d.** hermano

2. Fill in the blank with the most appropriate word: *Los hijos de mi madre _____.*

   **a.** son mis hermanos

   **b.** son mis hermanas y hermanos

   **c.** somos yo y mis hermanos

   **d.** all of the above

3. Choose the correct alternate way of saying *Uso el ascensor de Elena.*

   **a.** Uso el ascensor suyo.

   **b.** Uso el ascensor suya.

   **c.** Uso la suya.

   **d.** Uso la de ella.

4. Choose the correct alternate way of saying *Veo los muebles de María.*

   **a.** Veo las suyas.

   **b.** Veo las de ella.

   **c.** Los veo de María.

   **d.** Veo los de ella.

5. Finish the sentence with a reasonable option, judging either by grammatical structure or by logical meaning: *No me gustan mis alfombras, pero me gusta _____.*

   **a.** el tuyo

   **b.** la suya

   **c.** las tuyas

   **d.** las de ella

# HOUR 15

# At the Office

CHAPTER SUMMARY

**LESSON PLAN:**
In this hour, you'll learn ...

- How to use vocabulary necessary for working in an office.
- How to use reflexive verbs.
- How to talk about the date (the names of the days of the week and the months).

Any transitive verb in Spanish can be transformed into a reflexive verb. The basic use for making a verb reflexive is to show that someone (or something) is doing something to him/her/itself, but there are other special uses for this type of verb as well.

Learning to use reflexive verbs involves learning the reflexive object pronouns as well as dealing with the use and meaning of this kind of verb. We'll start with the reflexive pronouns to make it possible, a little further on, to illustrate the uses and meanings with examples.

## LEARN THE REFLEXIVE OBJECT PRONOUNS

You already know how to use several kinds of personal pronouns: subject pronouns, direct object pronouns, indirect object pronouns, and possessive pronouns. The following table shows the reflexive object pronouns compared with the direct and indirect object pronouns.

**Comparative Object Pronouns: Direct, Indirect, and Reflexive**

| Direct | Indirect | Reflexive |
| --- | --- | --- |
| me | me | me |
| te | te | te |
| lo | le | se |
| la | le | se |
| nos | nos | nos |
| os | os | os |
| los | les | se |
| las | les | se |

GO TO ▶
To review the use and placement of indirect and direct objects, see Hours 11 and 12, respectively.

You can see that the reflexive object pronouns are identical to the direct and indirect object pronouns for the subjects represented by the pronouns *yo*, *tú*, *nosotros/as*, and *vosotros/as*. The pronoun that is new to you, the one that is uniquely reflexive, is *se*, which is the reflexive object pronoun for the grammatical third person (*él, ella, usted, ellos, ellas, ustedes*). As you'll see, it is also used with the infinitive verb in the abstract—that is, when no particular person is referred to.

Now that you know the reflexive object pronouns, you can move on to their use and meaning.

## USE THE TRUE REFLEXIVE

You can transform any transitive verb into a reflexive verb, in English and in Spanish. A reflexive verb is one in which the subject and the object are identical. That is to say, the one performing the action of the verb is also the one receiving the action of that same verb. Another way to say this is that the one doing the action of the verb is doing it to him-, her-, or itself.

**JUST A MINUTE**

A transitive verb is one that can take an object, such as *to see*, whereas an intransitive verb is one that doesn't take an object, such as *to swim*.

For example, the verb *ver* means *to see*. It can be used with direct object pronouns—for example, *verlo* (to see him or it), *verla* (to see her or it). The infinitive verb *verse* means *to see oneself*.

The verb *decir*, as you know, means *to say* or *to tell*. It can be used with either direct or indirect object pronouns. *Decirlo* means *to say it*, whereas *decirle* means *to tell (to) him* or *her*. The infinitive verb *decirse* means *to say to oneself*.

GO TO ▶
For a different meaning of the plural reflexives, see the lesson on reciprocal verbs later in this hour.

You know the verb *lavar*; it means *to wash*. *Lavar* can be used with a direct object pronoun: *lavarlo* (to wash him or it), or *lavarla* (to wash her or it). The infinitive verb *lavarse* means *to wash oneself*. Keep in mind that in English, we often don't bother to use *-self* with many verbs, including *to wash*. (For example, we can say, "He's washing [up] right now.") We feel it's understood in English, but in Spanish it has to be made clear.

Take a look at the following sentences with the reflexive verb *verse*:

(*Yo*) *Me veo.* (I see myself.)

(*Tú*) *Te ves.* (You see yourself.)

(*Él*) *Se ve.* (He sees himself.)

*(Ella) Se ve.* (She sees herself.)

*(Usted) Se ve.* (You see yourself.)

*(Nosotros) Nos vemos.* (We see ourselves.)

*(Vosotros) Os veis.* (You see yourselves.)

*(Ellos) Se ven.* (They see themselves.)

*(Ellas) Se ven.* (They see themselves.)

*(Ustedes) Se ven.* (You see yourselves.)

Study the following sentences and practice saying them aloud:

*(Yo) Me veo en el espejo.*
I see myself in the mirror.

*¿(Tú) Te ves?*
Do you see yourself?

*Él se dice que no puede ser.*
He tells himself it can't be.

*Uds. se dicen que es verdad.*
You tell yourselves it's true.

*(Nosotros) Nos lavamos a menudo.*
We wash up (wash ourselves) often.

*El jefe se afeita en la oficina.*
The boss shaves (himself) at the office.

*Os decís que no importa.*
You tell yourselves it doesn't matter.

*María se lavó esta mañana.*
María washed up (herself) this morning.

New verbs used in the preceding sentences:

- afeitar(se)
- cortar(se)
- peinar(se)

Explanation: *Afeitar* means *to shave* (someone else, the direct object). Used reflexively, *afeitarse* means *to shave* (oneself). *Peinar* means *to comb* (something, someone's hair); when used reflexively (even if the word for hair is not used), it means *to comb one's hair*. *Cortar* means *to cut*; when used reflexively, of course, it means *to cut oneself*.

Related nouns:

| | |
|---|---|
| el corte (m.) | cut |
| el corte de pelo (m.) | haircut |

## USE REFLEXIVE VERBS WITH BODY PARTS

In English, we use the possessive adjective when we refer to what someone does to a part of his or her body. (For example, He washed *his* face.) In Spanish, the normal procedure is different, because it's assumed that whatever a person is doing to a body part, it is part of his or her own body, unless otherwise indicated. In Spanish, you would use the reflexive form of the verb, and the definite article before the relevant body part. Compare English and Spanish in the following sentences:

| | |
|---|---|
| He washed his face. | (Él) Se lavó la cara. |
| She combed her hair. | (Ella) Se peinó el cabello. |
| They shaved their legs. | Se afeitaron las piernas. |
| They'll brush their teeth soon. | Se lavarán los dientes pronto. |
| We dry our hands. | Nos secamos las manos. |
| They wash their faces. | Se lavan la cara. |
| We hurt our heads. | Nos lastimamos la cabeza. |

Note that the singular form of the noun is used for the body part if each person in the group has *only one* of those body parts (*cara, cabeza*). If each person has more than one, then the plural is used (*piernas, dientes, manos*).

**PROCEED WITH CAUTION**

If you were to say *Nos lastimamos las cabezas* in the last sentence above, people would picture you as having more than one head each.

Note: The word *cabello* refers to hair, but specifically of the head, "a head of hair." The general word for hair, which can also be used for the hair on the head, or anyplace else, is *el pelo*. A single hair is *un pelo*.

## USE REFLEXIVE VERBS WITH CLOTHING

In English, we use the possessive adjective when we refer to what someone does to his or her clothing. In Spanish, the normal procedure is different because it's assumed that whatever a person is doing to clothing, he or she is doing to his or her own clothes, unless otherwise indicated. In Spanish, you would use the reflexive form of the verb and the definite article before the relevant article of clothing. Compare English and Spanish in the following sentences:

| | |
|---|---|
| He puts his hat on. | Se pone el sombrero. |
| We took off our coats. | Nos quitamos el abrigo. |
| She removed her shoes. | Ella se quitó los zapatos. |
| They donned their mufflers. | Se pusieron la bufanda. |

**JUST A MINUTE**

As with parts of the body, if each person in a group has only one of the articles of clothing mentioned, the singular is used, as in the second and fourth sentence.

## CUT THROUGH THE IDIOMATIC DISGUISES

As you've noticed in the previous sample sentences, some English idioms don't mesh very well with the Spanish way of expressing the same thought. The verb *poner*, you'll remember, means *to put* or *to place*. When it's used reflexively in Spanish (*ponerse*), literally, *to put to oneself*, it has the same underlying meaning as the English *to put on* with reference to clothing. The verb *quitar* means *to take away* or *to remove*. When it's used reflexively in Spanish (*quitarse*), literally, *to take away from oneself* or *to remove from oneself*, it has the same semantic charge as the English *to take off* with reference to clothing.

Do not be confused when you encounter different meanings for verbs when they are not shown in their reflexive form. For example, the verb *levantar* means *to lift* or *raise*, but it is commonly shown in its reflexive form, *levantarse*, which means *to get up*. At first sight, there doesn't seem to be a connection between getting out of bed and lifting a heavy weight or raising the window. But if you understand the literal meaning of the verb, and know how reflexive verbs work in Spanish, there's no mystery to the connection. The basic meaning of *levantar* is that of lifting or raising something. If it's used reflexively, meaning that someone is doing this raising or lifting to him or herself (*I raise myself at 7:00 A.M. = Me levanto a las siete de la mañana), it's perfectly clear how getting up and raising or lifting something are essentially the same thing. The only difference lies in the object: whom or what are you raising? If it's yourself, the English idiom is *to get up*.

It might help to recognize this connection more quickly if you think that *levantar* means *to raise,* and the more formal English for *to get up* is *to rise.* This is not a coincidence.

Following is a vocabulary list of common reflexive verbs in Spanish, which might not seem to mesh with the same verb when not reflexive, and the idiomatic English equivalent.

**Spanish Verbs, as Transitive and as Reflexive**

| Transitive | English | Reflexive | English |
| --- | --- | --- | --- |
| acostar (ue) | to put to bed | acostarse (ue) | to go to bed |
| despertar (ie) | to awaken, wake up | despertarse (ie) | to awaken, wake up |
| levantar | to raise, lift | levantarse | to get up |
| bañar | to bathe | bañarse | to take a bath |
| duchar | to give a shower | ducharse | to take a shower |
| lavar | to wash | lavarse | to get washed |
| poner | to put, place | ponerse | to put on (clothes) |
| quitar | to take away | quitarse | to take off (clothes) |

If you said, "*Se llevó los zapatos,*" this would mean that he or she carried the shoes off, and could suggest shoplifting.

## USE THE VERBS RECIPROCALLY

When the subject of a reflexive verb is plural, it is possible to understand it in the reciprocal sense rather than in the reflexive sense. In other words, instead of several people doing something to themselves, it could be taken to mean they're doing something to *each other*. See the following sentences:

*Se lavan la cara.* (They wash each other's faces.)

*Nos lastimamos la cabeza.* (We hurt each other's heads.)

*Se pusieron la bufanda.* (They put their mufflers on each other.)

*Nos quitamos el abrigo.* (We took off each other's coats.)

## Make Reflexive or Reciprocal Clearer

Because, in the case of a plural subject with a reflexive verb, the very literal meaning is more like *They wash to them the face, *We hurt us the head, *They put to them the muffler, and *We removed us the coat, the sentences can be taken to mean either that the people involved performed these actions on themselves (reflexive), or on each other (reciprocal). The context, as well as the logic, will make the meaning clear.

However, it is possible to make this difference absolutely explicit. If you need to make it clear that a plural subject is doing something reflexively (doing it to them/our/yourselves), you can add *a sí mismos (mismas)* when the subject is *ellos, ellas,* or *Uds.,* or *a nosotros/as mismos/as* or *a vosotros/as mismos/as* when the subject is *nosotros/as* or *vosotros/as.*

If, on the other hand, you want to clarify that plural subjects are doing something reciprocally (doing it to each other), you can add *el uno al otro* (the one to the other) if only two people are involved, or *los unos a los otros* (the ones to the others) if more than two people are involved.

See the following examples of explicit reflexive reference:

*Se lavan la cara a sí mismos.* (They wash their own faces.)

*Nos lastimamos la cabeza a nosotros mismos.* (We hurt our own heads.)

*Se pusieron la bufanda a sí mismos.* (They put their mufflers on themselves.)

*Nos quitamos el abrigo a nosotros mismos.* (We took off our own coats.)

See the following examples of explicit reciprocal reference:

*Se lavan la cara el uno al otro.* (They wash each other's faces.)

*Nos lastimamos la cabeza los unos a los otros.* (We hurt each others' heads.)

*Se pusieron la bufanda el uno al otro.* (They put mufflers on each other.)

*Nos quitamos el abrigo los unos a los otros.* (We took off each others' coats.)

Note that the *el (los) uno(s)* and *el (los) otro(s)* can be made feminine (*la (las) una(s)* and *la (las) otra(s)* when either the *one(s)* or the *other(s)* (or both) is (are) exclusively women. If you say, for example, "*Se lavan la cara el uno a la otra*" (or "*... la una al otro*"), you're clearly showing that one man and one woman are involved in this reciprocal action.

## USE REFLEXIVE FOR THE ACCIDENTAL

If you did something by accident rather than on purpose, in Spanish you would often make it appear that it was not you who did it, but that the event happened to you. In other words, if you broke your leg, you would say what would literally mean *The leg broke itself to me*, which, of course, involves the reflexive use of the verb: *Se me rompió la pierna*. You're saying that *you* didn't do it; the *leg* did it to you. The most common verbs used in this way are: *romper* (to break), *olvidar* (to forget), *perder* (to lose), and *caer* (to fall, used for to drop). See the following examples, and practice saying them aloud:

*Se me rompió la pierna.*
I broke my leg. (Itself to me broke the leg.)

*Se me olvidaron los libros.*
I forgot the books. (Themselves to me forgot the books.)

*Se les perdió todo el dinero.*
They lost all their money. (Itself to them lost all the money.)

*¿Se te cayeron los cheques?*
Did you drop the checks? (Themselves to you fell the checks?)

*Sí, se me cayeron.*
Yes, I dropped them. (Yes, themselves to me they fell.)

**GO TO** ▶
To review irregular preterit tense verbs such as *cayeron*, see Hour 5.

With regard to the last Spanish sample sentence, *caer* means *to fall*, and *dejar caer* (to let fall) is what is used in Spanish for the English verb *to drop*. No single verb means *to drop*. *He dropped it* would be *Lo dejó caer*. The verb *caer* is often used reflexively (*caerse*) with no difference in meaning, just as the word *down* added to the English verb *to fall* (He fell down) adds nothing to the meaning.

## USE THE ANONYMOUS SUBJECT

Sometimes the action of the verb is more important than the subject. There are many techniques to de-emphasize the subject. Look at the following list for examples in both English and Spanish:

- In English, we can use the word *one*, as in *One doesn't smoke here*. Spanish does exactly the same thing: *Uno no fuma aquí*.

- In English, we can use a nonspecific *they*, as in *They say it's going to rain*. Spanish does the same, but goes one step further by omitting *ellos*: *Dicen que va a llover*.

- In English, we often use the pronoun *you*, pronounced *yuh*, as in *Yuh don't smoke here*. Spanish can do the same, as in *Ud. No fuma* (*Tú no fumas*) *aquí*.

- In English, the passive voice can be used for the same purpose in many (but not all) cases. For example, we can say *Many books are sold here* instead of *One sells many books here*. Spanish, too, can use the passive voice for anonymity: *Muchos libros son vendidos*; however, it is not used as frequently as it is in English.

**GO TO** ▶
For a review of the passive voice, see Hour 10.

## USE REFLEXIVE VERBS WITH ANONYMOUS SUBJECTS

Let's look at the five different ways we can express this anonymous subject sentence, *Many books are sold here* or *One sells many books here*, in Spanish:

- **One.** *Uno vende muchos libros aquí.*
- **They.** *Venden muchos libros aquí.*
- **You (Yuh).** *Ud. vende muchos libros aquí.*
- **Passive voice.** *Muchos libros son vendidos aquí.*
- **Reflexive.** *Aquí se venden muchos libros.*

The subject of the fourth sentence is *muchos libros*, so, naturally, the verb ends with *-n*, the unvarying sign of the third person plural (*ellos*). In the last sentence, the verb, with the telltale object pronoun *se*, is reflexive (subject and object are identical). The sentence very literally means *Many books sell themselves here*.

### PROCEED WITH CAUTION

Spanish can't "speak itself," but a person *is* capable of doing things to him- or herself, so don't say, for example, "*Se mató Juan,*" for the meaning *Juan was killed*, because it means *Juan killed himself*. Instead, simply add the personal *a* after the verb: *Se mató a Juan.*

If the subject were singular, then the verb would reflect this by being in the third person singular: *Aquí se vende un libro por día.*

Study the following examples, and practice saying them aloud:

(1) *La puerta se abrió.* (The door [was] opened.)

(2) *Las puertas se abrieron.* (The doors [were] opened.)

(3) *Aquí se habla español.* (Spanish is spoken here.)

(4) *Aquí se hablan español e inglés.* (Spanish and English are spoken here.)

(5) *Se quiere tener éxito.* (People want to be successful.)

(6) *Se alquilan apartamentos.* (Apartments for rent.)

(7) *Se busca empleado.* (Employee wanted [sought, looked for].)

Literally, sentence 1 means *The door opened itself.* Because the subject (*puerta*) is singular, the verb is singular. This is true of sentence 3, in which the subject is the singular *español;* of sentence 5, in which the subject is *tener éxito;* and of sentence 7, in which the subject is *empleado.*

The subject of sentence 2 is the plural *puertas,* so the verb is plural. This is also true of sentence 4, in which the subject is the *español e inglés* (*two* languages); and of sentence 6, in which the subject is the plural *apartamentos.*

Often, there is no grammatical subject at all. For example, the English sentence *One doesn't speak here,* or *You don't talk here,* would be, using the reflexive verb for the nonspecific subject in Spanish, *Aquí no se habla.* The English sentences have a grammatical subject (even though nonspecific): *One* or *You.* But there is no visible subject in the Spanish counterpart. It could be thought of as literally meaning *It doesn't speak itself here.* As you know, *it* as a subject is implicit, but not expressed. When there is no visible subject, the third person singular form of the verb is always used. Practice with the following examples:

*No se fuma aquí.* (No smoking here. [One doesn't smoke here].)

*Si se desea, se puede.* (If one wishes, one can.)

*Se trabaja en esta oficina.* (One works [You work] in this office.)

*Se archiva de esta manera.* (One files in this manner.)

*Se llega a las nueve en punto.* (One arrives at nine o'clock on the dot.)

Often the reflexive verb with the anonymous/invisible subject is a verb of informing, or believing, followed by the relative pronoun *que* and another clause that tells what the information or belief is. In this case, the verb is always singular. Practice saying the following sentences:

*Se dice que va a llover.*
They say (that) it's going to rain.

*Se informa que habrá guerra.*
It is reported that there will be war.

*Se cree que el jefe no vendrá hoy.*
It is believed that the boss won't come today.

*Se piensa que la secretaria trabaja demasiado.*
It is thought (people think) that the secretary works too much.

## USE OFFICE TERMINOLOGY

The following is a useful vocabulary list referring to office work.

### Vocabulario para la Oficina

| Spanish | English |
|---|---|
| la agenda (f.) | agenda |
| la agenda de compromisos (f.) | appointment book |
| anunciar | to announce |
| archivar | to file |
| el archivero (m.) | file cabinet; file clerk |
| el archivo (m.) | files |
| el bolígrafo (m.) | ballpoint pen |
| el buzón (m.) | mail box |
| el cadete (m.) | office boy, trainee; cadet |
| la carpeta (f.) | file, dossier |
| la carta (f.) | letter (written communication, not alphabet) |
| la cita (f.) | appointment; date |
| citar | to make an appointment |
| comercial (adj.) | commercial, business |
| el compromiso (m.) | appointment; commitment; arbitration; engagement, betrothal; compromising situation |
| la computadora (f.) | computer |
| la copiadora (f.) | copier |
| el correo (m.) | mail; post office |
| el correo electrónico (m.) | electronic mail (e-mail) |

*continues*

*continued*

| Spanish | English |
|---|---|
| el departamento (m.) | department |
| echar al correo | to mail |
| el/la ejecutivo/a (m./f.) | executive |
| el e-mail (m.) | e-mail |
| escribir | to write |
| escribir a computadora | to write on the computer |
| el escritorio (m.) | desk |
| la estampilla (f.) | (postage) stamp |
| la etiqueta (f.) | label |
| el fax (m.) | fax |
| la goma (f.) | rubber; rubber band |
| la impresión de una computadora (f.) | computer printout |
| imprimir | to impress; to print |
| la impresora (f.) | printer |
| el/la jefe (m./f.) | boss |
| el lápiz (m.) | pencil |
| llegar a tiempo | to arrive on time |
| llegar temprano | to arrive early |
| llegar tarde | to arrive late |
| el mensaje (m.) | message |
| meter | to put (something) into (something) |
| la oficina (f.) | office |
| el/la oficinista (m./f.) | office worker, clerk |
| la pantalla (f.) | screen (for movie, TV, computer) |
| el papel (m.) | paper; piece of paper |
| el ordenador (m.) | computer (in Spain only) |
| la pluma (estilográfica) (f.) | pen |
| la regla (f.) | rule; ruler |
| el reloj (m.) | clock; watch |
| la reunión (f.) | meeting; get-together |
| reunirse | to meet; gather together |
| el sacapuntas (m.) | pencil sharpener |
| el/la secretario/a (m./f.) | secretary |

| Spanish | English |
| --- | --- |
| el sello (m.) | (postage) stamp |
| el sello de goma (m.) | rubber stamp |
| el sobre (m.) | envelope |
| el sueldo (m.) | salary |
| el sujetador (m.) | fastener |
| el sujetapapeles (m.) | paper clip |
| sujetar | to hold down; to hold fast |
| el tablero de anuncios (m.) | bulletin board |
| la tecla (f.) | key (of keyboard) |
| el teclado (m.) | keyboard |
| las tijeras (f. pl.) | scissors |
| el timbre (m.) | bell, buzzer; (postage) stamp (Mexico) |
| la tinta (f.) | ink |

**TIME SAVER**

Spanish-speakers often use the English abbreviation for electronic mail: *e-mail*. Sometimes *un emilio* is used in a very informal, jocular tone.

Study the following sentences, and practice saying them:

*El oficinista se prepara para trabajar.*
The clerk gets ready (prepares himself) for work.

*Se escriben muchas cartas comerciales.*
Many business letters are written.

*Nos escribimos a menudo.*
We write to each other often.

*Se puede decir o "el correo electrónico" o "el e-mail."*
One can say either "electronic mail" or "e-mail."

*No se escribe con lápiz; se usa bolígrafo.*
You don't write in pencil; you use a (ballpoint) pen.

*Se echaron las cartas al correo.*
The letters were mailed (were thrown into the mail).

*En la reunión se habló de los sueldos.*
Salaries were discussed at the meeting.

*Se reunieron para café.*
They got together for coffee.

*En la oficina se trabaja mucho.*
At the office one works hard.

*Se llamó al presidente.*
The president was called.

## LEARN THE DAYS OF THE WEEK

In business, it helps to know on what day of the week you're supposed to meet a client. Learn the following vocabulary:

| | |
|---|---|
| el día | day |
| la semana | week |
| el domingo | Sunday |
| el lunes | Monday |
| el martes | Tuesday |
| el miércoles | Wednesday |
| el jueves | Thursday |
| el viernes | Friday |
| el sábado | Saturday |

Note: To make plural the days that end with -*s*, only change the definite article to plural: *Monday = el lunes; Mondays = los lunes.* If you do something on a certain day, the word *on* is not translated: *Voy el martes = I'm going on Tuesday; Voy los martes = I go on Tuesdays.*

## LEARN THE MONTHS

It would be very inconvenient to know the day but not the month you are to meet a client. Study the following list:

| | |
|---|---|
| enero | January |
| febrero | February |

| marzo | March |
| abril | April |
| mayo | May |
| junio | June |
| julio | July |
| agosto | August |
| septiembre | September |
| octubre | October |
| noviembre | November |
| diciembre | December |

Additional vocabulary: *el mes* (the month); *los meses del año* (the months of the year).

---

**PROCEED WITH CAUTION**

The first of the month is *el primero,* but all the rest use the cardinal numbers: *el dos, el tres, el cuatro, el cinco,* and so on.

To give dates, use the definite article, then the number, then *de*, then the month; for example, *Hoy es el primero de junio* (Today is June first); *Es el veinticinco de enero* (It's January 25). *Hoy es lunes, el quince de octubre de 2005.* (Today is Monday, October 15, 2005.) Remember that the year would be given as *dos mil cinco*.

GO TO ▶
See Hour 8 to review the numbers in the thousands.

## THE 30-SECOND RECAP

During this hour, you've learned how to use reflexive verbs for several purposes, and you've learned how to use vocabulary necessary for working in an office, including dates (days of the week, months, years).

## HOUR'S UP!

Review this hour's work, and then test yourself by answering the following questions. Remember, don't look back at the corresponding pages while taking the quiz.

1. Choose the phrase that is equivalent to the one given: *Dicen que va a llover.*

   **a.** Se dicen que va a llover.

   **b.** Uno dicen que va a llover.

   **c.** Se dice que va a llover.

   **d.** All of the above.

2. Choose the phrase that is equivalent to the one given: *Aquí se habla inglés.*

   **a.** Aquí hablan inglés.

   **b.** Aquí tú hablas inglés.

   **c.** Aquí uno habla inglés.

   **d.** All of the above.

3. Choose the phrase that is equivalent to the one given: *No se sabe.*

   **a.** No es sabido.

   **b.** Uno no sabe.

   **c.** Nadie sabe.

   **d.** All of the above.

4. Choose the closest, most correct, most normal Spanish translation: He broke his head.

   **a.** Rompió su cabeza.

   **b.** Se rompió su cabeza.

   **c.** Su cabeza fue rota.

   **d.** Se le rompió la cabeza.

5. Choose the closest, most correct, most normal Spanish translation: We forgot our appointment.

   **a.** Se nos olvidó nuestra cita.

   **b.** Nos olvidó nuestra cita.

   **c.** Olvidamos nuestra cita.

   **d.** Le nos olvidó nuestra cita.

# Hour 16

# At the Mall

## CHAPTER SUMMARY

**LESSON PLAN:**

In this hour, you'll learn ...

- How to use the present perfect tense.
- How to handle two object pronouns (direct and indirect) with the same verb.
- How to talk about shopping.

If you ever intend to go shopping in a Spanish-speaking country, or even in many parts of the United States, there are a number of lexical items you would want to be able to use. Fortunately, you already know the numerical system, which will help you with prices. Learn the vocabulary in the following table.

### Vocabulario para Ir de Compras

| Spanish | English |
| --- | --- |
| el abrigo (m.) | overcoat |
| el algodón (m.) | cotton |
| alto/a | high; tall |
| el anillo (m.) | ring (plain band) |
| el anillo de boda (m.) | wedding ring |
| bajo/a | low; short (stature) |
| barato/a | cheap, inexpensive |
| la blusa (f.) | blouse |
| la bota (f.) | boot |
| el botón (m.) | button |
| el calcetín (m.) | sock (Spain) |
| la camisa (f.) | shirt |
| la campera (f.) | zipper jacket |
| caro/a | expensive, costly |
| el centro (de la ciudad) (m.) | downtown; center (of the city) |
| el centro comercial (m.) | shopping center, plaza |
| el collar (m.) | necklace |

*continues*

### Vocabulario para Ir de Compras (continued)

| Spanish | English |
| --- | --- |
| el comercio (m.) | business, commerce; store (Argentina/Uruguay/Chile) |
| la compra (f.) | purchase |
| el/la comprador/a (m./f.) | buyer, shopper |
| comprar | to buy, to purchase |
| costar (ue) | to cost |
| el cuello (m.) | collar; neck |
| la chaqueta (f.) | jacket |
| el/la dependiente/a (m./f.) | store clerk, salesperson |
| el dinero (m.) | money |
| la falda (f.) | skirt |
| fino/a | fine |
| la galería comercial (f.) | shopping mall |
| la ganga (f.) | bargain, good deal |
| gastar | to spend (money, not time) |
| la gorra (f.) | cap (with visor) |
| el gorro (m.) | cap (without visor) |
| grande | big, large |
| el impermeable (m.) | raincoat |
| ir de compras | to go shopping |
| la lana (f.) | wool |
| el lino (m.) | linen |
| la media (f.) | stocking; sock (Latin America) |
| mediano/a | medium |
| el mercado (m.) | market |
| el negocio (m.) | business deal; store (Argentina/Uruguay/Chile) |
| el nilón (m.) | nylon |
| el pantalón (m.) | trousers |
| pequeño/a | small, little |
| la plata (f.) | silver; money |
| el precio (m.) | price |
| la pulsera (f.) | bracelet; watch band; wrist bandage |
| regalar | to give (as a gift), regale |

| Spanish | English |
| --- | --- |
| el regalo (m.) | gift, present |
| regatear | to haggle, to bargain |
| la ropa (f.) | clothes, clothing |
| la ropa interior (f.) | underwear |
| la seda (f.) | silk |
| la sandalia (f.) | sandal |
| el sombrero (m.) | hat (with brim) |
| la sortija (f.) | ring |
| el suéter (m.) | sweater |
| el supermercado (m.) | supermarket |
| el tamaño (m.) | size |
| la tarjeta (de crédito) (f.) | (credit) card |
| la tela (f.) | cloth |
| el/la tendero/a (m./f.) | shopkeeper |
| la tienda (f.) | store, shop |
| el traje (m.) | suit |
| el traje de baño (m.) | bathing suit |
| valer | to be worth |
| valor | value; valor |
| el/la vendedor/a (m./f.) | seller, vendor |
| vender | to sell |
| la venta (f.) | sale |
| el vestido (m.) | dress |
| vestir(se) (i) | to wear; to dress (to get dressed) |
| la zapatería (f.) | shoe store |
| el zapato (m.) | shoe |

### Modismos (Idioms)

| | |
| --- | --- |
| A menos de | At less than |
| ¿Cuánto vale? | How much is it? (How much is it worth?) |
| ¿En qué puedo servirle? | How may I help you? (In what can I serve you?) |
| Me las llevo. | I'll take them. |
| quedarse con | to keep (to stay with) |

*continues*

**Vocabulario para Ir de Compras** (continued)

| Spanish | English |
| --- | --- |
| ¿Qué le parece? | What do you think? (What does it seem to you?) |
| Ir de compras | to go shopping |

**JUST A MINUTE**

In Spain, *medias* are *stockings,* and *calcetines* are *socks.* In Latin America, *medias* are both (stockings and socks).

Practice saying the following sentences aloud:

*Hija mía, mañana vamos a la galería (comercial).*
Daughter, tomorrow we're going to the mall.

*¿Es que vamos de compras, Mamá?*
(Is it that) we're going shopping, Mom?

*Claro, y vamos a gastar mucho dinero.*
Of course, and we're going to spend a lot of money.

*¿Y, qué compraremos?*
And, what will we buy?

*¿Bueno, necesitamos mucha ropa, no?*
Well, we need a lot of clothing, don't we?

*Es verdad. Yo necesito unas faldas nuevas.*
It's true. I need some new skirts.

**JUST A MINUTE**

*Bathing suit* in some Latin American countries is *la malla,* which in Texas Spanish refers to stretch material used in tights. Elsewhere it means *mesh* or *netting* or *coat of mail.* Bathing suit in Cuba is *la trusa.*

## LEARN USEFUL IDIOMS (*MODISMOS ÚTILES*)

The following list introduces some useful idioms that might come in handy on your shopping trip:

- *Es verdad.* (It's true.)
- *¿No es verdad?* Literally, *Isn't it true?* This is a common "tag" question, added to a positive statement, equivalent to the English *Isn't that right?*

(or Isn't it? or Aren't you? or Isn't he? or True? or Right? or Don't you? or Doesn't she?). For example, *Él sabe, ¿no es verdad?* (He knows, doesn't he?) or *Necesitamos mucha ropa, ¿no es verdad?* (We need a lot of clothes, don't we?) or *Es bonito, ¿no es verdad?* (It's pretty, isn't it?).

In the same way that we shorten this tag question from Isn't it true? to simply True? or Isn't that right? to Right? Spanish-speakers often shorten *¿No es verdad?* to either *¿Verdad?* or to the simple *¿No?*

- *Tú vienes, ¿no es verdad?* (You're coming, aren't you?)
- *Tú vienes, ¿verdad?* (You're coming, right?)
- *Tú vienes, ¿no?* (You're coming, right?)

**JUST A MINUTE**

The English translations in the preceding bulleted list are not literal; they're just likely equivalents. The English for all three of the preceding sentences could just as well have been *You're coming, isn't that so?*

- *¿Qué va?* Literally, *What goes?* It is used when you are surprised at what the other person said or did, or if you're surprised at the situation. It could just as well be translated as *Are you kidding?* or *What do you mean?* or *Give me a break!* or even *Heck, no!* or *Heck, yes!*
- *Aquí tiene Ud.* (or *Aquí tienes*, and so on). Literally, *Here you have*, is used in Spanish when giving someone something. In English we say, "Here's …."

Study the following sentences, and practice saying them aloud:

**El dependiente:** *Buenos días, señor. ¿En qué puedo servirle?* (Good morning [or Good day], sir. How can I help you?)

**Víctor:** *Estoy buscando unas camisas y quizás un par de pantalones.* (I'm looking for some shirts and perhaps a pair of pants.)

**El dependiente:** *Muy bien. Aquí tiene Ud. camisas muy finas. ¿Qué le parece?* (Very well. Here are (you have) some very fine shirts. What do you think?)

**Víctor:** *Ah, sí, son muy lindas. ¿Cuánto valen?* (Oh, yes, they're very nice [pretty]. How much are they?)

**El dependiente:** *Se venden a doscientos cuarenta pesos cada una.* (They sell for 240 pesos each.)

**Víctor:** *Hombre, ¡son muy caras!* (Man, they're very expensive!)

**El dependiente:** *Puede ser, señor, pero, Ud. puede ver, son bonitas.* (Maybe so [it can be], sir, but, you can see, they're good-looking [pretty].)

**Víctor:** *Es verdad. Yo podría comprar tres camisas a un precio más bajo.* (It's true. I could buy three shirts at a lower price.)

**El dependiente:** *Bueno, si nos compra tres camisas, puede llevárselas a doscientos pesos cada una. Un total de seiscientos pesos. ¡Una ganga!* (Well, if you buy three shirts from us, you can take them home (carry them off) for 200 pesos each. A total of 600 pesos.)

**Víctor:** *Le doy quinientos pesos por las tres.* (I'll give you 500 pesos for the three of them.)

**El dependiente:** *Ah, no. Lo siento, señor, pero no puedo venderlas a menos de quinientos cincuenta pesos por las tres camisas.* (Oh, no. I'm sorry, sir, but I can't sell them at less than 550 pesos for the three shirts.)

**Víctor:** *Muy bien. Muy bien. Me las llevo.* (Okay. Okay. I'll take them [with me].)

## LEARN THE COLORS

Knowing the words for colors will be helpful if you go shopping. Study the following list:

| | |
|---|---|
| amarillo/a | yellow |
| azul | blue |
| blanco/a | white |
| (color) café (m.) | brown |
| colorado/a | red |
| gris | gray |
| marrón | brown |
| morado/a | purple |
| anaranjado/a | orange |
| negro/a | black |
| pardo | brown |
| purpúreo/a | purple |
| rojo/a | red |
| rosado/a | pink |
| verde | green |
| violeta (f.) | violet |

**GO TO** ▶

For a review of the indirect object pronouns, including the placement of object pronouns in general, see Hour 11.

**JUST A MINUTE**

All but two of the colors are adjectives. *Café* and *violeta* are nouns used to describe colors (coffee color and violet); as such, they don't agree in number or gender with the nouns they modify.

Study the following list of sentences using the vocabulary from this hour. Notice how the words for colors agree with the terms they modify:

*Quiero comprar una camisa azul y otra blanca.*
I want to buy one blue shirt and another white (one).

*¿Aquí se venden blusas amarillas o verdes?*
Are yellow or green blouses sold here?

*¿Prefiere Ud. un sombrero gris o (color) café?*
Do you prefer a gray or brown hat?

*Me gustaría comprar una gorra roja.*
I'd like to buy a red cap.

*Busco un par de pantalones marrones de lana.*
I'm looking for a pair of brown woolen trousers.

## HANDLE DOUBLE-OBJECT PRONOUNS

Up to this point, you've learned to use the indirect object pronouns, the direct object pronouns, and the reflexive object pronouns. But you've been handling them separately. Now it is time to learn to use them together—that is, as objects of the same verb at the same time. We do this in English all the time, as in the sentence *I gave it to him.* Now you'll learn how to do this in Spanish.

### PLACE THE PRONOUNS IN ORDER

You've already learned the position of object pronouns, whether direct, in-direct, or reflexive, with relation to the verb. Now, when you use more than one object pronoun with a verb, you need to know the order in which to place them with relation to each other.

When you have two object pronouns (three is extremely rare) of the same verb, the order in which to place them is invariably as follows: The reflexive pronoun is always first; the indirect object pronoun is always second; the direct object pronoun is always last (reflexive + indirect + direct).

We're going to take sentences with verbs that have two objects; one will be in the form of a noun, and the other will in the form of a pronoun. We're going to change these sentences so that both objects will be in the form of a pronoun. In this way, you'll see two object pronouns working together.

These sentences have an indirect object pronoun and a direct object noun, which will be transformed into a direct object pronoun:

> *Carlos me da los lápices.* (Carlos gives me the pencils.)
>
> *Carlos me los da.* (Carlos gives them to me.)
>
> *Yo te dí el cuaderno.* (I gave you the notebook.)
>
> *Yo te lo dí.* (I gave it to you.)
>
> *Ellas nos dijeron la verdad.* (They told us the truth.)
>
> *Ellas nos la dijeron.* (They told it to us.)
>
> *María os escribió unas cartas.* (María wrote you some letters.)
>
> *María os las escribió.* (María wrote them to you.)

Notice, in the preceding sentences, that in each case of two object pronouns, the indirect object pronoun (*me, te, nos, os*) always precedes the direct object pronouns (*los, lo, la, las*). This is always the case.

You may have noticed that none of the preceding sample sentences have two third person object pronouns. This was not an oversight; there is a special peculiarity that takes place in the case of two third person object pronouns. What happens in this case can be stated in the following manner:

If …

- There are two object pronouns of the same verb,
- One is direct, the other is indirect,
- Both are grammatically third person,
- Then the first one (always the indirect object pronoun), will change to *se.*

(Keep in mind that *Ud.* and *Uds.*, although semantically second person, are considered grammatically third person.)

---

Let's take a look at an example containing two object pronouns both in the third person; here's the first stage:

*Ricardo dio las revistas a María.*
Ricardo gave María the magazines.

In the next stage, the indirect object noun (María) is transformed into the third person indirect object pronoun *le* (to him, to her, to it) while the direct object noun (*revistas*) remains unchanged:

*Ricardo le dio las revistas.*
Ricardo gave her the magazines.

In the next stage, the direct object noun (*revistas*) is transformed into the third person feminine plural direct object pronoun *las* (them), while the indirect object pronoun (María) remains unchanged:

*Ricardo las dio a María.*
Ricardo gave them to María.

In the final stage, you would expect to bring down the *le* from the previous example first (because the indirect object pronoun always precedes the direct object pronoun), and then bring down the *las* right after it, forming *\*Ricardo le las dio*. But this does not happen. The first of the two object pronouns, *le*, is transformed into *se* because it is in front of a third person direct object pronoun:

*Ricardo se las dio.*
Ricardo gave them to her.

Remember, if there is any chance that the "*se*" (or the "*le*," for that matter) will not be easily identified by context, you can always add "*a él*," "*a ella*," "*a Ud.*," and, in the case of "*se*" for "*les*," "*a ellos*," "*a ellas*," or "*a Uds.*" Or you can add *a* plus a noun, whether common or proper (someone's name). For example, *Se las dio a ella,* or *Se las dio a María.* (For a review of this matter, see the lesson on indirect object pronouns in Hour 11.)

Keep in mind that the sentence of the first stage, although grammatically correct, 9 times out of 10 would have the redundant *le* in front of the verb, even though the specific direct object noun (María) is mentioned. It would come out *Ricardo le dio las revistas a María.* (This matter, too, can be reviewed in the lesson on indirect object pronouns in Hour 11.)

**PROCEED WITH CAUTION**

Even though both words sound the same and are spelled the same, there is absolutely no connection between the reflexive pronoun *se* and the *se* resulting from *le* or *les*. Do not confuse the meaning.

Study the following sentences for understanding, then practice saying them aloud, picturing who does what to whom, and with what:

(1) *María me trajo un regalo.* (María brought me a gift.)

(2) *María me lo trajo.* (María brought it to me.)

(3) *Yo le dí un collar (a ella).* (I gave her a necklace.)

(4) *Yo se lo dí (a ella).* (I gave it to her.)

(5) *Te compraron una camisa.* (They bought you a shirt.)

(6) *Te la compraron.* (They bought it for you.)

(7) *Roberto le dio dos regalos (a Ud.).* (Roberto gave you two gifts.)

(8) *Roberto se los dio (a Ud.).* (Roberto gave them to you.)

(9) *Elena me aceptó las joyas.* (Elena accepted the jewels from me.)

(10) *Elena me las aceptó.* (Elena accepted them from me.)

Sentences 3, 4, 7, and 8 show the change from *le* or *les* to *se* in front of direct object pronouns beginning with the letter *l*.

**JUST A MINUTE**

There is no plural form of *se;* it converts from either the singular *le* or the plural *les.*

## USE THE VERB *IRSE*

You've already learned to use the reflexive verbs (true reflexive and reciprocal usage) as well as for anonymous subjects. You've also seen how certain reflexive verbs seem to be almost unrelated to the nonreflexive form of the same verb, if you go by the English translation. You've learned to understand the real meaning behind them by thinking in Spanish. There is one important and commonly used verb, which is intransitive, but is commonly used as a reflexive verb. The difference in signification is subtle, yet very real.

You are very familiar with the intransitive verb *ir* (to go). The verb is also used reflexively, *irse* (roughly, to go away).

When you use the verb *ir*, the important concept in your mind is the place to which you're going, not the place you're leaving. Whether or not you mention the place to which you're going, you have it in mind. See the following examples:

**GO TO** ▶

For an explanation of the oft-heard expression *¡Vámonos!*, see the lesson on commands in Hour 19.

> *¿Adónde vas ahora?* (Where are you going now?)
>
> *Voy al centro comercial.* (I'm going to the mall.)
>
> *¿Adónde fueron Uds. ayer?* (Where did you go yesterday?)
>
> *Fuimos al cine.* (We went to the movies.)
>
> *¿Adónde vamos a ir mañana?* (Where are we going to go tomorrow?)
>
> *Vamos a ir a Taco Bell.* (We're going to go to Taco Bell.)
>
> *¿Cuándo van Uds.?* (When are you going?)
>
> *Vamos a las dos.* (We're going at two o'clock.)

Although no destination is mentioned in the last two sentences, you can assume that the two people have a specific destination in mind because *ir* is used.

When you use the reflexive verb *irse*, the main idea in your mind is *not* the place to which you're going; rather, it is the place from which you're going *away*. You're referring to leaving the place you are in, and not being specific about any possible destination—*irse* is about going away, leaving, or getting out of a location, not about heading for a specific destination. This makes it practically synonymous with *salir* (to leave) in most cases. See the following examples:

> *Me voy y no vuelvo.* (I'm going [away] and not coming back.)
>
> *Ella se fue ayer.* (She went away [left] yesterday.)
>
> *Nos vamos de aquí.* (We're getting out of here.)
>
> *Se irían, pero ….* (They would leave, but ….)
>
> *¿Te vas mañana?* (Are you going away tomorrow?)

In the second sentence, to inquire about where she went, you would de-reflexivize the verb by saying "*¿Adónde fue?*"

## UNDERSTAND *IRSE PARA*

You should know, however, that in the dialects of the Caribbean and other areas, and in very colloquial language, the reflexive *irse* is used with the preposition *para* to mean *to go to*, or *to head for*, with a specific destination in mind.

See the following examples:

*¿Para dónde te vas?* (Where are you heading?)

*Me voy para el centro.* (I'm heading downtown [the center].)

*¿Para dónde se fue ella?* (Where did she go?)

*Se fue para la tienda.* (She went to the store.)

In many areas, certainly including the ones in which the *irse para* is used as described in the preceding exercise, the common pronunciation of *para* is *pa* (*Me voy pa la tienda*).

## TELL WHAT YOU HAVE DONE

Present perfect tense: You know how to talk about events in the present, the past, and the future, and events that are conditional. There is a tense, in English and Spanish, which refers to actions that have taken place at some indeterminate time before the present, and which are still relevant to the present. This tense is called the present perfect.

**GO TO** ▶

For a review of the formation of the past participle and its use as an adjective, see Hour 9.

In both English and Spanish, the present perfect is a compound tense; that is, the verbs have two parts: a helping verb (auxiliary verb) plus the past participle. You have already mastered the past participle; you've used it as an adjective to describe conditions, and you've used it with *ser* to form the passive voice. Now you're going to learn to use it as part of the present perfect tense.

In English, the helping verb placed in front of the past participle is *to have*. To see how similar the Spanish present perfect tense is to the English, glance at these English examples:

I have eaten. (I've eaten.)

Have you seen her?

We have not (seen her). (We haven't.)

They have been here for an hour. (They've been here ....)

Has he left yet?

No, he has not (left). (No, he hasn't [left].)

The use of the auxiliary verb *to have* plus the past participle to form the present perfect tense has as its purpose to speak of an event that took place some time before right now. But you don't tell exactly at what point in the past.

You know how to form the Spanish past participle. The helping verb is *not* the usual word that actually means *to have* or *to possess* (*tener*), but the specialized verb *haber*. For the present perfect tense, *haber* will be conjugated in the present tense, just as the English verb *to have* is conjugated in the present tense for the same purpose. Learn the conjugation of *haber* in the present tense by studying the following table.

**Present Tense of Auxiliary Verb *Haber***

| Subject Pronoun | Haber | Subject Pronoun | Haber |
| --- | --- | --- | --- |
| yo | he | nosotros/as | hemos |
| tú | has | vosotros/as | habéis |
| él | ha | ellos | han |
| ella | ha | ellas | han |
| usted | ha | ustedes | han |

As you can see, the verb *haber* in the present tense is highly irregular. Only the *vosotros/as* form is regular, coming directly from the infinitive form of the verb.

In previous lessons, the past participle agreed with the noun it referred to in number and gender. This is *not* the case when it is part of a compound (perfect) tense. When used with the auxiliary verb *haber*, it is part of a compound tense; this means it is not being used as an adjective, but rather is part of a verb system. As such, it is invariable, and will always end in the letter *-o*.

**GO TO** ▶

You've used *haber* for a different purpose, and with the peculiar form *hay* in third person singular present tense. See Hour 12 for the lesson on *haber*.

Study the following sentences, and then practice saying them aloud:

(Yo) *He comprado un traje nuevo.* (I've bought a new suit.)

*¿Has sabido el precio del abrigo?* (Have you found out the price of the coat?)

*Ya hemos comido.* (We've already eaten.)

*¿Qué han hecho ellos?* (What have they done?)

*Han vendido las perlas.* (They've sold the pearls.)

*¿Habéis ido al cine?* (Have you gone to the movies?)

*No, todavía no hemos ido.* (No, we haven't gone yet [still haven't gone].)

*¿Han visto Uds. el collar de oro?* (Have you seen the gold necklace?)

*Sí, lo hemos visto.* (Yes, we've seen it.)

### Understand *Ya* and *Todavía*

Notice the vocabulary items *ya* and *todavía* in the third and seventh sentences in the previous list. *Ya* means *already*, and, therefore, refers to the beginning or end of an action at a point in time prior to another specified time: *Ya he comido* = *I've already eaten* (that is, before now). It is sometimes used in a way that makes it very close to the meaning of *ahora* (now): *¡Vamos ya!* (Let's go already [now]!)

---

**JUST A MINUTE**

The idiom *ya no* plus a verb means *no longer* or *anymore*. *Ya no vive aquí* = *He no longer lives here* or *He doesn't live here anymore*.

---

*Todavía* means *still*; it refers to the continuation in the present of an action or situation that started in the past. (*Estamos comiendo todavía* = *We're still eating*.)

In some contexts, they can both be translated into English by the ambiguous word *yet*. Don't let this confuse you. Think in terms of *already* and *still* (beginning or end of an action prior to a certain time as opposed to an act continuing from the past). See the following sentences:

(1) *¿Han comido ya?* (Have they eaten yet? [Have they already eaten?])

(2) *No, no han comido todavía.* (No, they haven't eaten yet. [They still haven't eaten.])

(3) *¿Ya se han ido?* (Have they gone away yet? [Have they gone away already?])

(4) *No, todavía no se han ido.* (No, they have not gone away yet. [No, they still haven't gone away.])

All four sentences can use the word *yet* in English. But if you limit yourself to a choice between *already* and *still*, the difference becomes clear. Sentences 1 and 3 ask if an action has taken place (finished eating; finished going away) before a specified time (*now* in these sentences), whereas sentences 2 and 4 refer to the continuation of a previous situation (*not* having eaten; *not* having gone away).

## Recognize a Literary Tense

In English, as you know, we can refer to an action that took place any time before the present (present perfect), without specifying when, by using the present tense of the auxiliary verb *to have* plus the past participle: I *have* eaten (*He comido*). We can also refer to an action that took place any time before some point in the *past*, by using the pluperfect (or past perfect) plus the past participle: I *had* eaten.

Spanish has two ways to show that an action took place before a point in the past. One of those ways, the *preterit perfect tense,* is not used very much in ordinary conversation; it is found, though, in literary texts. Because you might come across this in your readings, it is treated in this lesson for recognition purposes. It is formed by using the preterit tense of the auxiliary verb *haber* plus the *past participle.* See the following table for the conjugation of *haber* in the preterit tense.

**Preterite Tense of the Auxiliary Verb *Haber***

| Subject Pronoun | Haber | Subject Pronoun | Haber |
|---|---|---|---|
| yo | hube | nosotros/as | hubimos |
| tú | hubiste | vosotros/as | hubisteis |
| él | hubo | ellos | hubieron |
| ella | hubo | ellas | hubieron |
| usted | hubo | ustedes | hubieron |

**GO TO ▶**
The third person singular form of *haber* in the preterit tense (*hubo*) has already been presented with the meaning *there was* or *there were.* See Hour 12.

Study the following sentences:

*Cuando llamó ella, yo ya hube salido.*
When she called, I had already gone out.

*Antes de irse, Carlos hubo comido.*
Before going away, Carlos had eaten.

*Se hubieron duchado cuando sonó el teléfono.*
They had taken a shower when the phone rang.

*Ya hubiste llegado cuando vine yo.*
You had already arrived when I came.

*Nos hubimos despertado antes que Ud.*
We had awakened before you.

**GO TO ▶**
The pluperfect tense is discussed in Hour 17.

This tense, the preterit perfect, which is not commonly used, is employed specifically to show that one thing had happened before another thing, which also happened in the past. In ordinary usage, the preterit tense or the pluperfect tense is used.

## QUIZ

## THE 30-SECOND RECAP

In this hour, you've learned to use the present perfect tense, to recognize the preterit perfect tense, and to handle two object pronouns (direct and indirect) of the same verb. You've also learned to speak about shopping at shops and malls, which involves verbs having to do with buying, selling, bargaining, and asking prices, and with nouns referring to clothing, jewelry, and colors.

## HOUR'S UP!

Review this hour's work, and then test yourself by taking the following quiz. Try not to refer back to the pages of this hour while actually taking the quiz.

1. Choose the correct transformation sentence with only object pronouns: *Carlos me dio dos libros.*

   **a.** Carlos me dos dio.

   **b.** Carlos me lo dio.

   **c.** Carlos me los dio.

   **d.** Carlos los me dio.

2. Choose the correct transformation sentence with only object pronouns: *Yo te dije la verdad.*

   **a.** Yo la te dije.

   **b.** Yo se la dije.

   **c.** Yo la se dije.

   **d.** Yo te la dije.

3. Choose the correct transformation sentence with only object pronouns: *Elena dio la tarjeta a los chicos.*

   **a.** Elena se la dio.

   **b.** Elena les la dio.

   **c.** Elena la les dio.

   **d.** Elena se los dio.

4. Choose the correct transformation sentence with only object pronouns: *Roberto regaló un sombrero a María.*

   **a.** Roberto se la regaló.

   **b.** Roberto se lo regaló.

   **c.** Roberto le lo regaló.

   **d.** Roberto le la regaló.

5. Choose the correct transformation sentence with only object pronouns: *Tú nos prestaste las esmeraldas*.

   a. Tú las nos prestaste.

   b. Tú nos las prestaste.

   c. Tú prestástelas a nosotros.

   d. Tú nos les prestaste.

6. Choose the best phrase or idiom to translate this English phrase: How may I help you?

   a. ¿En qué puedo servirle?

   b. ¿Cómo es Ud.?

   c. ¿Cómo está Ud.?

   d. ¡Para servirle a Ud.?

7. Choose the best phrase or idiom to translate this English phrase: How much is it (asking about the price)?

   a. ¿Cómo mucho es?

   b. ¿Cuántos son?

   c. ¿Cuánto vale Ud.?

   d. ¿Cuanto vale?

8. Choose the best phrase or idiom to translate this English phrase: I'll take them (with me).

   a. Me los tomo.

   b. Los tomaré.

   c. Me los llego.

   d. Me los llevo.

9. Give the best English translation: *No lo hemos roto todavía*.

   a. We hadn't broken it yet.

   b. We haven't broken it yet.

   c. We haven't ruptured him yet.

   d. We hadn't ruptured him yet.

**10.** Give the best English translation: *Ya han comido*.

    **a.** They're still eating.

    **b.** They still haven't eaten.

    **c.** They haven't eaten yet.

    **d.** They've already eaten.

# HOUR 17
# At the Market

## CHAPTER SUMMARY

**LESSON PLAN:**
In this hour, you'll learn ...

- How to shop at the market for food.
- Some of the differences between the prepositions *por* and *para*.
- How to form the infinitive perfect tense.

To shop for food, you'll need to have a vocabulary dealing with the places to buy the food (the grocery store, the butcher's, the fish shop, the market, the supermarket), as well as the vocabulary referring to the food products themselves. We're going to divide the vocabulary into various sections, in order to make it easier for you to seek out the words you want.

## FIND THE RIGHT PLACE

The following table identifies the places where you can buy (*comprar*) various kinds of *comestibles* (foodstuffs).

### *Vocabulario para Dónde Comprar Comestibles*

| Spanish | English |
| --- | --- |
| la abarrotería (f.) | grocery store |
| el abarrotero (m.) | grocer |
| los abarrotes (m. pl.) | groceries |
| el almacén (m.) | warehouse; grocery store; general store |
| el almacenero (m.) | owner of *almacén* |
| la bodega (f.) | grocery store (Caribbean) |
| el bodeguero (m.) | grocery store keeper (Caribbean) |
| la carnicería (f.) | butcher shop |
| el carnicero (m.) | butcher |
| el comercio (m.) | store; commerce; business |
| comestible (adj./m.) | edible; food product |

*continues*

### Vocabulario para Dónde Comprar Comestibles   (continued)

| Spanish | English |
|---|---|
| los comestibles (m. pl.) | foodstuffs, food |
| el (super)mercado (m.) | (super)market |
| el negocio (m.) | store; business; deal |
| la pescadería (f.) | fish market |
| la tienda (f.) | store |
| la tienda de abarrotes (f.) | grocery store |
| la tienda de comestibles (f.) | grocery store |
| la tienda de ultramarinos (f.) | grocery store (Spain) |
| los ultramarinos (m. pl.) | imported foods; groceries (Spain) |

**PROCEED WITH CAUTION**

Although there are many words for grocery, *grocería* is not one of them. Be careful not to use it; in Latin American Spanish, it sounds exactly like *grosería*, which means *vulgarity, coarse language or behavior*, or *dirty word*.

In most Latin American countries, the word *almacén* is usually employed with the meaning of department store. In other countries it means *grocery store*, whereas in Spain it refers to a warehouse. The word for *wine cellar* in Spain and elsewhere (*bodega*) refers to a grocery store in Puerto Rico (and in New York City).

**JUST A MINUTE**

You should know that *la libra* is the weight of a pound, and that *la onza* means *ounce*.

## NAME THE MEAT

Study the following list of words for meat, fowl, fish, and seafood.

### Vocabulario para Carnes y Fruta de Mar

| Spanish | English |
|---|---|
| **Carnes de Cuadrúpedos (Meat of Four-Legged Animals)** | |
| el biftec. bistec (m.) | beefsteak |
| la carne (f.) | meat; flesh |
| la carne de cerdo (f.) | pork |

| Spanish | English |
| --- | --- |
| la carne de carnero (f.) | mutton |
| la carne de oveja (f.) | mutton |
| la carne de res (f.) | beef |
| la carne de ternera (f.) | veal |
| la carne de vaca (f.) | beef |
| la carne molida (f.) | ground meat |
| la carne picada (f.) | chopped meat |
| la costilla (f.) | rib |
| la chuleta (f.) | chop |
| el hígado (m.) | liver |
| el jamón (m.) | ham |
| la lengua (de vaca) (f.) | (beef) tongue |
| el lomo (m.) | pork loin |
| la morcilla (f.) | blood sausage; blood pudding |
| el riñón (m.) | kidney |
| la salchicha (f.) | pork sausage |
| el salchichón (m.) | sausage |
| el solomillo (m.) | loin of beef, sirloin |
| el venado (m.) | venison |

### Carnes de Aves (Poultry)

| Spanish | English |
| --- | --- |
| el ala (f.) | wing |
| el ave (f.) | poultry (one bird) |
| las aves (f. pl.) | poultry |
| la gallina (f.) | hen |
| el gallo (m.) | rooster, cock |
| el muslo (m.) | thigh; drumstick |
| el pavo (m.) | turkey |
| la pechuga (f.) | breast; breast meat |
| la perdiz (f.) | partridge |
| el pollo (m.) | chicken |

### Fruta de Mar (Seafood)

| Spanish | English |
| --- | --- |
| la almeja (f.) | clam |
| el arenque (m.) | herring |

*continues*

**Vocabulario para Carnes y Fruta de Mar** (continued)

| Spanish | English |
|---|---|
| el atún (m.) | tuna |
| el bacalao (m.) | codfish |
| el calamar (m.) | squid |
| el camarón (m.) | shrimp (one) |
| los camarones (m. pl.) | shrimp (many) |
| el cangrejo (m.) | crab |
| la fruta de mar (f.) | seafood |
| la langosta (f.) | lobster |
| los mariscos (m. pl.) | shellfish |
| la merluza (f.) | hake |
| la oreja marina (f.) | abalone |
| la ostra (f.) | oyster |
| el pescado (m.) | fish |
| el pulpo (m.) | octopus |
| el salmón (m.) | salmon |
| la sardina (f.) | sardine |

**GO TO** ▶
*El ave* is a feminine noun; the plural for it is *las aves. El ala* is a feminine noun (plural, *las alas*). For an explanation of using *el* with a feminine noun, see Hour 2.

Note: In Spanish there is no difference between "meat" and "flesh."

**PROCEED WITH CAUTION**

While *langosta* means *lobster* in the ordinary context, you might read or hear about *langostas* darkening the sky and eating all the grain, causing a famine. This is because the same word also means *locust*.

In Puerto Rico, the word for a very common type of crab in the area, which is served in restaurants all over the island, is *juey* (plural, *jueyes*).

## NAME THE FRUITS AND VEGETABLES

Study the following list of fruits and vegetables.

**PROCEED WITH CAUTION**

The term *judía verde,* in the context of food, doesn't need the adjective *verde* (green). However, *judía* meaning *green bean* is limited in use strictly to Spain. The same word is the feminine form of *judío,* which means *Jewish.*

## Vocabulario de Frutas y Legumbres

| Spanish | English |
| --- | --- |
| el aguacate (m.) | avocado |
| el albaricoque (m.) | apricot |
| la alcachofa (f.) | artichoke |
| el ananá (m.) | pineapple |
| el apio (m.) | celery |
| la arveja (f.) | pea |
| la banana (f.) | banana |
| la calabaza (f.) | squash; gourd; pumpkin |
| el calabacín (m.) | squash |
| la cereza (f.) | cherry |
| la col (f.) | cabbage (Spain) |
| la coliflor (f.) | cauliflower |
| el choclo (m.) | ear of corn; corncob |
| el durazno (m.) | peach |
| el elote (m.) | ear of corn; corncob (Mexico) |
| la frambuesa (f.) | raspberry |
| la fresa (m.) | strawberry |
| el frijol (m.) | bean |
| el gandul (m.) | pigeon pea |
| el garbanzo (m.) | chick pea |
| el guisante (m.) | pea |
| el haba (f.) | fava bean, broadbean |
| la habichuela (f.) | green bean; bean (Caribbean) |
| el hongo (m.) | mushroom |
| la judía (verde) (f.) | green bean |
| la lechuga (f.) | lettuce |
| la legumbre (f.) | vegetable; legume, pod vegetable |
| la lenteja (f.) | lentil |
| el limón (m.) | lemon; lime |
| el maíz (m.) | corn, maize |
| el mango (m.) | mango |
| la manzana (f.) | apple |

*continues*

### Vocabulario de Frutas y Legumbres  (continued)

| Spanish | English |
| --- | --- |
| la mazorca (de maíz) (m.) | ear of corn; corncob |
| el melocotón (m.) | peach |
| el melón (m.) | melon |
| la mora (f.) | blueberry |
| la naranja (f.) | orange |
| la palta (f.) | avocado |
| la papa (f.) | potato (Latin America) |
| la papaya (f.) | papaya |
| la patata (f.) | potato (Spain) |
| la pasa (f.) | raisin |
| el pepino (m.) | cucumber |
| la pera (f.) | pear |
| la piña (f.) | pineapple |
| el plátano (m.) | banana; plantain |
| el pomelo (m.) | grapefruit |
| el poroto (m.) | pea |
| el repollo (m.) | cabbage (Latin America) |
| la sandía (f.) | watermelon |
| la seta (f.) | mushroom |
| el rábano (m.) | radish |
| el tomate (m.) | tomato |
| la toronja (f.) | grapefruit |
| la uva (f.) | grape |
| la verdulería (f.) | vegetable market |
| la verdura (f.) | vegetable; greenness |
| la zanahoria (f.) | carrot |
| el zapallo (m.) | squash |
| la zarzamora (f.) | blackberry |

**PROCEED WITH CAUTION**

In Cuba and Venezuela, *papaya* has acquired another meaning, and is not used in mixed company. The word for this tropical fruit in Cuba is *fruta bomba* and in Venezuela is *lechosa*.

# Speak of Movement Through vs. Movement Toward

*Por* versus *para:* The similar prepositions *por* and *para* illustrate once again why translation is not a great aid in learning a foreign language. Both prepositions can be translated to mean *for* and *by* (among other things, to, because of, and so on). They are *not* interchangeable; in fact, they are used to express very different ideas. Thought of in translation, their differences are very confusing; therefore, it is very important to understand the subtleties of their usage in Spanish.

An effective means of uncovering the differences between the very similar *por* and *para* is to visualize the concepts involved with each preposition. Picture the preposition *por*as being represented by a box with two arrows. Both arrows point in the same direction, but one arrow lies inside the box, while the other arrow is outside the box. Can you visualize this? The reason that this will help you internalize the function of *por* is that the principal idea underlying this preposition is that of movement *through* a space, or *alongside* a space.

Picture the preposition *para* as being represented by a box with an arrow *not* inside or alongside it, but aiming at it, being shot toward it. The underlying concept of *para* is that of movement *toward* a space, movement in the direction of that space.

## Talk of Physical Space

If you have those images in your mind, one associated with *por*, the other with *para*, we can now take some concrete examples to illustrate their use.

*Por:* The space represented by the box can be physical, geographical space. If you use *por*, you're talking about either moving through a physical space or alongside it. Study the following examples for understanding, and then practice saying them aloud, visualizing what the Spanish words mean:

(1) *Viajé por España hace un mes.* (I traveled through Spain a month ago.)

(2) *¿Quieres caminar por el parque?* (Do you want to walk through the park?)

(3) *Pasaremos por las montañas.* (We'll pass through the mountains.)

(4) *Proclaman la noticia por toda Europa.* (They proclaim the news throughout all Europe.)

(5) *Anduvo por la calle rápidamente.* (He walked along the street quickly.)

In sentence 1, the box represents the geographical space named Spain. You're saying you were the arrow that moved through that space. You can bend the arrow, or picture it moving in a circular fashion, but always within the space called Spain. In sentence 2, you're talking about passing through the physical space that is the park; the box has whatever shape the park has, and is filled with grass, trees, flowers, and benches; but it's still represented by a box, an enclosure. In sentence 3, the box contains the mountains through which we're going to pass. In sentence 4, the geographical space is larger than Spain; it's all Europe, but it's still the box through which the news is being proclaimed. In sentence 5, the box represents the street through which the person walked. (You could also think of the buildings as being the space, and he passed alongside them.)

Notice that the English translations of *por* in the five sentences above were variously *through*, *throughout*, and *along*(*side*). This doesn't change the image of the arrow within or beside the box. Other English prepositions might have been used to translate *por* as well.

*Para:* The space we're referring to is still physical, geographical space. But with the preposition *para*, we're not talking about passing through the space, or alongside the space; we haven't reached that space yet. This preposition is the one that represents movement toward that space, aiming at that space, trying to reach it. Study the following sentences for understanding, and then practice saying them aloud, picturing what is happening:

(1) *Mañana salgo para España.* (Tomorrow I leave for Spain.)

(2) *¿Quieres irte para el parque?* (Do you want to head toward the park?)

(3) *Mañana me voy para las montañas.* (Tomorrow I'm off to the mountains.)

(4) *La noticia es para toda Europa.* (The news is for all Europe.)

(5) *Salió rápidamente para la calle.* (He left quickly for [toward] the street.)

In sentence 1, the subject of the verb is not going to move through the space called Spain; he or she is merely going to move toward it, aim at it. In sentence 2, you're asking if someone wants to move in the direction of the space called the park, not through it. In sentence 3, you're saying you're going to be moving, not through the geographical space called the mountains, but toward that space. In sentence 4, you're not saying that the news is being proclaimed throughout the space called Europe, but that it's for Europe, in the sense that it's destined for Europe, that it's aimed at Europe, that it's going to be heading toward Europe. In sentence 5, he didn't walk along the street, he hasn't reached that street yet; he's only moving toward it, heading in that direction, aiming at reaching that street.

Notice the various English ways of translating *para* in the preceding sentences (head toward, to be off to, for). Other expressions could have been used, but they all follow the idea of the arrow flying toward a box, aiming at it.

## TALK OF TIME

*Por:* That box doesn't have to represent physical, geographical space. Instead, it can represent a block of time. If you're using the preposition *por,* you're talking about moving through that block of time. *Por,* in speaking of time, is very close in meaning to *durante* (during). Study the following sentences for understanding; then practice saying them aloud, picturing the scene:

(1) *Estuviste en Inglaterra por dos meses.* (You were in England for two months.)

(2) *María estuvo en casa por tres horas.* (María was at home for three hours.)

(3) *Vivían en México por un año escolar.* (They lived in Mexico for one school year.)

(4) *Leyeron novelas por varias horas.* (They read novels for several hours.)

(5) *Veías la televisión por cuatro horas diarias.* (You used to watch TV for four hours a day.)

In sentence 1, the box represents a block of time called *two months*; you moved through that block of two hours while you were in England. Visualize that box, label it *two months*, and picture yourself as the arrow passing through that box and time period. In sentence 2, María moved through a box that represents the block of time called *three hours* while she stayed at home. In sentence 3, *they* passed through the box that represents *one school year* while they were living in Mexico. In sentence 4, *they* moved through the block of time called *several hours* while reading novels. In sentence 5, you used to move through a block of time called *four hours* every day, while watching television.

In all five sentences, the person involved is an arrow moving through a box that represents a time period, a temporal space. Visualize this as you say the sentences aloud.

*Para:* When using the preposition *para* to talk about a block of time, there is no movement through that block of time; the arrow is not moving inside the box. Instead, the arrow is aiming at the block of time, heading for it. When it reaches the edge of the time period, the wall of the box, it will stop and not enter. In using *para* to speak of time, you'll be talking of a deadline, a cutoff date. Nothing is going to happen within that space of time; something is supposed to happen at that time, by that time. That time is the destination for the arrow. Study the following sentences for meaning, and then practice saying them aloud, feeling the meaning underlying them:

(1) *Quiero que Uds. me devuelvan los libros para el viernes.* (I want you to return the books to me by Friday.)

(2) *Quiero que lo hagas para mañana.* (I want you to do it by tomorrow.)

(3) *Los informes deben estar listos para el miércoles.* (The reports should be ready by/for Wednesday.)

(4) *¿Para cuándo puede Ud. hacerlo?* (By when can you do it?)

(5) *Para las cinco.* (By five o'clock.)

**GO TO** ▶
Sentences 1 and 2 employ the present subjunctive. To review the subjunctive with verbs of wishing and wanting, see Hour 12. For more information on the subjunctive, refer to Hour 13.

In sentence 1, you want those books returned by Friday (not *during* Friday) at the latest. Friday is the time those people will have to aim at; to have the books returned *by* Friday will be their goal. When you've arrived at the block of time called Friday, the time for traveling with those books is over.

The same basic situation exists in the other sentences. In sentence 2, *tomorrow* is the time aimed at, not entered and passed through. In sentence 3, the same can be said about Wednesday; picture the arrow heading for the wall of the box called Wednesday, not penetrating it, because the window of opportunity stops when those reports reach that time period called Wednesday. It can't go beyond. Sentence 4 asks when the wall will be reached, when this person thinks the deadline should be. Sentence 5 answers, telling us that the point aimed at is five o'clock, not beyond that.

Notice that both *by* and *for* could be the English prepositions used in some of these sentences. In all cases, the arrow aiming at the box is the underlying concept.

## TALK OF CAUSE VS. GOAL

The space represented by the box does not have to represent physical space, or even a block of time. It can be more abstract; it can speak of the *Why?* and *What for?* of actions and situations.

Think of the box as having turned into a target, in the middle of which is a bull's-eye. Now the arrow is aimed at the bull's-eye and the illustration represents a goal, or something you are shooting for. We can use *para* to represent our aspirations and goals. Study the following sentences employing *para* to show goals, then practice saying them aloud:

(1) *Trabajo para ganar dinero.* (I work in order to earn money.)

(2) *Estudian para aprender.* (They study [in order] to learn.)

(3) *Él come poco, para no engordar.* (He eats little [He doesn't eat much], so as not to gain weight [fatten].)

(4) *Ella toma vitaminas para suplementar su dieta.* (She takes vitamins [in order] to supplement her diet.)

(5) *Estamos aquí para verlo a Ud.* (We're here to see you.)

**PROCEED WITH CAUTION**

To show purpose/goal in English, we use *in order to* and *so as to,* but usually shorten these expressions to a simple *to.* This *to,* when representing purpose or goal is not equivalent to Spanish *a* or to the infinitive verb; it represents *para.*

In sentence 1, the purpose of your working is to earn money. Because we are discussing an action involving achieving a goal, *para* is used. In sentence 2, they're aiming at the goal of learning when they study; their purpose in studying is to learn. In other words, learning is the target at which they shoot the arrow. In sentence 3, he has a goal; he's aiming to avoid gaining weight. His purpose in eating very little, not eating much, is to ensure he does not gain weight. In sentence 4, her target is to supplement her diet; this is her goal, what she's aiming at by taking vitamins. In sentence 5, our target is labeled *to see you.* We are here for the purpose of seeing you, in order to see you, or simply *to see you.*

## LEARN TO ASK WHY

If you're asking someone a question about his or her purpose or goal in doing something, you use the phrase *¿Para qué?* Study the following questions and answers, and practice saying them aloud. Then make up your own questions and answers, using the preposition *para.* But be sure your questions deal with purpose, goals, and aims:

*¿Para qué trabaja Ud.?*
What are you working for?

*Trabajo para ganar dinero.*
I work in order to earn money.

*¿Para qué estudian?*
What are they studying for?

*Estudian para aprender.*
They study (in order) to learn.

*¿Para qué come tan poco él?*
Why does he eat so little?

*Él come poco para no engordar.*
He eats little (doesn't eat much) so as not to gain weight (fatten).

In each of the preceding sentences, the question, no matter how it comes out in English, asks to know what the goal is, what the purpose is, what is being aimed at by the person being questioned. You know this because the question contains the expression *¿Para qué?* The answer invariably has the preposition *para* plus an infinitive in it, because it responds to the question with an answer telling of the goal.

### PROCEED WITH CAUTION

 Many students, thinking in English, will say something like *Trabajo ganar dinero*, translating word for word from *I work to earn money*. But that Spanish sentence has no meaning. The preposition *para* must be inserted to speak of purpose.

## Discuss the Cause of an Action

When you want to know the cause of an action or of being in a particular situation, the question you ask is *¿Por qué?* You're *not* asking for someone's purpose or goal; you're asking about what *caused* the situation to which you're referring. Study the following sentences, and then practice saying them aloud:

(1) *¿Por qué trabaja Ud.?* (Why do you work?)

(2) *Trabajo porque antes no tenía dinero.* (I work because I had no money before.)

(3) *¿Por qué estudian?* (Why do they study?)

(4) *Estudian porque no quieren fracasar.* (They study because they don't want to fail.)

(5) *¿Por qué come tan poco él?* (Why does he eat so little?)

(6) *Él come poco porque temía por su salud.* (He doesn't eat much because he feared for his health.)

All the preceding questions ask about the cause of an action or a situation; they ask what happened first, what landed people in their present situation. Sentence 1 asks about what happened first that propelled the other person into working. The answer tells us that the person had first been in the dilemma of having no money. There is absolutely no direct reference to purpose or goals, although you can easily draw your own conclusions.

**JUST A MINUTE**

When he says "*Trabajo porque antes no tenía dinero,*" giving the cause, you can think to yourself "*Trabaja para ganar dinero,*" thinking of his goal.

Sentence 3 asks about what happened first to push these people into studying. The answer tells us that their fear of failure, which was present first, propelled them into studying. Sentence 5 shows a desire to find out what prior situation existed that caused the condition of eating so little; the answer tells us that this prior condition was his fear of poor health, or his desire for good health.

Note: The answer to a *¿Por qué?* question will have *por* in it somewhere. The answer sentences have the word *porque* (because) because it is followed by a conjugated verb. Otherwise, it would have been a simple *por*. This *por* answer (or unsolicited statement) will appear as …

- *porque* before a conjugated verb.
- *por* before an infinitive (unconjugated verb) or a noun.

For example, the second sentence could have been expressed, instead of with *porque* plus the conjugated verb *tenía*, as *por* before either an infinitive verb or before a noun. See the following alternative sentences:

*Trabajo por no tener dinero antes.*
I work because of not having money before.

*Trabajo por falta de dinero.*
I work because of lack of money.

The first alternative sentence, using *por* plus an infinitive, shows the cause, the situation existing before, as *no tener dinero* (not having money); not having money propelled him into working. The second sentence, employing *por* plus the noun *falta* (lack), shows the cause—the prior situation—as *falta de dinero* (lack of money); this is what pushed him into the box of working.

**TIME SAVER**

*Por* looks toward the *past,* at the bowman; *para* looks toward the *future,* at the target.

Imagine that a reporter travels to the state prison to (*para*) interview a criminal. If the reporter were to ask the criminal in English, "Why are you here?" or more colloquially, "What are you in for?" he is not asking the prisoner what his purpose was in coming to reside in this jail, what goals he hopes to accomplish, and what he's aiming at. The reporter obviously wants to know what the prisoner did that landed him in jail. He's looking backward. He wants to know the cause of his incarceration, so the question would have to start with *¿Por qué …?*

The prisoner's answer would contain some form of *por:* either *porque* plus a conjugated verb, *por* plus an infinitive, or *por* plus a noun.

If the prisoner were to ask the reporter in English "Why are you here?" or more informally, "What are you doing here?" he would probably not be thinking that something happened first to make the reporter come to this prison (although it's possible, but not probable); he would want to know what the reporter was aiming at, what his goal was, what his purpose was. He's looking ahead, not backward. The prisoner's question would start with *¿Para qué …?*

The following table has some new vocabulary for you to study.

### Vocabulario Nuevo

| Spanish | English |
| --- | --- |
| la cárcel (f.) | jail |
| el periódico (m.) | newspaper |
| el/la periodista (m./f.) | journalist, reporter |
| la prisión (f.) | prison |
| el/la prisionero/a (m./f.) | prisoner |
| robar | to rob, to steal |
| el robo (m.) | robbery, theft |

See the following possible conversation between the reporter and the prisoner:

**Prisionero:** *¿Para qué está Ud. aquí?* (Why are you here?)

**Periodista:** (*Estoy aquí*) *para hablar con Ud.* ([I'm here] to talk with you.)

*Periodista:* *¿Y, por qué está Ud. aquí?* (And why are you here?)

*Prisionero:* *Estoy aquí porque robé un banco.* (I'm here because I robbed a bank.)

The fourth sentence uses *porque* plus the conjugated verb *robé*. He could just as well have answered with *por* plus an infinitive, or *por* plus an noun. See the following alternative ways the prisoner might have responded.

**PROCEED WITH CAUTION**

It would have been laughable if the reporter had asked the prisoner *¿Para qué está Ud. aquí?* This would imply that the prisoner had some goal in mind and went to jail of his own volition (in order) to accomplish that goal.

*Estoy aquí por robar un banco.*
I'm here for (because of) robbing a bank.

*Estoy aquí por haber robado un banco.*
I'm here for (because of) having robbed a bank.

*Estoy aquí por robo.*
I'm here for (because of) robbery.

**GO TO ▶**
There are more uses for the prepositions *por* and *para* than we've dealt with in this hour. You'll be working with them in Hour 18.

## USE THE INFINITIVE PERFECT TENSE

Notice the use of the infinitive form of the helping verb *haber* plus the past participle *robado* in the preceding second sentence. This is a case of a compound tense with an infinitive auxiliary verb; it is the infinitive perfect tense. See the following examples:

*El haberme visto es peligroso.* (Having seen me is dangerous.)

*No me gusta haber recibido la carta.* (I don't like having received the letter.)

*No me gusta haberla recibido.* (I don't like having received it [the letter].)

*Me gustaría haberlo hecho.* (I would like to have done it.)

*No debes haber dicho que sí.* (You shouldn't have said yes.)

## THE 30-SECOND RECAP

In this hour, you've learned how to shop at the market for foodstuffs. You've also begun to learn some of the differences between the prepositions *por* and *para,* and have learned to use the infinitive perfect tense.

## Hour's Up!

Review this hour's work, and then test yourself by taking the following quiz. For best results, don't check back through the pages of this hour while actually taking the quiz.

1. Choose the logical ending for the sentence: *En una tienda de legumbres se compran …*

    **a.** chuletas de cerdo.

    **b.** zanahorias.

    **c.** almejas.

    **d.** alas de pollo.

2. Choose the logical ending for the sentence: *En un negocio de frutas de mar se compran …*

    **a.** pulpos.

    **b.** pomelos.

    **c.** costillas.

    **d.** alas de pollo.

3. Choose the correct expression according to context: *Voy a dormir _____ tener sueño.*

    **a.** por

    **b.** para

    **c.** porque

    **d.** para que

4. Choose the correct expression according to context: *Quiero tener el dinero _____ el viernes.*

    **a.** por

    **b.** para

    **c.** porque

    **d.** para que

5. Choose the correct expression according to context: *Me voy, _____ no quiero estar aquí.*

    **a.** por

    **b.** para

    **c.** porque

    **d.** para que

# Hour 18

# Dining Out

## Chapter Summary

**LESSON PLAN:**

In this hour, you'll learn ...

- About the past perfect tense.
- More about the uses of *por* and *para*.
- The most common prepositions and prepositional objects.
- Vocabulary necessary for dining at restaurants.

In order to get a feeling for the various tenses, think of the present tense as a ship on which you're a passenger. It keeps moving forward (1:00, 1:05, 1:20, 9:00, 11:00), but it's always the present. Today you say "I speak" because it's your present; tomorrow you'll still say "I speak" because it will then be your present, and in 10 years, you'll still say "I speak" because that will then be your present. So the boat named *the present* keeps moving forward, but is still called *the present*.

The preterit tense is like a buoy dropped in the water at a specific point. When you say "I spoke yesterday at five o'clock," your boat (the present) keeps moving farther and farther from that buoy, but the buoy stays at that specific point in the ocean of time.

The present perfect tense is like a flag flying from the mast of *the present*; it is affixed to no specific point in the past. It vaguely refers to a nonspecified time before the present, but which is still relevant to the present.

The past perfect is like a flag tied to some buoy back there. The buoy represents a specific point in the past, but the past perfect vaguely refers to an unspecified time before the time or event represented by the buoy, and still relevant to that buoy. The past perfect is to the preterit what the present perfect is to the present.

GO TO ▶
For a review of the present perfect, see Hour 16.

# USE THE PAST PERFECT TENSE

You're familiar with several of the perfect (compound) tenses: present perfect, preterit perfect, and infinitive perfect. The preterit perfect, however, is not used very often in ordinary conversation. Because of this, in order to talk about events that took place at some time before a point in the past, you'll want to learn the past perfect tense (also called the pluperfect).

The past perfect tense, like all compound tenses, is formed with two elements: the verb *haber* plus the past participle. For the past perfect tense, the helping verb *haber* is conjugated in the imperfect tense.

**Past Perfect Tense Using *Hablar***

| Subject Pronoun | Haber | Past Participle of Hablar |
|---|---|---|
| yo | había | hablado |
| tú | habías | hablado |
| él | había | hablado |
| ella | había | hablado |
| Ud. | había | hablado |
| nosotros/as | habíamos | hablado |
| vosotros/as | habíais | hablado |
| ellos | habían | hablado |
| ellas | habían | hablado |
| Uds. | habían | hablado |

As you can see, *haber* in the imperfect tense is perfectly regular. (For a review of the imperfect tense, see Hour 6.)

Practice saying the following sentences aloud, picturing their meanings:

*Anoche, cuando te vi, yo ya había comido.*
Last night, when I saw you, I had already eaten.

*Ya habían recibido las noticias.*
They had already received the news.

*El lunes pasado, ya lo habíamos comprado.*
Last Monday, we had already bought it.

*¿Habías almorzado cuando llegaron?*
Had you eaten when they arrived?

*Sí, y también (había) cenado.*
Yes, and (I had) eaten dinner, too.

In all of the preceding five sentences, whether stated explicitly or not, the verb in the past perfect tense refers to an action that had taken place at an unspecified time *before* a certain point in the past, or before some action that took place in the past.

GO TO ▶
To review the formation of the past participle, see Hour 9.

Note: In the fifth sentence, because we already know we're dealing with the past perfect tense because of the question in the fourth sentence, we can omit the helping verb *haber* in both English and Spanish. The *I had* in English and the *había* in Spanish are understood. It's as though the *cenado* of the fifth sentence were mentally attached to the helping verb of the fourth sentence (with the change of subject understood, of course). But the helping verb can be omitted only in a case like this, when it's absolutely understood.

**PROCEED WITH CAUTION**

Just as in English you would never say *"I eaten dinner," you would never say in Spanish *"(*Yo*) *cenado*." We wouldn't know if you *have* eaten, or *had* eaten, or *will have* eaten, or *would have* eaten, and so on, or, without the pronoun, who the subject is.

GO TO ▶
To review *por* and *para* with space, time, cause, and purpose, as well as the explanation of the arrow and the box, see Hour 17.

## Continue Learning *Por* and *Para*

You've learned to use the prepositions *por* and *para* in dealing with physical space, with periods of time, and with cause (*por*) and purpose (*para*). You've worked with the image of the arrow and the box to understand the underlying psychological implications of these prepositions. There are many other uses of these two words. Let's take a look.

### Do It for Someone's Sake

When you want to say that someone did (does, will do, would do, and so on) something for someone else's sake, use *por*. When you say to someone "I did it for you," this means *I did it for your sake*, which means *I did it to benefit you in some way*. If you switched careers for Jennifer, then, actually, Jennifer (or your desire to please her) was the original *cause* of your switching careers.

Note: *For the sake of* will usually come out simply as *for*, which means so many things in English.

Practice saying the following sentences aloud:

*Víctor cambió de carrera por Elena.*
Víctor changed careers for Elena.

*Lo hizo por ella.*
He did it for her.

*Él se sacrificó por la causa.*
He sacrificed himself for the cause.

*Por sus padres, se fue.*
For his parents' sake, he went away.

*Murió por la patria.*
He died for his country.

The fourth sentence is ambiguous; it can be taken to mean that he went away for his parents' sake, to benefit them in some way. Or it could be taken to mean he went away *because of his parents*, which might, but doesn't necessarily, leave a different impression. After all, it could suggest that his parents were impossible to live with, for example. In either case, though, those parents are still the cause.

## Do It on Someone's Behalf

The idea behind the English expressions *on behalf of* or *on account of* is close to the idea of *for the sake of* (although the second expression can also be synonymous with *because of*), but is not exactly the same. Sometimes *on behalf of* comes close to meaning *instead of*. There is a thin line between these concepts at times. Either way, the Spanish preposition *por* is used:

*El Sr. Pérez no pudo venir; yo estoy aquí por él.*
Mr. Pérez could not come; I'm here on his behalf.

*González lo hizo por Rodríguez.*
González did it on behalf of Rodríguez.

*Acepto el honor por mi padre, quien no puede estar presente.*
I accept the honor on behalf of my father, who cannot be present.

*Por todos mis amigos, le felicito a Ud.*
On behalf of all my friends, I congratulate you.

*Carmen asistió, por toda la oficina.*
Carmen attended on behalf of the entire office.

In English, the first sentence could just as well have ended with *on Mr. Pérez's account*, or *because of Mr. Pérez*, or, with a somewhat different slant, *instead of Mr. Pérez*. Either way, there is still a close connection with the idea of cause, one thing happening first, causing the second thing to happen. The fact that Mr. Pérez couldn't come is the cause of my coming.

There are more precise expressions: *de parte de* only means *on behalf of*, whereas *a causa de* only means *because of*. *En nombre de* means *in the name of*.

Be very careful: The same English sentence might be expressed in two different ways (one with *por,* one with *para*), depending on the deeper meaning:

Elena bought the lamp for him.

It seems like a simple sentence with only one possible meaning. However, this simplicity is deceptive. It could mean that Elena bought a lamp to give to him. He is the recipient of the lamp. The lamp is destined for him. This means that *para* is the preposition to use. The sentence in Spanish would be this:

Elena compró la lámpara para él.

However, the same English sentence could mean that he was going to buy the lamp to give to someone else (for example, his mother). His mother, not he (him) is the lamp's final destination. In this case, Elena did him a favor and bought the lamp in his stead, on his behalf. With this meaning, the Spanish sentence would be this:

Elena compró la lámpara por él.

## Talk About Exchange

When you talk about exchanging one thing for another, whether it's a case of barter or purchase with currency, you use the preposition *por.* It may be stretching a point to say this use of *por* is related to the idea of *cause,* but if it works, think of it that way. If I pay you five dollars for your book, then you could say that my giving you the five dollars is the *cause* of your giving me the book. After all, you wouldn't have done it otherwise.

Practice saying the following sentences aloud:

*Te doy mi sombrero por tu camisa.*
I'll give you my hat for your shirt.

*Te doy cinco dólares por la camisa.*
I'll give you five dollars for the shirt.

*¿Qué me darás por mi libro?*
What will you give me for my book?

*Te daré mis revistas por tu libro.*
I'll give you my magazines for your book.

## BE VAGUE ABOUT LOCATION

GO TO ▶
Sentence 2 uses a command form of the verb. See Hour 19 for the lesson on commands.

The adverbs *aquí* and *acá* mean *here* (near the person speaking). The adverb *ahí* means *there* in the sense of being near the listener. *Allí* and *allá* mean *there* or *out there* or *yonder*, far from both the speaker and the listener. Usually, *aquí* is taken to be a shade more precise than *acá*, and *allí* is taken to be more precise than *allá*. It is customary in most Spanish-speaking areas to use *acá* and *allá* with verbs of motion (going, coming, flying, swimming, running, and so on, somewhere), but there's no strict rule involved:

*Estoy aquí.* (I'm here.)

*Ven acá.* (Come here.)

*Carlos está allí.* (Carlos is over there.)

*Carlos fue allá.* (Carlos went out there.)

*Me voy para allá.* (I'm heading over there.)

GO TO ▶
Sentence 5 uses *Me voy para ....* For a review of the reflexive verb *irse* plus the preposition *para*, see Hour 16.

The preposition *por* can be used to make a physical location vague; that is, it can be used in front of *aquí* or *acá* or in front of *ahí*, or in front of *allí* or *allá*. When *por* is placed in front of these words, the effect is similar to our placing the word *around* in front of *here* or *there*. It speaks of the general area, the approximate, rather than the exact, location of something or someone. Compare the following sentences, and practice saying them aloud:

*Carlos está aquí.* (Carlos is [right] here.)

*Carlos está por aquí.* (Carlos is around here [somewhere].)

*Dejé el menú allí.* (I left the menu [right] out there.)

*Dejé el menú por allí.* (I left the menu around there [somewhere].)

## REFER TO INSTRUMENT OR AGENT

The preposition *por* is used to talk about the means or instrument by which something was done or the agent by whom it was done. Study the following sentences, and practice saying them aloud:

*Me llamaron por teléfono.*
They phoned me. (They called me by telephone.)

*Fui por avión.*
I went by plane.

*Mandaron el mensaje por el correo.*
They sent the message by mail (or through the mail).

Don Quijote de la Mancha, *por Miguel de Cervantes ....*
*Don Quixote of La Mancha,* by Miguel de Cervantes ....

*El libro fue escrito por Cervantes.*
The book was written by Cervantes.

**GO TO** ▶
For a review of the passive voice, see Hour 10.

## CONSIDER THE CIRCUMSTANCES

The preposition *para* is used to mean *for* in the sense of *considering the fact that ...* or *with a view to the fact that ...* or *in spite of the fact that.* The following examples will make this clear:

*Para (ser) un norteamericano, habla muy bien el español.*
For (being) an American, he speaks Spanish very well.

*Para haber estudiado por dos años, no sabe mucho.*
For having studied for two years, he doesn't know much.

*Vicky sabe mucho para estar en primer grado.*
Vicky knows a lot for being in first grade.

*No es muy fuerte para un atleta.*
He's not very strong for an athlete.

*Para un locutor de la televisión, no habla muy claramente.*
For a television announcer, he doesn't speak very clearly.

The first sentence could just as well have been translated as *Considering the fact that he's an American, he speaks Spanish very well,* or *Despite the fact that he's an American, he speaks Spanish very well.* The same type of transformation could be made with the rest of the five sentences.

## GIVE YOUR OPINION

The preposition *para* can be used with the meaning of *as far as I'm* (or he's, she's, and so on) *concerned,* or *In my* (or his, her, etc.) *opinion.* Study the following sentences:

*Para mí, no es importante.*
As far as I'm concerned, it's not important.

*Para ella, es ridículo.*
In her opinion, it's ridiculous.

*Para nosotros, no vale mucho.*
In our opinion, it's not worth much.

*Para los niños, es cómico.*
As far as the children are concerned, it's funny.

## USE PREPOSITIONS AND THEIR OBJECTS

You've learned a great many pronouns up until now: the subject pronoun, the direct object pronoun, the indirect object pronoun, and the reflexive object pronoun. There is one more object pronoun you should know: the prepositional object pronouns. The previous sentences use the preposition *para* plus the objects of the preposition. First, however, it would be useful to learn some more prepositions.

### LEARN MORE PREPOSITIONS

By now, you're thoroughly familiar with the complicated case of the prepositions *por* and *par*(a). You've also been using the preposition *de* (from, of, or belonging to), and the preposition *a*, meaning *to* and used as the untranslatable *personal a*. Learn the following prepositions as well.

**Spanish Prepositions**

| Spanish | English |
| --- | --- |
| a la derecha (de) | to the right (of) |
| al lado de | beside |
| alrededor de | around |
| arriba de | above |
| bajo | under, underneath, below |
| con | with |
| debajo (de) | under, underneath, below |
| delante (de) | in front (of) |
| dentro (de) | inside (of); within |
| detrás (de) | behind, in back (of) |
| encima (de) | on top (of) |
| en | in, into; on |
| enfrente (de) | facing, opposite; in front (of) |
| entre | between, among |
| excepto | except |
| fuera (de) | outside (of) |

| Spanish | English |
|---------|---------|
| a la izquierda (de) | to the left (of) |
| junto a | next to |
| sin | without |
| sobre | on, on top of; over |
| según | according to |

**JUST A MINUTE**

*En* can mean either *in* or *on*. To be more specific, you can use *dentro de* for *inside of* or *encima de* or *sobre* for *on* (top of).

*Debajo de* refers to physical position: *un libro debajo de otro* (one book under another); *está debajo de la mesa* (it's under the table). *Bajo* is more abstract: *bajo la luna llena* (beneath the full moon); *bajo la influencia del alcohol* (under the influence of alcohol).

Many of the preceding prepositions that need *de* are used as prepositions only in combination with that preposition *de*. Otherwise, they are adverbs. See the following sentences showing these prepositions used as adverbs:

*Él fue a la derecha.*
He went (to the) right.

*Hay que ir a la izquierda.*
It's necessary to go (to the) left.

*María está fuera.*
María's outside.

*La casa de Carlos está enfrente.*
Carlos's house is across the way.

*Elena vive arriba.*
Elena lives upstairs.

Others are somewhat altered:

*Salgamos afuera.*
Let's go outside.

*Roberto vive abajo.*
Roberto lives down below (or downstairs).

*Hay que seguir adelante.*
One must continue onward.

*Se quedaron atrás.*

They were left (remained) behind.

---

**TIME SAVER**

 In colloquial speech, some of these expressions can be used as interjections taking the place of a command (the command verb understood, not expressed): *¡Fuera!* (Out!); *¡Adentro!* (Inside!); *¡Adelante!* (Foreward!); *¡Atrás!* (Back!).

## LEARN THE PREPOSITIONAL OBJECTS

Examine the following table of prepositional object pronouns; the left column contains the subject pronouns you already know, and the right column shows the prepositional object pronouns for the same person.

**Pronouns as Objects of Prepositions**

| Subject Pronouns | Prepositional Object Pronouns |
| --- | --- |
| yo | mí |
| tú | ti |
| él | él; sí |
| ella | ella; sí |
| usted | usted; sí |
| nosotros/as | nosotros/as |
| vosotros/as | vosotros/as |
| ellos | ellos; sí |
| ellas | ellas; sí |
| ustedes | ustedes; sí |

Note: The preposition *mí* has a written accent mark over the vowel to distinguish it in writing from the possessive adjective *mi* (my). The preposition *ti* does not have a written accent mark, because there is no other word that's spelled the same; there is nothing to contrast it with.

No doubt, you were happy to notice that there are very few new items among the pronouns that are objects of prepositions.

The prepositional object pronouns are exactly the same as the subject pronouns, with the following exceptions:

- *mí* (instead of *yo*)
- *ti* (instead of *tú*)

Note the double entries for the third person; they involve the prepositional object pronoun *sí*. This is the prepositional object pronoun that corresponds to the pronouns for the reflexive object of the verb for the third person (*se*). It is used when the third person is doing something to him-, her-, or itself. Often, the *sí* is augmented by adding *mismo* or *misma* after it. See the following sentences:

> *Carlos dijo para sí ...*
> Carlos said to himself ...
>
> *Carlos se dijo (a sí mismo) ...*
> Carlos said to himself ...
>
> *Conchita se miró (a sí misma).*
> Conchita looked at herself.

The first sentence uses an idiom that is synonymous with the second sentence.

Something unusual happens with the combination of the preposition *con* and three of the prepositional object pronouns: *mí, ti,* and *sí*. They become *conmigo, contigo,* and *consigo*.

### PROCEED WITH CAUTION

Three prepositions—*entre, excepto,* and *según*—do not take prepositional object pronouns; they take the subject pronouns: *entre tú y yo* (between you and me); *excepto yo* (except me); and *según tú* (according to you).

Practice saying the following sentences aloud:

> *Este regalo es para ti.* (This gift is for you.)
>
> *¿Para mí?* (For me?)
>
> *Bueno, no es para ellos.* (Well, it's not for them.)
>
> *La ensalada está delante de Ud.* (The salad is in front of you.)
>
> *El camarero está detrás de nosotros.* (The waiter is behind us.)
>
> *Elena va con ellos.* (Elena is going with them.)
>
> *Y ellos van conmigo.* (And they're going with me.)
>
> *Lo hago (o) contigo o sin ti.* (I'll do it [either] with you or without you.)
>
> *Ella trajo sus libros consigo.* (She brought her books with her.)
>
> *¿Vas con él o conmigo?* (Are you going with him or with me?)

Note that the next-to-last sentence above uses *consigo* because it's considered reflexive, because *she* is the one who brought it, and *she* is the one it is with (with herself). The subject is the same person as the object of the preposition.

**JUST A MINUTE**

The tendency in most of Spanish America, unlike Spain, is *not* to use the reflexive prepositional object pronoun with *con*. For example, instead of *Ella trajo sus libros consigo*, a Latin American speaker would use *Ella trajo sus libros con ella*.

## DINE OUT IN SPANISH

You already have acquired a vocabulary for buying food at the market. To order meals in restaurants, you'll need additional lexical items. Study the following vocabulary.

### *Para Comer en un Restaurante* (To Eat in a Restaurant)

| Spanish | English |
| --- | --- |
| el aderezo (m.) | dressing (for salad) |
| a fuego lento | over a low fire |
| el ajo (m.) | garlic |
| al horno | baked |
| a la parrilla | grilled, charbroiled |
| al punto | medium rare |
| la almendra (f.) | almond |
| el almíbar (m.) | syrup |
| asar | to roast |
| el asado (m.) | barbecue |
| el ambiente (m.) | atmosphere; surroundings; environment |
| atender (ie) | to attend to; to take care of |
| atender mesas | to wait on tables |
| el arroz (m.) | rice |
| el azúcar (m.) | sugar |
| la azucarera (f.) | sugar bowl |
| bien asado/a | well-done |
| el berro (m.) | watercress |

| Spanish | English |
| --- | --- |
| bien cocido/a | well-done |
| el cochinillo (m.) | suckling pig (Spain) |
| el bizcocho (m.) | sponge cake; biscuit |
| el caldo (m.) | broth; clear soup |
| el/la camarero/a (m./f.) | waiter (server) |
| la cena (f.) | dinner; supper |
| el cóctel (m.) | cocktail; cocktail party |
| la comida (m.) | meal; food |
| la copa (f.) | wine glass |
| la crema (f.) | cream |
| crudo/a | raw |
| el cubierto (m.) | table setting |
| la cuchara (f.) | spoon; soup spoon |
| la cucharilla (f.) | little spoon; teaspoon |
| la cucharita (f.) | little spoon; teaspoon |
| el cucharón (m.) | big spoon; ladle |
| el cuchillo (m.) | knife |
| la cuenta (f.) | bill, check, tab |
| champiñones (m. pl.) | mushrooms |
| dejar una propina | to leave a tip |
| dulce | sweet |
| elegante | elegant, fancy |
| la ensalada (f.) | salad |
| el entremés (m.) | hors d'oeuvre |
| el escaparate (m.) | shop or restaurant window |
| el flan (m.) | flan, caramel-covered custard |
| freír (i) | to fry |
| frito/a | fried |
| la fuente (f.) | fountain, spring; tureen |
| la fuente para sopa (f.) | soup tureen |
| la galleta (f.) | cracker; biscuit; cookie |
| gusto (m.) | taste |
| el helado (m.) | ice cream |

*continues*

**Para Comer en un Restaurante (To Eat in a Restaurant)   (continued)**

| Spanish | English |
| --- | --- |
| el horno (m.) | oven |
| hornear | to bake |
| el huevo (m.) | egg |
| el lechón (m.) | suckling pig |
| el lujo (m.) | luxury |
| lujoso/a | luxurious |
| el mantel (m.) | tablecloth |
| la manteca (f.) | lard (Argentina/Uruguay: butter) |
| la mantequilla (f.) | butter |
| la mesa (f.) | table |
| el/la mesero/a (m.f.) | waiter (server) |
| la mostaza (f.) | mustard |
| el/la mozo/a (m./f.) | waiter, waitress (server) |
| la nuez (las nueces) (f.) | walnut(s) |
| la paella (f.) | Spanish dish of rice, shellfish, chicken, and meat |
| pagar | to pay |
| el pan (m.) | bread |
| el pan tostado (m.) | toast |
| picante | spicy, hot |
| el pimentero (m.) | pepper shaker |
| la pimienta (f.) | pepper (condiment) |
| el pimiento (m.) | pepper (vegetable) |
| el plato (m.) | plate; dish |
| el plato fuerte (m.) | main dish |
| el pocillo (m.) | coffee cup (Argentina/Uruguay) |
| poco asado/a | rare |
| poco cocido/a | rare |
| la porción (f.) | serving |
| el postre (m.) | dessert |
| preparar | to prepare |
| probar | to try (out); to test; to taste |
| la propina (f.) | tip |

| Spanish | English |
|---|---|
| el puré de papas (patatas) | mashed potatoes |
| el queso (m.) | cheese |
| el restaurán, restaurante, restorán (m.) | restaurant |
| rico/a | delicious |
| el sabor (m.) | flavor |
| saborear | to taste, to savor |
| sabroso/a | delicious |
| la salsa (f.) | sauce |
| la sal (f.) | salt |
| el sándwich (m.) | sandwich |
| la servilleta (f.) | napkin |
| servir (i) | to serve |
| la sopa (f.) | soup |
| tarjeta de crédito (m.) | credit card |
| la tarta (f.) | tart; pie; filled pastry |
| la taza (f.) | cup |
| la torta (f.) | cake |
| la tortilla (f.) | omelet (Spain); tortilla (Mexico) |
| la tostada (f.) | toast |
| la vitrina (f.) | shop or restaurant window |

**PROCEED WITH CAUTION**

In Mexico, the vulgar slang meaning of *huevo* is so prevalent that a substitute word is usually used: *blanquillo* (little white one).

**GO TO** ▶

To review names of meats, vegetables, and fruits, see Hour 17.

## EL RESTAURANTE

Read the following story for comprehension. The vocabulary comes either from previous lessons or from the present lesson (except for the English in parentheses).

Ricardo Montero, con su esposa María Victoria ("Vicky") fueron a cenar con sus amigos, los Gómez, Víctor y Adela. Decidieron ir a un restaurán elegante llamado El Horno de Oro. Les dieron una mesa junto al escaparate. Primero pidieron cócteles. Luego, el mesero les trajo el caldo, pero no estaba bastante caliente. Se quejaron (complained) al camarero, y él lo devolvió a la cocina, y volvió con un caldo bien caliente. Nadie quería entremeses. Cuando llegaron los platos fuertes, Ricardo tenía un biftec, poco asado, con papas fritas y una ensalada de berro. Vicky había pedido chuletas de cerdo, bien asado, con papas al horno y una ensalada de lechuga y tomates. Víctor se preocupaba mucho por el problema del colesterol; por eso (therefore), pidió el salmón asado, no frito, en una salsa de limón, pero sin mantequilla, con una ensalada de berro sin aderezo. Adela, que desaprueba (disapproves) de la matanza (slaughtering) de animales, pidió el plato vegetariano, que consistía en arroz con varias formas de habichuelas y varias formas de queso, más o menos como una paella sin pollo, mariscos ni carne. Naturalmente, también pidió la ensalada de lechuga con tomates. Encontró un trozo (bit, piece) de jamón en la ensalada; y siendo muy tímida, lo sacó y lo puso debajo de la mesa. De postre, Ricardo comió un rico queso con uvas, y café negro, sin azúcar. Vicky prefirió un helado italiano con café con leche y unos bizcochos. Víctor, que tenía miedo a los postres muy ricos, pidió el platillo ("plato pequeño") de frutas variadas y un vaso de leche desnatada (skimmed). De postre, Adela pidió zapallo en almíbar y una taza de té. Ya que (since, because) habían recibido buen servicio del mozo, le dejaron una buena propina.

## THE 30-SECOND RECAP

In this hour, you've analyzed the connection between the grammatical tenses and actual time. You've learned the past perfect tense, as well as more about the uses of *por* and *para*. You've also learned the most common prepositions, as well as the prepositional objects; and you've learned vocabulary necessary for dining at restaurants.

## HOUR'S UP!

Review this hour's work, and then test yourself by answering the following questions. Remember, don't go back to check the lessons in this hour while actually taking the quiz.

1. Choose *por* or *para*: *Se sacrificó _____ la patria.*

   **a.** *por*

   **b.** *para*

**2.** Choose *por* or *para*: *Pagué cinco pesos* _____ *la camisa.*

    **a.** *por*

    **b.** *para*

Answer the following questions about the story called *"El Restaurante."* (You may consult with the story while doing this.)

**3.** Their table was located …

    **a.** on top of the fire escape.

    **b.** next to the fire escape.

    **c.** next to the window.

    **d.** next to the fireplace.

**4.** The soup was brought to the table …

    **a.** twice.

    **b.** by the owner.

    **c.** three times.

    **d.** by the customers.

**5.** Vicky had …

    **a.** pork chops, rare, with French fries.

    **b.** steak, rare, with French fries.

    **c.** pork chops, well-done, with baked potato.

    **d.** the vegetable plate.

**6.** Choose the correct answer: The past perfect tense is like …

    **a.** a ship.

    **b.** a buoy.

    **c.** a flag on the ship.

    **d.** a flag on the buoy.

**7.** Choose the correct answer: *Ellos* _____ *cenado.*

    **a.** habríamos

    **b.** habíamos

    **c.** habían

    **d.** haberían

**8.** Choose the correct answer: Ella va _____.

    **a.** con me

    **b.** conmigo

    **c.** con mí

    **d.** conmego

**9.** Adela had …

    **a.** paella (rice, chicken, shellfish, meat).

    **b.** rice, beans, and cheese.

    **c.** paella without rice.

    **d.** vegetables only.

**10.** Choose the correct translation: Between you and me.

    **a.** Entre ti y mí.

    **b.** Entre te y me.

    **c.** Entre tú y yo.

    **d.** Entre tú y mí.

# Dialect Vocabulary

**LESSON PLAN:**

In this hour, you'll learn ...

- The future perfect tense.
- How to give commands.
- Vocabulary of various dialects.

Y ou've already learned to use several of the compound (or perfect) tenses (present perfect, preterit perfect, past perfect, and infinitive perfect). It will now be easy for you to learn the future perfect tense.

## TALK ABOUT THE FUTURE PERFECT

The future perfect tense is used to represent an event that will have taken place at an indeterminate time before a specific time in the future: By tomorrow, at 9:00 A.M., I'll have eaten. We don't know exactly at what time he will eat, or even if it will be on that same day or the day before; we only know it is at some point *before* tomorrow, 9:00 A.M.

We form the future perfect tense by combining the future tense of the auxiliary verb *haber* with the past participle. In the future tense, *haber* drops the *-e-* from the infinitive ending before adding the typical endings of the future tense. See the following table, which shows the future tense of *haber* in conjunction with the past participle of the verb *ver* as an example of the future perfect tense.

**Future Perfect Tense with the Verb *Ver***

| Subject Pronoun | Future of Haber | Past Participle of Ver |
|---|---|---|
| yo | habré | visto |
| tú | habrás | visto |
| él | habrá | visto |
| ella | habrá | visto |

*continues*

**Future Perfect Tense with the Verb _Ver_**   (continued)

| Subject Pronoun | _Future_<br>_of Haber_ | _Past Participle_<br>_of Ver_ |
| --- | --- | --- |
| usted | habrá | visto |
| nosotros/as | habremos | visto |
| vosotros/as | habréis | visto |
| ellos | habrán | visto |
| ellas | habrán | visto |
| ustedes | habrán | visto |

Study the following sentences, and practice saying them aloud, feeling the meaning:

> _Mañana a las nueve de la mañana, ya habré desayunado._
> Tomorrow at nine A.M., I'll already have had breakfast.
>
> _El profesor habrá dictado su clase._
> The professor will have given his class.
>
> _¿Habremos visto al decano?_
> Will we have seen the Dean?
>
> _¿Cuánto habrá hecho Ud. para mañana?_
> How much will you have done by (for) tomorrow?
>
> _Habré escrito veinte páginas._
> I'll have written twenty pages.

## TALK OF PROBABILITY

You remember that the future tense can also be used to refer to probability or wondering in the present. The future perfect tense can be used similarly, for wondering about what someone has done, or talking about what someone probably has done (must have done). For example, the second sentence above could mean _The professor must have given his class_ or _The professor has probably given his class._ See the following sentences, which use the future perfect tense to refer to matters of probability:

**GO TO** ▶
For a review of the future tense to express wonder and probability in the present, see Hour 6.

> _¿Habrán venido ya?_
> I wonder if they've already come (come yet).
>
> _No creo. No habrán llegado todavía._
> I don't think (so). They probably haven't arrived yet (still haven't arrived).

*¿Quiénes habrán sido?*
Who could they have been?

*Habrán sido los jefes de los departamentos.*
They must have been the department chairpersons.

*¿Qué habrá visto ella?*
I wonder what she has seen. (What could she have seen?)

*Habrá recibido sus notas.*
She must have received her grades.

# GIVE ORDERS IN SPANISH

In English, the subject of commands is usually not expressed, but is always understood to be the second person you. When we say "Go away!" it's clear that we want the person we're talking to (second person) to obey the command. In other words, we mean *You! Go away!*

In Spanish, too, the subject of a command is the second person. However, as you know, there are many different subject pronouns that translate as you: *tú, usted, vosotros, vosotras,* and *ustedes.* The command is different, depending on which of the above subject pronouns is the subject of your command.

**GO TO ▶**
It would be advisable to review the formation of the present subjunctive in Hour 12.

In other words, the form of the command depends on the person(s) you're talking to.

## COMMAND BY SUBJUNCTIVE

To give commands to people you refer to using *usted* or *ustedes,* the command form is the same as the present subjunctive tense (which you've already studied).

Naturally, the subjunctive/command form of the verb agrees with the subject pronoun. For the singular *usted,* the verb will end with a vowel, whereas for the plural *ustedes,* it will end with -*n*. Study the following commands for Ud., and practice saying them aloud:

*¡Hable (Ud.)!* (Speak!)

*¡No hable (Ud.)!* (Don't speak!)

*¡Viva (Ud.) aquí!* (Live here!)

*¡No viva (Ud.) aquí!* (Don't live here!)

*¡Coma (Ud.)!* (Eat!)

*¡No coma (Ud.)!* (Don't eat!)

Study the following commands for the plural *Uds.*, and practice saying them aloud:

*¡Hablen (Uds.)!* (Speak!)

*¡No hablen (Uds.)!* (Don't speak!)

*¡Vivan (Uds.) aquí!* (Live here!)

*¡No vivan (Uds.) aquí!* (Don't live here!)

*¡Coman (Uds.)!* (Eat!)

*¡No coman (Uds.)!* (Don't eat!)

---

**JUST A MINUTE**

You can include or exclude the subject pronoun *Ud.* and *Uds.* with the command. It's more courteous to include it, but in a series of commands, once is enough. For example, *¡Venga Ud! ¡Hable y coma!*

## Place Object Pronouns with Commands

You've learned where to place the object pronouns with relation to the verb in all the tenses you've studied up to this point. With reference to commands, there are two simple rules:

- **Affirmative command.** Attach the object pronoun to the end of the verb.
- **Negative command.** Place the object pronoun in front of the verb.

Study the following examples, and practice saying them aloud:

*¡Hábleme Ud.!* (Speak to me!)

*¡No me hable Ud.!* (Don't speak to me!)

*¡Cómala!* (Eat it!)

*¡No la coma!* (Don't eat it!)

*¡Tráigame los libros!* (Bring me the books!)

*¡Tráigamelos!* (Bring them to me!)

*¡Díganles la verdad!* (Tell them the truth!)

*¡Dígansela!* (Tell it to them!)

*¡No se la digan!* (Don't tell it to them!)

## COMMAND WITH FAMILIARITY

When speaking to people you address as *tú* or *vosotros/as*, the command forms are more complex.

If the *tú* command is *negative*, use the present subjunctive form of the verb. Practice saying the following sentences aloud:

¡*No me hables* (*tú*)! (Don't speak to me!)

¡*No la comas!* (Don't eat it!)

¡*No vivas aquí!* (Don't live here!)

¡*No vengas!* (Don't come!)

¡*No vayas!* (Don't go!)

Note: The subjunctive form of the verb as the negative command for *tú* ends with *-s*, as you would expect.

A special command form (*not* subjunctive) is used for *tú* if the command is *affirmative*. With a handful of exceptions, the formula for constructing the affirmative command with *tú* is as follows:

GO TO ▶
To review the present tense, see Hours 3 and 4.

- Take the él/ella/Ud. form of the verb, present tense.
- Use this form as the command for *tú*.

See the following examples:

¡*Háblame* (*tú*)! (Speak to me!)

¡*Cómela!* (Eat it!)

¡*Vive aquí!* (Live here!)

¡*Llega a tiempo!* (Arrive [Get there] on time!)

¡*Tráemelos!* (Bring them to me!)

¡*Llévales la llave!* (Take the key to them!)

¡*Llévasela!* (Take it to them [to him, to her]!)

The negative commands for *tú* are simple enough if you retain your knowledge of the present subjunctive. The affirmative commands are just as easy, if not more so, if you remember the present indicative tense. The problem is that the negative commands are so different from the affirmative commands.

Study the following table for the affirmative and negative commands with *tú*, and practice by saying aloud the examples of the two rightmost columns.

**Affirmative and Negative Commands with *Tú***

| Infinitive | Present Tense | Affirmative | Negative |
|---|---|---|---|
| hablar | Él habla. | ¡Habla (tú)! | ¡No hables (tú)! |
| comer | Él come. | ¡Come! | ¡No comas! |
| vivir | Él vive aquí. | ¡Vive aquí! | ¡No vivas aquí! |
| traer | Él me lo trae. | ¡Tráemelo! | ¡No me lo traigas! |
| llevar | Él se la lleva. | ¡Llévasela! | ¡No se la lleves! |
| llegar | Él llega a tiempo. | ¡Llega a tiempo! | ¡No llegues a tiempo! |
| coger | Él lo coge. | ¡Cógelo! | ¡No lo cojas! |
| escribir | Él me escribe. | ¡Escríbeme! | ¡No me escribas! |
| cocinar | Él cocina. | ¡Cocina! | ¡No cocines! |
| correr | Él corre. | ¡Corre! | ¡No corras! |

All negative commands are subjunctive; there are no exceptions. However, although almost all verbs follow the rule that the *tú* affirmative command form is the same as the *él* form of the present tense, a handful of verbs are irregular in the affirmative. The irregular affirmative command forms for *tú* are all one-syllable words. The negative command for these are regular; they're still subjunctive.

Study the following table, and practice saying the affirmative and negative commands until they sound natural to you.

**Irregular Affirmative Commands with *Tú***

| Infinitive | Affirmative Command | Negative Command |
|---|---|---|
| decir (to say) | di | no digas |
| hacer (to do, to make) | haz | no hagas |
| ir (to go) | ve | no vayas |
| poner (to put) | pon | no pongas |
| salir (to leave, to go out) | sal | no salgas |
| ser (to be) | sé | no seas |
| tener (to have) | ten | no tengas |
| venir (to come) | ven | no vengas |

Because of the difference between negative and affirmative *tú* commands, you'll find it even more important than ever to drill with each form of the same verb.

**JUST A MINUTE**

Contrary to the situation with *Ud.,* the inclusion of the pronoun *tú* with the command sounds less courteous, and more imperious, than its omission.

The affirmative command for the irregular verb *ir* with *tú* is exactly the same as the affirmative command for the regular verb *ver*. In a different context, the word *ve* could also mean *he/she/it sees*. You might have noticed, as well, that the affirmative command form of the verb *venir* with *tú* looks and sounds exactly like the word that means *they see*. Furthermore, the affirmative command of the verb *ser* for *tú* looks and sounds just like the word that means *I know*. But there really is no chance of confusion; the context will clarify the meaning.

**GO TO ▶**
To review the difference between *ir* and the reflexive *irse,* see Hour 16.

Practice saying the following sentences aloud, picturing the meaning (noticing the difference between affirmative and negative, and between *tú*, on one hand, and *Ud.* and *Uds.*, on the other hand):

> *¡Profesor, venga Ud. a la fiesta!* (Professor, come to the party!)
>
> *Pero, no venga muy tarde.* (But, don't come very late.)
>
> *¡Paco, ven a la fiesta!* (Paco, come to the party!)
>
> *¡Pero, no vengas muy tarde!* (But, don't come very late!)
>
> *Dígamelo, profesor.* (Tell it to me, professor.)
>
> *No me lo diga, profesor.* (Don't tell it to me, professor.)
>
> *Dímelo, Margarita.* (Tell it to me, Margarita.)
>
> *No me lo digas, Margarita.* (Don't tell it to me, Margarita.)
>
> *Abran Uds. los libros.* (Open your books.)
>
> *No abran Uds. los libros.* (Don't open your books.)
>
> *Abre el libro, amigo.* (Open your book, [my] friend.)
>
> *No, no lo abras.* (No, don't open it.)

Only when the *vosotros/as* command is *negative* do you use the present subjunctive form of the verb. Practice saying the following sentences aloud:

> *¡No me habléis (vosotros)!* (Don't speak to me!)
>
> *¡No la comáis!* (Don't eat it!)

*¡No viváis aquí!* (Don't live here!)

*¡No vengáis!* (Don't come!)

*¡No vayáis!* (Don't go!)

A special command form (*not* subjunctive) is used for *vosotros/as* if the command is *affirmative:*

1. Start with the infinitive of the verb.
2. Detach the final *-r.*
3. Replace the final *-r* with *-d.*

Note: In formal writing, the rule for affirmative *vosotros* commands, as given in all grammar books, is followed, yet most Spaniards in ordinary conversation simply use the infinitive as the command for *vosotros.*

This rule has absolutely no exception; all *vosotros/as* affirmative commands are regular.

See the following examples:

*¡Hablad (vosotros)!* (Speak!)

*¡Comed!* (Eat!)

*¡Vivid aquí!* (Live here!)

*¡Decídmelo!* (Tell it to me!)

*¡Dádmelos!* (Give them to me!)

You'll need to remember that the affirmative commands for *vosotros/as* are very different from the negative commands (subjunctive). Study the two forms side by side, and then practice saying them aloud.

### Affirmative and Negative Commands with *Vosotros/as*

| Infinitive | Affirmative Command | Negative Command |
| --- | --- | --- |
| hablar | ¡Habladme! | ¡No me habléis! |
| comer | ¡Comedlo! | ¡No lo comáis! |
| vivir | ¡Vivid aquí! | ¡No viváis aquí! |
| venir | ¡Venid acá! | ¡No vengáis acá! |
| ir | ¡Id a casa! | ¡No vayáis a casa! |

Note: If you use a reflexive verb as a command for *vosotros/as,* the object pronoun *os* is handled normally for *negative* commands; you place it in front of the verb: *No os sentéis* (Don't sit down); *No os vistáis* (Don't get dressed); *No os vayáis* (Don't go away).

However, when you use a reflexive verb as a command for *vosotros/as* in an *affirmative* command, the object pronoun *os* is attached to the end of the verb, as is normal with affirmative commands; but, in addition, you drop the *-d* ending first: *Sentaos* (Sit down); *Vestíos* (Get dressed).

*Exception:* The verb *ir* keeps the *-d: Idos* (Go away).

## Express Commands Indirectly

Indirect commands are employed when you are not talking directly to the person(s) you want to carry out the action of the verb. For indirect commands, the subjunctive is always used. The sentence structure is as follows:

1. Start with the relative pronoun *que*.
2. Place the object pronouns, if there are any.
3. Use the subjunctive form of the verb.
4. Place the rest of the sentence, if there is any more, after the verb.

If the subject pronoun is needed for clarity, or desired for emphasis, it can be placed either right after *que* or after the verb.

The English equivalent of the indirect command is something like *Let them ...*, *Make them ...*, or *Have them ....*

Study the following sentences, and practice saying them aloud:

*Que lo hagan ellos.* (Let them do it.)

*¡Que (él) venga en seguida!* (Have him come right away!)

*Que se preocupe ella.* (Let her worry.)

*¡Que salgan inmediatamente!* (Make them leave immediately!)

*Que se vayan, si quieren.* (Let them go away, if they want to.)

---

**JUST A MINUTE**

Think of the indirect command as having a mental *Quiero*, or *Mando*, or *Aconsejo* before the *que*: (*Quiero*) *que lo hagan ellos.*

## USE ANOTHER EQUIVALENT OF *LET'S*

You've been using *vamos a* plus the infinitive as the equivalent of the English exhortation *Let's* plus a verb. This is the most common way, but there is another, perhaps more literary or elegant, way of achieving the same effect. Simply use the present subjunctive in the *nosotros* form of the verb. The rule for the placement of the object pronouns is the same as for all commands: Attach the object pronoun to the end of the verb when it's an affirmative command, but place it in front of the verb when it's a negative command. Study the following sentences; they show the *vamos a* method, the subjunctive method, and the English equivalent.

**Two Methods of Exhortation (Let's)**

| VAMOS A + Infinitive | Subjunctive | English |
|---|---|---|
| Vamos a hablar. | Hablemos. | Let's talk. |
| Vamos a comer. | Comamos. | Let's eat. |
| Vamos a vivir. | Vivamos. | Let's live. |
| Vamos a hacerlo. | Hagámoslo. | Let's do it. |
| Vamos a verla. | Veámosla. | Let's see her (or it). |

Note: The subjunctive *vayamos* is very rarely used as an affirmative exhortation; instead, the present tense *vamos* is almost always used to mean *let's go* or *let's* whatever the next infinitive says (in addition to its meaning of *we go* or *we're going*). On the other hand, the negative *No vamos* is never taken to mean *Let's not go* or *Let's not* whatever the next infinitive means; it only means *We don't go, We're not going,* or *We're not going to* plus the following infinitive.

The equivalent of *Let's not go* is the subjunctive: *No vayamos.* See the following examples:

> ¡*Vamos!* (Let's go!)
>
> ¡*No vayamos!* (Let's not go!)
>
> ¡*Vamos a comer!* (Let's eat!)
>
> ¡*Comamos!* (Let's eat!)
>
> ¡*No comamos!* (Let's not eat!)

**PROCEED WITH CAUTION**

In a negative *vosotros* command, you might think the *No os* ... is *Nos* ... because, in rapid speech, the two letters *o* next to each other tend to blend together.

Note: If the verb is reflexive, drop the final *-s* from the subjunctive *nosotros/as* form (if affirmative) before attaching the reflexive object pronoun *nos* to the end of the verb. See how this works with the sample verb *sentarse* (to sit down):

- Infinitive: *sentarse*
- Subjunctive of *sentar* with *nosotros* = *sentemos*
- Drop final *-s* = *\*sentemo*
- Add *nos* = *sentemo + nos*
- Result: *sentémonos*

Compare the affirmative and negative reflexive commands with *nosotros* as the subject in the following table.

**Affirmative and Negative Reflexive Exhortations**

| Infinitive | Affirmative Command | Negative Command |
| --- | --- | --- |
| *sentarse* (to sit) | sentémonos | no nos sentemos |
| *lavarse* (to wash) | lavémonos | no nos lavemos |
| *levantarse* (to get up) | levantémonos | no nos levantemos |
| *afeitarse* (to shave) | afeitémonos | no nos afeitemos |
| *quejarse* (to complain) | quejémonos | no nos quejemos |
| *ponerse* (to put on ...) | pongámonos ... | no nos pongamos ... |

Note: Whereas ¡*Vamos*! is *Let's go* (to a specific place), ¡*Vámonos*! means *Let's go* (away from here)! Drop the final *-s* of *vamos* and then add the reflexive *nos*.

## UNDERSTAND DIALECT VOCABULARY

Over time, languages spoken in widely separated areas of the world develop differences, mainly in vocabulary and in pronunciation; these differences are what form dialects. In the United States, we put *gas* (gasoline) in the *truck*, and reach our apartment by means of an *elevator*. In Britain, they put *petrol*

**GO TO** ▶
For pronunciation differences among Spanish dialects, see Hour 23.

in the *lorry*, and reach their apartment by means of a *lift*. In this hour, you will familiarize yourself with some important differences in vocabulary of several dialects.

## DIFFERENT WORDS, SAME MEANING (FOODS)

Many foods have one name in some regions, but another name in other regions. The following list provides a sampling of these differences. The English word is followed by the various Spanish terms and the region in which they are used.

- **Abalone.** In Spain and elsewhere, this is *oreja marina*, whereas in Chile it is *loco*, which also means *crazy*. In other countries, *loco* only means *crazy*.

- **Avocado.** In Spain, Mexico, and the Caribbean, this is *aguacate*; in Peru, Chile, and Argentina, it is *palta*.

- **Cabbage.** In Spain, it is *col* (f.), whereas in all Spanish America it is *repollo*.

- **Banana.** In most of South America, the word is *banana*. In Cuba, it is *guineo*, whereas in other regions bordering the Caribbean it is *plátano*. However, *plátano* in Cuba means *plantain*. In some regions, *plátano* is used for both bananas and plantain.

- **Bean.** In Mexico and Central America, the common word is *frijol* (pl. *frijoles*), which usually refers to a kidney bean. You can specifically refer to red beans (*frijoles colorados*) and black beans (*frijoles negros*). In Colombia, the word is accented on the first syllable (*fríjol, fríjoles*). In Argentina and Uruguay, the word for beans is *poroto*.

  In the Caribbean, the word *habichuela* is a general term for all kinds of beans. To be specific, you can say *habichuela verde* for a green bean, *habichuela negra* for a black bean, and so on.

  In Mexico, a green bean is *ejote*, whereas in Spain it is *judía (verde)*.

- **Peas.** In Spain, *guisantes*, whereas in Argentina and Uruguay, *arvejas*. In Puerto Rico, *petipuás*.

- **Pineapple.** In Spain, Mexico, Central America, the Caribbean, and northern South America, *piña*, whereas in the southern regions of South America it is *ananá*.

- **Turkey.** The word for this bird is *pavo* in every Hispanic country except Mexico and neighboring parts of Central America, where it is *guajolote*.

## SAME WORD, DIFFERENT MEANING: ARGENTINA AND SPAIN

Many Spanish words have one meaning in one country but a different meaning in another country. The following table compares words that differ in meaning between Spain and Argentina, two centers of film production and literature.

| Word | Spain | Argentina |
|------|-------|-----------|
| aguinaldo | Christmas gift to postman, etc. | overtime pay |
| alcahuete | pimp, procurer | police informer |
| almacén | warehouse | grocery store |
| bronca | fight, argument | anger, rage |
| cachete | slap | cheek; buttock |
| cartera | wallet, billfold | woman's handbag |
| coger | to take, seize | have sex |
| cuadra | stable (for horses) | city block |
| currar | (slang) to work | to trick |
| encajar un golpe | to receive a blow | to hit, strike |
| facha | (1) fascist; (2) appearance | appearance |
| felices pascuas | Merry Christmas | Happy Easter |
| frigorífico | refrigerator | meat-packing plant |
| funcionario | public servant | government official |
| gallego | Galician | any Spaniard |
| género | any merchandise | cloth |
| guapo | handsome | tough guy |
| jugo | liquid extracted from anything *except* fruit | liquid extracted from anything *especially* fruit |
| ligar | to join/combine | to receive a beating |
| manteca | lard | butter |
| mozo/a | young man/woman | waiter/waitress |
| ole | cheer (for one's team) | jeer (for other team) |

*continues*

*continued*

| Word | Spain | Argentina |
|------|-------|-----------|
| paro | unemployment | labor strike; heart attack |
| polla | penis | horse race |
| pollera | female chicken vendor | skirt |
| putear | to annoy | to insult |
| saco | bag, sack | jacket |
| zapatillas | house slippers | athletic footwear |

**JUST A MINUTE**

In Spain, *fruit juice* is *zumo*.

Don't be discouraged by these differences. You have a solid base in Spanish. If you stay in a country for a month or two, you will pick up the local terminology, just as you would in English whether in the United States, Britain, Australia, or any other anglophone area.

## THE 30-SECOND RECAP

In this hour, you've learned to use the future perfect tense, as well as how to give commands in Spanish, both directly and indirectly. You've also learned about differences in dialect vocabulary.

## HOUR'S UP!

**QUIZ**

Review this hour's work, and then see how you're doing by taking the following quiz. Remember, for accurate results, don't check back in the pages of this hour while actually testing yourself.

1. *¿Qué habrá hecho Carlos?* can mean …
   - **a.** What will Carlos have done?
   - **b.** I wonder what Carlos has made.
   - **c.** What could Carlos have made?
   - **d.** I wonder what Carlos has done.
   - **e.** What will Carlos have made?
   - **f.** All of the above.

2. *Ellos nos habrán dicho la verdad* can mean …
   a. They will have told us the truth.
   b. They probably have told us the truth.
   c. They must've told us the truth.
   d. They will have said the truth to us.
   e. All of the above.

3. Choose the phrase that will turn the original phrase from an affirmative command into a negative one: *¡Dímelo!*
   a. ¡No me lo diga!
   b. ¡No dímelo!
   c. ¡No me lo digas!
   d. ¡No dígasmelo!
   e. All of the above.

4. Choose the phrase that will turn the original phrase from an affirmative command into a negative one: *¡Mírala!*
   a. ¡No la mira!
   b. ¡No la mires!
   c. ¡No la mire!
   d. ¡No mírala!
   e. None of the above.

5. Choose the phrase that will turn the original phrase from an affirmative command into a negative one: *¡Venga acá!*
   a. ¡No venga acá!
   b. ¡Venga no acá!
   c. ¡No vengas acá!
   d. ¡No vienes acá!
   e. None of the above.

6. Choose the phrase that will turn the original phrase from an affirmative command into a negative one: *¡Ponéoslo!*
   a. ¡No ponéoslo!
   b. ¡No os lo pongáis!
   c. ¡No os lo poned!
   d. ¡No pongáisoslo!
   e. ¡No os pongáislo!

**7.** Choose the phrase that will turn the original phrase from an affirmative command into a negative one: *¡Vete!*

    **a.** ¡No te vayas!

    **b.** ¡No te ves!

    **c.** ¡No te ve!

    **d.** ¡No te vayáis!

    **e.** ¡No vete!

**8.** Choose the alternate way of saying ¡Comamos!

    **a.** ¡Comeremos!

    **b.** ¡Comemos!

    **c.** ¡Tenemos que comer!

    **d.** ¡Vamos a comer!

    **e.** ¡Debemos de comer!

**9.** If you were to encajar un golpe, would you be more comfortable in Spain or in Argentina?

**10.** Would you be more comfortable jogging in zapatillas in Spain or in Argentina?

**QUIZ**

# PART V

# Business, Travel, and Service Industries

# Hour 20
# Travel and Hotel

**LESSON PLAN:**
In this hour, you'll learn ...

- How to use the conditional perfect tense.
- Whether to use the subjunctive or indicative mood in adjective clauses.
- How to speak about travel, travel agents, and hotel accommodations.

This hour will help you communicate your needs when traveling, to travel agents and hotel personnel. There will be occasions on which you will want to talk about what you would have done, if conditions had been right. This hour will show you how to do that with the conditional perfect tense. You will also learn when to use the subjunctive and when not to in adjective phrases.

## LEARN THE CONDITIONAL PERFECT

The conditional perfect tense is used to refer to actions, events, or states that have not taken place because certain *conditions* were not in effect. It's called the conditional perfect tense precisely because it refers to actions whose reality is conditional; those conditions were not met, so the events did not take place. See the following English sentences for examples:

- I would have gone if they had invited me. Here my going relied on their inviting me. I did not go because they did not invite me. The condition for my going was not met.

- He would have been a good worker *if* he hadn't been lazy. This sentence means he has not been a good worker, because the condition for his being a good worker (not being lazy) was not met.

- We would have gone to the beach *if* we had known how to swim. This means we have not gone to the beach, because we hadn't known how to swim; knowing how to swim was the unmet condition.

- Who would have done such a thing (*if* given the opportunity)? This means we are wondering who, under the right conditions (opportunity), would have committed the act in question.

The same sense of unfulfilled plans can be seen in contrasting English sentences that predict completed events by projecting into the future perfect, with English sentences that project from the past into an unfulfilled past future:

(1) He says he will have gone.

(2) He said he would have gone (but he didn't go).

(3) I think I'll have had lunch by then.

(4) I thought I would have had lunch by then (but I had not).

(5) They promise they will have completed the task.

(6) They promised they would have completed the task (but they didn't).

**TIME SAVER**

The conditional perfect tense relates to the past tense (said, etc.) the way the future perfect tense relates to the present tense (says, etc.).

The first verb in each of the odd-numbered sentences (*says*, *think*, and *promise*) is in the present tense, and is followed by a verb in the future perfect tense (*will have gone*, *I'll have had*, and *they will have*). The future perfect tense is used in these sentences to project what will have happened some time after the verb in the present tense.

The even-numbered sentences merely shift the sentences from the present into the past. Because the first verb (*said*, *thought*, and *promised*) has been shifted from the present tense to the past tense, the verbs that had been in the future perfect tense in the odd-numbered sentences are shifted to the conditional perfect tense (*would have gone*, *I'd have*, and *would have completed*). The conditional perfect tense is used in these sentences to project what would have happened (but didn't) at some time after the verb in the past tense.

## FORM THE CONDITIONAL PERFECT TENSE

You know that any verb that is irregular in the future tense is irregular in exactly the same way in the conditional tense. The conditional perfect tense is formed by using the conditional tense of the auxiliary verb *haber* plus the past participle. In the conditional tense, *haber* drops the *-e-* of the infinitive ending before adding its endings. See the following table, which shows the conditional tense of *haber* with the past participle of *ver* as an example of the conditional perfect tense.

**Conditional Perfect Tense with *Ver***

| Subject Pronoun | Conditional of Haber | Past Participle of Ver |
|---|---|---|
| yo | habría | visto |
| tú | habrías | visto |
| él | habría | visto |
| ella | habría | visto |
| usted | habría | visto |
| nosotros/as | habríamos | visto |
| vosotros/as | habríais | visto |
| ellos | habrían | visto |
| ellas | habrían | visto |
| ustedes | habrían | visto |

Study the following sentences, and practice saying them aloud:

> *Ella no lo habría hecho si …*
> She wouldn't have done it if …
>
> *Yo habría comido si …*
> I would have eaten if …
>
> *Yo habría ido si …*
> I would have gone if …
>
> *López habría sido un buen trabajador si …*
> López would have been a good worker if …
>
> *Habríamos ido a la playa si ….*
> We would have gone to the beach if ….
>
> *¿Quién habría hecho tal cosa?*
> Who would have done such a thing?

Whether they explicitly say so or it's implicit, every one of the preceding sentences suggests an *if*, meaning *under certain conditions*. For example, the next-to-last sentence implies *if the opportunity had presented itself*, and the last sentence implies *if something else had (or had not) taken place*.

## TALK OF PAST PROBABILITY

You remember that the conditional tense can be used, in addition to talking of what could have been, to refer to probability or wondering in the past (just as the future tense can be used to refer to probability or wondering in the present). The conditional perfect tense can be used similarly, for wondering about what someone had done or talking about what someone probably had done before some point in the past.

GO TO ▶
For a review of the conditional tense to express wonder and probability in the past, see Hour 7.

When the word *si* is omitted, the previous six sentences could be interpreted as follows (depending on the context):

She probably hadn't done it.

I probably had eaten.

I probably had gone.

López had probably been a good worker.

We probably had gone to the beach.

I wonder who had done such a thing.

See the following sentences, which use the conditional perfect tense, but in contexts in which you know you're either wondering (questioning) or talking about the probability of an event that might have taken place (or not taken place) at an unspecified time, before some specified point in the past:

*¿Habrían venido antes de las cinco?*
I wonder if they had come before five o'clock.

*No creo. No habrían llegado.*
I don't think (so). They probably hadn't arrived.

*¿Quiénes habrían sido?*
I wonder who they had been.

*Habrían sido los jefes de los departamentos.*
They'd probably been the department chairpersons.

*¿Qué habría visto ella?*
I wonder what she had seen.

*Habría recibido sus notas.*
She'd probably received her grades.

*¿Qué habría hecho yo para que se enojara?*
I wonder what I had done to make her angry.

GO TO ▶
The last sentence ends with the word *enojara*, which is in the imperfect subjunctive. For the lesson on that tense, see Hour 22.

# Take a Vacation in Spanish

To prepare to take a vacation in a Spanish-speaking country, you'll need to know terms related to travel arrangements and hotel accommodations.

## Make Travel Arrangements

If you need to make arrangements to travel, the following vocabulary will be indispensable.

**JUST A MINUTE**

The word (*el*) *mar* is usually masculine; in poetic usage (and sometimes among sea-farers) it can be *la mar* (feminine).

### Vocabulario para Viajar

| Spanish | English |
| --- | --- |
| abordar | to board |
| a bordo | onboard |
| la aduana (f.) | customs |
| aéreo/a | air |
| el aeroplano (m.) | airplane |
| el aeropuerto (m.) | airport |
| el aire (m.) | air |
| la agencia de viajes (f.) | travel agency |
| el/la agente de viajes (m./f.) | travel agent |
| el/la auxiliar de vuelo (m./f.) | flight attendant |
| el/la asistente de vuelo (m./f.) | flight attendant |
| aterrizar | to land |
| el avión (m.) | airplane |
| la azafata (f.) | stewardess; flight attendant (female) |
| bajar | to go down; to get off (a conveyance) |
| el barco (m.) | ship |
| el billete (m.) | ticket (Spain); bill (currency) |
| el boleto (m.) | ticket (Lat. Amer.) |
| cambiar | to change; to exchange |
| cambiar un cheque | to cash a check |

*continues*

### *Vocabulario para Viajar* (continued)

| Spanish | English |
|---|---|
| la clase turista (f.) | tourist class |
| el cheque (de viajero) (m.) | (traveler's) check |
| los derechos de aduana (m. pl.) | customs duty |
| desembarcar | to disembark; to deplane |
| despegar | to take off |
| desplazar | to move, shift; to displace; to travel |
| el desplazamiento (m.) | movement, shifting; displacement; travel |
| el destino (m.) | destination; destiny |
| embarcar | to embark; to board (put passengers on board) |
| embarcarse | to embark; to board (to get onboard) |
| el equipaje (m.) | luggage, baggage |
| la escala (f.) | stop (at a port or airport); stopover |
| esperar | to wait; to hope; to expect |
| la excursión (f.) | excursion, tour |
| facturar la(s) maleta(s) | to check baggage |
| el/la guía (m./f.) | guide (person) |
| la guía (f.) | guide (book) |
| hacer escala en | to stop (or stop over) at |
| hacer la(s) maleta(s) | to pack (one's bags) |
| de ida | one way |
| de ida y vuelta | round trip |
| el impuesto (m.) | tax |
| ir de vacaciones | to go on vacation |
| la llegada (f.) | arrival |
| la maleta (f.) | suitcase |
| el mar (m.) | sea |
| la natación (f.) | swimming (the activity) |
| el pasaje (m.) | passage; ticket (for travel) |
| el pasaporte (m.) | passport |
| (de) primera clase | first class |
| el puerto (m.) | port; harbor |

| Spanish | English |
|---------|---------|
| reclamar | claim, demand; reclaim, recover, take back |
| el reclamo de equipaje (m.) | baggage claim |
| la reservación (f.) | reservation, booking |
| reservar | to reserve; to book (passage, rooms, etc.) |
| la sala de espera (f.) | waiting room |
| la salida (f.) | exit; departure |
| la sección de fumar (f.) | smoking section |
| la sección de no fumar (f.) | no smoking section |
| el seguro (m.) | insurance |
| seguro/a | sure; secure; safe |
| el sol (m.) | the sun |
| subir | to go up; to get on (a conveyance) |
| la tarifa (f.) | fare, ticket prices |
| tramitar | to transact, to negotiate, to take necessary steps |
| los trámites (m. pl.) | procedures, steps, formalities |
| la transacción global (f.) | package deal |
| transbordar | to transfer; to transship |
| el transbordo (m.) | transfer, (plane) connection; transshipment |
| el transporte (m.) | transportation |
| el transporte aéreo | air transportation |
| el transporte marítimo | sea transportation |
| trasladar | to transfer |
| el traslado (m.) | transfer, transferal |
| el turismo (m.) | tourism |
| el/la turista (m./f.) | tourist |
| turístico/a | having to do with tourists, tourism |
| las vacaciones (f. pl.) | vacation |
| la vacuna (f.) | vaccination; "shot" |
| el valor (m.) | value; valor |
| el viaje (m.) | trip, voyage |

*continues*

### Vocabulario para Viajar  (continued)

| Spanish | English |
| --- | --- |
| viajar | to travel |
| el visado (m.) | visa |
| la visa (f.) | visa |
| volar (ue) | to fly |
| el vuelo (m.) | flight |
| de vuelta | return; returned |
| la vuelta (f.) | return; stroll; drive |
| el yate (m.) | yacht |

**JUST A MINUTE**

The word *aeroplano* is somewhat old-fashioned; *avión* is more popular.

Read the following sentences, and practice saying them aloud:

*Juan Gómez trabaja mucho. Un día decidió ir de vacaciones.*
Juan Gómez works hard. One day he decided to go on vacation.

*Fue a la agencia de viajes "El Sol" a comprar un pasaje de ida y vuelta para San Juan, capital de Puerto Rico.*
He went to the "El Sol" travel agency to buy a round-trip ticket to San Juan, the capital of Puerto Rico.

**JUST A MINUTE**

Even though *para* would ordinarily be used for *to* when it means *in order to,* you can use *a* if it comes after a verb of motion, as before *comprar* (based on *Fue*) in the previous sentence.

*La agente de viajes, Rita Méndez, le convenció a hacer una transacción global.*
The travel agent, Rita Méndez, convinced him to take a package deal.

*La transacción incluía el desplazamiento aéreo, el traslado desde el aeropuerto hasta el hotel, y el precio del hotel por catorce días y trece noches.*
The deal included air transportation, transfer from the airport to the hotel, and the price of the hotel for 14 days and 13 nights.

*Gómez le preguntó si el precio también incluía la comida.*
Gómez asked her if the price included meals as well.

*La agente le contestó que sólo incluía un desayuno que consistía en panecillos, tostadas, o medialunas con café, chocolate, o té.*

The agent answered (to him) that it only included a breakfast that consisted of rolls, toast, or croissants, with coffee, (hot) chocolate, or tea.

*La agente le reservó el vuelo 428 que despegaría del Aeropuerto Kennedy a las cuatro de la tarde y aterrizaría en Puerto Rico a las nueve y veinte de la noche, con transbordo en Atlanta.*

The agent booked him on flight 428, which would take off from Kennedy Airport at 4:00 p.m. and would land in Puerto Rico at 9:20 p.m., with a connection through Atlanta.

## CHECK-IN AND TOUR

If you need to handle check-in, arrange for sightseeing, and deal with other matters at a hotel, the following vocabulary for lodging and tours will help.

### PROCEED WITH CAUTION

 Many countries use *ventilador* for an electric fan. In those countries, *abanico eléctrico* will sound comical (a handheld fan connected to electricity), whereas in other countries it is the normal term.

### *Vocabulario para Alojamiento y Excursiones*

| | |
|---|---|
| el abanico (m.) | fan |
| el abanico eléctrico (m.) | (electric) fan |
| el acondicionador de aire (m.) | air conditioner |
| el aire acondicionado (m.) | air conditioning ("conditioned air") |
| el alojamiento (m.) | lodging |
| alojar | to lodge; to give lodging |
| alojarse (en) | to stay (at) |
| arreglar (ie) | to arrange; to put in order; to fix up |
| el arreglo (m.) | arrangement |
| ascender (ie) | to ascend, to go up |
| el ascensor (m.) | elevator |
| la aventura (f.) | adventure |
| aventurero/a | adventurous; adventurer |
| el baúl (m.) | steamer trunk |

*continues*

## *Vocabulario para Alojamiento y Excursiones* (continued)

| | |
|---|---|
| el billete (m.) | bill (paper money); ticket (Spain) |
| el bosque (m.) | woods, forest |
| el bosque tropical (m.) | rain forest |
| el botón (m.) | button |
| los botones (m. pl.) | buttons |
| el botones (m.) | bellboy |
| la caja (f.) | box; cash register; checkout counter |
| el/la cajero/a (m./f.) | cashier; checkout clerk |
| la cama matrimonial (f.) | double bed |
| la cama para una persona (f.) | single bed |
| la camarera (f.) | waitress; chambermaid |
| el carro público (m.) | fixed-route taxi (Puerto Rico) |
| el catre (m.) | cot |
| la cola (f.) | tail; line (of people), queue |
| la criada (f.) | maid |
| el dinero en efectivo (m.) | cash |
| el elevador (m.) | elevator |
| el/la empleado/a (m./f.) | employee; clerk |
| entender (ie) | to understand; to hear |
| la entrada (f.) | entrance; ticket (to theater, movie, etc.) |
| la excursión (f.) | excursion, tour |
| el/la gerente/a (m./f.) | manager |
| la guagua (f.) | bus (Caribbean, Canary Islands) |
| la habitación (f.) | room |
| hacer cola | to form a line (of people), to queue up |
| el hospedaje (m.) | lodging |
| hospedar | to lodge, to give lodging, to "put up" |
| hospedarse (en) | to lodge (oneself), to take lodging, to stay (at) |
| la inspección (f.) | inspection |
| inspeccionar | to inspect |
| marcharse | to go away, to leave |
| la mesita de noche (f.) | night table |
| el motel (m.) | motel |

### Vocabulario para Alojamiento y Excursiones

| | |
|---|---|
| pagar la cuenta | to check out (pay the bill) |
| la palma (f.) | palm (of hand); palm tree |
| la palmera (f.) | palm tree |
| la piscina (f.) | swimming pool |
| la propina (f.) | tip; gratuity |
| la recepción (f.) | reception; reception desk |
| recoger | to collect, to pick up, to gather |
| registrarse | to check in (a hotel); to register |
| reír(se) | to laugh |
| la salida (f.) | exit |
| la selva (f.) | jungle |
| el servicio (m.) | service |
| los servicios (m. pl.) | services; bathroom (in a public place) |
| servir (i, i) | to serve; to give service; to be of use |
| sonreír (i, i) | to smile |
| tropical | tropical |
| el trópico (m.) | the tropics |
| la valija (f.) | suitcase, valise |
| el ventilador (m.) | (electric) fan |

**JUST A MINUTE**

A variant of *alojamiento* in some parts of Spanish America is *el alojo*. Synonymous with these nouns is *hospedaje*.

The verb *entender* (*ie*) is the usual word for *to understand*, but can also mean *to hear*. *No te entiendo* means *I don't understand you*, or *I don't hear you*, or *I didn't quite catch that*. It's not always clear if the problem is with comprehension or hearing.

The verb *comprender* is involved strictly with comprehension, and suggests a deeper kind of understanding than *entender* (*ie*). *No te comprendo* suggests that there is a different mind-set between the two people.

Notice that the *singular* masculine *el botones* refers to *the bellboy*. No doubt the word's origin has to do with the shiny buttons bellboys used to have on their uniforms.

Study the following sentences:

*Después de bajar del taxi, Gómez entró al hotel y fue directamente a la recepción.*
After getting out of the taxi, Gómez went into the hotel and went straight to the reception desk.

*El empleado buscó su nombre en la computadora, y le dijo que todo estaba arreglado.*
The clerk looked up his name on the computer, and told him everything was taken care of.

*El empleado le dio la llave, y llamó al botones.*
The clerk gave him the key, and called the bellboy.

*Gómez le preguntó al botones, "¿Dónde está el ascensor?" y el botones dijo, "¿Cómo?" sin entender.*
Gómez asked the bellboy, "Where's the elevator?" and the bellboy said "What?" without understanding.

*El empleado sonrió y dijo, "Aquí decimos, 'el elevador.'"*
The clerk smiled and said, "Here we say, 'el elevador.'"

*El botones recogió las maletas, y los dos entraron al ascensor, y ascendieron al tercer piso.*
The bellboy picked up the suitcases, and the two (of them) rode up to the third floor.

*Gómez le dio una propina al botones, e inspeccionó la habitación.*
Gómez gave the bellboy a tip, and inspected the room.

*Al próximo día, después de desayunar en el comedor, se puso el traje de baño y pasó la mañana nadando en la piscina.*
The next day, after having breakfast, he put on his bathing suit and spent the morning swimming in the pool.

*Un día, siendo aventurero, viajó en carro público a las montañas del interior, para visitar los bonitos pueblos de Aibonito y Barranquitas.*
One day, being adventurous, he traveled by "*carro público*" to the mountains of the interior, to visit the beautiful towns of Aibonito and Barranquitas.

In the seventh sentence, *e* is used instead of *y* for *and*. This is common practice when the next word begins with the letter *i* or the combination *hi*.

# USE THE SUBJUNCTIVE IN ADJECTIVE CLAUSES

Up until now, you've used the subjunctive mood in noun clauses and in impersonal expressions. Now, you're going to learn to use the subjunctive mood in adjective clauses.

**GO TO** ▶
To review the uses of the subjunctive mood studied previously, see Hours 12 and 13.

An adjective clause is a clause that is used as an adjective. For example, the English sentence *I'm looking for a house that has four bathrooms* has two clauses: *I'm looking for a house* is the main clause, and *that has four bathrooms* is the adjective clause. The clause *that has four bathrooms* behaves like an adjective, because it describes the noun (house) of the main clause.

## BE SPECIFIC; USE INDICATIVE

If the antecedent (the noun of the main clause) refers to a specific, definite person or thing, then the verb in the adjective clause that describes that antecedent will not be subjunctive; it will be indicative (in whatever tense the situation calls for). It's not referring to that shadowy, doubtful, unreal world of the subjunctive; it's reporting on a fact, something real. See the following examples:

(1) *Busco un hotel que **tiene** un restaurante.*
I'm looking for a hotel that has a restaurant.

(2) *Ella quisiera visitar una ciudad que **está** en Sudamérica.*
She'd like to visit a city that's in South America.

(3) *Voy a llamar a un agente de viajes que **sabe** lo que hace.*
I'm going to call a travel agent who knows what he's doing.

(4) *Conocemos a la señora que **hablará** mañana.*
We know the lady who will speak tomorrow.

(5) *¿Quién es el hombre que **cantó** ayer?*
Who is the man who sang yesterday?

In this type of sentence, Spanish gives us more information than an English sentence of the same type. Precisely because the indicative is used (rather than the subjunctive) in the adjective clauses, we know that the person or thing referred to is a definite, specific entity existing in the real world.

Notice that any of the indicative tenses can be used. The first three sentences of the previous list are in the present indicative tense; however, the fourth sentence is in the future indicative, and the last sentence is in the preterit indicative tense.

Because of the use of the indicative, sentence 1 tells us that the speaker has a specific hotel in mind; he could probably give you its name. He may just have forgotten the hotel's location. This doesn't make it any less real or less specific. He just can't find it. Sentence 2 tells us that she has a definite, specific South American city in mind; if you were to ask her which city it is, she could tell you. The speaker of sentence 3 has a specific travel agent in mind, and he's going to call him. In sentence 4, we're saying that we're acquainted with a specific woman, and that she's going to speak tomorrow. In sentence 5, the speaker doesn't know the name of the man who sang yesterday, it's true, but he has a definite, specific man in mind. He knows that this man sang yesterday, and he might have even seen and heard him sing; he just wants someone to give the man's name or otherwise identify him.

## USE THE SUBJUNCTIVE WHEN BEING VAGUE

If the noun of the main clause (the antecedent) is nonspecific, then you will use the subjunctive form of the verb in the adjective clause. See the following examples:

(1) *Busco un hotel que* **tenga** *un restaurante.*
I'm looking for a hotel that has a restaurant.

(2) *Ella quisiera visitar una ciudad que* **esté** *en Sudamérica.*
She'd like to visit a city that's in South America.

(3) *Voy a llamar un agente de viajes que* **sepa** *lo que hace.*
I'm going to call a travel agent who knows what he's doing.

(4) *¿Conocen Uds. una señora que* **hable** *español?*
Do you know a lady who speaks Spanish?

(5) *¿Hay un hombre aquí que* **cante** *bien?*
Is there a man here who sings well?

**JUST A MINUTE**

Sentences 3 and 4 of the earlier (indicative) series have the personal *a* in front of *un agente* and *una señora,* respectively; however, the third and fourth sentences of the previous (subjunctive) series omit it. The *a* is often omitted when a *specific* human being is not the object of the verb.

Note: Sentences 1 through 3 in the earlier (indicative) series are exactly the same in English as the first three sentences in the previous series, yet the Spanish sentences are different. Because the verbs of the previous series were in the indicative, we know the antecedents were specific. But in this series, because the verbs are in the subjunctive, we know the antecedents are non-specific or indefinite. Spanish sentences with an adjective clause, then, provide more information than English sentences of the same type.

Sentence 1, by using the subjunctive *tenga*, lets us know that the speaker does *not* have a specific hotel in mind; he doesn't even know if such a hotel exists.

In sentence 2, the speaker tells us that someone (*ella*) would like to visit a city that's in South America. We can tell from the use of the subjunctive *esté* that she doesn't have a specific city in mind.

In sentence 3, the speaker, by using the subjunctive, makes it clear that this travel agent is not a specific person. The speaker doesn't have a specific travel agent in mind; he's just hoping to locate one. He can't use the indicative to report that a hypothetical person knows what he's doing.

Sentences 4 and 5 of the earlier ( indicative) series can't be made subjunctive. That's because sentence 4 says we know the lady. If we know her, she must be a definite person. Because we can report these things as facts, we can't use the subjunctive. In sentence 5, we don't know the man's name—that's why we're asking who he is—but he is a definite, specific, flesh-and-blood human being, so we used the preterit indicative to report that he actually sang.

The final two Sentences 4 and 5 of the second group are different. The subjunctive *hable* in sentence 4 tells us that we'd like to find a woman who speaks Spanish, but we don't have a specific woman in mind. We're only asking (and hoping) that the people to whom we're talking know such a person. In the sentence 5, we're asking if there is any man here who sings well. This means we don't know if such a man even exists—not in the whole world, just *here*. Obviously, if we're asking this question, we don't have a specific man in mind who sings well.

**TIME SAVER**

Whenever you *ask* if someone or something exists, the antecedent must be nonspecific, and the adjective clause will use the subjunctive.

Sentences 4 and 5 of this latter series could be changed to show we have a specific person in mind. See the following sentences:

*¿Conocen Uds. a **la** señora que **habla** español?*
Do you know *the* lady who speaks Spanish?

*Sí, hay un hombre aquí que **canta** bien.*
Yes, there is a man here who sings well.

The first of these alternate sentences now has not only the indicative *habla* instead of the subjunctive *hable*, but also has the definite article *la* instead of the indefinite article *una*. The indicative indicates we're talking about a specific person who, we can report, actually speaks Spanish well. The definite article is a dead giveaway, too, that we're talking about a specific person.

## USE THE SUBJUNCTIVE FOR NONEXISTENCE

You have seen that you use the subjunctive mood in adjective clauses when the antecedent is nonspecific, because you can't report that a person who does not definitely exist does or doesn't perform an act. It stands to reason, then, that you certainly can't report that a person who definitely does *not* exist can do or not do something.

**TIME SAVER**

Using the indicative in an adjective clause for a nonexistent antecedent would make as much sense as using an adjective to describe what doesn't exist: *This house, which doesn't exist, is blue.*

Rule: When the antecedent of the adjective clause is nonexistent, use the subjunctive.

Study the following sentences:

*No hay ningún hombre aquí que **cante** bien.*
There is no man here who sings well.

*No conozco a ningún agente de viajes que **sepa** lo que hace.*
I don't know any travel agent who knows what he's doing.

*No existe el hombre a quien no le **guste** la aventura.*
The man doesn't exist who doesn't like adventure.

*No veo nada aquí que me **guste.***
I don't see anything here I like.

*No hay ningún estudiante en la clase que **hable** chino.*
There is no student in the class who speaks Chinese.

## The 30-Second Recap

In this hour, you've learned to use the conditional perfect tense, and whether to use the subjunctive mood or the indicative mood in adjective clauses. You've also learned to speak about travel, travel agents, and hotel accommodations.

## Hour's Up!

Look this hour over again, and then see how you're doing by answering the following questions. You'll have a better idea of your progress if you don't consult with the lessons involved while taking the quiz.

1. The conditional perfect tense …
   a. Refers to lost opportunities.
   b. Speaks of what might have been.
   c. Either states or implies an "if."
   d. All of the above.

2. An adjective clause …
   a. Modifies a noun in the main clause.
   b. Always has a subjunctive verb.
   c. Always has an indicative verb.
   d. None of the above.

3. Choose the best translation: *Yo no habría ido.*
   a. I haven't gone.
   b. I hadn't gone.
   c. I wouldn't have gone.
   d. I won't have gone.

4. Choose the best translation: *¿Quién habrá hecho tal cosa?*
   a. I wonder who has done such a thing.
   b. I wonder who had done such a thing.
   c. I wonder who would have done such a thing.

5. Choose the best translation: *Yo habría reservado el vuelo 25 para mi desplazamiento al Perú.*

   a. I had reserved seat 25 for my tour of Peru.

   b. I would have reserved seat 25 for my tour of Peru.

   c. I had booked flight 25 for my trip to Peru.

   d. I would have booked flight 25 for my trip to Peru.

6. Choose the best translation: Habrían llegado ayer.

   a. They would've arrived yesterday.

   b. I wonder if they've arrived yesterday.

   c. They had arrived yesterday.

7. Choose the best translation: ¿Habías comido?

   a. Have you eaten?

   b. Had you eaten?

   c. Would you have eaten?

8. Choose the best translation: Le dí una propina al botones.

   a. I gave propane to the mailman.

   b. I tipped the bellboy.

   c. I gave a tip for (bringing) my buttons.

   d. I tipped over the buttons.

# Hour 21
# At the Doctor's

CHAPTER SUMMARY

**LESSON PLAN:**
In this hour, you'll learn …

- How to use the subjunctive present perfect tense.
- How to refer to existence in the subjunctive.
- How to talk about medical problems to doctors and dentists.
- How to talk about this, these, that and those.
- How to use two different words for "but."

In case you need the services of a doctor or dentist in a Spanish-speaking country, it will be helpful to be able to discuss your symptoms and understand the doctor's or dentist's questions. First, however, you will strengthen your grasp of the Spanish language by dealing with the subjunctive present perfect tense.

## FORM THE PRESENT PERFECT SUBJUNCTIVE

The present perfect subjunctive, like all compound tenses, is composed of the auxiliary verb *haber* plus the past participle. (For a review of the formation of the past participle, see Hour 9.) In this case, you will conjugate *haber* in the present subjunctive. See the following for the present subjunctive conjugation of *haber*:

- haya
- hayas
- haya
- hayamos
- hayáis
- hayan

### KNOW WHEN TO USE THE PRESENT PERFECT SUBJUNCTIVE

The present perfect subjunctive is used to refer to an event that took place at some indeterminate time before the present, but when the subjunctive is called for, for any of the reasons you've already learned (doubt, denial, wishing or wanting, emotion, and so on). For example: I doubt (that) he's arrived. The present perfect is used in English because his arriving took place at some indeterminate time before the present. The subjunctive is needed in Spanish because that arrival (or nonarrival) is a noun clause following the verb *doubt*.

**TIME SAVER**

 Use the present perfect subjunctive whenever two factors are present: The English is in the present perfect, and the subjunctive is called for.

Practice saying the following sentences aloud:

> *Dudo que Roberto haya llegado.*
> I doubt that Roberto has arrived.

> *Me alegro de que lo hayas hecho.*
> I'm glad you've done it.

> *No creemos que hayan salido.*
> We don't believe (that) they've left.

> *Es triste que María se haya ido.*
> It's sad that María has gone away.

> *¿Cree Ud. que yo haya dicho tal cosa?*
> Do you believe (that) I've said such a thing?

**GO TO ▶**
To review the reasons for using the subjunctive, see Hours 12, 13, and 20.

> *Lamentan que hayamos venido tarde.*
> They're sorry (that) we've come late.

> *Es lástima que ella no haya estudiado.*
> It's a pity (that) she hasn't studied.

## Refer to Existence in the Subjunctive

You've used the verb *haber*, not only as a helping verb in compound tenses, but also to show *existence* in all the indicative tenses. Naturally, *haber* can also be used in the subjunctive mood to show existence. See the following examples:

> *¿Crees que haya una fiesta mañana?*
> Do you think there will be a party tomorrow?

> *Dudo que haya tres enfermeras en el consultorio.*
> I doubt there are three nurses in the doctor's office.

> *Es lástima que no haya mucha gente aquí.*
> It's too bad there aren't many people here.

*Es posible que haya dificultades.*
It's possible there are (or there will be) difficulties.

*Quiero que haya paz.*
I want there to be peace.

## TALK ABOUT HEALTH

If you're in a Spanish-speaking country and need to talk to doctors or dentists, you'll need a battery of terms relating to parts of the body, to ailments, and to symptoms. You'll also need to understand the medical advice you're given. The following three vocabulary lists will be of help. The first list covers the parts of the body.

### JUST A MINUTE

In other contexts, *muñeca* also means a *doll* (a human-shaped child's toy).

### Vocabulario para las Partes del Cuerpo

| Spanish | English |
| --- | --- |
| el abdomen (m.) | abdomen |
| el ano (m.) | anus |
| el antebrazo (m.) | forearm |
| el apéndice (m.) | appendix |
| la articulación (f.) | joint |
| el bazo (m.) | spleen |
| la boca (f.) | mouth |
| el brazo (m.) | arm |
| bucal | relating to the mouth |
| la cabellera (f.) | hair (of the head, head of hair) |
| el cabello (m.) | hair (of the head, head of hair) |
| la cabeza (f.) | head |
| la cara (f.) | face |
| cardíaco/a | cardiac, (of the) heart |
| el carrillo (m.) | cheek |
| la ceja (f.) | eyebrow |

*continues*

### Vocabulario para las Partes del Cuerpo  (continued)

| Spanish | English |
| --- | --- |
| el cerebro (m.) | brain |
| el colon (m.) | colon |
| la columna (vertebral) | spine |
| el corazón (m.) | heart |
| corporal | corporal; relating to the body |
| la costilla (f.) | rib |
| la coyuntura (f.) | joint |
| el cráneo (m.) | cranium |
| el cuello (m.) | neck |
| el cuero cabelludo (m.) | scalp |
| el cuerpo (m.) | body |
| el dedo (m.) | finger; toe |
| el diente (m.) | tooth |
| la espalda (f.) | back |
| las espaldas (f. pl.) | shoulder blades |
| el espinazo (m.) | spine, backbone |
| estomacal | relating to the stomach |
| el estómago (m.) | stomach |
| la garganta (f.) | throat |
| la glándula (f.) | gland |
| el hígado (m.) | liver |
| el hueso (m.) | bone |
| la ingle (f.) | groin |
| el labio (m.) | lip |
| la lengua (f.) | tongue |
| la mano (f.) | hand |
| la mandíbula (f.) | jaw, mandible |
| la mejilla (f.) | cheek |
| el meollo (m.) | marrow |
| la muela (f.) | molar |
| la muñeca (f.) | wrist |
| el músculo (m.) | muscle |
| el muslo (m.) | thigh |

| Spanish | English |
| --- | --- |
| la nalga (f.) | buttock |
| las narices (f. pl.) | nostrils |
| la nariz (f.) | nose |
| nasal | nasal, of the nose |
| la nuca (f.) | nape (of neck) |
| el oído (m.) | ear (internal) |
| el ojo (m.) | eye |
| el ombligo (m.) | navel, bellybutton |
| oral | oral, of the mouth |
| la oreja (f.) | ear (outer shell) |
| la pantorrilla (f.) | calf |
| el párpado (m.) | eyelid |
| el pecho (m.) | chest; breast |
| los pechos (m. pl.) | breasts |
| el pelo (m.) | hair |
| el pene (m.) | penis |
| la penicilina (f.) | penicillin |
| la pestaña (f.) | eyelash |
| el pezón (m.) | nipple |
| el pie (m.) | foot |
| la piel (f.) | skin |
| la pierna (f.) | leg |
| el pómulo (m.) | cheekbone |
| psicosomático/a | psychosomatic |
| el pulmón (m.) | lung |
| la quijada (f.) | jaw |
| la rodilla (f.) | knee |
| los senos (m. pl.) | breasts |
| los senos nasales (m. pl.) | sinus cavities |
| somático/a | somatic, relating to the body |
| el testículo (m.) | testicle |
| la tiroides (f.) | thyroid |
| el tobillo (m.) | ankle |

*continues*

### Vocabulario para las Partes del Cuerpo  (continued)

| Spanish | English |
| --- | --- |
| umbilical | umbilical; relating to the navel |
| el útero (m.) | uterus, womb |
| la vagina (f.) | vagina |
| las ventanas de la nariz (f. pl.) | nostrils |
| la vértebra (f.) | vertebra |
| la vesícula biliar (f.) | gall bladder |
| el vientre (m.) | womb; abdomen; belly |
| la vulva (f.) | vulva |

**PROCEED WITH CAUTION**

Don't confuse *pezón*, which is a human nipple, with *tetilla (de biberón)*, the nipple on a bottle.

The following list provides useful terms for describing medical problems and treatments.

**PROCEED WITH CAUTION**

Don't confuse *la cura* with *el cura* (the priest). If you ask for *el cura*, people will think you're dying.

### Vocabulario para Condiciones Médicas y Curaciones

| Spanish | English |
| --- | --- |
| la anestesia (f.) | anesthesia |
| anestesiar | to anesthetize |
| anestésico/a | anesthetic |
| el/la anestesiólogo/a (m./f.) | anesthesiologist |
| el/la anestesista (m./f.) | anesthetist |
| el antibiótico (m.) | antibiotic |
| antihistamínico/a | antihistamine |
| antiinflamatorio/a | anti-inflammatory |
| artrítico/a | arthritic |
| la artritis (f.) | arthritis |
| arrancar | pull out, rip out |

| Spanish | English |
| --- | --- |
| auscultar | to listen (with a stethoscope) |
| la calentura (f.) | fever |
| el cardenal (m.) | bruise, welt; cardinal |
| la carie (f.) | cavity (in tooth) |
| el catarro (m.) | head cold |
| la cirujana (f.) | surgeon (female) |
| el cirujano (m.) | surgeon (male) |
| la cirujía (f.) | surgery |
| cirúrgico/a | surgical |
| la cura (f.) | treatment (medical); cure |
| la curación (f.) | treatment (medical); cure |
| curar | to treat (medical problem); to cure |
| la curita (f.) | band-aid |
| la diarrea (f.) | diarrhea |
| la diabetes (f.) | diabetes |
| doler (ue) | to hurt, to ache (produce pain, ache) |
| el dolor (m.) | pain, ache; sorrow |
| embarazada | pregnant |
| encinta | pregnant |
| la enema (f.) | enema (apparatus) |
| enfermo/a | ill, sick |
| la epidemia (f.) | epidemic |
| epidémico/a | epidemic |
| estar bien | to be well, in good health |
| el estetescopio (m.) | stethoscope |
| el examen (m.) | examination |
| examinar | to examine |
| extraer | to extract |
| la fiebre (f.) | fever |
| la fiebre amarilla (f.) | yellow fever |
| la fractura (f.) | fracture |
| fracturar | to fracture |
| la gonorrea (f.) | gonorrhea |

*continues*

### *Vocabulario para Condiciones Médicas y Curaciones*    (continued)

| Spanish | English |
| --- | --- |
| la gripe (f.) | flu, grippe |
| la herida (f.) | wound |
| herir (ie, i) | to wound |
| la hernia (f.) | hernia |
| la inflamación (f.) | inflammation |
| la influenza (f.) | influenza |
| la jaqueca (f.) | headache |
| lastimar | to hurt, to cause physical harm |
| lastimarse | to hurt oneself |
| la lavativa (f.) | enema (procedure) |
| la llaga (f.) | sore, wound, ulcer |
| llagar | to wound, to injure |
| el mal (m.) | sickness, disease; epilepsy |
| mareado/a | nauseous; dizzy; seasick, motion sick |
| el mareo (m.) | nausea; motion sickness; dizziness |
| el medicamento (m.) | medicament, medicine |
| la medicina (f.) | medicine |
| la náusea (f.) | nausea |
| la operación (f.) | operation |
| operar | to operate |
| palpar | to palpate |
| el paludismo (m.) | malaria |
| la papera (f.) | goiter |
| las paperas (f. pl.) | mumps |
| la pulmonía (f.) | pneumonia |
| reconocer | to recognize; to examine (medically) |
| el reconocimiento (m.) | recognition; medical examination |
| el resfriado (m.) | cold (illness) |
| el resfrío (m.) | cold (illness) |
| romper | to break |
| sacar | to take out, to extract |
| sanar | to heal, to cure; to recover, to regain health |

| Spanish | English |
| --- | --- |
| sanear | to improve; to sanitize; to make healthy |
| sano/a | healthy, fit; healthful, wholesome |
| el sarampión (m.) | measles |
| el SIDA (m.) | AIDS |
| la sífilis (f.) | syphilis |
| el síntoma (m.) | symptom |
| sintomático/a | symptomatic |
| sufrir (de) | to suffer (from) |
| taladrar | to drill |
| el taladro (m.) | drill |
| la temperatura (f.) | temperature |
| la tos (f.) | cough |
| la tos ferina (f.) | whooping cough |
| toser | to cough |
| la sinusitis (f.) | sinusitis |
| la tablilla (f.) | splint |
| la úlcera (f.) | ulcer |
| la varicela (f.) | chicken pox |
| la venda (f.) | bandage; blindfold |
| el vendaje (m.) | bandage; bandaging |
| la viruela (f.) | small pox |
| el yeso (m.) | plaster; plaster cast |

**JUST A MINUTE**

*Lastimar* is to cause physical damage; *doler* (*ue*) is to ache. *Me lastimé la pierna = I hurt my leg. Me duele la pierna = My leg hurts (me).*

*Cabello* and *cabellera* refer only to the hair on the head, to the whole head of hair. *Cabello* can refer to a single hair of the head, and can be pluralized. *Pelo* can refer collectively to all the hair on the body, or to an individual hair, and can be pluralized.

You'll want to know terms relating to medical personnel, hospitals, doctors' offices, and dentists' offices. Study the following vocabulary.

### Vocabulario para Personal Médico y Sitios

| Spanish | English |
| --- | --- |
| la botica (f.) | drugstore (old-fashioned) |
| el/la boticario/a (m./f.) | druggist (old-fashioned) |
| la clínica (f.) | clinic; private hospital |
| el consultorio (m.) | doctor's office; consulting room |
| el/la dentista (m./f.) | dentist |
| el/la doctor/a (m./f.) | doctor (M.D. or Ph.D.) |
| la enfermera (f.) | nurse (female) |
| el enfermero (m.) | nurse (male) |
| el/la facultativo/a (m./f.) | doctor, physician |
| la farmacéutica (f.) | pharmacist (female) |
| el farmacéutico (m.) | pharmacist (male) |
| farmacéutico/a | pharmaceutical |
| los farmacéuticos (m. pl.) | pharmaceuticals |
| la farmacia (f.) | pharmacy |
| el hospital (m.) | hospital |
| la inyección (f.) | injection; "shot" |
| la jeringa (f.) | syringe |
| la jeringuilla (f.) | syringe |
| el médico (m.) | doctor (M.D.); physician (male) |
| el/la odontólogo/a (m./f.) | dentist |
| el/la optómetra (m./f.) | optometrist |
| el/la paciente/a (m./f.) | patient |
| el/la recepcionista (m./f.) | receptionist |
| la receta (f.) | prescription; recipe |
| recetar | to prescribe; to write a prescription |

The noun *dolor* can be used with the preposition *de* plus a part of the body to speak of the location of the ache or pain:

| | |
| --- | --- |
| dolor de cabeza | headache |
| dolor de muela | toothache |
| dolor de estómago | stomach ache |

The following are some typical questions and answers that might pass between patient and doctor:

*¿Qué tiene Ud., señora?*
What's the matter with you, ma'am?

*Tengo dolor de cabeza.*
I have a headache.

*¿Y, tiene fiebre?*
And, do you have a fever?

*No, doctor.*
No, doctor.

*¿Desde cuándo tiene Ud. dolor de cabeza?*
How long have you had a headache?

*Ya hace tres días.*
It's been three days now.

*Abra Ud. la boca, por favor.*
Open your mouth, please.

*Aaaaaah.*
Aaaaaah.

*Le he examinado la boca, la garganta, los oídos, y los ojos.*
I've examined your mouth, your throat, your ears, and your eyes.

*¿Y, qué tal, doctor?*
And how is everything, doctor?

*Muy bien, de veras.*
Actually, very well.

*¿Entonces, qué me pasa?*
So, what's happening to me?

*No estoy seguro. Dígame, señora, ¿Ud. lee mucho?*
I'm not sure. Tell, me, ma'am, do you read much?

*Sí, doctor, leo muchísimo.*
Yes, doctor, I read a great deal.

*Mire, señora, yo sugiero que visite al optómetra.*
Look, ma'am, I suggest you visit the optometrist.

Practice saying aloud the following expressions:

*¿Dónde le duele?*
Where do you hurt? (Where does it hurt you?)

*Me duelen los oídos.*
My ears hurt (me).

*¿Cuál es la fecha de su nacimiento?*
What is your birthdate?

*¿Está Ud. embarazada?*
Are you pregnant?

*Sí, estoy encinta.*
Yes, I'm pregnant.

*¿De cuántos meses?*
How many months?

*¿Cómo se lastimó Ud.?*
How did you hurt yourself?

*Me caí por la escalera.*
I fell down the stairs.

*¿Cómo se le rompió la pierna?*
How did you break your leg?

*Se me rompió esquiando.*
I broke it skiing.

*¿Ha tenido Ud. la vacuna contra el tétano?*
Have you had the anti-tetanus shot?

*Sí, pero, hace doce años.*
Yes, but twelve years ago.

*¿Por qué no vino al consultorio más temprano?*
Why didn't you come to the (doctor's) office earlier?

*Yo habría ido ayer, pero tuve que trabajar.*
I would have gone yesterday, but I had to work.

### PROCEED WITH CAUTION

 Even though *muela* specifically means *molar*, a toothache is called *dolor de muela*, no matter which tooth is involved. Don't let this confuse you.

# Learn the Demonstratives

The following adjectives and pronouns are called demonstrative because they *demonstrate*, in the sense that they point out where something is located. In most dialects of modern American English, there are only four demonstratives:

- this (singular, near the person speaking)
- these (plural, near the person speaking)
- that (singular, away from the speaker)
- those (plural, away from the speaker)

## Use the Demonstrative Adjectives

The Spanish system is more complicated than the English one. Because they are adjectives and have to agree in number and gender with the nouns they modify, there will be four forms in each position: masculine singular, masculine plural, feminine singular, feminine plural.

In addition, instead of only two positions involved (near the speaker, away from the speaker) as in English, there are three positions: (1) near the speaker, (2) near the listener, (3) far from both speaker and listener. Three (positions) times 4 (number and gender) makes 12 forms of the demonstrative adjective in Spanish. Study and learn the demonstrative adjectives in the following table.

**TIME SAVER**

There are parts of the United States and Britain where there still are three positions: *this, that,* and *yonder,* with the same positional meanings as the Spanish.

### *Adjetivos Demonstrativos* (Demonstrative Adjectives)

| Adjective | Noun | Number | Gender | English |
|-----------|------|--------|--------|---------|
| este | hospital | singular | masculine | this hospital |
| estos | hospitales | plural | masculine | these hospitals |
| esta | farmacia | singular | feminine | this pharmacy |
| estas | farmacias | plural | feminine | these pharmacies |
| ese | médico | singular | masculine | that doctor |
| esos | médicos | plural | masculine | those doctors |
| esa | doctora | singular | feminine | that doctor |

*continues*

### *Adjetivos Demostrativos* (Demonstrative Adjectives)   (continued)

| Adjective | Noun | Number | Gender | English |
|-----------|------|--------|--------|---------|
| esas | doctoras | plural | feminine | those doctors |
| aquel | cirujano | singular | masculine | that surgeon |
| aquellos | cirujanos | plural | masculine | those surgeons |
| aquella | cirujana | singular | feminine | that surgeon |
| aquellas | cirujanas | plural | feminine | those surgeons |

You can see that translation doesn't help much, because the last two groups (*ese* and *aquel*) are translated in the same way. Think in terms of position, as described earlier. Perhaps it would help if you thought of yourself saying "that doctor" when you say "*ese médico*," but picture the doctor being relatively close to the person to whom you're speaking. On the other hand, think of yourself saying "that surgeon (way out there)" when you say "*aquel cirujano*," and picture the surgeon being far away from both you and your listener.

### TIME SAVER

The demonstratives referring to a position near the speaker (*este,* etc.) and the demonstratives referring to a position near the listener (*ese,* etc.) differ only in that the first-mentioned ones have the letter *t* in them, whereas the second-mentioned ones do not.

These are somewhat peculiar adjectives; *este* and *ese* do not end with an *-o* in the masculine singular, yet the masculine plural ends with *-os. Aquel* does not simply add an *-es* to the consonant *l* to become plural; it first doubles the *l* into *ll* and then adds *-os.* The feminine forms all have that double *ll.*

Keep in mind that in a conversation, in both English and Spanish, the speaker and listener keep changing positions. Otherwise, it would not be a conversation; it would be a speech. In English, when you refer to a book near you, you call it *this book,* but when the other person speaks, he or she refers to the very same book as *that book.* A typical English conversation would go like this, if the book is near Bob:

**Bob:** Do you like *this* book?

**Stacey:** No, I don't like *that* book.

The same type of exchange happens in Spanish as well. Study the following exchange, and practice saying the sentences aloud, as you picture what is being referred to. Roberto has the stethoscope, but Elena has the medicine:

> **Roberto:** *¿Quiere Ud. usar **este** estetescopio?*
> Do you want to use this stethoscope?
>
> **Elena:** *¿Ese estetescopio? No, gracias. Prefiero **aquel** estetescopio allá.*
> That stethoscope (near you)? No, thanks. I prefer that stethoscope over there.
>
> **Roberto:** *¿Bueno, quiere darme **esa** medicina que tiene?*
> Well, will you (do you want to) give me that medicine you have (near you)?
>
> **Elena:** *Sí, le doy **esta** medicina que tengo.*
> Yes, I'll give you this medicine that I have.

## USE THE DEMONSTRATIVE PRONOUNS

The 12 demonstrative adjectives you have just learned become demonstrative pronouns when you use them without nouns. You do this when you and your listener already know what the noun is. For example, if you both (or you all) know you're talking about hospitals, and you want to ask about someone's preference, you wouldn't say "Which hospital do you prefer, this hospital or that hospital?" You'd probably ask, "Which one do you prefer, this one or that one?" leaving out the word *hospital*.

Notice that in English, we don't save any breath doing that, because we insert the word *one* instead of *hospital*. But in Spanish, you don't insert the word that means *one* or any other word; you simply drop the noun, if everyone knows what it is. This automatically turns the demonstrative from an adjective into a pronoun.

First, let's see how repetitive (and, in Spanish, long-winded) sentences are if they repeat the noun that we all know we're talking about.

> *Entre todos los hospitales, prefiero este hospital.*
> Out of (among) all the hospitals, I prefer this hospital.
>
> *Yo no; yo prefiero aquel hospital.*
> I don't; I prefer that hospital (out there).
>
> *Esta medicina no sirve; esa medicina, sí.*
> This medicine is no good; that medicine (near you) is.

Now study the following sentences; they don't repeat the noun. When the noun is omitted, the demonstrative takes its place, and even though it's the same word, it is now called a demonstrative pronoun (instead of adjective). Essentially, it's the same word with a different name:

> *Entre todos los hospitales, prefiero éste.*
> Out of (among) all the hospitals, I prefer this one.
>
> *Yo no; yo prefiero aquél.*
> I don't; I prefer that one (out there).
>
> *Esta medicina no sirve; ésa sí.*
> This medicine is no good; that one (near you) is.

One technicality: The only difference between the 12 demonstrative adjectives you've learned and the 12 demonstrative pronouns is in the writing system, not the speaking system. Notice, in the five preceding sentences, a written accent mark is placed over the automatically stressed vowel. This is a technical device used to differentiate in writing the demonstrative adjectives from the demonstrative pronouns; otherwise, they are exactly identical.

Three *extra* demonstrative pronouns: Whereas the 12 demonstrative adjectives have their counterpart in the 12 demonstrative pronouns you've just studied, three demonstrative pronouns have no counterpart among the demonstrative adjectives:

- esto
- eso
- aquello

Notice: Unlike the demonstratives you learned earlier, the three extra demonstrative pronouns all end with the letter *-o*. The 12 previous pronouns (and their adjective counterparts) are either masculine singular, masculine plural, feminine singular, or feminine plural. In other words, they agree in number or gender with (or take the place of) nouns.

The three additional demonstrative pronouns are called *neuter*. Think about it: If all nouns in Spanish are either masculine or feminine, no noun is neuter. Then ask yourself, what nouns would any of these three neuter pronouns represent? The answer is: *none*.

Then what are these three demonstrative pronouns used for? They have two purposes:

- To refer to an entire idea which can't be pinned down to a specific noun
- To refer to an unidentified object

Let's take a look at an example of a demonstrative pronoun that refers to an idea that can't be nailed down to a specific noun. You tell someone you're going to get up tomorrow at 8:00 A.M., take a shower, have breakfast, jog to work, work from 9:00 to 5:00, have dinner, then go dancing, go home, and go to bed. Your friend says "That's nice."

How do you say "That's nice" in Spanish in this particular case? Do you use the masculine singular *éste?* The feminine singular *ésa?* The plurals *ésos* or *ésas?* Because the *that* refers to the whole idea just expressed, and *cannot be pinned down to a specific noun*, then *that* can't agree with any noun in the whole Spanish language, masculine or feminine (and certainly not plural). You use the neuter demonstrative pronouns.

As to which one of the three to use, it's not very precise, because you can't actually point to a physical object and locate its position. Usually, if you're the one speaking, and you associate the idea with the person to whom you're speaking, you would use *eso* (you're saying "that idea mentally near you" to the listener). If it's an idea you associate with yourself, you would say *esto*. And if it's an idea you consider remote from both of you (that stuff going on over in China) you would use *aquello*.

Now look at an example of a demonstrative pronoun that refers to an unidentified object. If you *ask* someone in English "What's that?" you don't know what *that* is. If you don't know what it is, then you don't know if it's masculine or feminine. You would have to use the neuter: *¿Qué es eso?* If this unidentified object is near you, you would say "*¿Qué es esto?*" And if it's way out over there, distant from you and the other person, you would say "*¿Qué es aquello?*"

Note that the three neuter demonstrative pronouns do not have written accent marks. This is because there are no neuter demonstrative adjectives from which to differentiate them.

## CONTRAST *SINO* WITH *PERO*

The words *pero* and *sino* can both translate into English as *but*. However, they are not used in the same way.

*Pero* is *but* in the sense of *nevertheless* or *still and all*; for example, *He's not smart, but he's a nice guy* is the same as saying *He's not smart; nevertheless, he's a nice guy. It's hot, but it's not humid* is the same as *It's hot; still and all, it's not humid.* See the following examples:

*No es inteligente, pero es una buena persona.*
He's not smart, but he is a good person.

*Hace calor, pero no hay humedad.*
It's hot, but there's no humidity.

*Quiero ir, pero no puedo.*
I want to go, but I can't.

*Sino,* on the other hand, can be used only if …

- You say something is *not* something.
- You then tell us what it really is.

In other words, *sino* is used to mean *but* or *but rather* or *but instead* when you say "It's not this way, but (rather) it's that way." You correct our thoughts about something by a negative statement (it's not like that), and then you complete the correction by telling us how it really is. See the following examples:

*No es grande, sino pequeño.*
It's not big, but small.

*No habla bien, sino mal.*
He doesn't speak well, but poorly.

*No es verde, sino rojo.*
It's not green, but red.

*No quiero hablar, sino cantar.*
I don't want to talk, but to sing.

*No vas a beber, sino comer.*
You're not going to drink, but to eat.

*Sino que:* The relative pronoun *que* is inserted after *sino* if what follows is a conjugated verb. Not an infinitive verb (as in the last two sentences), but a conjugated verb (*No un verbo infinitivo, sino un verbo conjugado*). See the following examples:

> *No habla, sino que canta.*
> She doesn't speak, but (instead) sings.
>
> *Nunca habla, sino que grita.*
> He never speaks, but (instead) shouts.
>
> *No caminan, sino que corren.*
> They don't walk, but (instead) run.

## THE 30-SECOND RECAP

In this hour, you've learned to use the subjunctive present perfect tense and the demonstratives (adjectives and pronouns), plus the use of *haber* for existence in the subjunctive. You've also learned to use two different words for *but* (*pero* and *sino*), as well as to talk about medical problems to doctors and dentists.

## HOUR'S UP!

It would be good to review this hour's work, and then test your progress by taking the following quiz, without, of course, going back to the lessons themselves while testing yourself.

1. Choose the most apt form of the verb: *Yo conozco a un hombre que ...*

   **a.** lo había visto.

   **b.** lo haya visto.

   **c.** lo han visto.

   **d.** None of the above.

2. Choose the most apt form of the verb: *No hay nadie que ...*

   **a.** lo haya hecho.

   **b.** lo ha hecho.

   **c.** lo hubo hecho.

   **d.** lo había hecho.

**3.** Choose the most apt form of the verb: *Sé que …*

    **a.** hay mucha gente.

    **b.** había mucha gente.

    **c.** habrá mucha gente.

    **d.** All of the above.

**4.** Choose the correct demonstrative pronoun: You're talking about a hospital that's near the person to whom you're talking.

    **a.** ésa

    **b.** eso

    **c.** aquélla

    **d.** aquello

    **e.** None of the above

**5.** Choose the correct demonstrative pronoun: You're talking about three female nurses who are way out there.

    **a.** aquéllas

    **b.** ésas

    **c.** aquéllos

    **d.** esos

    **e.** None of the above

**6.** Give the most logical answer: *Si se te ha roto la pierna, debes …*

    **a.** ir al odontólogo.

    **b.** tomar antibióticos.

    **c.** usar una jeringa.

    **d.** usar una tablilla.

## CHAPTER SUMMARY

**LESSON PLAN:**

In this hour, you'll learn ...

- How to use the imperfect subjunctive tense.
- Terminology used in business and banking.

U p to this point, you have been using the many tenses of the indicative mood, and one tense of the subjunctive mood: the present subjunctive tense. There is another tense in common use within the subjunctive mood: the imperfect subjunctive tense.

## FORM THE IMPERFECT SUBJUNCTIVE TENSE

The imperfect subjunctive tense is based on the preterit indicative tense. Therefore, it is very important that you review the rules for the preterit tense. To form the imperfect subjunctive tense, you ...

- Start with the *ellos* form of the preterit tense.
- Remove the *-ron* ending.
- Add the endings *-ra, -ras, -ra, -ramos, -rais, -ran.*

Study the following demonstration of the formation of the verb *hablar* in the imperfect subjunctive tense:

- **Infinitive.** Hablar
- ***Ellos* in preterit.** Hablaron
- **Remove *-ron.*** Habla *-ron*
- **Result.** Habla
- **Add *-ra.*** Habla + *-ra*
- **Result.** Hablara
- **Entire conjugation.** (*Yo*) *hablara*, (*tú*) *hablaras*, (*él*) *hablara*, (*nosotros*) *habláramos*, (*vosotros*) *hablarais*, (*ellos*) *hablaran*

You may wonder why we bothered with using the *ellos* form of the preterit tense instead of starting with the infinitive verb. The reason is that, although there are no irregular verbs in the imperfect subjunctive tense, there are a great many irregular verbs in the preterit tense. Because we use the preterit form as the base of the imperfect subjunctive, we must be aware of verbs that are irregular in the preterit. Study the conjugation of verb *decir*, and see how different the imperfect subjunctive is from the infinitive:

- **Infinitive.** Decir
- ***Ellos* in preterit.** Dijeron
- **Remove -*ron*.** Dije -*ron*
- **Result.** Dije
- **Add -*ra*.** Dije + -*ra*
- **Result.** Dijera
- **Entire conjugation.** *Dijera, dijeras, dijera, dijéramos, dijerais, dijeran*

As an example, study the following table of the conjugation of four sample verbs, taken at random, in the imperfect subjunctive tense.

**Conjugation of Verbs in the Imperfect Subjunctive Tense**

| Subject Pronoun | Comer | Poner | Ser | Cantar |
| --- | --- | --- | --- | --- |
| yo | comiera | pusiera | fuera | cantara |
| tú | comieras | pusieras | fueras | cantaras |
| él | comiera | pusiera | fuera | cantara |
| ella | comiera | pusiera | fuera | cantara |
| usted | comiera | pusiera | fuera | cantara |
| nosotros/as | comiéramos | pusiéramos | fuéramos | cantáramos |
| vosotros/as | comierais | pusierais | fuerais | cantarais |

| Subject Pronoun | Comer | Poner | Ser | Cantar |
|---|---|---|---|---|
| ellos | comieran | pusieran | fueran | cantaran |
| ellas | comieran | pusieran | fueran | cantaran |
| ustedes | comieran | pusieran | fueran | cantaran |

Study the following sentences, and practice saying them aloud:

*Elena dudaba que vinieran.*
Elena doubted (that) they would come.

*Queríamos que hablaras.*
We wanted you to speak.

*Fue imposible que lo hiciera ella.*
It was impossible for her to do it.

*Pregunté si había una casa que tuviera cuatro baños.*
I asked if there was a house that had (might have) four bathrooms.

*Mandaron que Roberto se fuera.*
They ordered Roberto to go away.

Important: There is a second structure for the imperfect subjunctive. Instead of adding -*ra*, ..., you can add -*se*, -*ses*, ... (*hablase, hablases, hablase, hablásemos, hablaseis, hablasen; dijese, dijeses, dijese, dijésemos, dijeseis, dijesen*). The -*ra* ending is more common in Spanish America; in Spain it's 50/50.

**GO TO** ▶
The imperfect subjunctive is easy to learn because all verbs are regular, but only if you thoroughly know the preterit tense, which has many irregularities. To review the preterit, see Hour 5.

## UNDERSTAND THE USAGE OF THE IMPERFECT SUBJUNCTIVE

The imperfect subjunctive tense is used for all the *same reasons* and situations that you've already learned with regard to the subjunctive mood in general. The only differences in its usage from that of the present subjunctive tense are in commands and in regard to the concept of *time*:

- The *present* subjunctive tense is used when talking about the present or the future. (There is no future subjunctive in common use.)

- The *imperfect* subjunctive tense is used when talking about the past or what is conditional.

Alternatively, we could say that if the subjunctive is required, use the *present* subjunctive *after* verbs in ...

- The present indicative tense.
- The future indicative tense.

If the subjunctive is required, use the *imperfect* subjunctive *after* verbs in …

- The imperfect indicative tense.
- The preterit indicative tense.
- The conditional indicative tense.

Compare the following sentences:

*Quiero que Ud. vaya a la oficina.*
I want you to go to the office.

*Querré que Ud. vaya a la oficina.*
I will want you to go to the office.

*Quería que Ud. fuera a la oficina.*
I wanted you to go to the office.

*Quise que Ud. fuera a la oficina.*
I wanted you to go to the office.

*Querría que Ud. fuera a la oficina.*
I'd want (I'd like) you to go to the office.

**GO TO** ▶
To review the situations in which you use the subjunctive mood, see Hours 12, 13, 19, and 20.

Now that you know how to form the imperfect subjunctive tense, and you know for what purposes to use it, study the following sentences, and then practice saying them aloud:

*Dudábamos que Pérez tuviera éxito.*
We doubted that Pérez would be successful (have success).

*Insistí en que la secretaria llegara más temprano.*
I insisted that the secretary arrive earlier.

*¿Deseaba Ud. que los viajantes estudiaran contabilidad?*
Did you want the traveling salespeople to study accounting?

*En ese momento, no creí que la compañía se declarara en bancarrota.*
At that moment, I didn't think the company might go bankrupt (might declare itself in bankruptcy).

*A Ud. le aconsejé que pusiera atención a la Bolsa.*
I advised you to pay attention to the stock market.

*Sentían mucho que la campaña publicitaria no tuviera resultado.*
They were very sorry that the advertising campaign didn't turn out well (didn't have results).

Notice how little translation helps; the English equivalents use expressions like *would be, come, to study, didn't turn out, might go,* and so on. This is because we have no real equivalent to the imperfect subjunctive in English, only a few traces of it.

## Do Business in Spanish

As always, a good Spanish-English dictionary, and even specialized dictionaries (in this case, on commercial Spanish) will be useful to someone who is involved in a specific aspect of the business world. The following table lists a very general vocabulary of business terminology.

**JUST A MINUTE**

*To sell for cash is vender al contado; to pay cash is pagar al contado.*

### Vocabulario Comercial

| Spanish | English |
| --- | --- |
| acusar recibo | to acknowledge receipt |
| el acuse de recibo (m.) | acknowledgement of receipt |
| la agencia publicitaria (f.) | advertising agency |
| el/la agente (m./f.) | agent |
| el/la agente comercial (m./f.) | sales representative |
| el/la agente publicitario/a (m./f.) | advertising agent |
| el anuncio (comercial) (m.) | advertisement, commercial |
| la campaña publicitaria (f.) | publicity/advertising campaign |
| la carta (f.) | letter (written communication) |
| la carta de crédito (f.) | letter of credit |
| la casa comercial (f.) | business, company |
| la comercialización (f.) | marketing (of new products) |
| comercializar | to market (a new product) |
| comercial | commercial, business |
| el/la comerciante (m./f.) | businessman, businesswoman; merchant |
| el comercio (m.) | commerce, business |
| la contabilidad (f.) | accounting; accountancy |
| el contador (m.) | accountant |
| la contadora (f.) | accountant |
| la contaduría (f.) | accountancy; accounting office |

*continues*

### Vocabulario Comercial   (continued)

| Spanish | English |
| --- | --- |
| contratar | to hire |
| el contrato (m.) | contract |
| correr con los gastos | to foot the bill; to pay the expenses |
| la correspondencia (f.) | correspondence |
| la cuenta (f.) | bill, invoice |
| el cheque (m.) | check |
| el departamento (m.) | department |
| el dinero (m.) | money |
| el dinero en efectivo (m.) | cash |
| el/la directora (m./f.) | director, manager |
| el/la ejecutivo/a (m./f.) | executive |
| la entrega (f.) | delivery |
| entregar | to deliver; to hand over |
| la fábrica (f.) | factory |
| el/la gerente/a (m./f.) | manager |
| el giro a la vista (m.) | sight draft |
| el giro postal (m.) | money order |
| la factura (f.) | bill; invoice |
| facturar | to invoice, to bill |
| enviar | to send |
| el envío (m.) | shipment |
| la firma (f.) | signature; firm |
| firmar | to sign |
| el hombre de negocios (m.) | businessman |
| la jefa (f.) | boss (woman) |
| la jefatura (f.) | leadership, management; headquarters |
| el jefe (m.) | boss (man) |
| el/la jerarca (m./f.) | high official; executive |
| la jerarquía (f.) | hierarchy, rank; scale |
| la letra de cambio (f.) | bill of exchange |
| el márketing (m.) | marketing |
| el mercadeo (m.) | marketing |

| Spanish | English |
| --- | --- |
| el mercado (m.) | market |
| la mercadería (f.) | merchandise |
| la mercancía (f.) | merchandise |
| el negocio (m.) | business; deal, transaction |
| la oficina (f.) | office |
| pagar | to pay |
| pagar a crédito | to pay in installments |
| pagar a plazos | to pay in installments |
| el pagaré (m.) | promissory note, I.O.U. |
| el pago (m.) | payment |
| la propaganda (f.) | propaganda; advertising |
| la publicidad (f.) | publicity; advertising |
| recibir | to receive |
| el recibo (m.) | receiving, receipt |
| el/la representante (m./f.) | representative; sales representative |
| el sindicato (laboral) (m.) | labor union |
| el subdirector (m.) | assistant manager (male) |
| la subdirectora (f.) | assistant manager (female) |
| solicitar | to solicit; to apply (for); to request |
| la solicitud (f.) | request; application |
| el/la tenedor/a de libros (m./f.) | bookkeeper |
| la teneduría de libros (f.) | bookkeeping |
| la venta (f.) | sale |
| el/la viajante (m./f.) | traveling salesperson |

**JUST A MINUTE**

Whereas the official word for marketing is *el mercadeo,* the English term *el márketing* very often is used, too. *La comercialización* is *marketing* (in the sense of making a new product known).

# WRITE BUSINESS LETTERS

If you are going to write business letters in Spanish, you will need to know certain basics.

## EL SALUDO

There are many kinds of salutations in Spanish business letters, just as there are in English. Study the following examples:

| | |
|---|---|
| Distinguido/a señor/señora: | Distinguished sir/madam: |
| Estimado/a señor/señora: | Esteemed sir/madam: |
| Estimable señor/señora: | Estimable sir/madam: |
| Estimados señores: | Esteemed sirs: |
| Señores: | Gentlemen: |
| Muy estimado señor Pérez: | Very esteemed Mister Pérez: |
| De mi mayor consideración: | Of my greatest consideration: |

The literal translations are provided, but, of course, in English we would use the terms *Dear sir, Dear Madam,* or *Dear Mr./Ms. Jones* for most of them.

Although abbreviations of titles (*Sr., Sra.,* …) can be used in the address (both inside and on the envelope), it is best to spell them out in the salutation (*señor, señora,* …).

### PROCEED WITH CAUTION

While *querido/a* (past participle of *querer*) is the literal equivalent of *dear,* and is used in friendly letters to good friends, it is considered overly affectionate in normal business letters.

## LA DESPEDIDA

As in English, there are several ways to close the letter before signing your name. Study the following:

| | |
|---|---|
| Atentamente. | Attentively. |
| De usted(es) atentamente. | Yours attentively. |
| Muy atentamente. | Very attentively. |
| Cordialmente. | Cordially. |
| Sinceramente. | Sincerely. |
| Con un saludo muy cordial. | With a very cordial greeting. |
| Saludo a Ud(s). muy atentamente. | I greet you very attentively. |
| Reciba Ud. mis mejores deseos. | Accept my best wishes. |
| Reciba Ud. mis mejores augurios. | Accept my best wishes. |

The last entry involves a peculiar use of the word *augurio* in Argentina and Uruguay. In most Spanish-speaking countries, *augurio* means *augury, omen,* or *foretelling*. However, in Argentina and Uruguay, through Italian influence, it is commonly used to mean *a wish for good things in the future*.

The expression (*Muy*) *Atentamente* can be preceded by *Soy de Ud(s)*.

## LA FIRMA

Just as in English, anywhere your company's name appears, it should be the official name with no attempt at translation. Then you sign your name. Under that, your name should be printed (in type), and under that, the name of your title and department should appear in Spanish translation.

**JUST A MINUTE**

In friendly letters, as opposed to business messages, you can close with *abrazos* (hugs), or *con un abrazo* (with a hug), between men, as well as with (*Muy*) *cordialmente* or *Con un saludo cordial*.

Study the following sample letter, which is for placing an order:

Librerías Valera, S.A. Avenida Cangallo 875 (1011) Buenos Aires, República Argentina Tel. 33-33-33 Fax: 33-33-34 E-mail: valera@hotmail.com

Atención: Depto. de Ventas

Estimados señores:

Les agradecemos por anticipado nos envíen tan pronto como sea posible cien (100) ejemplares de su libro, *Aprenda inglés sin profesor en un día*. Les ruego los envíen según el precio referido en su catálogo, $18.50 el ejemplar, con el descuento acostumbrado de 25% (veinticinco por ciento), de esta manera resultando el precio para nosotros a $13.87 cada ejemplar, llegando a un total de $1.387 (mil trescientos ochenta y siete dólares) más el costo de envío.

Liquidaremos su factura con el descuento correspondiente tan pronto la recibamos en esta casa.

Atentamente,

(firma)

Eduardo Ricci, Gerente, Departamento de Adquisiciones

The letter is addressed to *Estimados señores* because the writer doesn't know the name of the person to whom he should write. If he knew it, he would write it more personally (for example, *Estimada señora Jones*).

The translation follows (omitting the letterhead and inside address):

Attention: Sales Department

Dear Sirs:

Please send us as soon as possible one hundred (100) copies of your book, *Aprenda inglés sin profesor en un día*. I request that you send them in accordance with the price mentioned in your catalogue, $18.50 per copy, with the usual discount of 25% (twenty-five percent), which in this way will come out to a price for us of $13.87 per copy, amounting to a total of $1,387 (one thousand three hundred eighty-seven dollars) plus shipping costs.

Payment of your invoice bearing the corresponding discount will be sent to you as soon as we receive it.

Sincerely,

(signature)

Eduardo Ricci, Manager, Acquisitions Department

In business letters, the relative pronoun *que* is sometimes omitted in front of a subjunctive verb, as in *Les agradecemos … nos envíen* and *tan pronto la recibamos* in the preceding Spanish letter.

The following table lists additional vocabulary for business letters.

### Vocabulario Adicional para la Correspondencia Comercial

| Spanish | English |
| --- | --- |
| acostumbrado/a | accustomed; customary, usual |
| acostumbrar | to accustom |
| acostumbrarse (a) | to become accustomed (to) |
| adjuntar | to attach, to include (with a letter), to enclose |
| el adjunto (m.) | attachment, enclosure |
| adquirir | to acquire, to obtain |
| la adquisición (f.) | acquisition |

| Spanish | English |
| --- | --- |
| agradecer | to thank |
| el anejo (m.) | attachment, enclosure, supplement, annex, appendix |
| anejo/a | attached, enclosed, annexed |
| el anexo (m.) | attachment, enclosure, supplement, annex, appendix |
| anexo/a | attached, annexed, appended |
| anticipadamente | in advance |
| anticipar | to advance, to move forward (for example, the date) |
| así | thus, so, in this way |
| el catálogo (m.) | catalogue |
| comunicar | to inform |
| comunicarse (con) | to communicate (with) |
| de esta manera | in this way |
| de este modo | in this way |
| la demora (f.) | delay |
| demorar | to delay |
| descontar (ue) | to discount |
| el descuento (m.) | discount |
| la despedida (f.) | dismissal; leave-taking, saying good-bye |
| despedir | to dismiss; to fire |
| despedirse (de) | to take leave (of), to say good-bye (to) |
| dicho/a | aforementioned (past participle decir) |
| fechar | to date |
| gracias anticipadas (f. pl.) | thanks in advance |
| lamentar | to lament, to be sorry, to regret |
| la liquidación (f.) | liquidation; settlement (of a debt); clearance sale |
| liquidar | to liquidate; to liquefy; to sell off; to pay off, to clear up (a debt) |
| el marco (m.) | frame |
| el membrete (m.) | letterhead |
| el mes corriente (m.) | the current month, this month |

*continues*

### Vocabulario Adicional para la Correspondencia Comercial (continued)

| Spanish | English |
| --- | --- |
| el motivo (m.) | motive, reason |
| la partida (f.) | item |
| el pedido (m.) | request; (commercial) order |
| pedir (i) | to request, to ask for; to order |
| por anticipado | in advance |
| por lo menos | at least |
| la presente (f.) | this letter |
| la queja (f.) | complaint |
| quejarse | to complain |
| la razón (f.) | reason (*see* tener razón) |
| referir (ie) | to mention |
| referirse (ie) a | to refer to |
| el resultado (m.) | result |
| resultar | to result, to turn out |
| revisar | to go over, to look over, to check |
| rogar (ue) | to request, to beg, to plead |
| la salud (f.) | health |
| saludar | to greet, to say hello to |
| el saludo (m.) | greeting |
| la salutación (f.) | salutation |
| S.A. (sociedad anónima) | Inc. |
| la sociedad (f.) | society |
| la sociedad anónima (f.) | corporation ("anonymous society") |
| según | according to |
| tan pronto como (sea posible) | as soon as (possible) |
| tener razón | to be right |
| tener toda la razón | to be completely right |

Note that the expression *la presente* is commonly used in business correspondence to refer to the letter in which the expression is found. It is understood to stand for *la carta presente* (the present letter).

## SEND A COMPLAINT

Because we've already discussed the format of a business letter, the following will include no more than the message:

> Les comunicamos que en su factura 2587-A fechada el 23 de noviembre, hay una partida de cien (100) marcos al precio de $23.00 cada uno.
>
> El pedido que habíamos pasado a ustedes fue de acuerdo con la lista de precios fechada el mes de septiembre. Esa lista muestra el precio de $16.00 para ese tipo de marco.
>
> Agradeceríamos que nos enviaran otra factura corregida o, por lo menos, nos explicaran el motivo por el que hayan sido obligados a aumentar el precio sin previo aviso.
>
> Atentamente,

Translation:

> We're informing you that in your invoice 2587-A dated November 23, there is an item of one hundred (100) frames at a price of $23.00 each.
>
> The order we sent you was in accordance with the September price list. That list shows a price of $16.00 for that type of frame.
>
> We would appreciate your sending us a corrected invoice, or, at least, explaining to us the reason that you have been obliged to increase the price without advance notice.
>
> Sincerely,

### JUST A MINUTE

Notice how much more courteous the apology is than the complaint. They correctly thank the complainer for pointing out the error.

Study the answer to this complaint:

> Lamentamos mucho nuestro error en mandarles una factura que muestra el precio de $23.00 cada uno, y les agradecemos que ustedes nos hayan indicado dicho error en su atenta carta del 3 de diciembre.
>
> Es verdad que la lista nueva de precios indica el precio de $23.00 por cada marco, pero ustedes ya habían hecho el pedido basándose en la lista anterior. Por eso, ustedes tienen toda la razón.

Con ésta adjuntamos otra factura que muestra el precio de $16.00 el marco. Háganos el favor de aceptar nuestras excusas por los inconvenientes que les hayamos causado.

Muy atentamente,

You can by now understand the above message without benefit of translation.

Note: It is common practice to refer to your customer's letter as *atenta carta* (attentive letter).

## SPEAK ABOUT BANKING AND INVESTMENTS

The following table lists general terms useful for the banking and financial fields.

**JUST A MINUTE**

*Ahorrar* means *to save* (in the sense of to put aside, to save up [usually money]). It does *not* mean to save from death, danger, or damnation; that verb is *salvar*.

### Vocabulario para la Banca y Asuntos Financieros

| Spanish | English |
| --- | --- |
| la acción (f.) | stock (share of capital stock); lawsuit |
| el/la accionista (m./f.) | stockholder, shareholder |
| acreditar una cuenta | to credit an account |
| el/la acreedor/a (m./f.) | creditor |
| el activo (m.) | assets |
| el/la agente de bolsa (m./f.) | stockbroker |
| ahorrar | to save |
| los ahorros (m. pl.) | savings |
| la anualidad (f.) | annuity |
| arrojar dividendos | to pay dividends |
| asentar | to enter (in the books) |
| el asiento (m.) | entry (in ledger, etc.) |
| la banca (f.) | banking |
| el banco (m.) | bank; bench |
| los bienes inmuebles (m. pl.) | real estate |
| los bienes muebles (m. pl.) | personal property |

| Spanish | English |
|---|---|
| los bienes raíces (m. pl.) | real estate |
| la Bolsa (de Valores) (f.) | The Stock Exchange |
| el bono (m.) | bond |
| el/la bonista (m./f.) | bondholder |
| deber | to owe; to ought to |
| el dinero (m.) | money |
| el/la corredor/a de bolsa (m./f.) | stockbroker |
| el dividendo (m.) | dividend |
| la escritura de propiedad (f.) | deed |
| la hipoteca (f.) | mortgage |
| hipotecario/a | mortgage (having to do with) |
| el impuesto (m.) | tax |
| invertir (ie) | to invest |
| la inversión (f.) | investment |
| la moneda (f.) | coin; currency |
| la sociedad (f.) | society; corporation |
| la sociedad anónima (f.) | corporation |
| la sociedad conyugal (f.) | joint ownership by husband and wife |
| la sociedad de personas (f.) | partnership |
| el/la socio/a (m./f.) | member; partner |
| la sucursal (f.) | branch, branch office; subsidiary |
| el talón (de cheques) (m.) | (check) stub |
| el/la tesorero/a (m./f.) | treasurer |
| la testamentaría (f.) | estate |
| el testamento (m.) | will |
| el título de propiedad (m.) | deed |
| traspasar por escritura | to deed |

**GO TO ▶**
While *propiedad inmueble* refers to *real estate, muebles* means *furniture*. To review vocabulary for household items, see Hour 14.

## USE SPECIAL IMPERFECT SUBJUNCTIVE

As you know, the imperfect subjunctive is used for the same reasons the present subjunctive is used, except that it used in speaking of the past and after verbs in the conditional tense. However, an additional use for this tense has no parallel with the present subjunctive. It is used in conditional sentences, in the if-clause, but only when referring to an action or situation that is contrary to fact.

This concept will become clearer with examples. Look at the following partial sentence in English:

If I saw her …

There is no way to translate that fragment into Spanish. This is because the translation could go one of two different ways, depending on what the rest of the sentence says.

## Do Not Use Subjunctive

You would think the sentence would necessarily refer to the past, because the verb *saw* seems to be in the preterit indicative tense. It might be, but it might not be.

Let's finish the sentence so that it actually does refer to the past:

If I saw her last night, I don't remember.

This if-clause definitely refers to the past, because the expression *last night* is very specific about it. The non-if-clause happens to be in the present tense. It could have been in any tense (I didn't notice; I won't remember tomorrow), *except* the conditional tense, as we'll see. This sentence is *not* contrary to fact. It doesn't imply that I didn't see her; it's perfectly noncommittal.

In this case, do *not* use the subjunctive, whether present or imperfect, in the if-clause. Because it is now obvious that the if-clause definitely refers to the past, use the preterit tense. The sentence will be this:

Si la vi anoche, no lo recuerdo.

---

**JUST A MINUTE**

The direct object pronoun *lo* would be included in Spanish. (I don't remember it [the incident].)

## Use Imperfect Subjunctive

What if the sentence turned out in the following manner?

If I saw her tomorrow, I wouldn't say hello.

This is a perfectly normal, everyday sentence in English. Yet, notice: What seems to be a verb in the past tense (saw) is followed by an adverb referring to the future (tomorrow). We don't usually think about this, but it puzzles foreigners who are studying English. It is what is left of the imperfect subjunctive in English. In other words, the English imperfect subjunctive, with very few exceptions, is spelled and pronounced exactly the same as the English preterit tense. This means, of course, that it can't be recognized out of context. It has disappeared as a distinct verbal form.

Another way to express the same thought in English is: If I *were to see* her tomorrow, I wouldn't say hello. (*Were* as opposed to *was* in this sentence is just about all that's left of the English imperfect subjunctive.)

Be that as it may, the important point for you to understand about Spanish is that it is *not* the Spanish preterit tense that is called for after the if in this kind of sentence. You want to use the imperfect subjunctive. The sentence would be this:

Si la viera mañana, no la saludaría.

**JUST A MINUTE**

In Spanish, to say hello is *saludar* (literally, to greet). The Spanish clause literally means *I wouldn't greet her.*

The rule is: In an if-clause, if the action or situation conveyed by the verb is contrary to fact—that is, if it isn't true, or even is unlikely—use the imperfect subjunctive. The speaker has not seen her recently, and thinks it unlikely he will see her tomorrow: The seeing is considered contrary to fact.

Thinking in English, we are not accustomed to having to consider whether an act or event is contrary to fact. For that reason, it may be difficult for you to think conceptually along those lines. Don't worry. There is an iron-clad mechanical clue to help you:

In both English and Spanish, if the non-if-clause is in the conditional tense, then the if-clause will be contrary to fact, and will take the imperfect subjunctive in Spanish. There is no exception to this, so you can't go wrong.

As you can see, *saludaría* in Spanish and *wouldn't say* in English are in the conditional tense. They always will be in the conditional tense if the if-clause is contrary to fact. The verb of the if-clause in Spanish, then, will be in the imperfect subjunctive tense.

If the verb of the non-if-clause is in *any other* tense (not the conditional), then the if-clause is *not* contrary to fact, and will *not* contain any kind of subjunctive verb. Compare and contrast the following sentences (keeping in mind that, just as in English, the if-clause can come either *before* or *after* the non-if-clause):

(1) Si *tenía* el dinero, lo *gasté*. (If I had the money, I spent it.)

(2) Si *tuviera* el dinero, lo *gastaría*. (If I had the money, I would spend it.)

(3) Yo *iré* si me *invitan*. (I will go if they invite me.)

(4) Yo *iría* si me *invitaran*. (I would go if they invited [were to invite] me.)

(5) Lo haremos si *podemos*. (We'll do it if we can [are able].)

(6) Lo *haríamos* si *pudiéramos*. (We would do it if we could [were able].)

(7) Si *llueve*, no *iré*. (If it rains, I won't go.)

(8) Si *lloviera*, no *iría*. (If it rained [were to rain], I wouldn't go.)

**GO TO ▶**
To review the conditional tense, see Hour 7.

Sentences 1, 3, 4, and 5 are not contrary to fact, so the if-clause does not contain the imperfect subjunctive, and the other clause does not contain the conditional tense. Sentences 2, 4, and 6 are contrary to fact, so the if-clause contains the imperfect subjunctive, and the other clause does not use the conditional tense.

To keep the concept simple, let's sum up by saying ...

- If the non-if-clause contains a verb in the conditional tense, the if-clause will have a verb in the imperfect subjunctive.

- If the non-if-clause contains a verb in any tense *except* the conditional, the if-clause will *not* contain a verb in the subjunctive.

Keep in mind: Under *no* circumstances will a verb in the *present* subjunctive appear in an if-clause.

## TALK ABOUT *AS IF*

The Spanish for *as if* is, as you would expect, *como si*. Think of the meaning of these expressions. By definition, *as if* and *como si* mean that what comes after these expressions is, by nature, contrary to fact. If you say "He acts as if he knew what he's doing," you're implying that he *doesn't* know what he's doing. The *knew* in that sentence would be in the imperfect subjunctive tense, because it comes after *if*, and is contrary to fact.

The English expression *as though* is synonymous with *as if;* both come out *como si* in Spanish.

Study the following sentences, and practice saying them aloud:

*Habla como si fuera el jefe.*
He talks as if he were the boss.

*Se porta como si supiera mucho.*
He behaves as though he knew a lot.

*Gasta dinero como si fuera un millonario.*
He spends money as if he were a millionaire.

*… Como si le importara (a ella).*
… As if she cared. (As if it mattered to her.)

*Nos pagan como si trabajáramos poco.*
They pay us as though we worked (very) little (didn't work much).

## THE 30-SECOND RECAP

In this hour, you've learned to use the imperfect subjunctive tense. You've also learned how to write business letters, along with terminology used in business and banking.

## HOUR'S UP!

Are you ready to test your knowledge of this hour's work? If so, you should probably review the hour. Then take the following quiz, but, for best results, don't look up the answers while taking the quiz.

1. Fill in according to grammatical rules: *Si María _____ la respuesta, habría contestado.*

     a. sabe

     b. supiera

     c. sepa

     d. supo

**2.** Finish according to grammatical rules: *Si estuvieran en dificultades, ellos lo …*

    **a.** sepan.

    **b.** supieron.

    **c.** sabrían.

    **d.** supieran.

**3.** Fill in according to grammatical rules: *Si Elena _____ ayer, no le hablé.*

    **a.** vino

    **b.** viniera

    **c.** venió

    **d.** venga

**4.** Finish according to grammatical rules: *Yo iría si tú …*

    **a.** fueras.

    **b.** irías.

    **c.** irás.

    **d.** vas.

**5.** Fill in according to grammatical rules: *Si ellos _____, yo también jugaría.*

    **a.** jugaron

    **b.** jugarán

    **c.** jugaran

    **d.** jugarían

**6.** Choose the ending that makes sense: *Si usted escribe anuncios comerciales, usted trabaja en …*

    **a.** la contaduría.

    **b.** una agencia de viajes.

    **c.** el departamento de ventas.

    **d.** una agencia publicitaria.

QUIZ

# HOUR 23

# Comparisons and Dialect Pronunciation

## CHAPTER SUMMARY

**LESSON PLAN:**
In this hour, you'll learn ...

- How to make equal and unequal comparisons in Spanish.
- To understand pronunciation in various dialects.

This hour will show you how to make comparisons in Spanish. It will also help you to understand the varied pronunciation patterns of Spanish speakers from various regions of the far-flung Hispanic world.

## COMPARE EQUALS

Comparisons, whether in English or Spanish, can be divided into two main types: comparisons of equality (one thing is as good as another), and comparisons of inequality (one thing is better or worse than another).

## TALK ABOUT EQUAL QUALITY

**A:** Modify adjectives: In English, when we compare equals in terms of quality, we use *as ... as*. For example, Bob is *as* tall *as* Brian. The Spanish formula is *tan ... como*.

Practice saying the following sentences aloud:

*Carlos es **tan** alto **como** Víctor.*
Carlos is as tall as Víctor (is).

*María es **tan** bonita **como** Elena.*
María is as pretty as Elena (is).

*Roberto es **tan** inteligente **como** yo.*
Roberto is as smart as I am.

*Aquellos hombres son **tan** fidedignos **como** el alcalde.*
Those men are as trustworthy as the mayor.

*Este banco es **tan** seguro **como** el otro banco.*
This bank is as reliable (sure, secure) as the other bank.

**GO TO** ▶

To review adjectives, see Hour 2. To review adverbs, see Hour 7.

**B:** Modify adverbs: In English, when we compare equals in terms of performance, we again use *as … as.* For this purpose, the Spanish formula again is *tan … como.* For example, *Yo escribo **tan** bien **como** Shakespeare.* (I write as well as Shakespeare.)

---

**PROCEED WITH CAUTION**

 Many of the following English sentences end with *do, does, is, are,* or *am* (either explicitly or implicitly); these are never stated in Spanish in this type of sentence.

Practice saying the following sentences aloud, while picturing what they mean:

*Éste habla tan bien como el otro.*
This (man) speaks as well as the other one.

*El tiempo transcurre tan velozmente como el viento.*
Time goes by as swiftly as the wind.

*Ella asiste tan frecuentemente como yo.*
She attends as frequently as I do.

*Yo me visto tan rápidamente como tú.*
I get dressed as fast as you do.

*Hágalo tan pronto como sea posible.*
Do it as soon as (it's) possible.

When *tan* is used without *como,* it speaks of *extent* and means *so* in English. The following sentences employ *tan* without *como;* there is no comparison involved.

*Éste habla **tan** bien.* (This [man] speaks so well.)

*El tiempo transcurre **tan** velozmente.* (Time goes by so swiftly.)

*Ella asiste **tan** frecuentemente.* (She attends so frequently.)

*Yo me visto **tan** rápidamente.* (I get dressed so fast.)

*Lo hizo **tan** pronto.* (He did it so soon.)

## TALK ABOUT EQUAL QUANTITY

**A:** Modify nouns: To compare equal quantities, English uses *as much + noun + as* (plural: *as many + noun + as*).

The Spanish formula is *tanto + noun + como.* The word *tanto,* when modifying a noun, is used as an adjective. This means that, because the masculine form ends with an *-o,* this adjective can take four forms, depending on the noun it modifies: *tanto, tantos, tanta, tantas.*

**PROCEED WITH CAUTION**

Never use \**tan mucho*(s) to mean as much/many instead of *tanto*(s)/*tanta*(s).

Practice saying the following sentences aloud:

> *González tiene **tanto** dinero **como** Vallejo.*
> González has as much money as Vallejo.

> *María tiene **tantos** inquilinos **como** Carlos.*
> María has as many tenants as Carlos.

> *Víctor puede beber **tanta** cerveza **como** Fernando.*
> Víctor can drink as much beer as Fernando.

> *El Banco de Buffalo tiene **tantas** hipotecas **como** este banco.*
> The Bank of Buffalo has as many mortgages as this bank.

> *La Argentina cosecha **tanto** trigo **como** el Canadá.*
> Argentina harvests as much wheat as Canada.

The following sentences employ *tanto/os/a/as* without *como*; there is no comparison:

> *González tiene **tanto** dinero.*
> González has so much money.

> *María tiene **tantos** inquilinos.*
> María has so many tenants.

> *Víctor puede beber **tanta** cerveza.*
> Víctor can drink so much beer.

> *El Banco de Buffalo tiene **tantas** hipotecas.*
> The Bank of Buffalo has so many mortgages.

> *La Argentina cosecha **tanto** trigo.*
> Argentina harvests so much wheat.

**B:** Modify verbs: *tanto* can also be used as an adverb to mean *so much*, or, with *como*, to mean *as much as*. As an adverb, it has only one unchanging form: *tanto*.

> *María habla **tanto**.* (María talks so much.)

> *María habla **tanto** como yo.* (María talks as much as I do.)

> *José estudia **tanto**.* (José studies so much.)

> *José estudia **tanto** como Ricardo.* (José studies as much as Ricardo.)

> *Comen **tanto**.* (They eat so much.)

> *Comen **tanto** como los caballos.* (They eat as much as horses.)

## COMPARE UNEQUALS

Inequality can be stated in English either by using *more* or *less*. The same is true in Spanish. Let's start by talking about *more*.

### MORE

**A:** Modify verbs: *más que = more than:* To say that someone does something *more* than someone else, the Spanish structure is very much like the English structure, so it will be very easy for you to learn quickly. Simply use the word *más* (more) plus the relative pronoun *que* after the verb. Practice saying the following sentences:

*Martínez trabaja* **más que** *Varela.*
Martínez works more than Varela.

*Yo pagué* **más que** *tú.*
I paid more than you (did).

*Ellos invierten* **más que** *nosotros.*
They invest more than we do.

*Escribimos* **más que** *ellos.*
We write more than they do.

*Ella sabe* **más que** *Ud.*
She knows more than you do.

If the comparison is implicit rather than explicit, then, just as in English, the word *más* (more) is used to modify the verb without *que* (than), as in the following sentences:

*Martínez trabaja* **más.** (Martínez works more.)

*Yo pagué* **más.** (I paid more.)

*Ellos invierten* **más.** (They invest more.)

**B:** Modify nouns: *más + noun + que = more + noun + than:* This structure is just like the English one, too. For that reason, it will be very easy to learn. Practice saying the following sentences:

> *Yo pagué **más** dinero **que** tú.*
> I paid more money than you did.

> *Ellos invierten **más** fondos **que** nosotros.*
> They invest more funds than we do.

> *Escribimos **más** cartas **que** ellos.*
> We write more letters than they do.

> *Ella sabe **más** canciones **que** Ud.*
> She knows more songs than you do.

> *¿Quién puede hacer **más** cosas **que** yo?*
> Who can do more things than I can?

**JUST A MINUTE**

The idiom *no poder con + someone* or *something* means not being able to put up with a certain person or situation. *No puedo con ella = I can't put up with her. No puedo con este trabajo = I can't stand this job.*

**C:** Modify adjectives: *más + adjective + que = more + adjective + than:* The English comparative system used with adjectives has certain peculiarities that you're accustomed to. Don't let it interfere with your Spanish. Actually, the Spanish system is much simpler.

The English peculiarity that can cause you problems if you're thinking in English rather than thinking in Spanish is illustrated in the following English sentences:

> Carlos is more intelligent than Roberto.

> Carlos is smarter than Roberto.

> Lola is more beautiful than Elena.

> Lola is prettier than Elena.

As you can see, there are a number of different ways in English to express comparisons. The Spanish system is intrinsically much more simple (or much simpler). In Spanish, we simply place the word *más* in front of the adjective.

Practice saying the following sentences aloud:

> *Carlos es **más** inteligente **que** Roberto.*
> Carlos is more intelligent than Roberto.

*Carlos es **más** inteligente **que** Roberto.*
Carlos is smarter than Roberto.

*Lola es **más** hermosa **que** Elena.*
Lola is more beautiful than Elena.

*Lola es **más** bonita **que** Elena.*
Lola is prettier than Elena.

*El sistema español es mucho **más** sencillo.*
The Spanish system is much more simple.

*El sistema español es mucho **más** sencillo.*
The Spanish system is much simpler.

Just as English has a couple of exceptions, so does Spanish.

See the following table for the Spanish equivalents of better and worse plus two more irregular comparative forms.

**Irregular Unequal Comparatives**

| Adjective | Comparative | English |
|-----------|-------------|---------|
| bueno/a | mejor | good/better |
| malo/a | peor | bad/worse |
| grande | mayor | big/greater; older |
| pequeño/a | menor | small/lesser; younger |

**PROCEED WITH CAUTION**

Do *not* use the word *más* with the four irregular comparatives. If you do, it will have the same effect as saying *"This is more better" in English.

There are actually two methods of showing unequal comparison for *grande* and for *pequeño*. However, the irregular comparatives *mayor* and *menor* have very different meanings from the regular comparatives *más grande* and *más pequeño*:

| | |
|--|--|
| más grande | bigger (physical size) |
| mayor | greater (importance); older |
| más pequeño | smaller (physical size) |
| menor | lesser (importance); younger |

Study the following expressions, and practice saying them aloud:

*Carlos es más grande que María.*
Carlos is bigger than María.

*Pero, María es mayor que Carlos.*
But, María is older than Carlos.

*Pedro es más pequeño que Rogelio.*
Pedro is smaller than Rogelio.

*Pero, Rogelio es menor que Carlos.*
But, Rogelio is younger than Carlos.

*Elena es mi hermana mayor.*
Elena is my older sister (big sister).

*Carlos es mi hermano menor.*
Carlos is my younger brother (kid brother).

*El Rey, don Carlos el mayor.*
King Charles the Greater.

*El Rey, don Carlos el menor.*
King Charles the Lesser.

The comparative *menor* can also be used as both the adjective and the noun meaning *minor*, whereas *mayor* can be used as both the adjective and the noun (military rank of) *major*, as well as the nouns *adult* or *elder*:

*Éste es un problema menor.* (This is a minor problem.)

*Éste es el problema menor.* (This is the lesser problem.)

*Éste es un problema mayor.* (This is a major problem.)

*Éste es el problema mayor.* (This is the greater problem.)

*Éste es el Mayor González.* (This is Major González.)

*Este film es para mayores de edad.* (This film is for adults.)

*Este film no es para menores de edad.* (This film is not for minors.)

*Hay que tener respeto para los mayores.* (It's necessary to respect one's elders.)

**JUST A MINUTE**

For the meaning of adult and minor, the expression *de edad* (of age) is customarily added.

**D:** The most: In English, we have not only the adjective and the comparative form of the adjective; we have the adjective, the comparative form of the adjective, and the superlative form of the adjective. For example:

- big, bigger, the biggest
- intelligent, more intelligent, the most intelligent
- good, better, the best
- bad, worse, the worst

The last entry in each of the items in the preceding list is the superlative. Spanish has *no special form* for the superlative, yet the same idea is certainly expressed. To convey the superlative concept, simply use the definite article with the comparative form of the adjective. Some examples follow:

- inteligente, más inteligente, el/la más inteligente
- grande, más grande, el/la más grande
- honrado, más honrado, el/la más honrado/a

Practice saying the following sentences aloud:

*Carlos es inteligente, y Marta es más inteligente que Carlos, pero Roberto es el más inteligente.*
Carlos is smart, and Marta is smarter than Carlos, but Roberto is the smartest.

*Mi casa es grande, y la casa tuya es más grande que la mía, pero la casa de Víctor es la más grande.*
My house is big, and your house is bigger, but Víctor's house is the biggest.

*Ricardo es un buen futbolista, Francisco es un mejor futbolista, y Víctor y Pedro son los mejores futbolistas.*
Ricardo is a good soccer player, Francisco is a better soccer player, and Víctor and Pedro are the best soccer players.

*Elena es una chica bonita, sí, pero Carmen es más bonita que ella, y María y Conchita son las (chicas) más bonitas.*
Elena is a pretty girl, yes, but Carmen is prettier than she is, and María and Conchita are the prettiest (girls).

*La clase de historia es interesante, pero la clase de biología es más interesante. Pero la clase de español es la (clase) más interesante.*
History class is interesting, but Biology class is more interesting. But Spanish (class) is the most interesting.

Note that the noun can be included, but, if known, does not have to be. Still, the definite article must agree with the noun, whether present or absent. If you're talking about the most interesting classes, you will use *las clases más interesantes*, or, if you know you're talking about classes, and omit the noun, it will be *las más interesantes*.

When we tell what group the superlative person or thing belongs to in English, we use the preposition *in*: He's the smartest kid *in* the class. Under these same conditions, Spanish uses the preposition *de*: *Es el chico más inteligente **de** la clase*.

## LESS

The Spanish word for *less* is *menos*. As the opposite of *más*, it can be used in the same way shown for *más*.

**JUST A MINUTE**

The idiom *no poder menos que* means *to be unable to help doing something;* for example, *No pude menos que reírme = I couldn't help laughing* (I could do no less than laugh).

Practice saying the following sentences:

*Martínez trabaja **menos que** Varela.* (Martínez works less than Varela.)

*Yo pagué **menos que** tú.* (I paid less than you.)

*Tengo menos libros que usted.* (I have fewer books than you.)

*Éste es el anuncio menos eficaz.* (This is the least effective ad.)

## BE FAMILIAR WITH DIALECT PRONUNCIATION

A language spoken in far-flung areas of the world is bound to develop dialect differences. The main differences are in vocabulary (see Hour 19) and pronunciation. Not knowing these differences will seriously interfere with communication. If you intend to deal with Spanish speakers from a particular region, you will want to become familiar with the variants you expect to come into contact with.

### RECOGNIZE THE CASTILIAN C AND Z

The pronunciation given in the table of consonant sounds for the letters *c* and *z* in Hour 1 is applicable to most of the Spanish-speaking world, but not to northern and central Spain. This area of Spain has a different pronunciation known as the *Castilian pronunciation*. In Castilian pronunciation, the *z* is pronounced like the English *th* in *think* and *tooth* (not in *the* and *this*). The letter *c* before an *e* or an *i* is pronounced the same way. In all other positions, the *c* is pronounced as shown in the table. See the following sampling of Castilian pronunciation of *c* before *e* or *i* and of *z* in all cases contrasted with Latin American:

**Castillian vs. Latin-American Pronunciation**

| Spanish Word | Castilian | Latin American |
|---|---|---|
| cinta | THEEN-tah | SEEN-tah |
| zorro | THOH-rroh | SOH-rro |
| paz | pahth | pahs |
| hacer | ah-THEHR | ah-SEHR |
| cinco | THEENG-koh | SEENG-koh |

## RECOGNIZE LETTERS *J* AND *G* IN DIFFERENT DIALECTS

The sounds represented by the letter *j* (and *g* before *e* or *i*) depend on the dialect. In the Caribbean area the letter *j* represents a sound that is almost exactly like the sound represented in English by the letter *h*. This pronunciation is true of Andalusia (the extreme south of Spain) and the Canary Islands, too. In central and northern Spain, however, the *j* represents a sound we don't have in English and which seems very harsh to us. It's like the sound in German *Ach!* or Scottish *loch*. The following pronunciation examples demonstrate this harsher sound:

| Juan | KHWAHN |
|---|---|
| jota | KHOH-tah |
| bajo | BAH-khoh |
| Javier | khah-BYEHR |

In most of Mexico and the Andes Mountains of South America, as well as Argentina and Uruguay, the *j* (and *g* before *e* or *i*) represents another sound we don't have in English. It's like the harsh-sounding *j* of central and northern Spain, but much more relaxed. You could say it's somewhere between the sound of English *h* and German *ch*.

## RECOGNIZE *Y* AND *LL* IN DIFFERENT DIALECTS

In some regions of the Hispanic world, the letter *y* and the letter *ll* are given separate pronunciations. However, in most of the Spanish-speaking world, *ll* is pronounced exactly as *y* is pronounced, so that *cayí* and *callí* sound the same. But the pronunciation of the *y* and the *ll* sound varies a great deal, depending on the dialect, as shown in the following table.

**Variant Pronunciations of *y* and *ll***

| Word | Variant 1 | Variant 2 | Variant 3 | Variant 4 |
|------|-----------|-----------|-----------|-----------|
| cayí | *kah-YOH* | *kah-YOH* | *kah-JOH* | *kah-ZHOH* |
| callí | *kah-LYOH* | *kah-YOH* | *kah-JOH* | *kah-ZHOH* |
| maya | *MAH-yah* | *MAH-yah* | *MAH-jah* | *MAH-zhah* |
| malla | *MAH-lyah* | *MAH-yah* | *MAH-jah* | *MAH-zhah* |

## RECOGNIZE THE LETTER *S* IN DIFFERENT DIALECTS

The *s* is extremely weak at the end of words and syllables in southern Spain, the Caribbean, and parts of coastal South America. In these zones, people either pronounce the *s* like the English *h* or it becomes silent altogether. The following table lists examples of this pronunciation (the double letter *hh* in these examples represents the sound of the letter *h* in English).

**Pronunciation of *s* at End of Syllables in Certain Dialects**

| Word | Weak s Pronunciation | Weaker s Pronunciation |
|------|----------------------|-------------------------|
| España | *Ehh-PAH-nyah* | *Ep-PAH-nyah* |
| escuela | *ehh-KWEH-lah* | *ek-KWEH-lah* |
| ¿Cómo estás? | *koh-moh-ehh-TAHH* | *koh-moh-et-TA* |
| Estoy bien. | *ehh-TOHY-BYEHN* | *et-TOHY-BYEHN* |
| ¿Qué es esto? | *keh-ehh-EHH-toh* | *keh-HEHT-toh* |
| los americanos | *loh-hhah-meh-ree-KAH-nohh* | *loh-ah-meh-ree-KAH-noh* |

**JUST A MINUTE**

The *s* is not as likely to be completely dropped at the end of a word if it is followed by a word that begins with a vowel, although it can happen (as in the last example).

## RECOGNIZE THE LETTERS *R* AND *L* IN DIFFERENT DIALECTS

There are variants of the pronunciation of the Spanish single *r*, but only at the end of syllables. Many Puerto Ricans pronounce the end-of-syllable *r* as *l*:

| | |
|---|---|
| arma | *AHL-mah* |
| amor | *ah-MOHL* |
| hablar | *ah-BLAHL* |
| puerto | *PWEHL-toh* |

In other dialect areas (for example, Panama and southern Spain), the opposite happens: the *l* at the end of syllables is pronounced like the single *r*:

| | |
|---|---|
| alma | *AHR-mah* |
| calma | *KAHR-mah* |
| general | *heh-neh-RAHR* |
| él | *EHR* |

In southern Spain (Andalusia), the *r* at the end of words tends to disappear:

| | |
|---|---|
| hablar | *ah-BLAH* |
| decir | *deh-SEE* |
| amor | *ah-MOH* |

## RECOGNIZE THE *RR* SOUND IN DIFFERENT DIALECTS

Pronunciations of the Spanish double *rr* sound vary widely. In many areas of the Andes, all the way from Colombia to northwest Argentina, the *rr* is pronounced something like the *s* in pleasure or the *z* in azure. See the following examples (remember that an *r* that begins a word is pronounced the same as an *rr*):

| | |
|---|---|
| Roberto | *zhoh-BEHR-toh* |
| la rosa | *lah-ZHOH-sah* |
| tierra | *TYEH-zhah* |
| perro | *PEH-zhoh* |
| guitarra | *gee-TAH-zhah* |

The double *rr* sound has two variants in Puerto Rico. Some people pronounce it as a simple aspiration (like the English *h*) followed by a single *r*:

| | |
|---|---|
| Roberto | *hroh-BEHL-toh* |
| la rosa | *lah-HROH-sah* |
| tierra | *TYEH-hrah* |
| perro | *PEH-hroh* |
| guitarra | *gee-TAH-hrah* |

Other Puerto Ricans pronounce the double *rr* consonant like the harsh guttural sound of the German *ch* in *Ach!* This is the same sound as the Scottish *ch* in *loch*. It also is the same pronunciation as the letter *j* in northern and central Spain:

| | |
|---|---|
| Roberto | *khoh-BEHL-toh* |
| la rosa | *lah-KHOH-sah* |
| tierra | *TYEH-khah* |
| perro | *PEH-khoh* |
| guitarra | *gee-TAH-kha* |

## THE 30-SECOND RECAP

In this hour, you've learned how to make equal and unequal comparisons in Spanish. You've also become familiar with vocabulary differences in various Spanish dialects.

## HOUR'S UP!

Take another glance at this hour's material, and then test your progress by taking the following quiz. Don't consult with the lessons while taking the quiz.

1. Choose the correct translation: Roberto is as tall as Víctor.

   **a.** Roberto es tanto alto como Víctor.

   **b.** Roberto es como alto como Víctor.

   **c.** Roberto es tan alto como Víctor.

**2.** Choose the correct translation: Elena has as many friends as María does.

   **a.** Elena tiene tantos amigos como María.

   **b.** Elena tiene tan amigos como María.

   **c.** Elena tiene tantos amigos como hace María.

**3.** Choose the correct translation: Pancho eats as much as Ricardo.

   **a.** Pancho come como mucho como Ricardo.

   **b.** Pancho come tanto como Ricardo.

   **c.** Pancho come tan como Ricardo.

**4.** Choose the correct translation: Víctor is taller than Roberto.

   **a.** Víctor es más alto que Roberto.

   **b.** Víctor es más alto como Roberto.

   **c.** Víctor es tan alto como Roberto.

**5.** Choose the correct translation: Pepe is my big brother.

   **a.** Pepe es mi hermano grande.

   **b.** Pepe es mi hermano mejor.

   **c.** Pepe es mi hermano mayor.

**6.** Choose the correct translation: Elena has fewer books than Pepita.

   **a.** Elena tiene pocos libros que Pepita.

   **b.** Elena tiene menos pocos libros que Pepita.

   **c.** Elena tiene menos libros que Pepita.

# Automotive

**LESSON PLAN:**

In this hour, you'll learn …

- The imperfect subjunctive compound tense.
- How to show existence in the imperfect subjunctive.
- How to use diminutive and augmentative endings on nouns.
- How to talk about automobiles and driving.
- How to know when to use the indicative or the subjunctive with time expressions.

This hour will help you to talk about cars and their maintenance. It will also sew up loose ends concerning the subjunctive mood, while showing how to make things sound bigger or smaller by special endings.

## FORM THE IMPERFECT SUBJUNCTIVE COMPOUND

The imperfect subjunctive compound, like all compound tenses, is composed of the auxiliary verb *haber* plus the past participle. In this case, you will conjugate *haber* in the imperfect subjunctive. See the following for the imperfect subjunctive conjugation of *haber*:

- hubiera
- hubieras
- hubiera
- hubiéramos
- hubierais
- hubieran

## KNOW WHEN TO USE IT

The imperfect subjunctive compound is used when you're referring to an event that took place at some indeterminate time before a specific point in the past, but that, for reasons you are now familiar with, need the subjunctive.

GO TO ▶
For a review of the formation of the past participle, see Hour 9.

GO TO ▶
To review the imperfect subjunctive, see Hour 22.

GO TO ▶
To review the reasons for using the subjunctive, see Hours 12, 13, and 20.

**TIME SAVER**

 You use the imperfect subjunctive compound whenever two factors are present: The English is in the past perfect (had done), and the subjunctive is called for.

Practice saying the following sentences aloud:

*Dudaba que Roberto hubiera llegado.*
I doubted that Roberto had arrived.

*Me alegraba de que lo hubieras hecho.*
I was glad (that) you had done it.

*No creíamos que hubieran salido.*
We didn't believe (that) they had left.

*Era triste que María se hubiera ido.*
It was sad that María had gone away.

*¿Creía Ud. que yo hubiera dicho tal cosa?*
Did you believe (that) I had said such a thing?

## REFER TO EXISTENCE IN THE IMPERFECT SUBJUNCTIVE

You've used the verb *haber*, not only as a helping verb in compound tenses, but also to show *existence*; you've done this in all the indicative tenses, and in the present subjunctive tense. Naturally, it can also be used in the imperfect subjunctive tense, when this tense is called for. See the following examples:

*¿Creías que hubiera una fiesta ese día?*
Did you think there would be a party that day?

*Dudaba que hubiera tres enfermeras en el consultorio.*
I doubted (that) there were three nurses in the doctor's office.

*Fue lástima que no hubiera mucha gente allí.*
It was too bad there weren't many people there.

*Era posible que hubiera dificultades.*
It was possible there might be difficulties.

*Quería que hubiera paz.*
I wanted there to be peace.

Notice the impossibility of an exact translation for the imperfect subjunctive tense (in the preceding cases, of the auxiliary verb *haber* in that tense), when dealing with a tense or mood that is no longer distinguishable in English.

The first sentence in the previous list, for example, could have been translated at least two other ways:

GO TO ▶
Compare the preceding sentences with their parallels in the present subjunctive perfect tense in Hour 21.

Did you think there might be a party that day?

Did you think there was a party that day?

The action or event indicated by the imperfect subjunctive can take place …

- At the same time as the verb triggering its use (that there was).
- At a time after the time of the triggering verb (that there would be).
- At a vague time that could be either simultaneous or after the time of the triggering verb (there might be).

For this same reason, the second sentence in the previous list, as an alternative to *there were*, could have been translated as *there would be* or *there might be*. The same is true of the other sentences.

## MAKE THINGS SMALLER AND BIGGER

There are endings placed on nouns in Spanish that make the noun seem smaller or bigger. Some endings are more common than others. Some endings tell you the speaker's feelings about the noun: whether he or she thinks affectionately, or dispassionately, or disparagingly about the noun.

### MAKE THINGS SMALLER/SHOW AFFECTION

An ending that makes a noun (even adjectives, at times) sound small is called a *diminutive ending*. Spanish is rich in these endings. The most common diminutive ending in Spanish is the ending *-ito/a* or *-cito/a*. See the examples in the following table.

### Lista de Sustantivos con Terminaciones Diminutivas

| Regular Noun | Noun with Diminutive Ending | English |
|---|---|---|
| libro | librito | little book |
| chico | chiquito | little boy |
| madre | madrecita | mommy |
| padre | padrecito | daddy |
| perro | perrito | little dog, doggy |
| casa | casita | little house, cottage |

*continues*

**Lista de Sustantivos con Terminaciones Diminutivas** (continued)

| Regular Noun | Noun with Diminutive Ending | English |
|---|---|---|
| Carmen | Carmencita | little Carmen |
| Pancho | Panchito | little Frank, Franky |
| joven | jovencito/a | very young person |
| viejo/a | viejito/a | little old man/woman |
| viejo/a | viejecito/a | little old man/woman |
| grande | grandecito/a | nice and big |

These endings can be attached to any noun (and sometimes adjectives).

Note: If the original noun ends with *o* or *a*, drop the vowel before adding *-ito/a*: for example, *libro/librito*; *casa/casita*.

With regard to differences in dialects, *mamá* and *papá* become *mamita* and *papito* in some regions, whereas in other dialects they become *mamacita* and *papacito*. Often these two terms (like mommy and daddy) are *mami* and *papi*.

**PROCEED WITH CAUTION**

These specific diminutive endings, *-ito/a* and *-cito/a*, do not necessarily show literal smallness; very often, they are used to show affection or to make someone or something sound "cute."

## MAKE THINGS SMALLER WITHOUT AFFECTION

The less frequent endings *-illo/a* and *-cillo/a* suggest smallness without any particular affection, perhaps at times even showing mild scorn:

| | |
|---|---|
| hombre : hombrecillo | little (no account) man |
| chico : chiquillo | little boy, "squirt" |

## MAKE THINGS SMALL AND NASTY

The diminutive endings *-uelo/a* and *-zuelo/a*, as well as the endings *-ucho/a*, make things sound small and nasty; they are definitely derogatory. They have a rather limited use:

| | |
|---|---|
| casa : casucha | shack, hovel |
| periódico : periodicucho | miserable newspaper, "rag" |
| mujer : mujerzuela | prostitute |

| traidor : traidorzuelo | dirty little traitor, sneak (*traidor* means traitor or treacherous). |
| joven : jovenzuelo/a | snot-nosed kid |

## MAKE THINGS BIG

Endings that indicate that the noun is large are *-ote/ota* and *-ón/ona*:

| hombre : hombrote | big man |
| mano : manota | big hand, "paw" (said of humans) |
| hombre : hombrón | big man |
| mujer : mujerona | big woman |
| colcha | bedspread |
| colchón | mattress |
| silla | chair |
| sillón | easy chair |
| casa : casona | mansion |
| pájaro : pajarote | large bird |

The augmentative endings *-azo* and *-aco* are also used in some limited cases. They not only imply big, but can be either neutral or derogatory:

| perro : perrazo | big, ugly, clumsy dog |
| español : españolazo | real, dyed-in-the-wool Spaniard |
| amigo : amigazo | old pal, crony |
| mano : manazo | big hand, "paw" |
| libro : libraco | huge, heavy book |
| pájaro : pajarraco | big, ungainly, ugly bird |

Note: Even though *pájaro* and even *pajarote* have but the single *-r-*, *pajarraco* contains a double *-rr-*. In colloquial usage, *pajarraco* is also applied to people considered to be *unscrupulous, underhanded, and cunning*.

## Learn Another Use of -azo

The ending -azo (but not -aza) is also used to signify a blow with the noun to which it's attached:

| | |
|---|---|
| el látigo (whip) | el latigazo (blow with a whip, whiplash, lash) |
| la mano (hand) | el manotazo (blow with hand, slap) |
| el pico (beak, bill) | el picotazo (peck) |
| la porra (club, bludgeon) | el porrazo (blow with a club) |
| la puerta (door) | el portazo (slamming of the door) |

Practice saying the following sentences:

*El caballo sintió el latigazo.*
The horse felt the lash.

*El detective le dio un manotazo al criminal.*
The detective slapped the criminal.

*El pájaro le dio un picotazo al gato.*
The bird pecked the cat.

*Después del porrazo, Don Quijote no pudo levantarse.*
After the beating, Don Quixote couldn't stand up.

*Al salir, dio un portazo.*
As he left (upon leaving), he slammed the door.

## Use al Plus the Infinitive

In Spanish, you can use the contraction al plus the infinitive form of the verb to be the equivalent of English upon or on plus the -ing form of the verb. In fact, this construction is more common in Spanish than its English equivalent. Practice saying the following sentences aloud:

*Al llegar, me llamó.* (Upon arriving, he called me.)

*Al hablar, me siento nervioso.* (Upon speaking, I feel nervous.)

*Al verla, la saludará.* (Upon seeing her, he will greet her.)

*No dije nada al saberlo.* (I said nothing on finding out about it.)

*Siempre me ha llamado al llegar.* (He has always called me upon arriving.)

Just as in English, it doesn't matter if the al + infinitive expression comes before or after the conjugated verb.

You will notice, then, that it's possible to translate a structure such as *al llegar* in several ways: *upon arriving, on arriving* (which, in themselves, indicate no tense), or *when he or she arrives* (first sentence), or *when he or she arrived* (fifth sentence).

Although the construction *al* plus the infinitive verb is more commonly used than it's English equivalent, *(up)on* plus the infinitive verb, the Spanish sentences could just as well have dispensed with it, and instead used a conjugated verb:

> Cuando llegó, me llamó.
>
> Cuando hablo, me siento nervioso.
>
> Cuando la vea, la saludará.

## DECIDE MOOD WITH TIME EXPRESSIONS

When you need to have a conjugated verb in an adverbial clause introduced by an expression of time, you will use either the indicative or the subjunctive mood, depending on certain factors.

### USE INDICATIVE WITH TIME EXPRESSIONS

Use the indicative *after* an expression of time, if …

- The action/situation happens all the time.
- The action/situation has already happened.

First, learn the time-related expressions in the following table.

### Expresiones Relacionadas con El Tiempo

| Spanish | English |
| --- | --- |
| al mismo tiempo que | at the same time |
| antes (de) que * | before * (see the following sidebar) |
| cuando | when |
| cuandoquiera que | whenever |
| después (de) que | after |
| en cuanto | as soon as |
| hasta que | until |
| mientras | while |
| tan pronto como | as soon as |
| una vez que | once |

**TIME SAVER**

 No need to think about *antes (de) que;* it *always* takes the subjunctive. By definition, the verb that comes after it has *not* yet happened with relation to the other verb.

Study the following sentences, and practice saying them aloud:

*Siempre me llama Carlos cuando llega.*
Carlos always calls me when he arrives.

*Me saludaban después (de) que yo entraba.*
They would (used to) greet me after I came in.

*Yo comí al mismo tiempo que ella salió.*
I ate at the same time (that) she left.

*Yo comía mientras ella dormía.*
I used to eat while she slept.

*Yo me levanté cuando oí el ruido.*
I got up when I heard the noise.

All the preceding situations report fact; they report things that happen all the time or that have already happened in the past. They're very much in the real world, and therefore do not require the subjunctive.

## Use the Subjunctive with Time Expressions

Use the subjunctive *after* an expression of time, if the action/situation takes place in the future with relation to the other verb; that is, it has/had not happened yet with relation to the other verb.

Study the following sentences, and practice saying them aloud:

*Querré usar el baño cuando lleguemos a la gasolinera.*
I'll want to use the bathroom when we get to the gas station.

*Llámeme Ud. tan pronto como llegue.*
Call me as soon as you get there.

*Antes (de) que lo hagas, consulta con el jefe.*
Before you do it, consult with the boss.

*Me saludarán después (de) que yo entre.*
They'll greet me after I go in.

*Yo comeré al mismo tiempo que ella salga.*
I'll eat at the same time (that) she leaves.

**GO TO ▶**
To review the direct object pronouns, see Hour 12.

# USE THE NEUTER DEFINITE ARTICLE

Up until this point, you have been using four definite articles (*el, los, la, las*). They always agree in number and gender with the noun they accompany. However, there is a fifth definite article in Spanish.

The fifth definite article is *lo*, and is neither masculine nor feminine; it is neuter.

---

**PROCEED WITH CAUTION**

Don't confuse the neuter definite article *lo* with the *lo* that is the masculine singular direct object pronoun.

---

Consider the following:

- The definite article *lo* is neuter.
- There are no neuter nouns in the Spanish language.

Then ask yourself the question: What kind of noun would *lo* accompany? The answer, of course, is: *no noun at all*. So, what does *lo* refer to?

*Lo* has two principal uses: *Lo* can be used with *que*, or it can be used with adjectives.

## USE *LO* WITH *QUE*

You remember that the other four definite articles can be placed directly before the relative pronoun *que* to mean *the one that*, if you and the person(s) to whom you're speaking already know what noun you're referring to. If we're talking about *libro*, then *el que tengo* means *the one I have*. If it's a question of more than one book, it's *los que tengo*. In each case, you simply dropped the noun, because it was known to everyone in the conversation.

Suppose you're talking about something you can't pin down to a specific noun; that's when you'd use the neuter definite article, *lo que*. There are more ways than one that we handle this situation in English:

- that which
- the thing that
- what

Don't confuse *lo que* with *¿qué?* just because they might both come out in English as *what*. *Lo que* does *not* ask a question.

Study the following sentences, and practice saying them aloud:

> *Lo que está sobre la mesa es un libro.* (What's on the table is a book.)
>
> *Lo que yo tengo es un catarro.* (What I have is a head cold.)
>
> *Lo que tú necesitas son unas vacaciones.* (What you need is a vacation.)
>
> *Ella tiene todo lo que necesita.* (She has everything [that] she needs.)
>
> *Él desea lo que tenemos nosotros.* (He wants what we have.)

However, every single one of those five sentences could have been translated with the highly formal *that which* .... The expression *lo que* stands for something that has not yet been identified, even if it's identified a couple of words *later* in the same sentence.

## Use *lo* with Adjectives

When you use the other four definite articles with adjectives, both the definite articles and the adjectives agree in number and gender with the nouns they modify. If the identity of the noun being modified is known by the people conversing, they don't bother expressing it; they drop it in both English and Spanish (but English substitutes the word *one*).

If you know you're talking about *libros*, then *el grande* is understood to mean *the big one*; it's short for *el libro grande*.

However, if you use the fifth definite article, *lo*, which is neuter, plus an adjective, what noun are you referring to? To absolutely *no* noun at all, because all Spanish nouns are either masculine or feminine; none are neuter. The fact is, you're referring to the essence of the quality encapsulated by the adjective, with no reference to any noun whatsoever.

We sometimes do this in English, but in extremely rare cases only. For example, we might say, "Look for the good, not the bad, in man." It has a limited use in English, but in Spanish is a structure that is prevalent. The translation problem: There is no one equivalent for it in English. Perhaps the closest English translation (in deep meaning, not surface structure) for a phrase like *Lo bueno* would be, depending on English usage and the particular context, something like this:

- The good part
- The good thing
- What's good
- Whatever is good
- Good things
- The good
- The good element

**TIME SAVER**

You could think of *lo* plus an adjective as a shortened form of *lo* plus *que* plus some form of *ser* plus the adjective: *Lo [que es] bueno ...; Lo [que será] malo ....*

Study the following sentences, and practice saying them aloud:

*Lo bueno es que no tienes que estudiar.*
The good part is (that) you don't have to study.

*Lo mejor es que te pagan.*
The best part is (that) they pay you.

*Lo estúpido de esta situación es ....*
The stupid thing about this situation is ....

*No me gusta lo verde.*
I don't like (whatever is) green.

*Me gusta lo bueno.*
I like good things.

*Busquen lo bueno de la vida.*
Seek the good in life.

*Y lo peor fue que no pude entrar.*
And the worst part was (that) I couldn't get in.

## TALK ABOUT CARS

If you're going to live in a Spanish-speaking country, automotive terminology will come in handy, for buying or renting a car, having one repaired, or simply purchasing gasoline. The following table lists very basic automotive vocabulary.

**PROCEED WITH CAUTION**

In Mexico, *camión* (truck everywhere else) is a bus, whereas *camión cargado* is a truck. In northern Mexico and the southwestern United States, *troca* is also used for truck. In Cuba, Puerto Rico, Dominican Republic, and the Canary Islands, the bus is *la guagua*.

### *Vocabulario Automovilístico*

| Spanish | English |
| --- | --- |
| el accidente (m.) | accident |
| aceitar | to oil, to lubricate |
| el aceite (m.) | oil |
| acelerar | to accelerate |
| el acelerador (m.) | accelerator |
| el acumulador (m.) | battery |
| alquilar | to rent, to lease |
| andar | to go, to run, to work (machine) |
| el aparcamiento (m.) | parking; parking lot |
| aparcar | to park |
| la armazón (f.) | chassis; framework |
| arrancar | to rip out; to start (a car) |
| asegurar | to insure; to assure |
| el asiento (m.) | seat |
| el auto (m.) | car, auto |
| el autobús (m.) | bus |
| el autocar (m.) | bus, motorcoach |
| automotor, -triz | automotive, automobile |
| el automóvil (m.) | automobile |
| el automovilismo (m.) | motoring; automobile industry |
| la batería (f.) | battery; set of drums |
| el baúl (m.) | trunk, boot (Brit.) |
| la bocacalle (f.) | intersection |
| la boleta (f.) | summons, ticket |
| la boleta por exceso de velocidad (f.) | speeding ticket |
| la bujía (f.) | spark plug |
| la caja de cambios (f.) | gear shift |
| la caja de velocidades (f.) | gear shift |

| Spanish | English |
| --- | --- |
| cambiar de velocidad | to shift gears |
| el cambio (m.) | transmission; change |
| el camino (m.) | road |
| el camión (m.) | truck, lorry (Brit.) |
| el carburador (m.) | carburetor |
| cargar | to charge; to load; to carry |
| el carnet de identidad (m.) | identity card |
| el carnet de manejar (m.) | driver's license |
| la carretera (f.) | highway |
| el carro (m.) | car |
| la carrocería (f.) | (auto) body; body shop; auto repair shop |
| el cobertizo (para autos) (m.) | carport |
| el coche (m.) | car |
| la colisión (f.) | collision, crash |
| conducir | to drive; to conduct, to lead |
| el/la conductor/a (m./f.) | driver |
| chocar (contra) | to crash (against) |
| el chofer; el chófer (m.) | driver |
| el choque (m.) | crash, collision |
| dar remolque a | to tow |
| de alquiler | rental, for rent |
| derecho | straight ahead |
| descompuesto/a | out of order, broken down, out of commission |
| el disco de tráfico (m.) | traffic light |
| doblar a la derecha | to make a right turn |
| doblar a la izquierda | to make a left turn |
| doblar la esquina | to turn the corner |
| la encrucijada (f.) | crossroads, intersection |
| engrasar | to grease, to oil |
| la entrada (f.) | entrance; driveway |
| el (tubo de) escape (m.) | exhaust (pipe) |
| la esquina (f.) | (street) corner |

*continues*

### *Vocabulario Automovilístico* (continued)

| Spanish | English |
|---|---|
| la estación de servicio (f.) | gas station, filling station |
| el estacionamiento (m.) | parking; parking space; parking lot |
| estacionar | to park |
| el faro (m.) | headlight |
| el faro trasero (m.) | rear light |
| frenar | to brake |
| el freno (m.) | brake |
| funcionar | to function, "go," "run" (machine) |
| el galón (m.) | gallon |
| el garaje (m.) | garage |
| la gasolina (f.) | gasoline, petrol (Brit.) |
| la gasolinera (f.) | gas station, filling station |
| la grasa (f.) | grease |
| guiar | to drive; to guide |
| el litro (m.) | liter (slightly over a quart) |
| lubricar | to lubricate |
| la luz de tráfico (f.) | traffic light |
| la llanta (f.) | tire |
| manejar | to drive; to manage |
| la máquina (f.) | machine; car |
| el motor (m.) | motor, engine |
| la multa (f.) | fine (payment for infraction) |
| la nafta (f.) | gasoline (Argentina) |
| el neumático (m.) | tire |
| el parabrisas (m.) | windshield, windscreen (Brit.) |
| parar | to stop |
| parquear | to park |
| el parqueo (m.) | parking; parking lot |
| la patente (f.) | license plate |
| el peaje (m.) | toll (for highway) |
| el petróleo (m.) | petroleum, (fuel) oil |
| la pila (f.) | battery |
| la pintura (f.) | painting; paint; paint job |

| Spanish | English |
| --- | --- |
| la placa (de matrícula) (f.) | license plate |
| remolcar | to tow |
| el remolque (m.) | towing; vehicle being towed |
| reparar | to repair |
| el retrovisor (m.) | rear-view mirror |
| la rueda (f.) | wheel |
| el salpicadero (m.) | dashboard |
| el seguro (m.) | insurance |
| el semáforo (m.) | traffic light |
| el tablero de instrumentos (m.) | dashboard |
| la velocidad (f.) | speed; gear |
| el velocímetro (m.) | speedometer |
| la ventanilla (f.) | window (of a car) |
| el volante (m.) | steering wheel |

**PROCEED WITH CAUTION**

If you need your steering wheel repaired, make sure you call it the *volante,* and not the *rueda,* which is one of the four wheels on which the car moves.

Study the following sentences, and practice saying them aloud:

*Carlos estaba conduciendo el coche por el camino, buscando la entrada a la carretera.*
Carlos was driving the car along the road, looking for the entrance to the highway.

*La encontró; se paró junto a la garita de peaje, pagó el peaje, y entró a la carretera.*
He found it; he stopped next to the toll booth, paid the toll, and entered the highway.

*Procediendo por la carretera, y cantando alegremente, oyó una sirena.*
Proceeding along the highway, and merrily singing, he heard a siren.

*Miró el tablero y notó con horror que el velocímetro indicaba que el coche estaba andando a más de doscientos kilómetros por hora.*
He looked at the dashboard and noticed with horror that the speedometer indicated (that) the car was moving at more than 200 kilometers per hour.

*Trató de frenar, pero los frenos no funcionaban bien.*
He tried to brake, but the brakes didn't work well.

*Finalmente, pudo parar. El policía llegó y le pidió su carnet de manejar.*
Finally, he managed to stop. The policeman arrived and asked him for his driver's license.

*El policía le informó a Carlos que el coche había necesitado tener una inspección el mes pasado.*
The policeman informed Carlos that the car had needed to be inspected the previous month.

## THE 30-SECOND RECAP

In this hour, you've learned the imperfect subjunctive compound tense, and to show existence in the imperfect subjunctive. You've learned to know when to use the indicative or the subjunctive with time expressions. You've also learned to use diminutive and augmentative endings on nouns, to use the neuter definite article (*lo*), and to talk about automobiles and driving. You've taken care of some loose ends, such as saying the equivalent of *upon doing something*, and using the *-azo* ending.

## HOUR'S UP!

Review the material of this hour, and then test your progress by taking the following quiz. Remember, it will be a more accurate test if you don't consult with the lessons while taking the quiz.

1. Complete this sentence correctly: *No creía que Carlos …*
   a. haya comido.
   b. ha comido.
   c. hubiera comido.
   d. había comido.
   e. habría comido.

2. Complete this sentence correctly: *Dudábamos que María …*
   a. haya comido.
   b. ha comido.
   c. hubo comido.
   d. hubiera comido.
   e. habría comido.

**3.** Complete this sentence correctly: *Sé que Víctor* …

    **a.** ha salido.

    **b.** haya salido.

    **c.** hubiera salido.

    **d.** haría salido

    **e.** None of the above.

**4.** Complete this sentence correctly: *Era lástima que Elena* …

    **a.** ha salido.

    **b.** había salido.

    **c.** hubiese salido.

    **d.** habrá salido.

    **e.** All of the above.

**5.** Choose the noun that agrees with the definite article *las*.

    **a.** mesa

    **b.** libro

    **c.** chicas

    **d.** coches

    **e.** Ninguno (none)

**6.** Choose the noun that agrees with the definite article *lo*.

    **a.** gasolina

    **b.** coche

    **c.** frenos

    **d.** placas

    **e.** Ninguno (none)

**7.** Choose the correct form of the verb: *Hazlo en cuanto* …

    **a.** llegas.

    **b.** llegues.

    **c.** llegaras.

    **d.** llegarás.

**8.** Choose the correct form of the verb: *Lo hice cuando* …

   **a.** llegué.

   **b.** llegue.

   **c.** llegara.

   **d.** llegaría.

**9.** Choose the correct form of the verb: *Siempre me llama tan pronto como* …

   **a.** llegó.

   **b.** llegaba.

   **c.** llegue.

   **d.** llega.

**10.** Choose the correct form of the verb: *María no podrá dormir hasta que ____ el nuevo coche.*

   **a.** reciba

   **b.** recibe

   **c.** recibió

   **d.** recibirá

# APPENDIX A
# Answer Key

**CHAPTER 1**

1. True   2. False   3. False   4. b.   5. c.
6. d.   7. a.   8. d

**CHAPTER 2**

1. b.   2. a   3. d.   4. d.   5. b.

**CHAPTER 3**

1. comen   2. viajo   3. piensa   4. pensamos
5. pides   6. pierdo   7. vivís   8. b
9. d   10. d

**CHAPTER 4**

1. d   2. b   3. a   4. a   5. c
6. c   7. a   8. d

**CHAPTER 5**

1. a   2. d   3. a   4. c   5. b
6. c

**CHAPTER 6**

1. e   2. e   3. c   4. a   5. d
6. e   7. d   8. d   9. d   10. b

## Chapter 7

1. c    2. d    3. b    4. a    5. a    6. c.    7. a.
8. e

## Chapter 8

1. d    2. d    3. a    4. d    5. b    6. c

## Chapter 9

1. d    2. e    3. a    4. d    5. b    6. a    7. e
8. e    9. a    10. b

## Chapter 10

1. c    2. e    3. a    4. d    5. b    6. b    7. a
8. d    9. d    10. a

## Chapter 11

1. d    2. b    3. c    4. c    5. d    6. d    7. c
8. d    9. b    10. d

## Chapter 12

1. c    2. a    3. d    4. b    5. d    6. b
7. false    8. true    9. a    10. d

## Chapter 13

1. c    2. a    3. a    4. d    5. c    6. b    7. d
8. a    9. d    10. c

## Chapter 14

1. b    2. d    3. a    4. d    5. b

## Chapter 15

1. c    2. d    3. d    4. d    5. a

## CHAPTER 16

1. c   2. d   3. a   4. b   5. b   6. a   7. d
8. d   9. b   10. d

## CHAPTER 17

1. b   2. a   3. a   4. b   5. c

## CHAPTER 18

1. a   2. a   3. c   4. a   5. c   6. d   7. c
8. b   9. b   10. c

## CHAPTER 19

1. f   2. e   3. c   4. b   5. a   6. b   7. a
8. d   9. Argentina   10. Argentina

## CHAPTER 20

1. d   2. a   3. c   4. a   5. d   6. a   7. b
8. b

## CHAPTER 21

1. a   2. a   3. d   4. e   5. a   6. d

## CHAPTER 22

1. b   2. c   3. a   4. a   5. c   6. d

## CHAPTER 23

1. c   2. a   3. b   4. a   5. c   6. c

## CHAPTER 24

1. c   2. d   3. a   4. c   5. c   6. e   7. b
8. a   9. d   10. a

# APPENDIX B
# Further Readings

You may want to consult other publications to deepen your knowledge of Spanish. Following is a list of general Spanish-English/English-Spanish dictionaries. You should own one of these to increase your vocabulary. If you are particularly interested in a career in a specific field of endeavor, there are specialized Spanish-English/English-Spanish dictionaries. Also included is a list of grammar books and a list of websites that will be useful to you.

## DICTIONARIES

### GENERAL SPANISH-ENGLISH/ENGLISH-SPANISH

*The American Heritage Larousse Spanish Dictionary: English/Spanish Español/Inglés*. Berkley Publication Group, 1992.

*The American Heritage Spanish Dictionary: Spanish/English English/Spanish* (hardcover). Houghton Mifflin Co., 1986.

*The American Heritage Spanish Dictionary: Spanish/English English/Spanish*. Houghton Mifflin Co., 1987.

*Compact American Spanish Dictionary*. American Heritage (editors). Houghton Mifflin Co., 1999.

Gramer, Margot. *Basic Oxford Picture Dictionary (Spanish/English Edition)*. Oxford University Press, 1996.

Lief, Philip. *Twenty-First Century Spanish-English/English-Spanish*. Dell Publishing Co., 1992.

### SPECIALIZED SPANISH-ENGLISH/ENGLISH-SPANISH

Collin, P. H. *Business Spanish Dictionary: Spanish-English/English-Spanish, Español-Inglés/Inglés-Español*. Peter Collin Publishing Ltd., 1999.

———. *Business Spanish Dictionary: Spanish-English/English-Spanish, Español-Inglés/Inglés-Español*. Peter Collin Publishing Ltd., 1997.

Headworth, Howard, and Sarah Steines. *English-Spanish Dictionary of Environmental Science and Engineering*. John Wiley & Son Ltd., 1997.

Kaplan, Steven M. *Dic Wiley's English-Spanish/Spanish-English Chemistry Dictionary = Diccionario De Química Inglés-Español/Español-Inglés*. Wiley-Interscience, 1998.

———. *Wiley's English-Spanish/Spanish-English Dictionary of Psychology and Psychiatry/Diccionario De Psicología y Psiquiatría Inglés-Español/ Español-Inglés*. John Wiley & Sons, 1997.

———. *English-Spanish/Spanish-English Electrical and Computer Engineering Dictionary = Diccionario De Ingienería Eléctrica y De Computadoras Inglés-Español/Español-Inglés*. John Wiley & Sons, 1996.

Kelz, Rochelle K. *Delmar's English-Spanish Pocket Dictionary for Health Professionals*. Delmar Publishing, 1997.

Real Estate Education Co., W. J. Allaway, et al. *Bienes Raíces: An English-Spanish Real Estate Dictionary*. Real Estate Education Co., 1995.

Rogers, Glen T. (ed.). *English-Spanish/Spanish-English Medical Dictionary = Diccionario Médico Inglés-Español/Español-Inglés*. McGraw-Hill, 1997.

## GRAMMAR BOOKS

De Bruyne, Jacques, et al. *A Comprehensive Spanish Grammar*. Blackwell Publishing, 1995.

Dueber, Julianne, et al. *1001 Pitfalls in Spanish*. Barrons Educational Series, 1997.

Jarvis, Ana C., et al. *Basic Spanish Grammar*. D.C. Heath & Co., 1996.

Noble, Judith, and Jaime Lacasa. *The Complete Handbook of Spanish Verbs*. Nat'l. Textbook Co., 1983.

Pérez, Ángeles, et al. *Cassell's Contemporary Spanish: A Handbook of Grammar, Current Usage, and Word Power*. IDG Books Worldwide, 1994.

Resnick, Seymour. *Essential Spanish Grammar*. Dover Publications, 1982.

Resnick, Seymour, and William Giuliano. *En Breve: A Concise Review of Spanish Grammar*. Holt Rinehart & Winston, 1997.

## WEBSITES

**amazon.com**
Look under "Spanish+grammar" and "Spanish-English dictionary."

**Google.com**
Look under "Spanish dictionary" and "Spanish grammar."

**www.umr.edu/~amigos/Virtual/**
*Basic Spanish for the Virtual Student*
Manuel Soto Arriví discusses Spanish grammar issues.

**www.columbia.edu/~fms5/**
*Spanish Language Drill*
Interactive drilling in Spanish grammar.

**www.studyspanish.com/**
*Learn Spanish: A Free Online Tutorial*
CD program for serious Spanish students.

**www.activa.arrakis.es/ind-en.htm**
General English-Spanish dictionary.

## JOURNALS

*Hispania*
Published by the American Association of Teachers of Spanish and Portuguese, Inc.

# Index